"Most congenial of innkeepers,
Your customer has entered.
Where would you like me to sit?
Those who must sit by the entrance
Cannot be at ease."

It's got a nice ring to it, doesn't it?
A song from the pirates of northern Europe.

—*Eiichiro Oda, 1997*

Eiichiro Oda began his manga career at the age of 17, when his one-shot cowboy manga **Wanted!** won second place in the coveted Tezuka manga awards. Oda went on to work as an assistant to some of the biggest manga artists in the industry, including Nobuhiro Watsuki, before winning the Hop Step Award for new artists. His pirate adventure **One Piece**, which debuted in **Weekly Shonen Jump magazine** in 1997, quickly became one of the most popular manga in Japan.

ONE PIECE VOL. 2
Gollancz Manga Edition

STORY AND ART BY EIICHIRO ODA

Translation/Andy Nakatani
English Adaptation/Lance Casselman
Touch-Up Art & Lettering/Bill Schuch
Cover Design/Sean Lee
Graphics & Layout/Sean Lee
Senior Editor/Jason Thompson
Graphic Novel Editor/Shaenon K. Garrity
UK Cover Adaptation/Sue Michniewicz

First published in Japan in 1997 by SHUEISHA Inc., Tokyo.
English publication rights in United Kingdom arranged by SHUEISHA Inc., through VIZ Media, LLC, U.S.A., Tuttle-Mori Agency, Inc., Japan, and Ed Victor Ltd., U.K.

This edition published in Great Britain in 2006 by
Gollancz Manga, an imprint of the Orion Publishing Group,
Orion House, 5 Upper St Martin's Lane, London WC2H 9EA,
and a licensee of VIZ Media, LLC.

1 3 5 7 9 10 8 6 4 2

A CIP catalogue record for this book is available from the British Library

ISBN-13 9 780 57507 869 7
ISBN-10 0 57507 869 3

Printed and bound at Mackays of Chatham, plc

PARENTAL ADVISORY
One Piece is rated 'T' for Teen. It may contain violence, language, alcohol or tobacco use, or suggestive situations. It is recommended for ages 13 and up.

The Orion Publishing Group's policy is to use papers that are natural, renewable and recyclable products and made from wood grown in sustainable forests. The logging and manufacturing processes are expected to conform to the environmental regulations of the country of origin.

www.orionbooks.co.uk

SHONEN JUMP GRAPHIC NOVEL

ONE PIECE

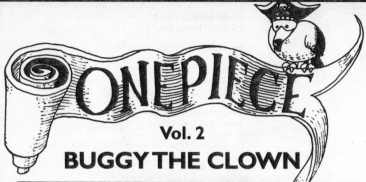

Vol. 2

BUGGY THE CLOWN

WANTED

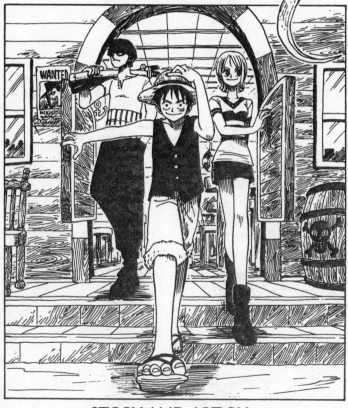

STORY AND ART BY

EIICHIRO ODA

THE STORY OF ONE PIECE
Volume 2

It is the Golden Age of Piracy. Countless pirates sail the seas, searching for legendary pirate Gold Roger's mysterious treasure, the "One Piece." Among them is Monkey D. Luffy, who grew up listening to the wild tales of buccaneer "Red-Haired" Shanks and dreaming of becoming a pirate himself. Having eaten the fruit of the Gum-Gum Tree, Luffy has the bizarre power to stretch like rubber—at the cost of being unable to swim!

Monkey D. Luffy

He ate the fruit of the Gum-Gum Tree, gaining stretchy powers. He wants to become King of the Pirates—and find his hero, "Red-Haired" Shanks.

"Red-Haired" Shanks

A pirate captain. He saved young Luffy's life, losing his own arm in the battle, and taught Luffy a love of the sea.

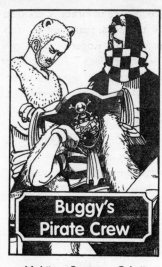

Buggy's
Pirate Crew

Mohji Buggy Cabaji

Now Luffy's quest to become the King of the Pirates has begun. He's found an unlikely friend and crewmate in the fearsome pirate hunter Zolo. But Luffy and Zolo are separated and run afoul of the ruthless pirate Captain Buggy and his gang. Meanwhile, Luffy meets Nami the thief, who specializes in robbing pirates. With an untrustworthy thief at his side and enraged pirates on his tail, Luffy's career on the high seas is already in big trouble. And he's about to learn the terrible secret of Captain Buggy's success...

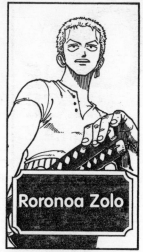

Roronoa Zolo

Although he's won fame as a pirate hunter, his true dream is to become the world's greatest swordsman.

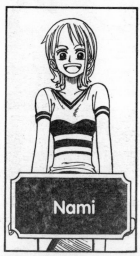

Nami

A freelance thief who targets pirates for her robberies.

Vol. 2
BUGGY THE CLOWN

CONTENTS

Chapter 9:
FEMME FATALE

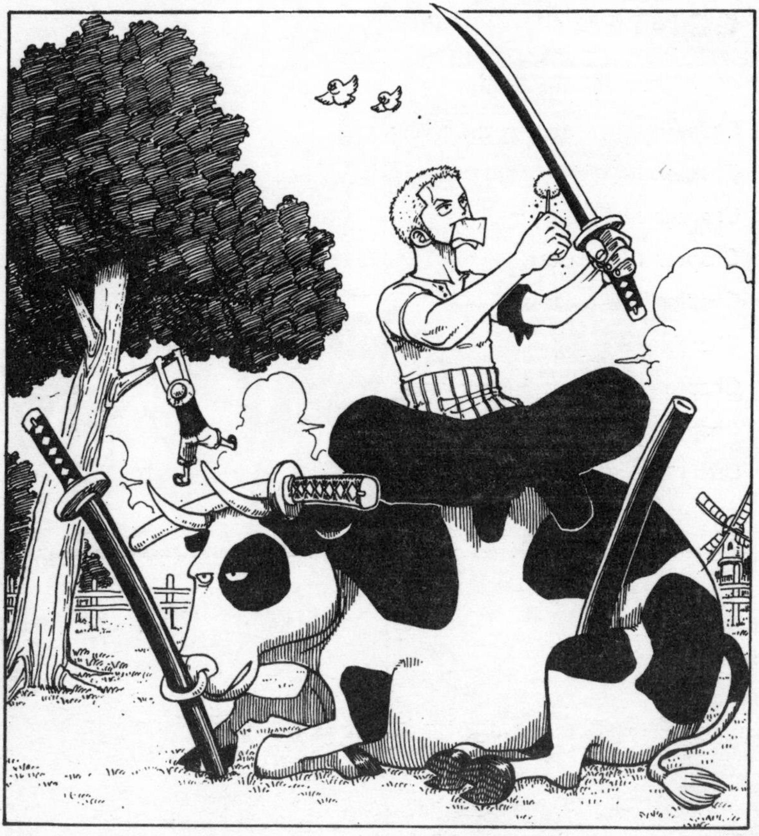

READ THIS WAY

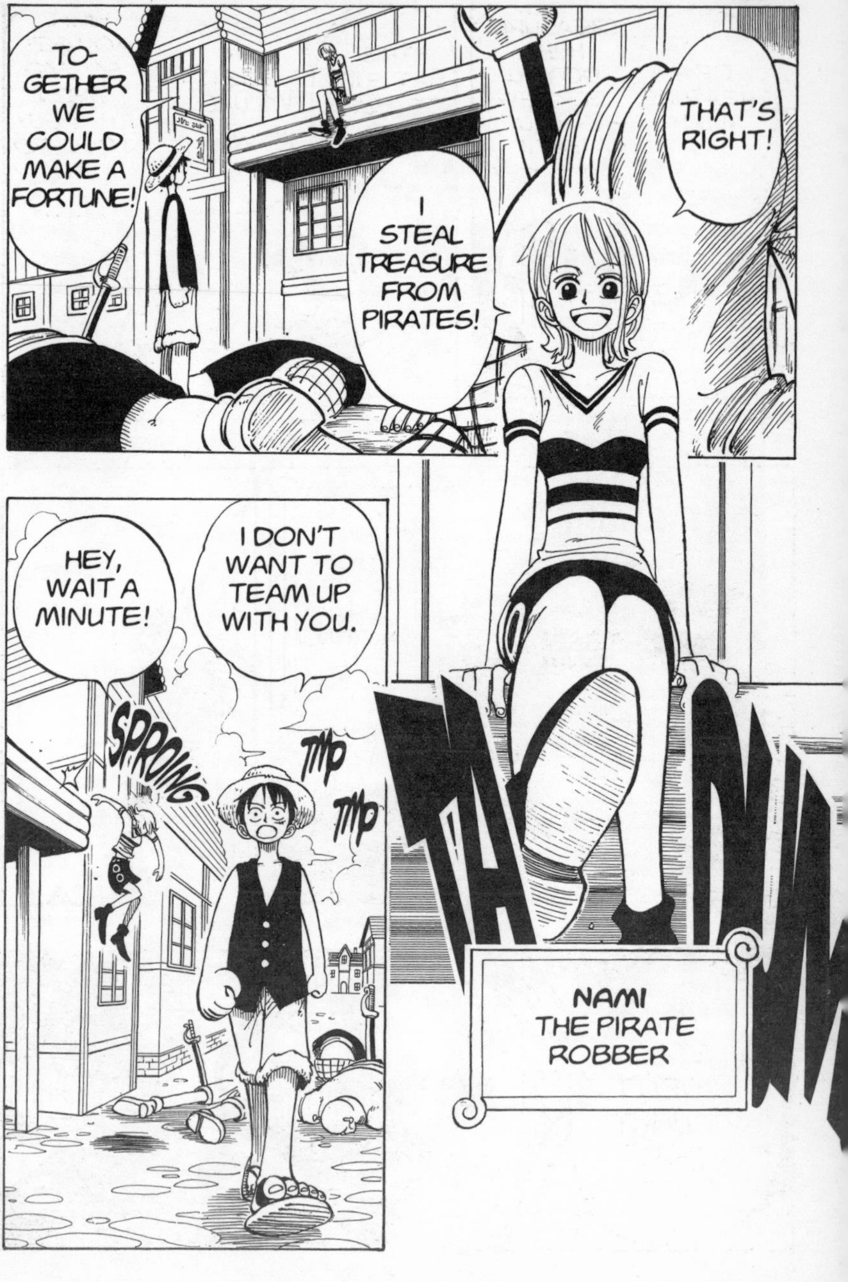
THAT'S RIGHT!
I STEAL TREASURE FROM PIRATES!
TO-GETHER WE COULD MAKE A FORTUNE!
NAMI THE PIRATE ROBBER
I DON'T WANT TO TEAM UP WITH YOU.
HEY, WAIT A MINUTE!
SPROING
TMP
TMP

READ THIS WAY

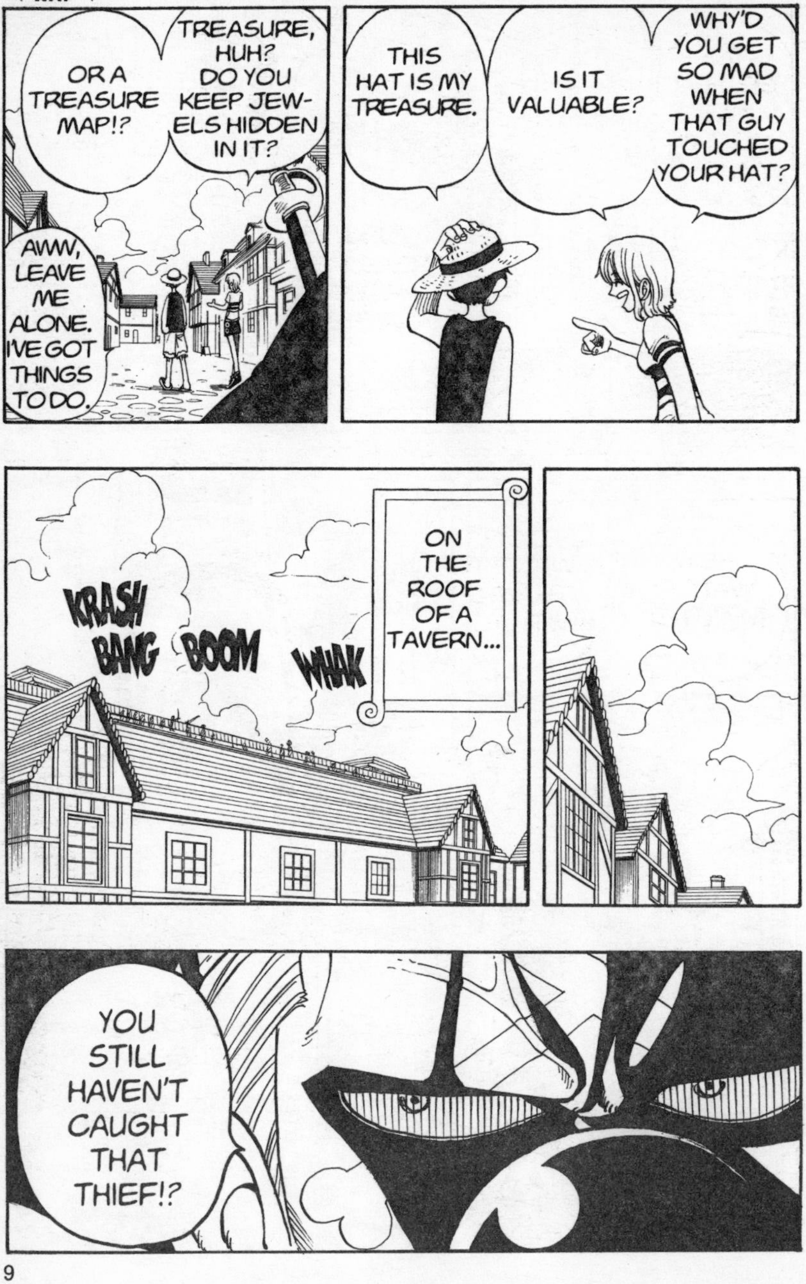

WHY'D YOU GET SO MAD WHEN THAT GUY TOUCHED YOUR HAT?
IS IT VALUABLE?
THIS HAT IS MY TREASURE.
TREASURE, HUH? DO YOU KEEP JEW-ELS HIDDEN IN IT?
OR A TREASURE MAP!?
AWW, LEAVE ME ALONE. I'VE GOT THINGS TO DO.
ON THE ROOF OF A TAVERN...
WHAK
BOOM
KRASH
BANG
YOU STILL HAVEN'T CAUGHT THAT THIEF!?

READ THIS WAY

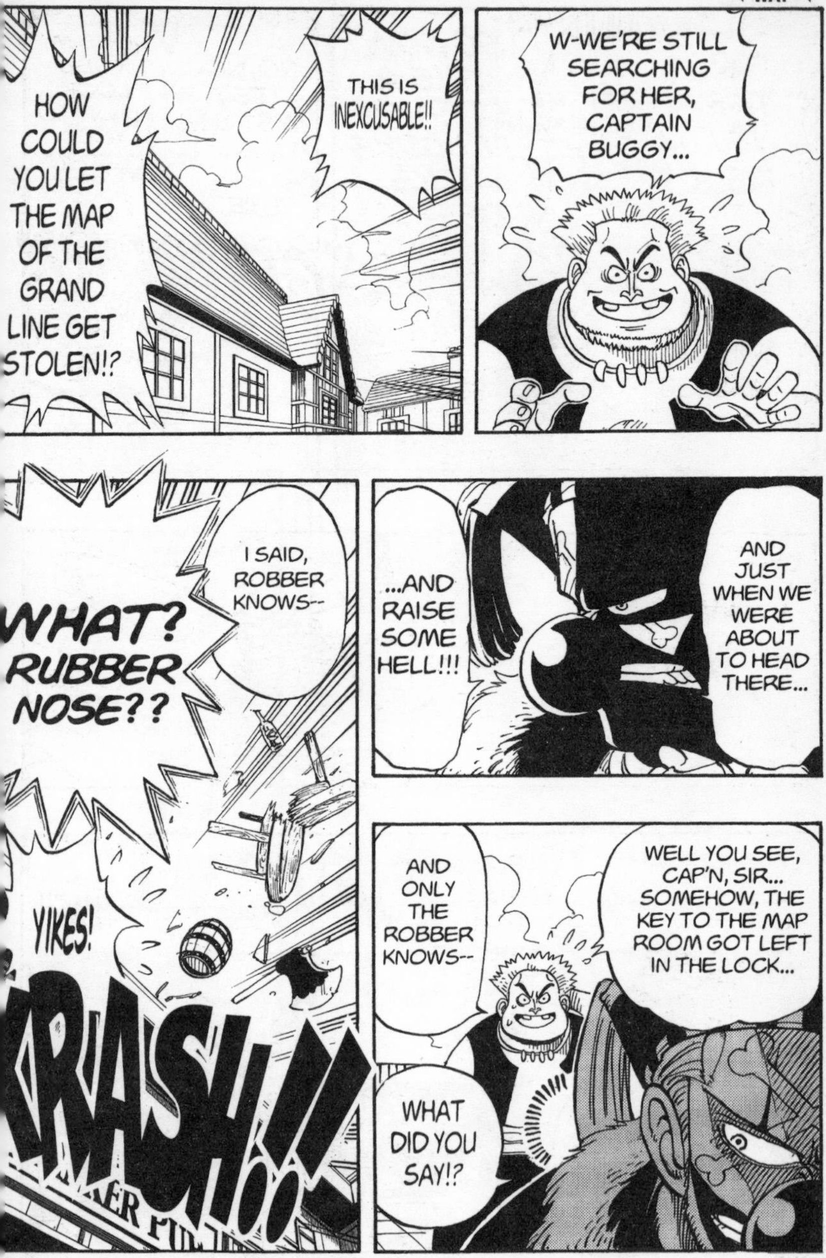
W-WE'RE STILL SEARCHING FOR HER, CAPTAIN BUGGY...
THIS IS INEXCUSABLE!!
HOW COULD YOU LET THE MAP OF THE GRAND LINE GET STOLEN!?
AND JUST WHEN WE WERE ABOUT TO HEAD THERE...
...AND RAISE SOME HELL!!!
WELL YOU SEE, CAP'N, SIR... SOMEHOW, THE KEY TO THE MAP ROOM GOT LEFT IN THE LOCK...
AND ONLY THE ROBBER KNOWS--
WHAT DID YOU SAY!?
I SAID, ROBBER KNOWS--
WHAT? RUBBER NOSE??
YIKES!
CRASH!!

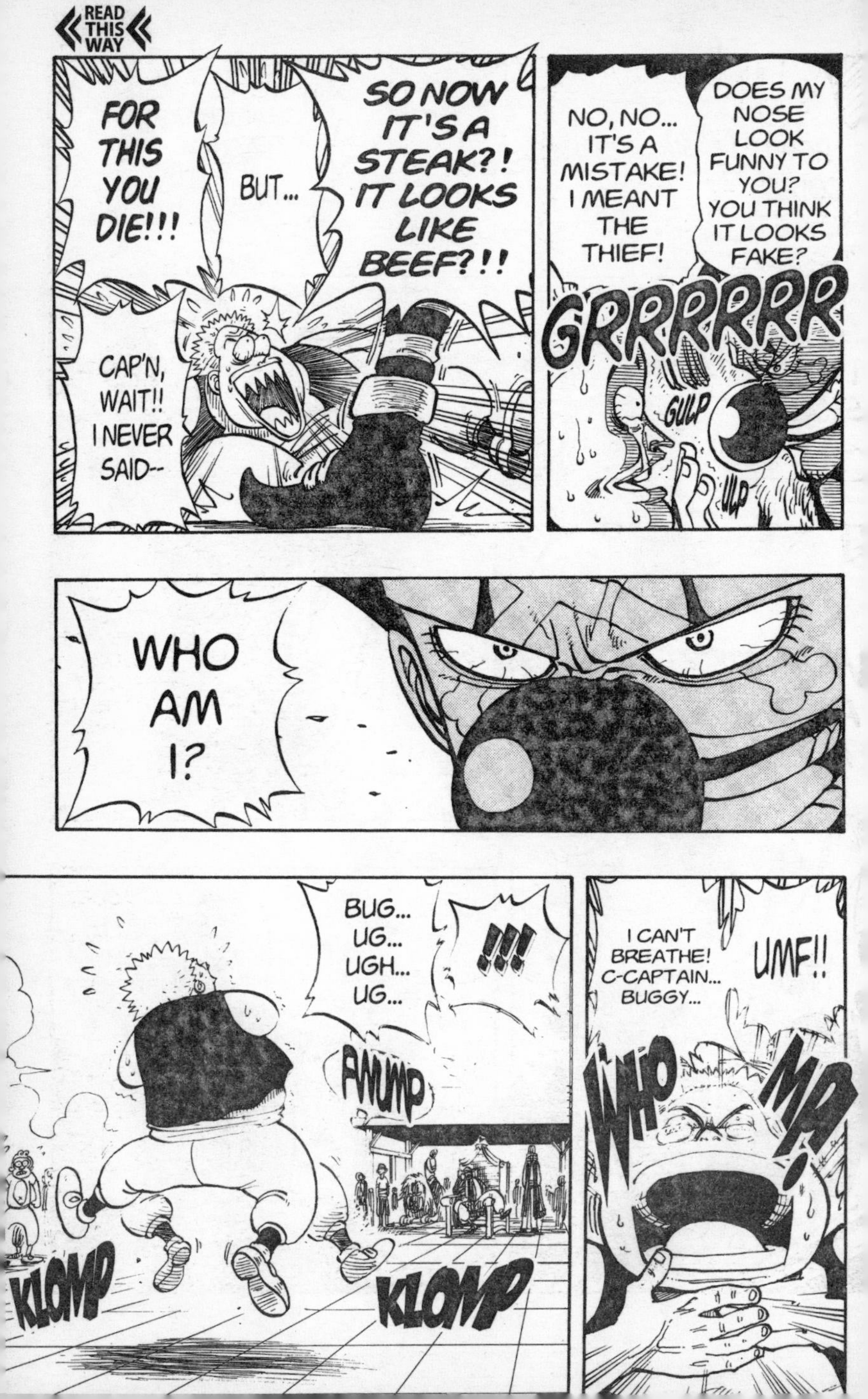
READ THIS WAY
DOES MY NOSE LOOK FUNNY TO YOU? YOU THINK IT LOOKS FAKE?
NO, NO... IT'S A MISTAKE! I MEANT THE THIEF!
GRRRRRR
GULP
ULP
SO NOW IT'S A STEAK?! IT LOOKS LIKE BEEF?!!
BUT...
FOR THIS YOU DIE!!!
CAP'N, WAIT!! I NEVER SAID--
WHO AM I?
UMF!!
I CAN'T BREATHE! C-CAPTAIN... BUGGY...
!!!
BUG... UG... UGH... UG...
FWUMP
KLOMP
KLOMP

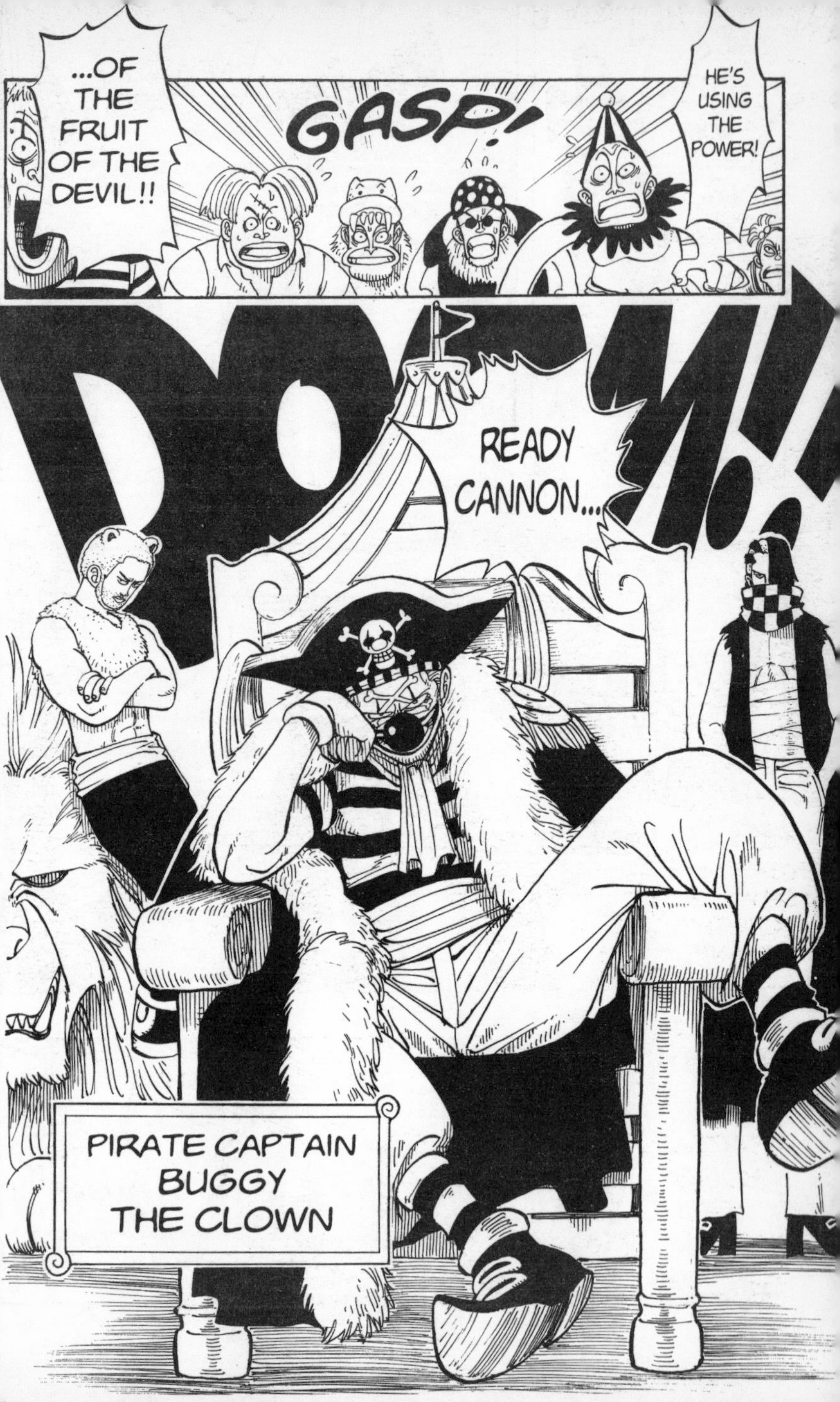
HE'S USING THE POWER!
GASP!
...OF THE FRUIT OF THE DEVIL!!
READY CANNON...
PIRATE CAPTAIN BUGGY THE CLOWN

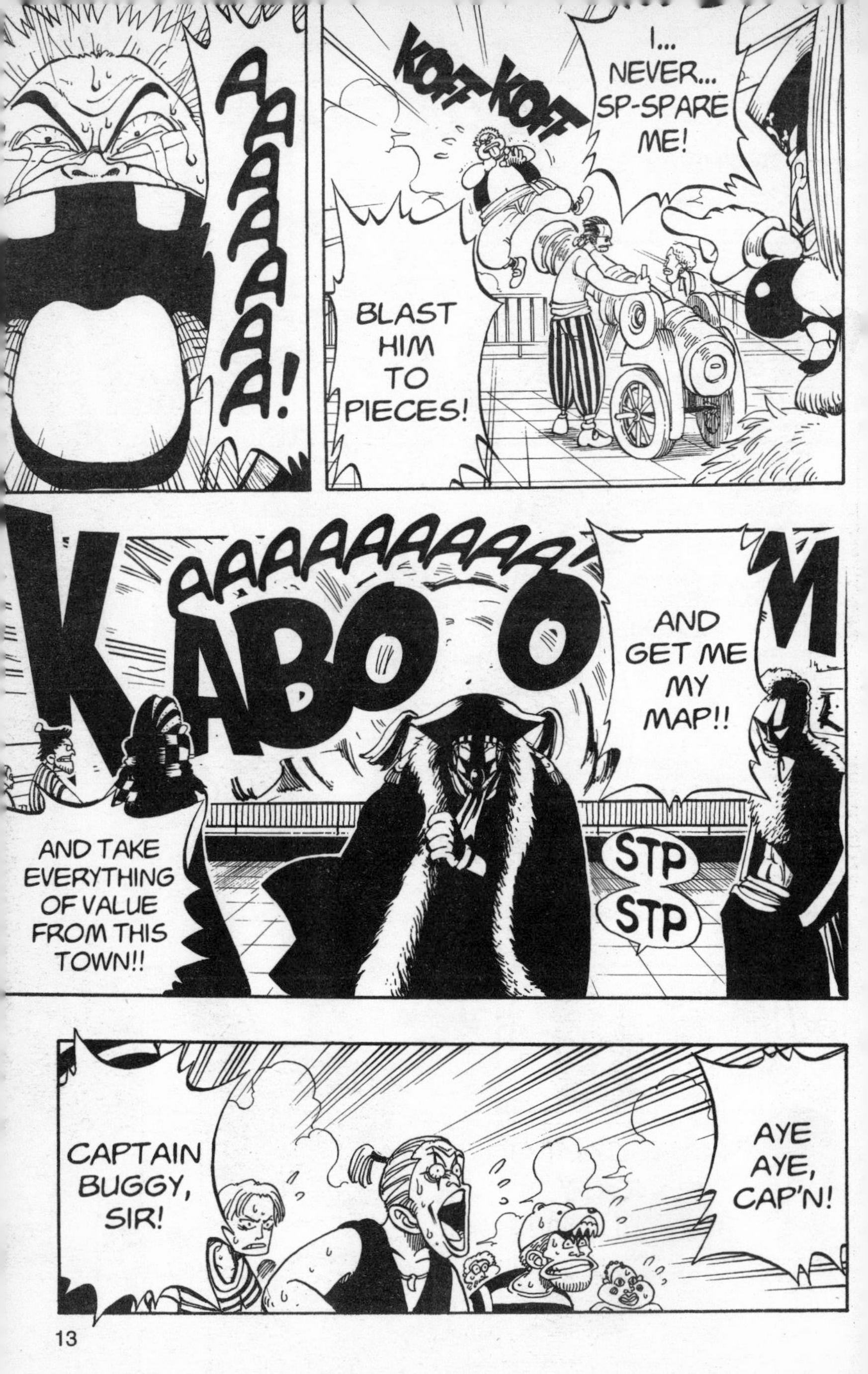
AAAAAAAA!
I... NEVER... SP-SPARE ME!
KOFF KOFF
BLAST HIM TO PIECES!
KABOOOM
AAAAAAAAA
AND GET ME MY MAP!!
AND TAKE EVERYTHING OF VALUE FROM THIS TOWN!!
STP
STP
AYE AYE, CAP'N!
CAPTAIN BUGGY, SIR!

READ THIS WAY

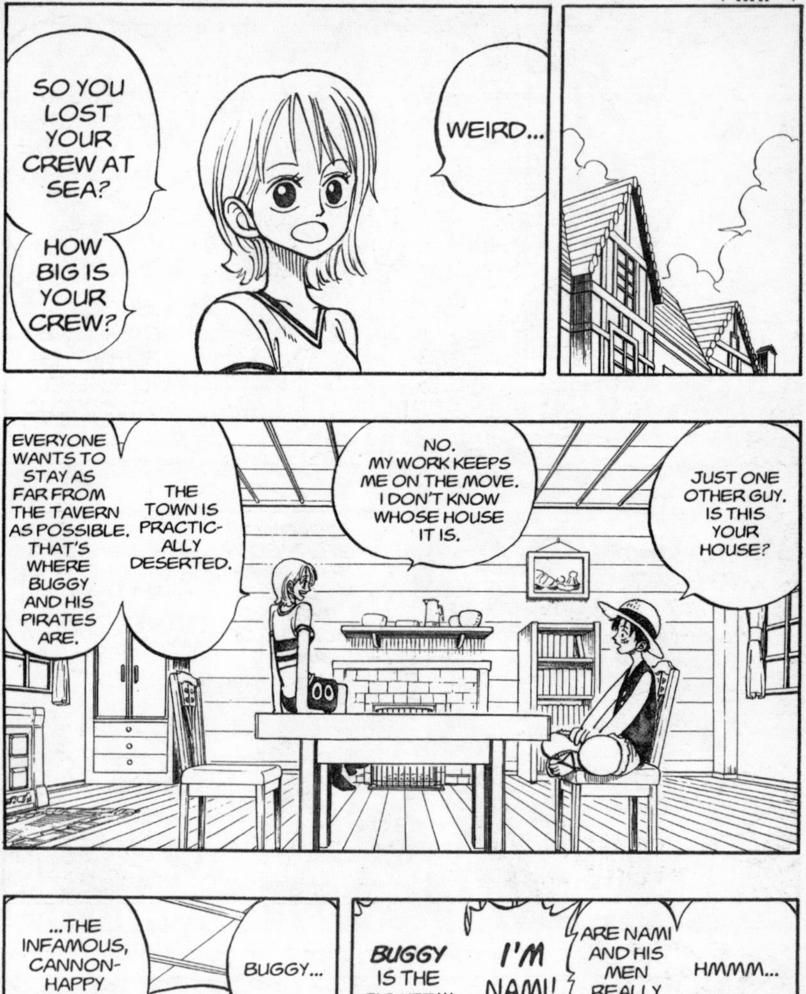
WEIRD...
SO YOU LOST YOUR CREW AT SEA?
HOW BIG IS YOUR CREW?
JUST ONE OTHER GUY. IS THIS YOUR HOUSE?
NO. MY WORK KEEPS ME ON THE MOVE. I DON'T KNOW WHOSE HOUSE IT IS.
THE TOWN IS PRACTICALLY DESERTED.
EVERYONE WANTS TO STAY AS FAR FROM THE TAVERN AS POSSIBLE. THAT'S WHERE BUGGY AND HIS PIRATES ARE.
HMMM...
ARE NAMI AND HIS MEN REALLY THAT SCARY?
I'M NAMI!
BUGGY IS THE PIRATE!!!
DON'T MIX ME UP WITH HIM!
BUGGY...
...THE INFAMOUS, CANNON-HAPPY BUCCANEER.

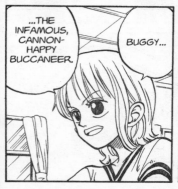

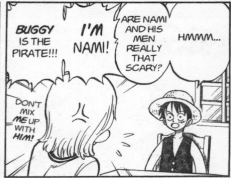

READ THIS WAY

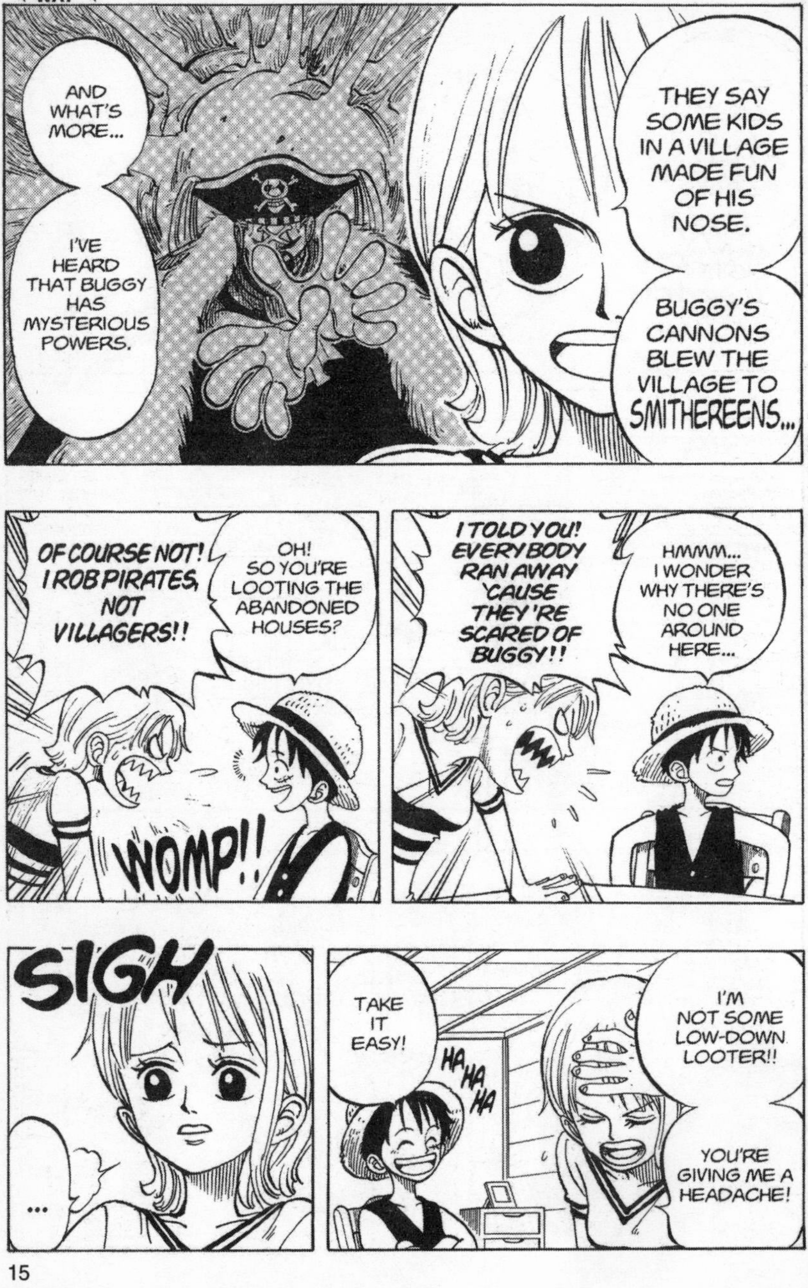

THEY SAY SOME KIDS IN A VILLAGE MADE FUN OF HIS NOSE.
BUGGY'S CANNONS BLEW THE VILLAGE TO SMITHEREENS...
AND WHAT'S MORE...
I'VE HEARD THAT BUGGY HAS MYSTERIOUS POWERS.
HMMM... I WONDER WHY THERE'S NO ONE AROUND HERE...
I TOLD YOU! EVERYBODY RAN AWAY 'CAUSE THEY'RE SCARED OF BUGGY!!
OH! SO YOU'RE LOOTING THE ABANDONED HOUSES?
OF COURSE NOT! I ROB PIRATES, NOT VILLAGERS!!
WOMP!!
I'M NOT SOME LOW-DOWN LOOTER!!
YOU'RE GIVING ME A HEADACHE!
TAKE IT EASY!
HA HA HA
SIGH
...

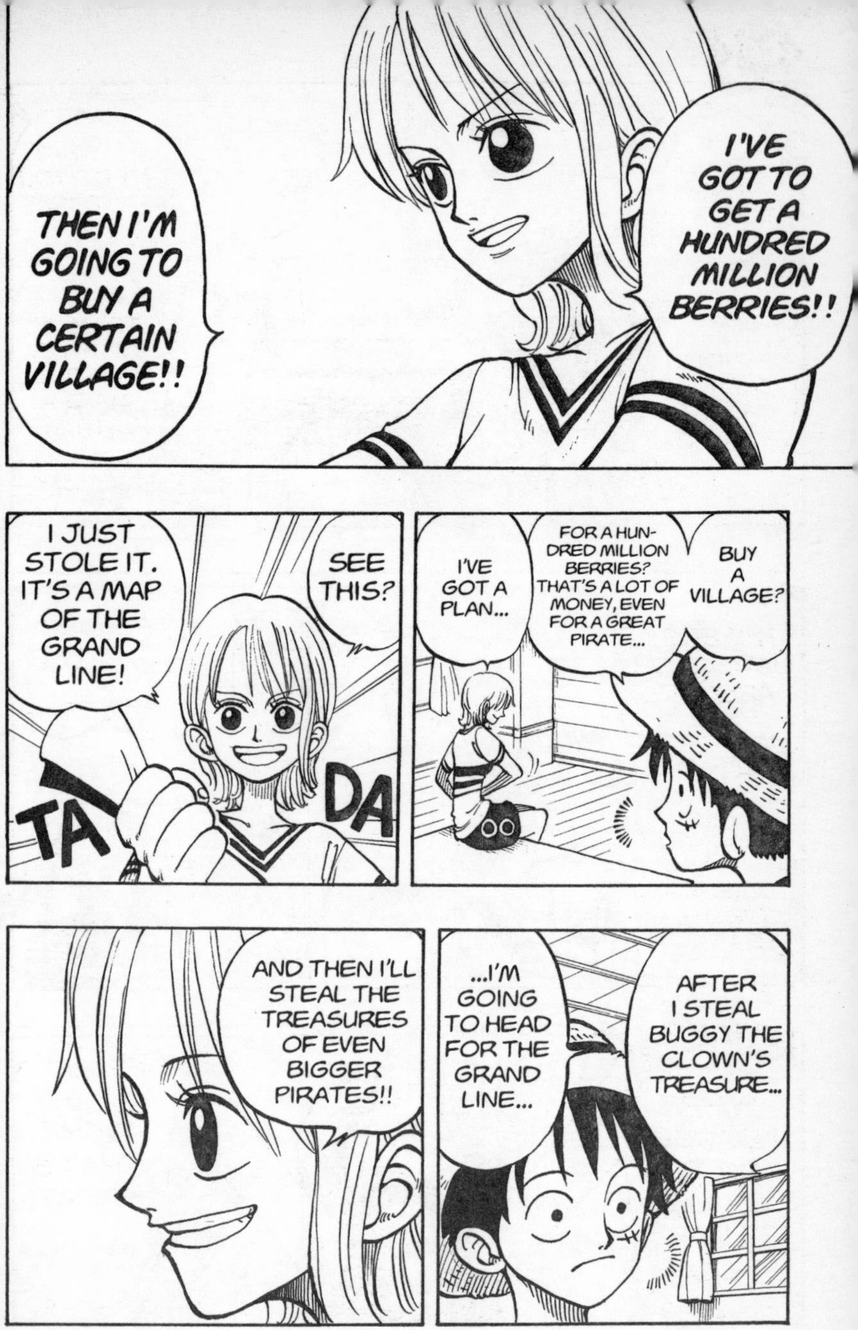
I'VE GOT TO GET A HUNDRED MILLION BERRIES!!
THEN I'M GOING TO BUY A CERTAIN VILLAGE!!
BUY A VILLAGE?
FOR A HUN-DRED MILLION BERRIES? THAT'S A LOT OF MONEY, EVEN FOR A GREAT PIRATE...
I'VE GOT A PLAN...
SEE THIS?
I JUST STOLE IT. IT'S A MAP OF THE GRAND LINE!
TA DA
AFTER I STEAL BUGGY THE CLOWN'S TREASURE...
...I'M GOING TO HEAD FOR THE GRAND LINE...
AND THEN I'LL STEAL THE TREASURES OF EVEN BIGGER PIRATES!!

READ THIS WAY

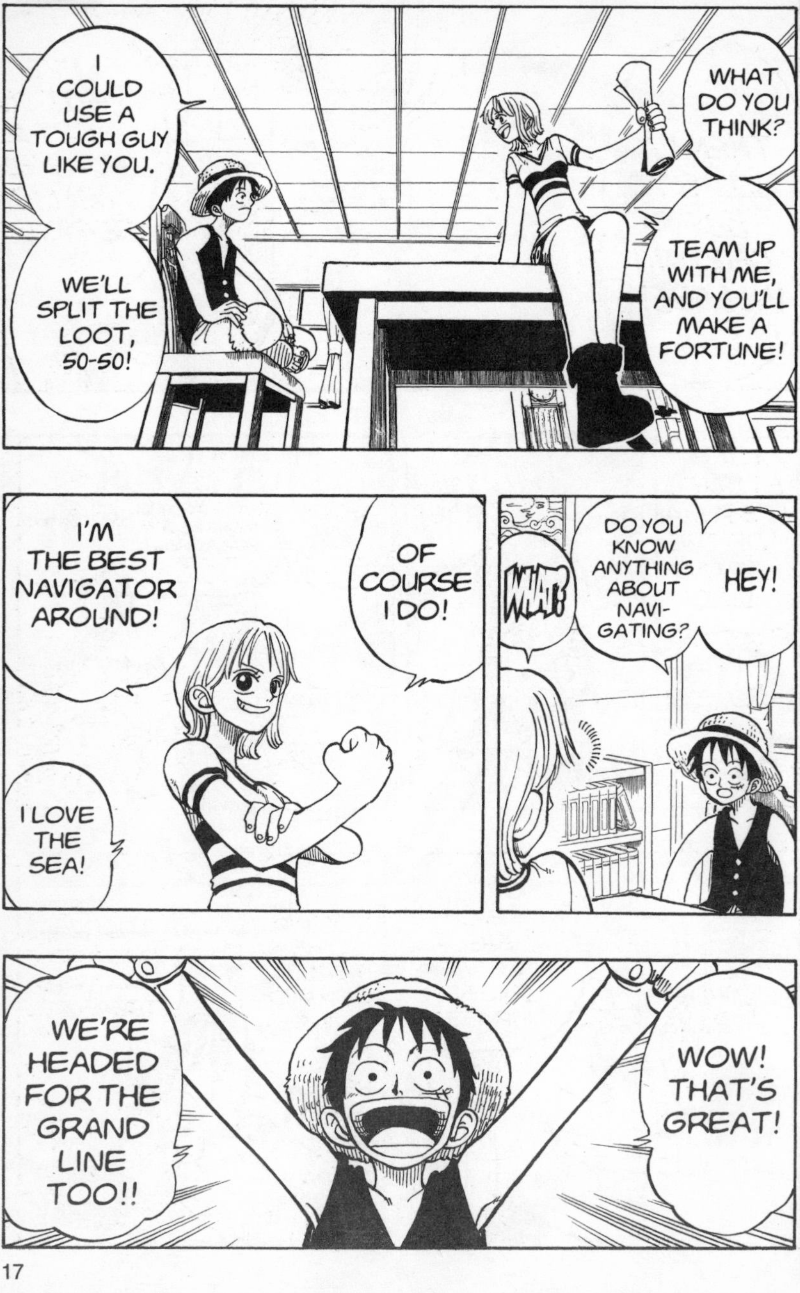
WHAT DO YOU THINK?
TEAM UP WITH ME, AND YOU'LL MAKE A FORTUNE!
I COULD USE A TOUGH GUY LIKE YOU.
WE'LL SPLIT THE LOOT, 50-50!
HEY!
DO YOU KNOW ANYTHING ABOUT NAVI-GATING?
WHAT?
OF COURSE I DO!
I'M THE BEST NAVIGATOR AROUND!
I LOVE THE SEA!
WOW! THAT'S GREAT!
WE'RE HEADED FOR THE GRAND LINE TOO!!

READ THIS WAY

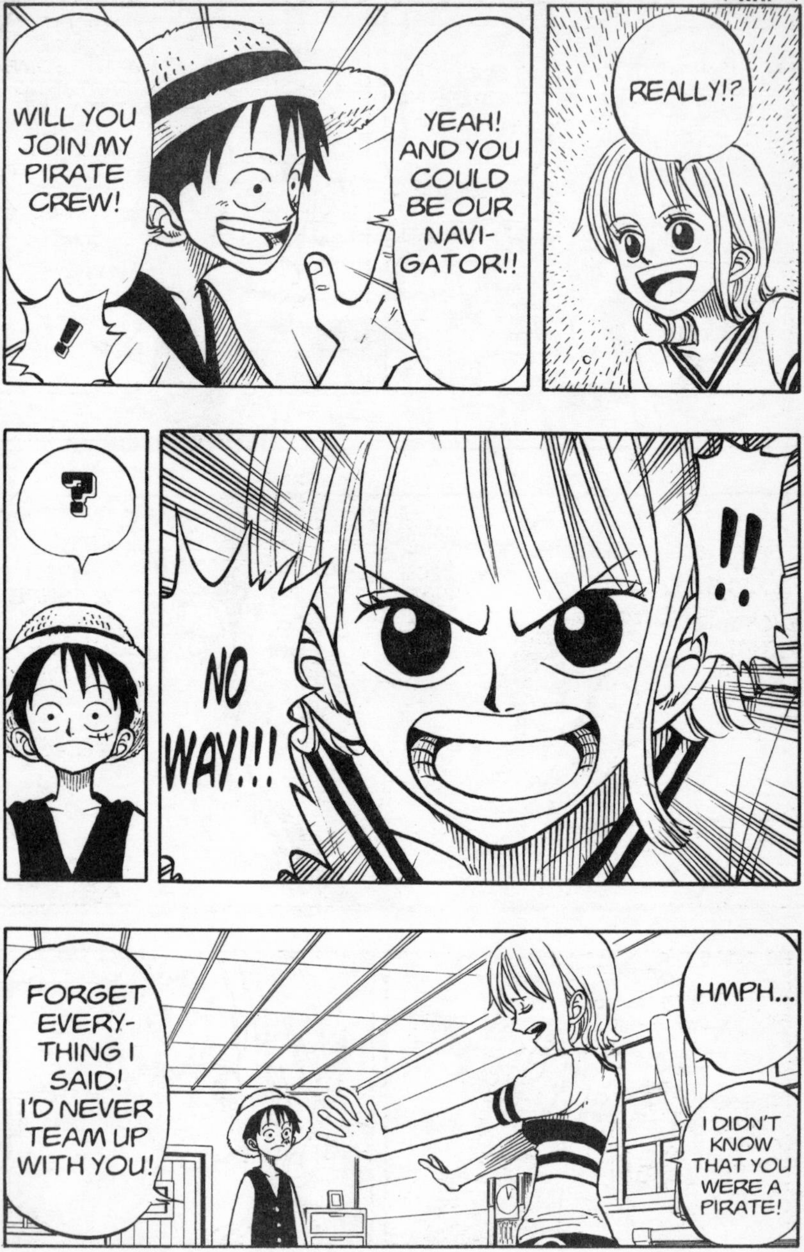
REALLY!?
YEAH! AND YOU COULD BE OUR NAVI-GATOR!!
WILL YOU JOIN MY PIRATE CREW!
!
!!
NO WAY!!!
?
HMPH...
I DIDN'T KNOW THAT YOU WERE A PIRATE!
FORGET EVERY-THING I SAID! I'D NEVER TEAM UP WITH YOU!

READ THIS WAY

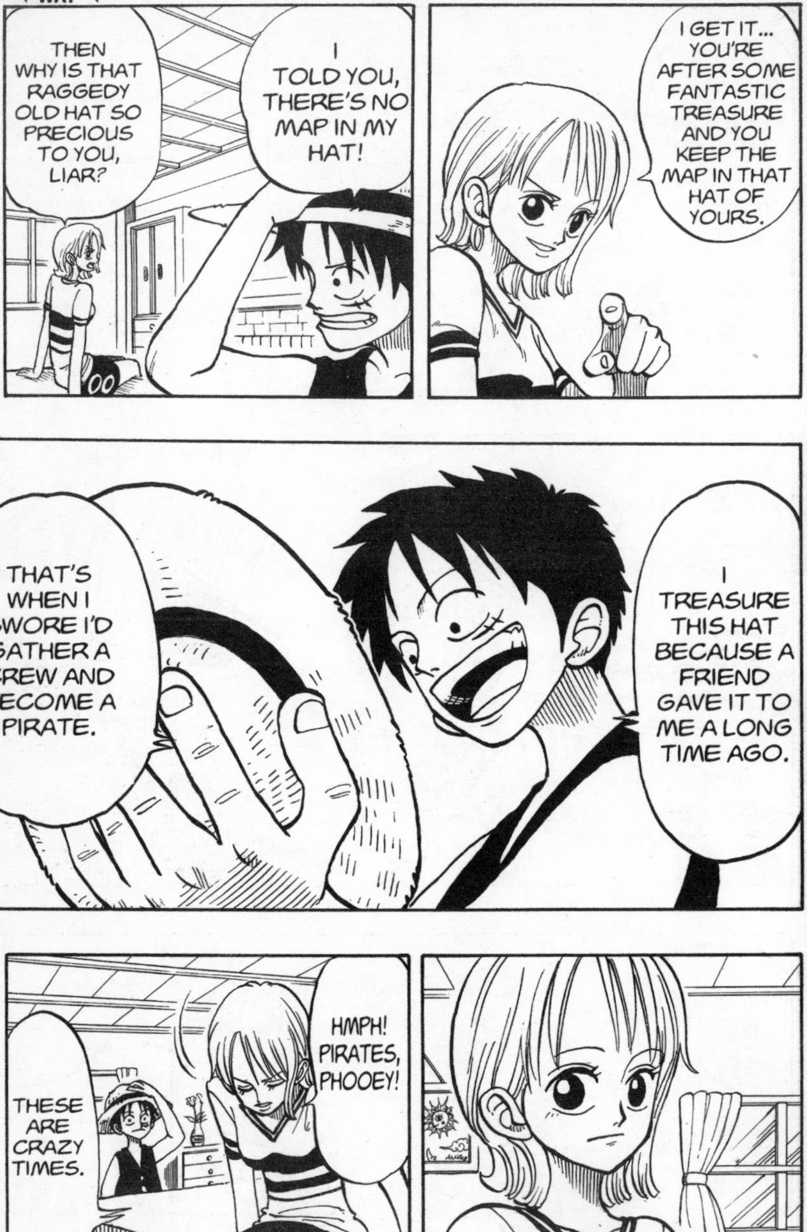

I GET IT... YOU'RE AFTER SOME FANTASTIC TREASURE AND YOU KEEP THE MAP IN THAT HAT OF YOURS.
I TOLD YOU, THERE'S NO MAP IN MY HAT!
THEN WHY IS THAT RAGGEDY OLD HAT SO PRECIOUS TO YOU, LIAR?
I TREASURE THIS HAT BECAUSE A FRIEND GAVE IT TO ME A LONG TIME AGO.
THAT'S WHEN I SWORE I'D GATHER A CREW AND BECOME A PIRATE.
HMPH! PIRATES, PHOOEY!
THESE ARE CRAZY TIMES.

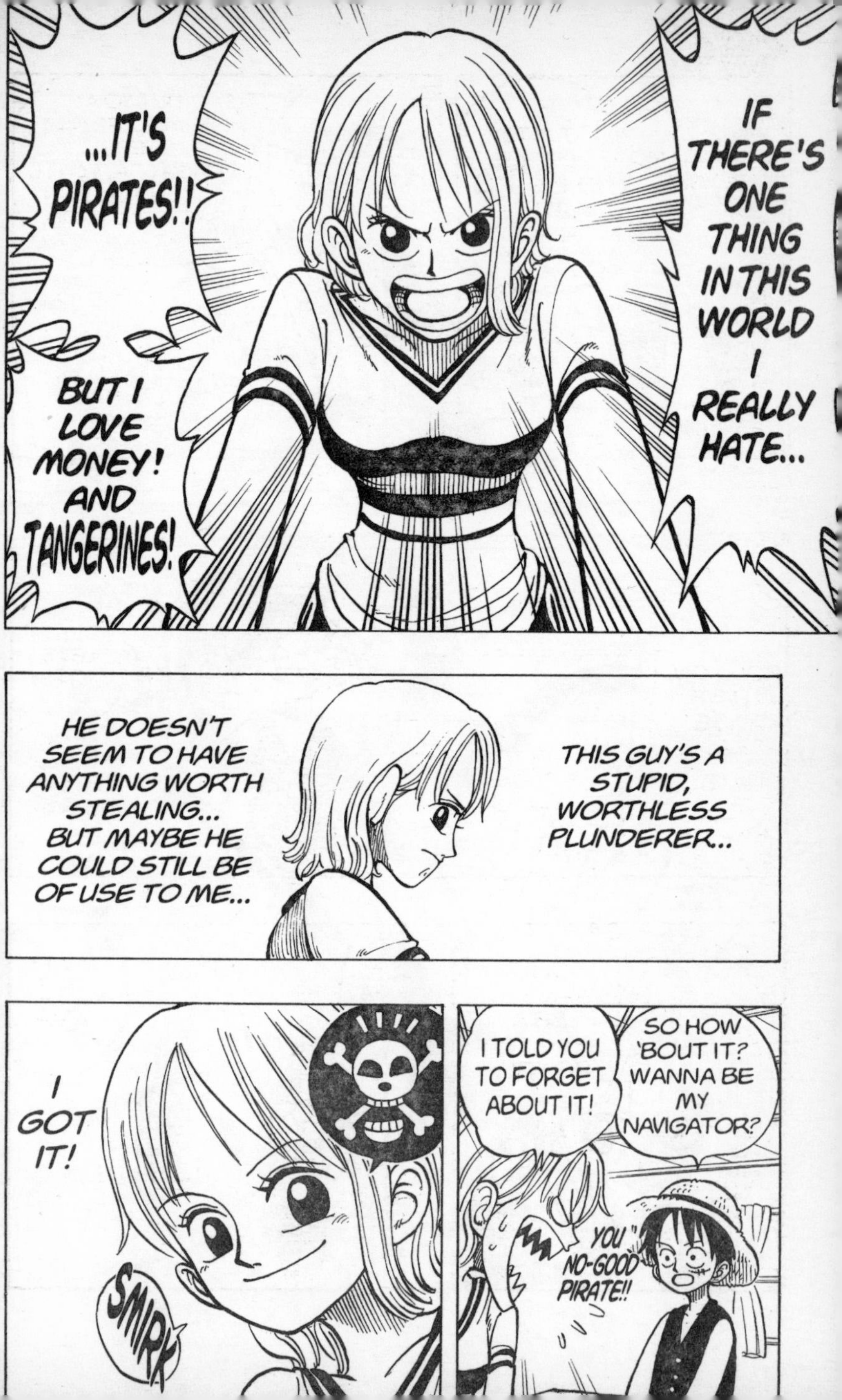
IF THERE'S ONE THING IN THIS WORLD I REALLY HATE...
...IT'S PIRATES!!
BUT I LOVE MONEY! AND TANGERINES!
THIS GUY'S A STUPID, WORTHLESS PLUNDERER...
HE DOESN'T SEEM TO HAVE ANYTHING WORTH STEALING... BUT MAYBE HE COULD STILL BE OF USE TO ME...
SO HOW 'BOUT IT? WANNA BE MY NAVIGATOR?
I TOLD YOU TO FORGET ABOUT IT!
YOU NO-GOOD PIRATE!!
I GOT IT!
SMIRK

READ THIS WAY

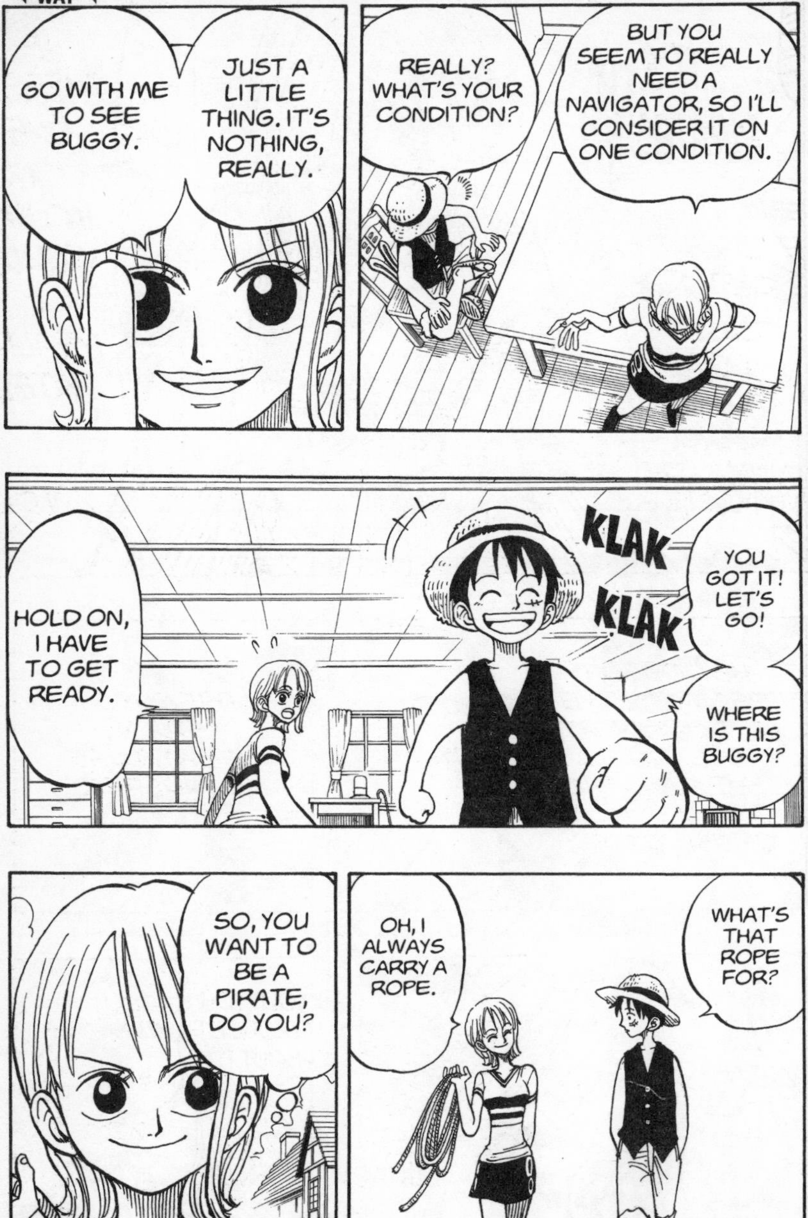
BUT YOU SEEM TO REALLY NEED A NAVIGATOR, SO I'LL CONSIDER IT ON ONE CONDITION.
REALLY? WHAT'S YOUR CONDITION?
JUST A LITTLE THING. IT'S NOTHING, REALLY.
GO WITH ME TO SEE BUGGY.
KLAK
KLAK
YOU GOT IT! LET'S GO!
WHERE IS THIS BUGGY?
HOLD ON, I HAVE TO GET READY.
WHAT'S THAT ROPE FOR?
OH, I ALWAYS CARRY A ROPE.
SO, YOU WANT TO BE A PIRATE, DO YOU?

READ THIS WAY

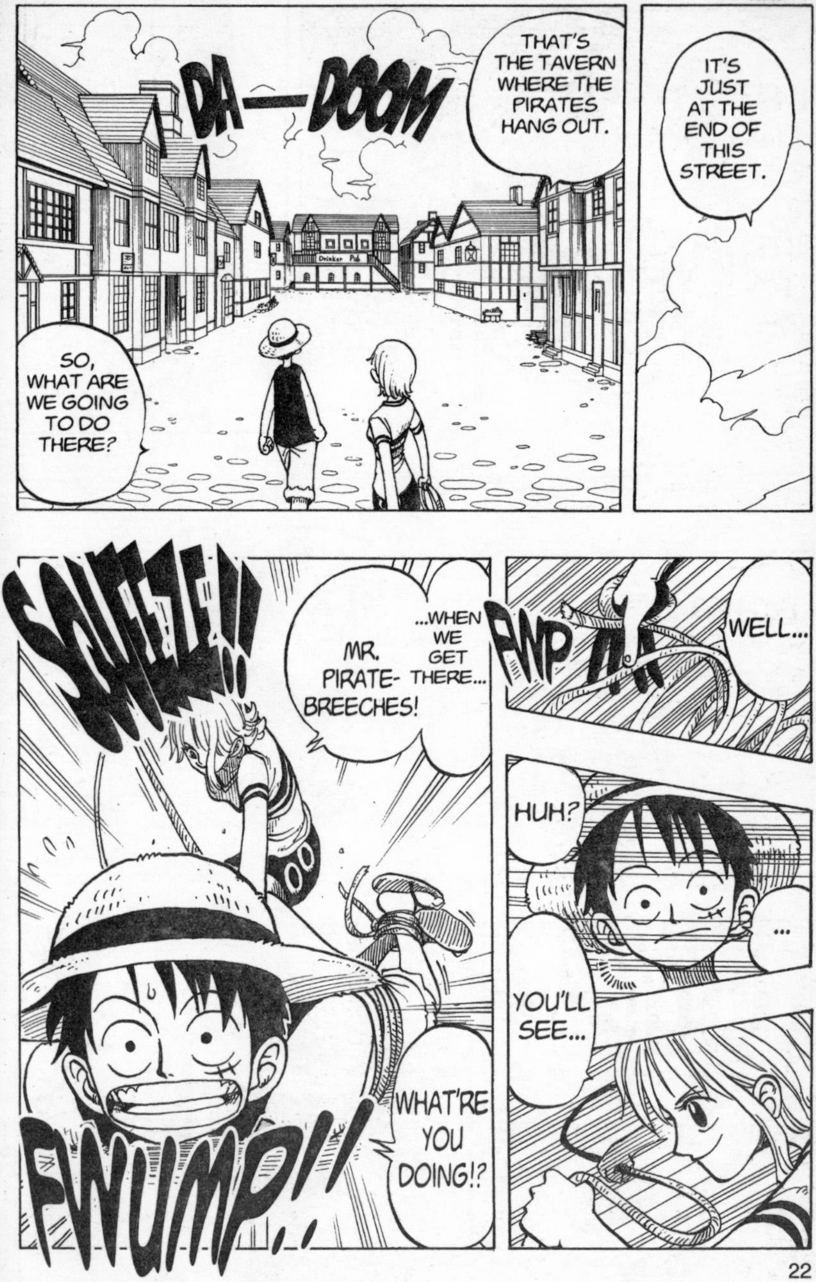
IT'S JUST AT THE END OF THIS STREET.
THAT'S THE TAVERN WHERE THE PIRATES HANG OUT.
DA—DOOM
SO, WHAT ARE WE GOING TO DO THERE?
WELL...
HUH?
...
YOU'LL SEE...
...WHEN WE GET THERE...
MR. PIRATE-BREECHES!
FWUMP!!
WHAT'RE YOU DOING!?

READ THIS WAY

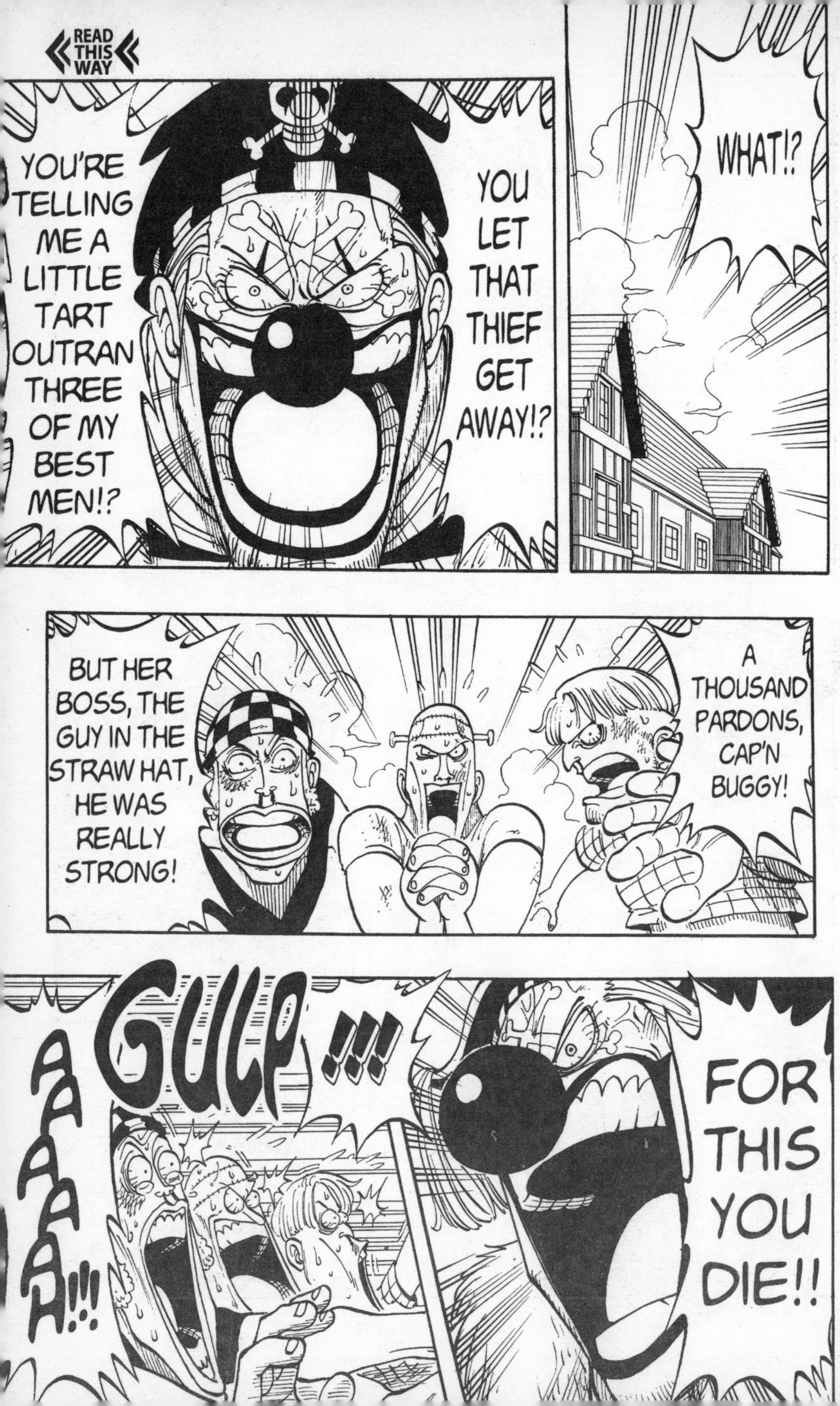

WHAT!?
YOU LET THAT THIEF GET AWAY!?
YOU'RE TELLING ME A LITTLE TART OUTRAN THREE OF MY BEST MEN!?
A THOUSAND PARDONS, CAP'N BUGGY!
BUT HER BOSS, THE GUY IN THE STRAW HAT, HE WAS REALLY STRONG!
FOR THIS YOU DIE!!
GULP!!!
AAAAAH!!!

READ THIS WAY

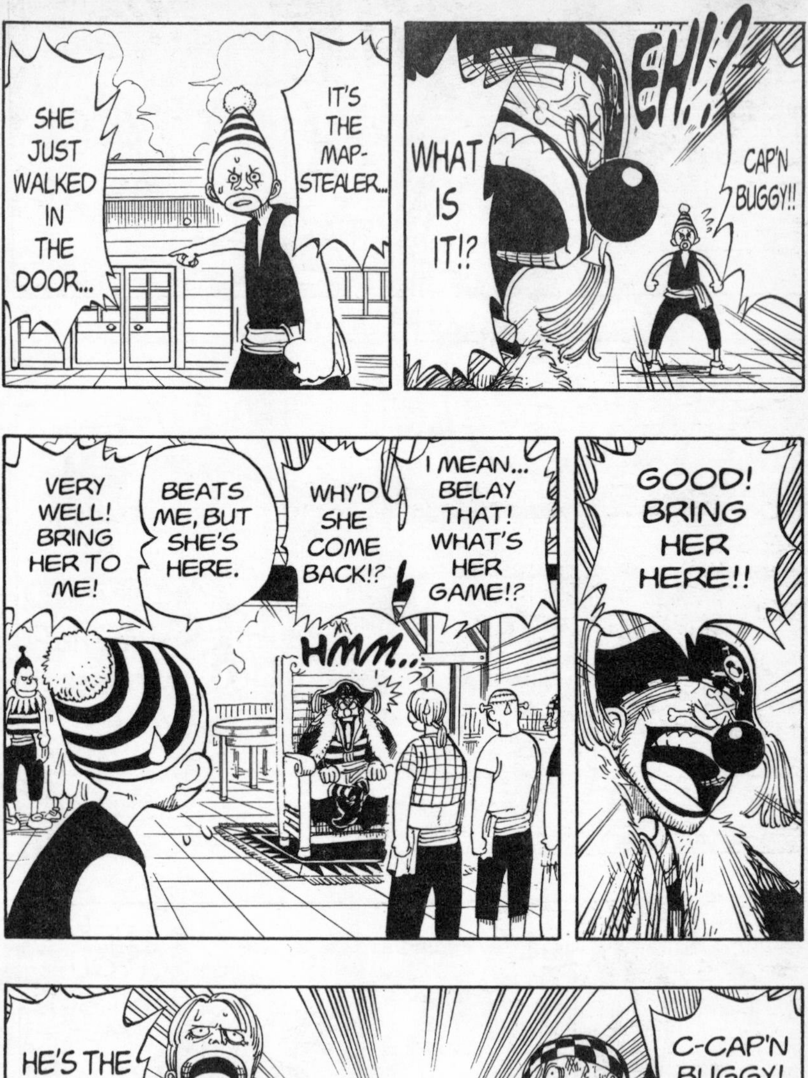
CAP'N BUGGY!!
EH!?
WHAT IS IT!?
IT'S THE MAP-STEALER...
SHE JUST WALKED IN THE DOOR...
GOOD! BRING HER HERE!!
I MEAN... BELAY THAT! WHAT'S HER GAME!?
HMM...
WHY'D SHE COME BACK!?
BEATS ME, BUT SHE'S HERE.
VERY WELL! BRING HER TO ME!
C-CAP'N BUGGY! IT'S *HIM!* SHE'S WITH *HIM!*
HE'S THE GUY WHO FELL OUT OF THE SKY!!

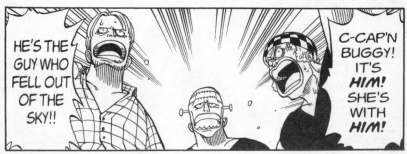

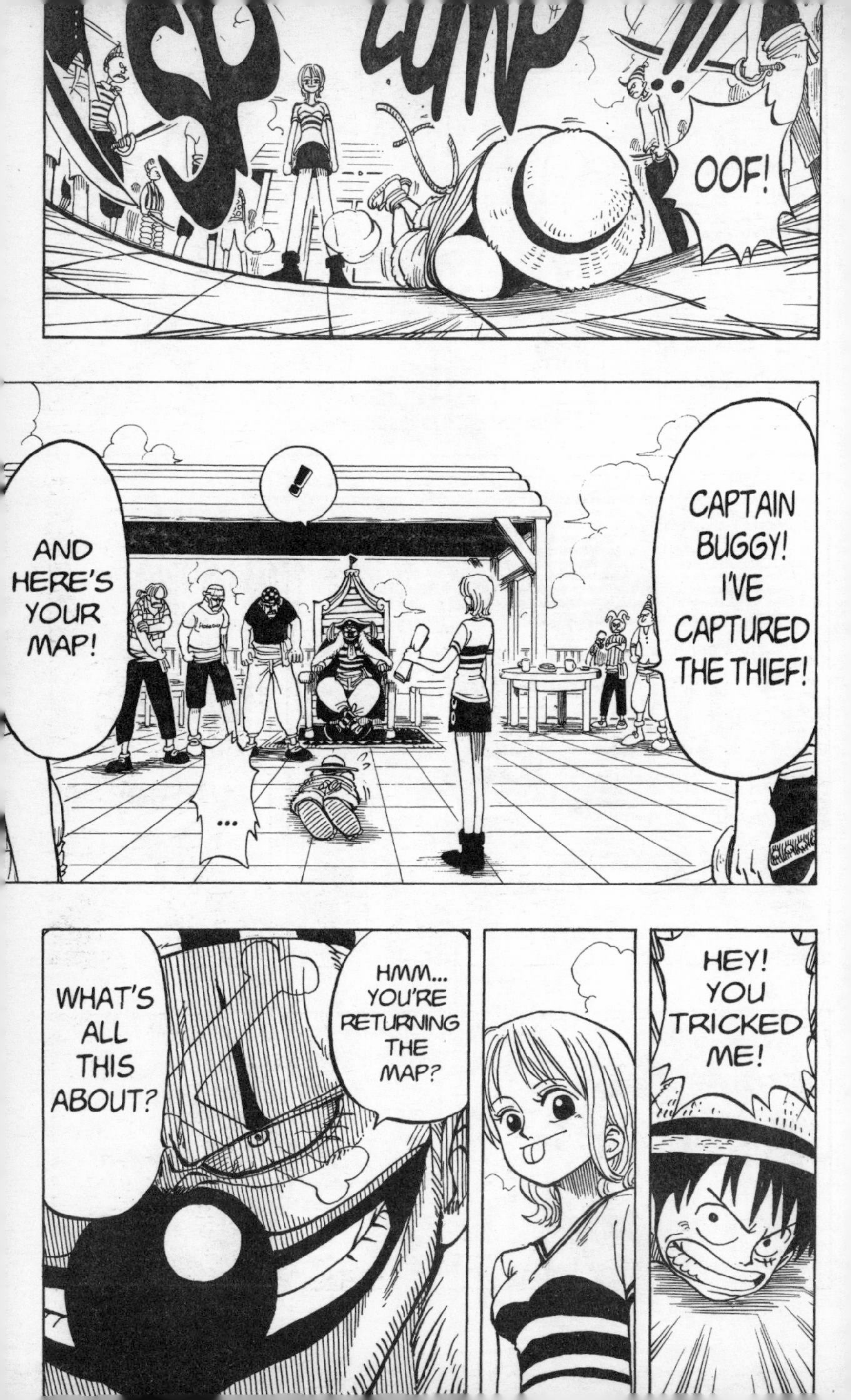
OOF!
CAPTAIN BUGGY! I'VE CAPTURED THE THIEF!
!
AND HERE'S YOUR MAP!
...
HEY! YOU TRICKED ME!
HMM... YOU'RE RETURNING THE MAP?
WHAT'S ALL THIS ABOUT?

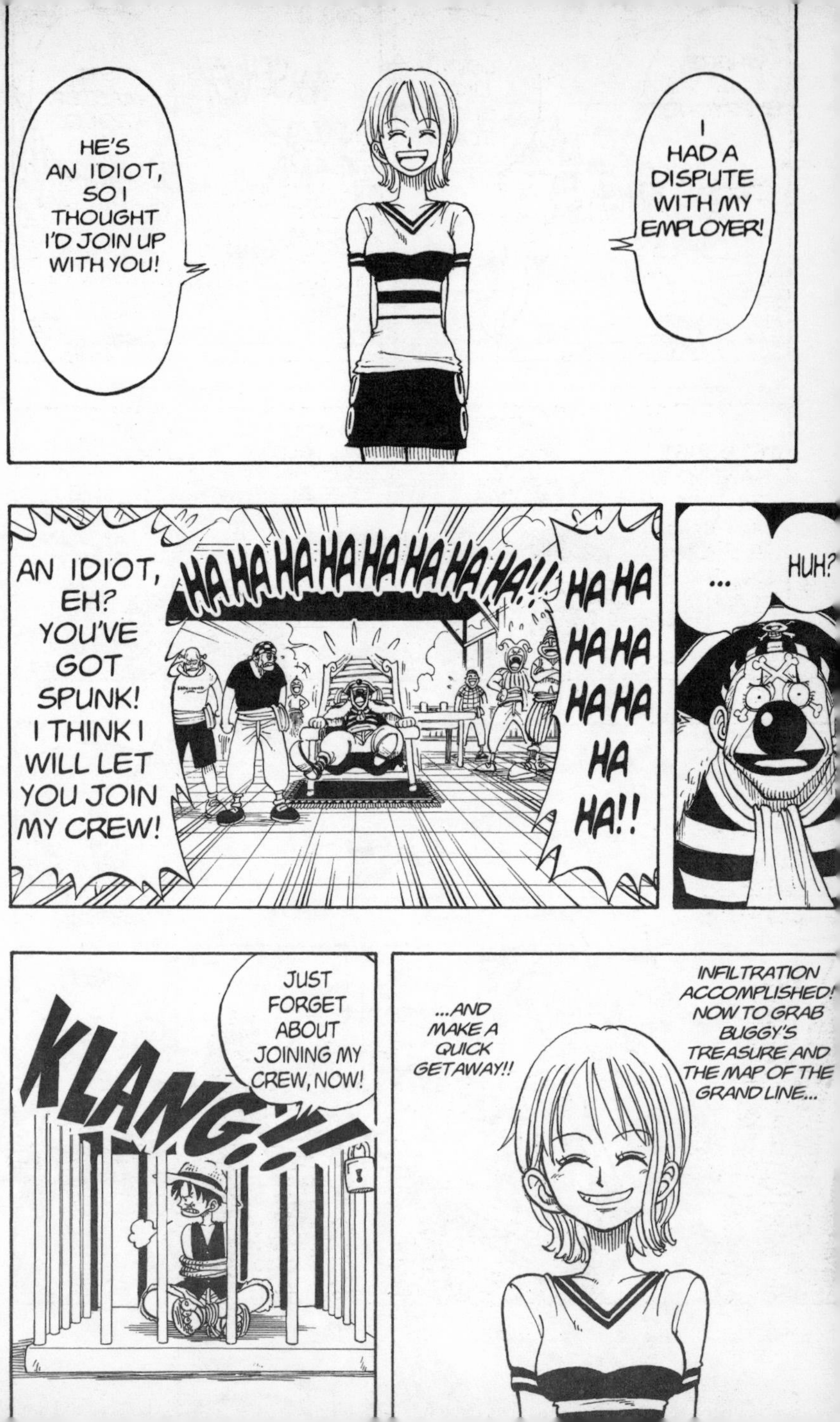
I HAD A DISPUTE WITH MY EMPLOYER!
HE'S AN IDIOT, SO I THOUGHT I'D JOIN UP WITH YOU!
... HUH?
HA HA HA HA HA HA HA HA HA HA HA!!
HA HA HA HA HA HA HA HA!!
AN IDIOT, EH? YOU'VE GOT SPUNK! I THINK I WILL LET YOU JOIN MY CREW!
INFILTRATION ACCOMPLISHED! NOW TO GRAB BUGGY'S TREASURE AND THE MAP OF THE GRAND LINE...
...AND MAKE A QUICK GETAWAY!!
JUST FORGET ABOUT JOINING MY CREW, NOW!
KLANG!!!

WHERE IS EVERYONE?

IT LOOKS LIKE A GHOST TOWN.

...

HEH HEHHEH

THIS IS IT, MASTER ZOLO.

WE'LL JUST HAVE TO TELL HIM THE TRUTH. IT'S ALL THAT GIRL'S FAULT!

WE'RE COMING BACK EMPTY-HANDED...

WHAT'LL WE TELL CAPTAIN BUGGY?

WELL YOU SEE, SIR... WE'VE TAKEN OVER THE TOWN.

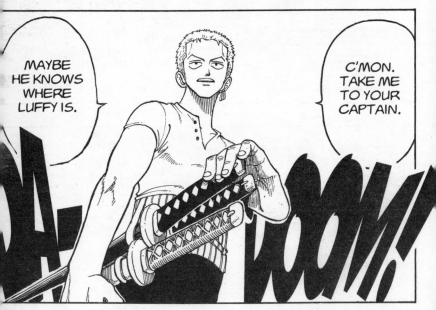

MAYBE HE KNOWS WHERE LUFFY IS.

C'MON. TAKE ME TO YOUR CAPTAIN.

One Piece Rough Sketch!

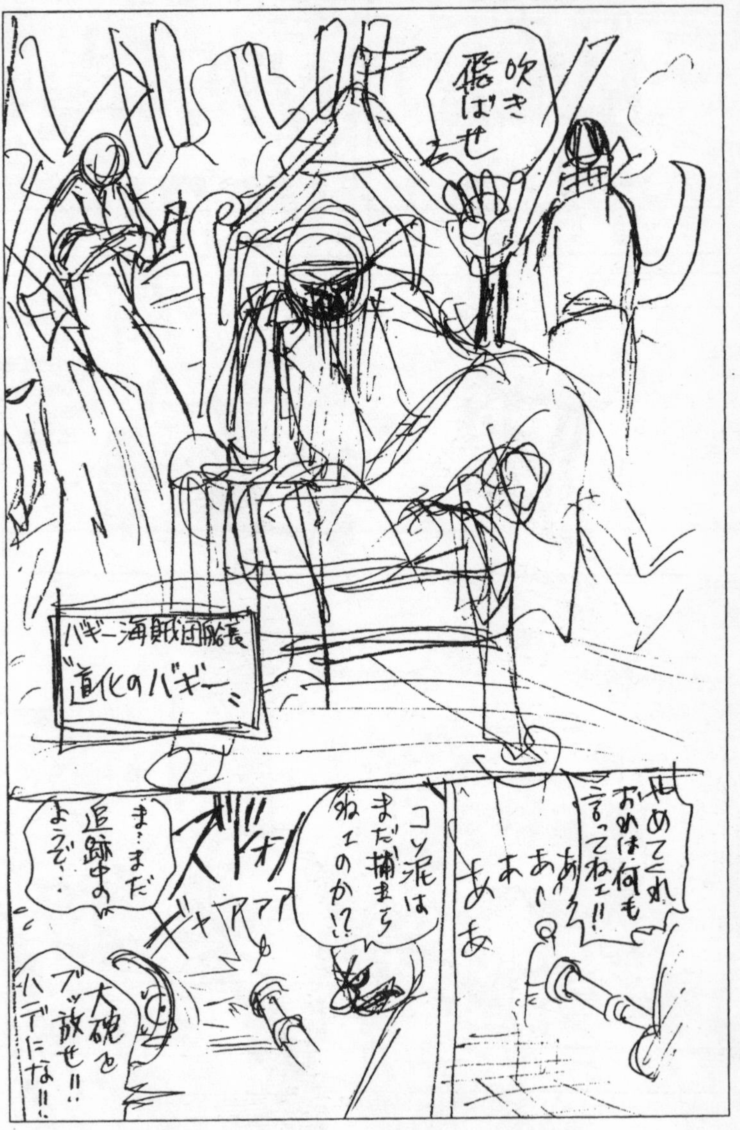
吹き飛ばせ
バギー海賊団船長
"道化のバギー"
やめてくれ おれは何も言ってねェ!!
あああああ
コソ泥はまだ捕まらねェのか!?
ドォン
ギャアア
ま…まだ追跡中のようで…
大砲をブッ放せ!! ハデにな!!

Chapter 10:
INCIDENT AT THE TAVERN

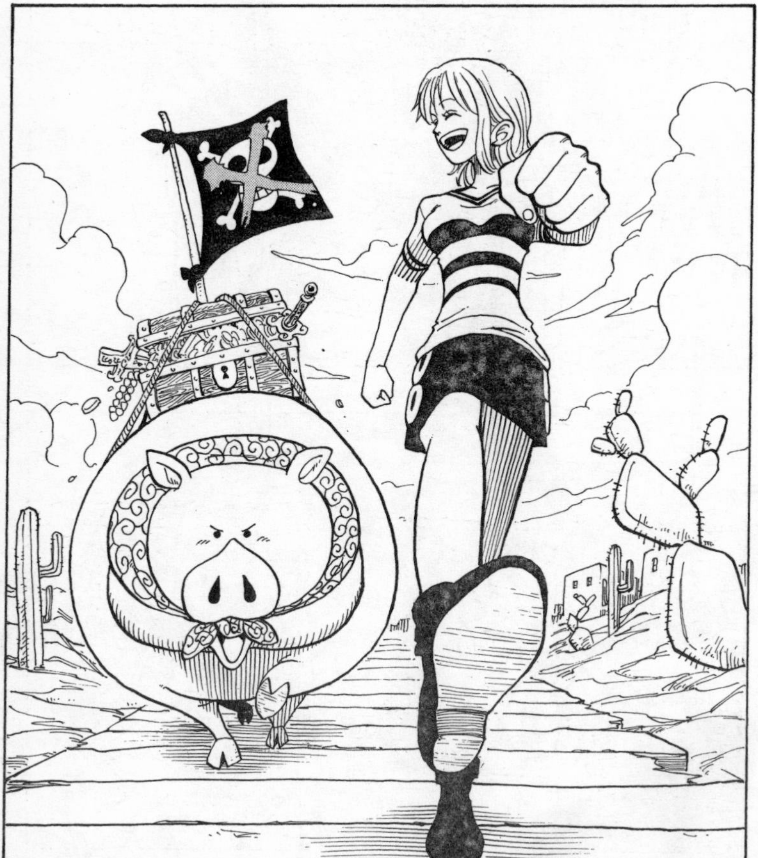

READ THIS WAY

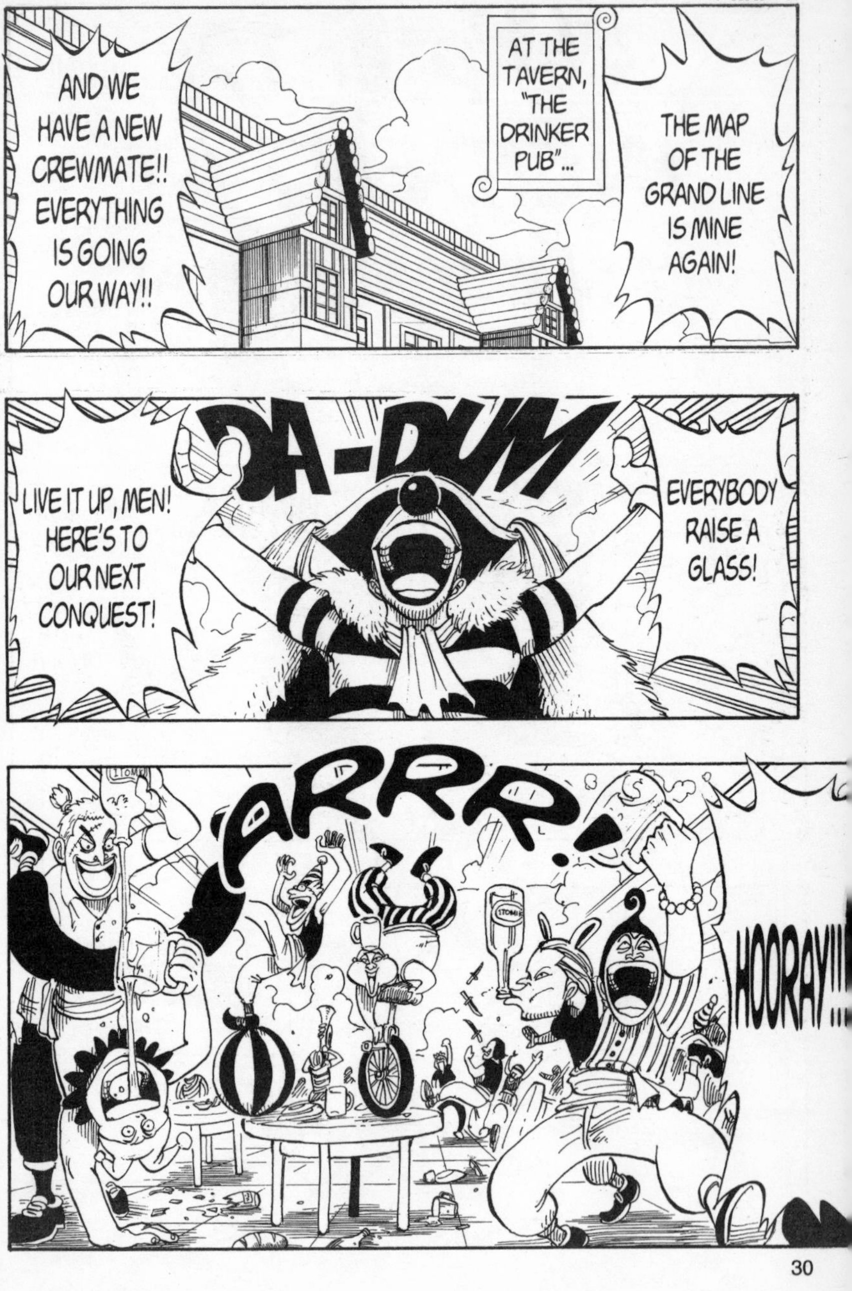
AT THE TAVERN, "THE DRINKER PUB"...
THE MAP OF THE GRAND LINE IS MINE AGAIN!
AND WE HAVE A NEW CREWMATE!! EVERYTHING IS GOING OUR WAY!!
DA-DUM
EVERYBODY RAISE A GLASS!
LIVE IT UP, MEN! HERE'S TO OUR NEXT CONQUEST!
ARRR!
HOORAY!!!

READ THIS WAY

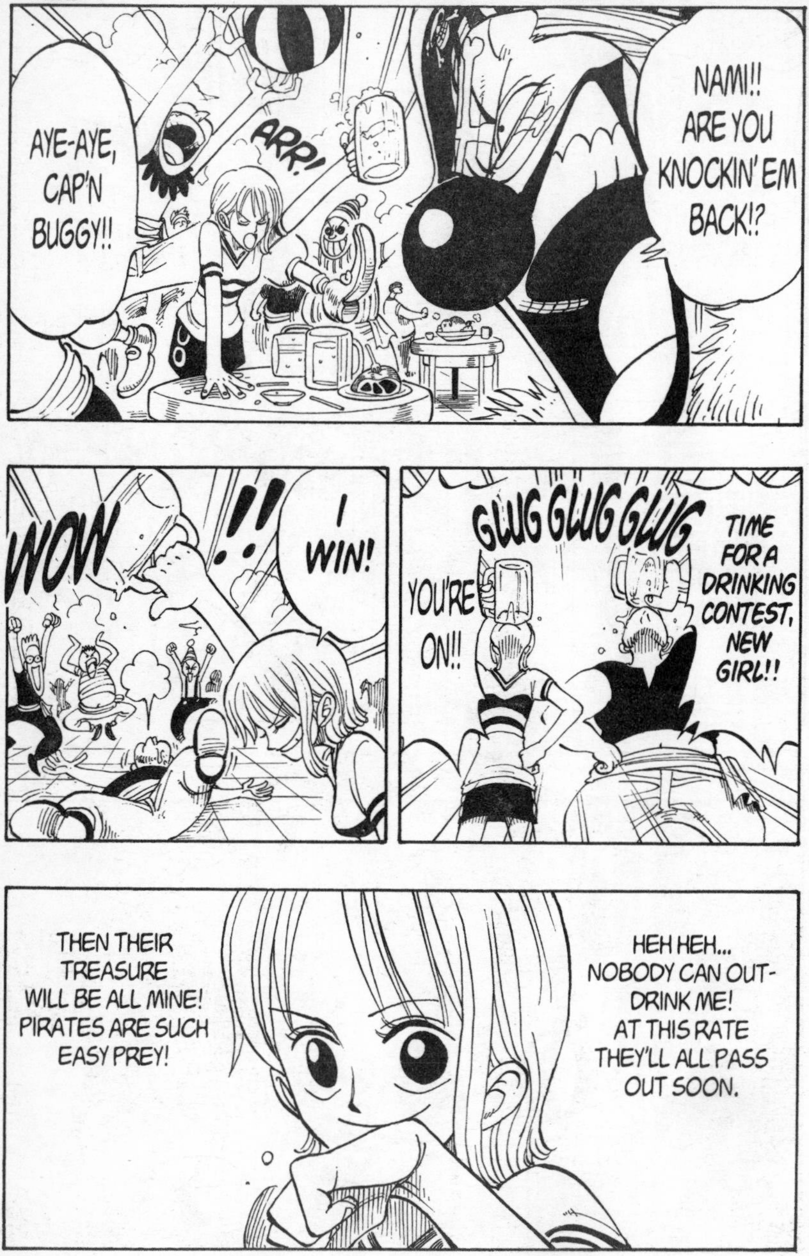
NAMI!! ARE YOU KNOCKIN' EM BACK!?
ARR!
AYE-AYE, CAP'N BUGGY!!
TIME FOR A DRINKING CONTEST, NEW GIRL!!
GLUG GLUG GLUG
YOU'RE ON!!
I WIN!
!!
WOW
HEH HEH... NOBODY CAN OUT-DRINK ME! AT THIS RATE THEY'LL ALL PASS OUT SOON.
THEN THEIR TREASURE WILL BE ALL MINE! PIRATES ARE SUCH EASY PREY!

READ THIS WAY

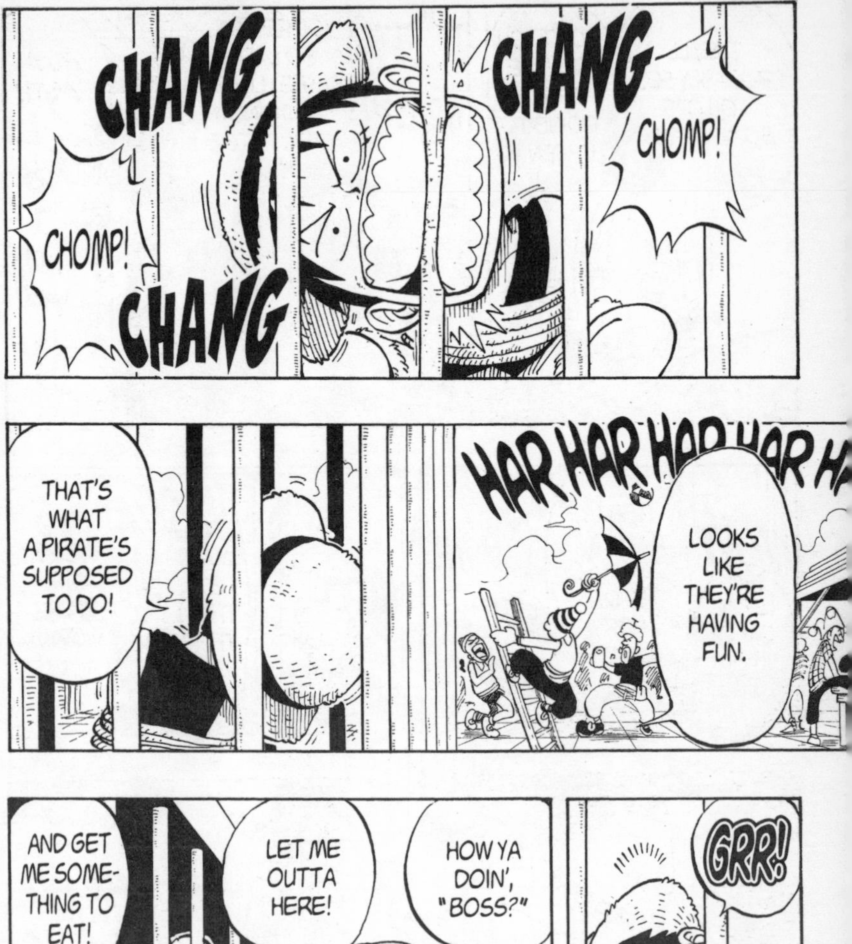
CHOMP!
CHANG
CHANG
CHOMP!
CHANG
HAR HAR HAR HAR
LOOKS LIKE THEY'RE HAVING FUN.
THAT'S WHAT A PIRATE'S SUPPOSED TO DO!
GRR!
HOW YA DOIN', "BOSS?"
LET ME OUTTA HERE!
AND GET ME SOME-THING TO EAT!
I'M STARVING!

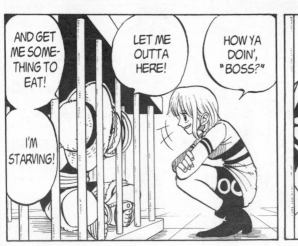

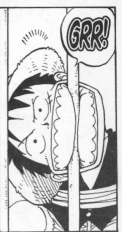

READ THIS WAY

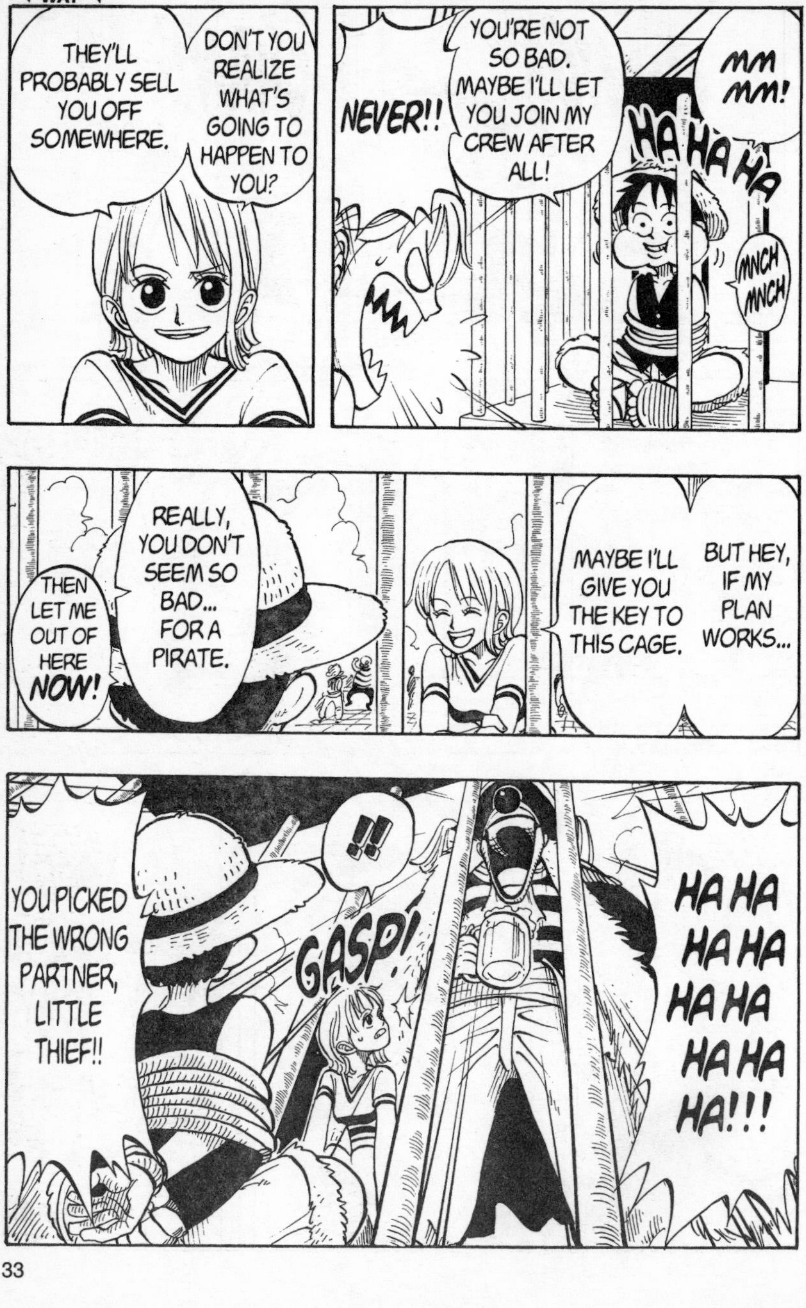
MM MM!
HA HA HA
MNCH MNCH
YOU'RE NOT SO BAD. MAYBE I'LL LET YOU JOIN MY CREW AFTER ALL!
NEVER!!
DON'T YOU REALIZE WHAT'S GOING TO HAPPEN TO YOU?
THEY'LL PROBABLY SELL YOU OFF SOMEWHERE.
BUT HEY, IF MY PLAN WORKS...
MAYBE I'LL GIVE YOU THE KEY TO THIS CAGE.
REALLY, YOU DON'T SEEM SO BAD... FOR A PIRATE.
THEN LET ME OUT OF HERE NOW!
HA HA HA HA HA HA HA HA HA!!!
!!
GASP!
YOU PICKED THE WRONG PARTNER, LITTLE THIEF!!

READ THIS WAY

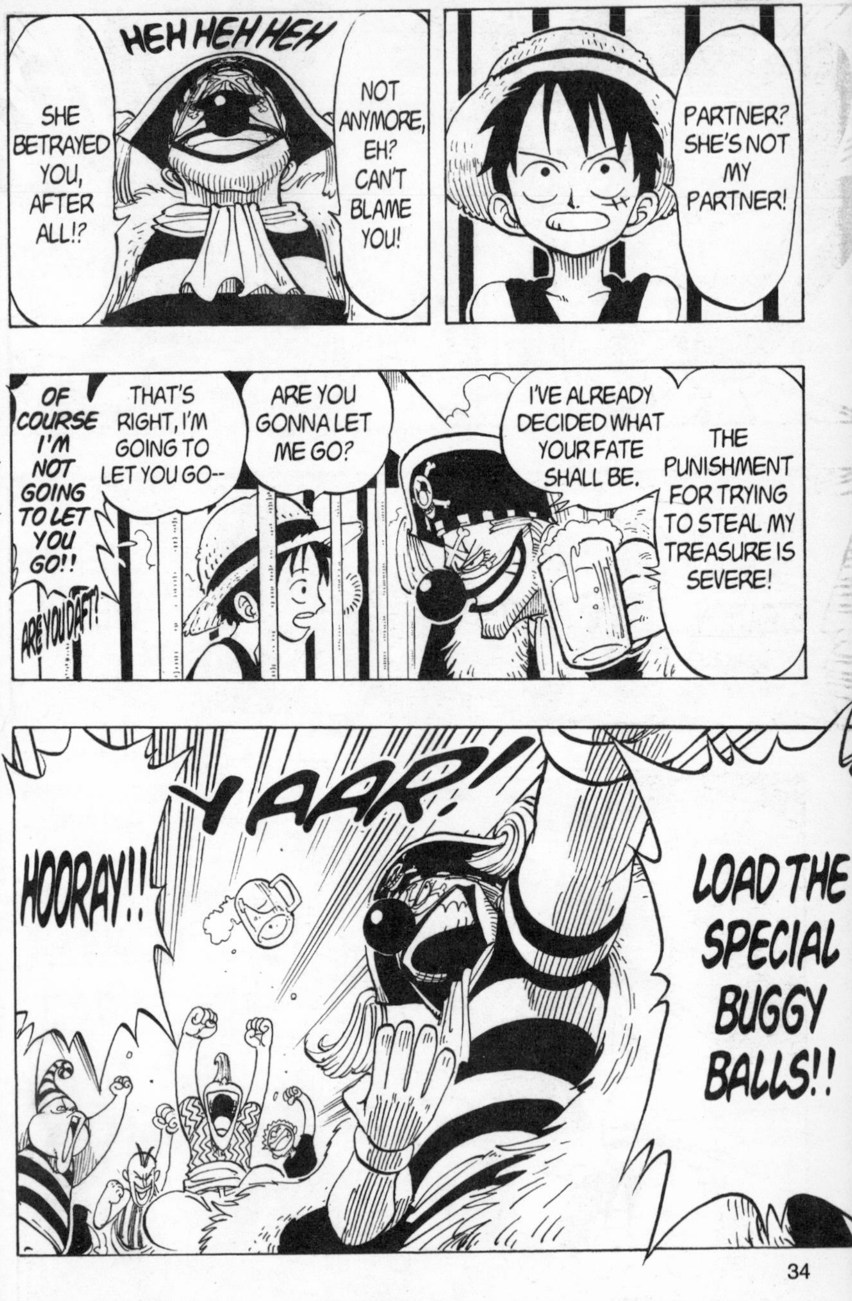
PARTNER? SHE'S NOT MY PARTNER!
HEH HEH HEH
NOT ANYMORE, EH? CAN'T BLAME YOU!
SHE BETRAYED YOU, AFTER ALL!?
THE PUNISHMENT FOR TRYING TO STEAL MY TREASURE IS SEVERE!
I'VE ALREADY DECIDED WHAT YOUR FATE SHALL BE.
ARE YOU GONNA LET ME GO?
THAT'S RIGHT, I'M GOING TO LET YOU GO--
OF COURSE I'M NOT GOING TO LET YOU GO!!
ARE YOU DAFT!
LOAD THE SPECIAL BUGGY BALLS!!
YAAR!
HOORAY!!

READ THIS WAY

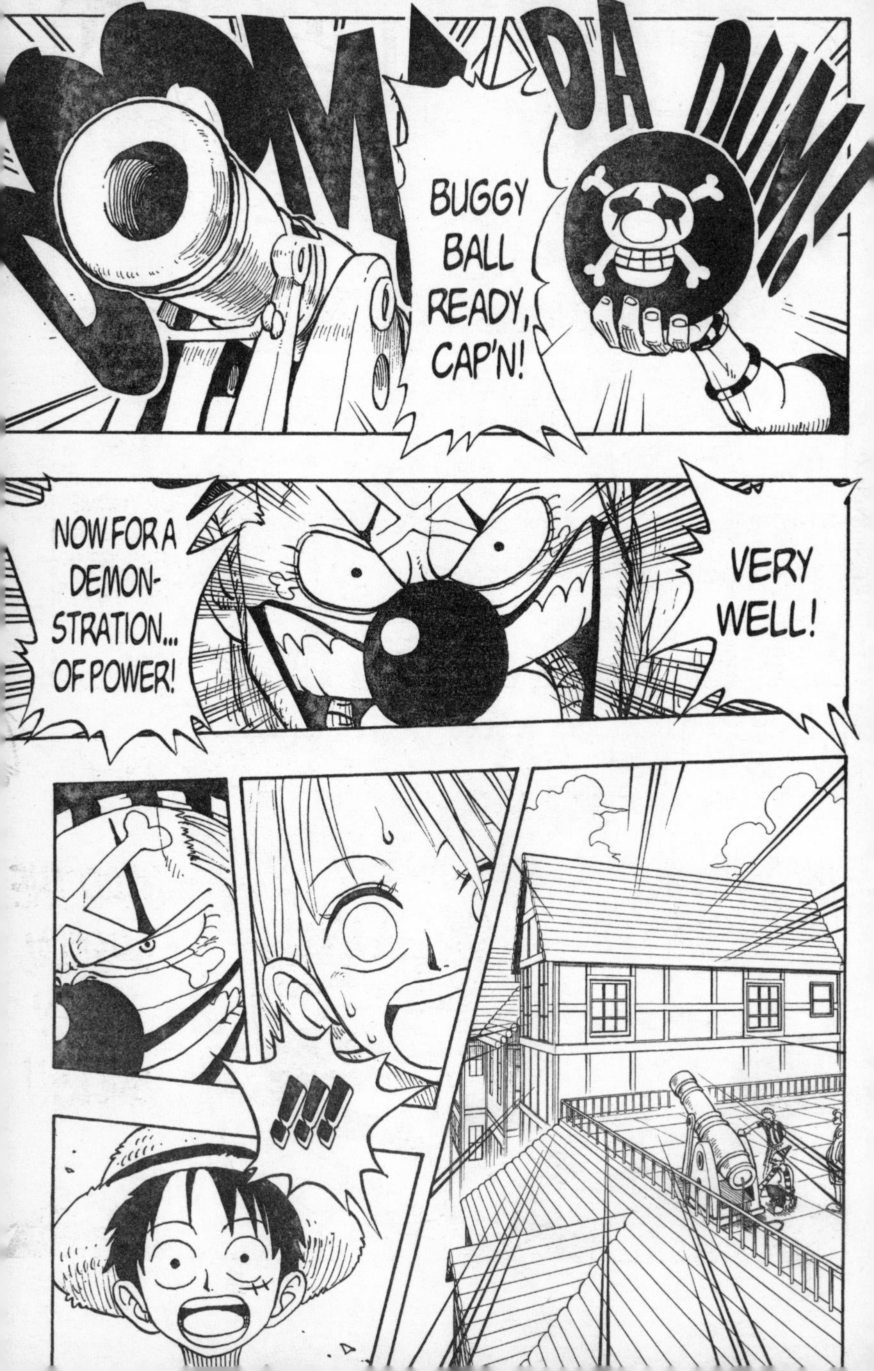
DA DUM!!
BUGGY BALL READY, CAP'N!
VERY WELL!
NOW FOR A DEMON-STRATION... OF POWER!
!!!

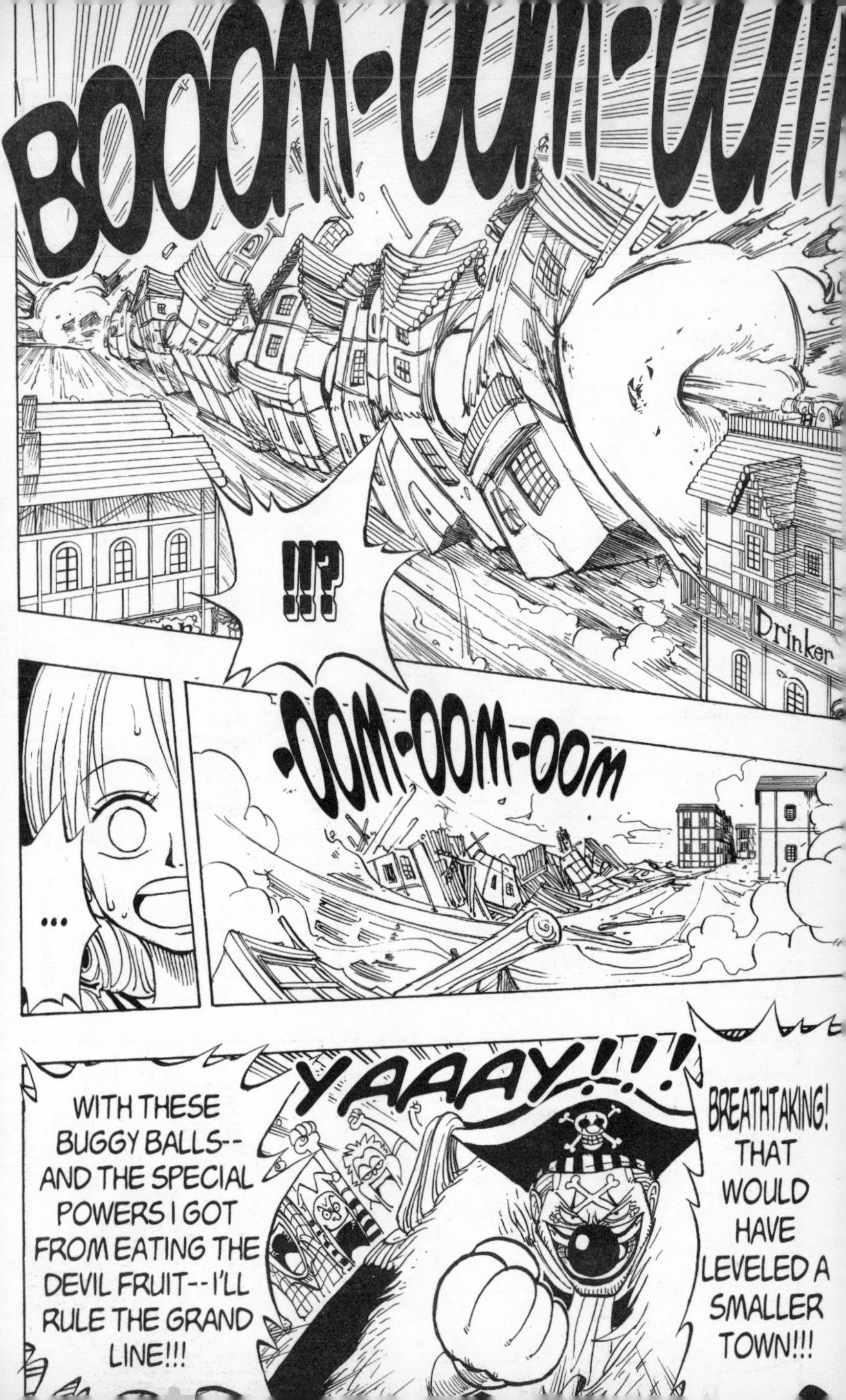

BOOM-UUM-UUM
!!?
Drinker
-OOM-OOM-OOM
...
YAAAY!!!
WITH THESE BUGGY BALLS--AND THE SPECIAL POWERS I GOT FROM EATING THE DEVIL FRUIT--I'LL RULE THE GRAND LINE!!!
BREATHTAKING! THAT WOULD HAVE LEVELED A SMALLER TOWN!!!

READ THIS WAY

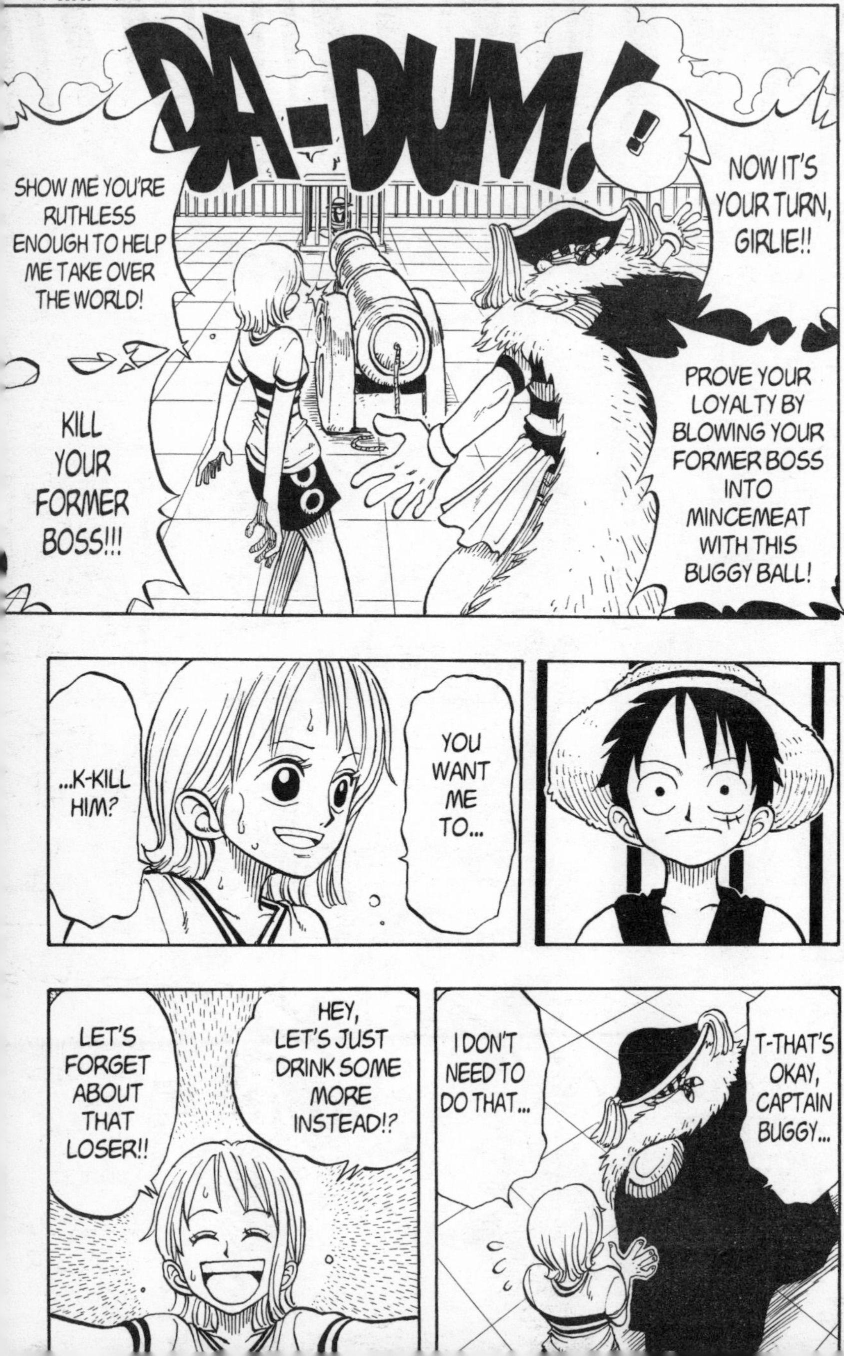
DA-DUM!
NOW IT'S YOUR TURN, GIRLIE!!
PROVE YOUR LOYALTY BY BLOWING YOUR FORMER BOSS INTO MINCEMEAT WITH THIS BUGGY BALL!
SHOW ME YOU'RE RUTHLESS ENOUGH TO HELP ME TAKE OVER THE WORLD!
KILL YOUR FORMER BOSS!!!
YOU WANT ME TO...
...K-KILL HIM?
T-THAT'S OKAY, CAPTAIN BUGGY...
I DON'T NEED TO DO THAT...
HEY, LET'S JUST DRINK SOME MORE INSTEAD!?
LET'S FORGET ABOUT THAT LOSER!!

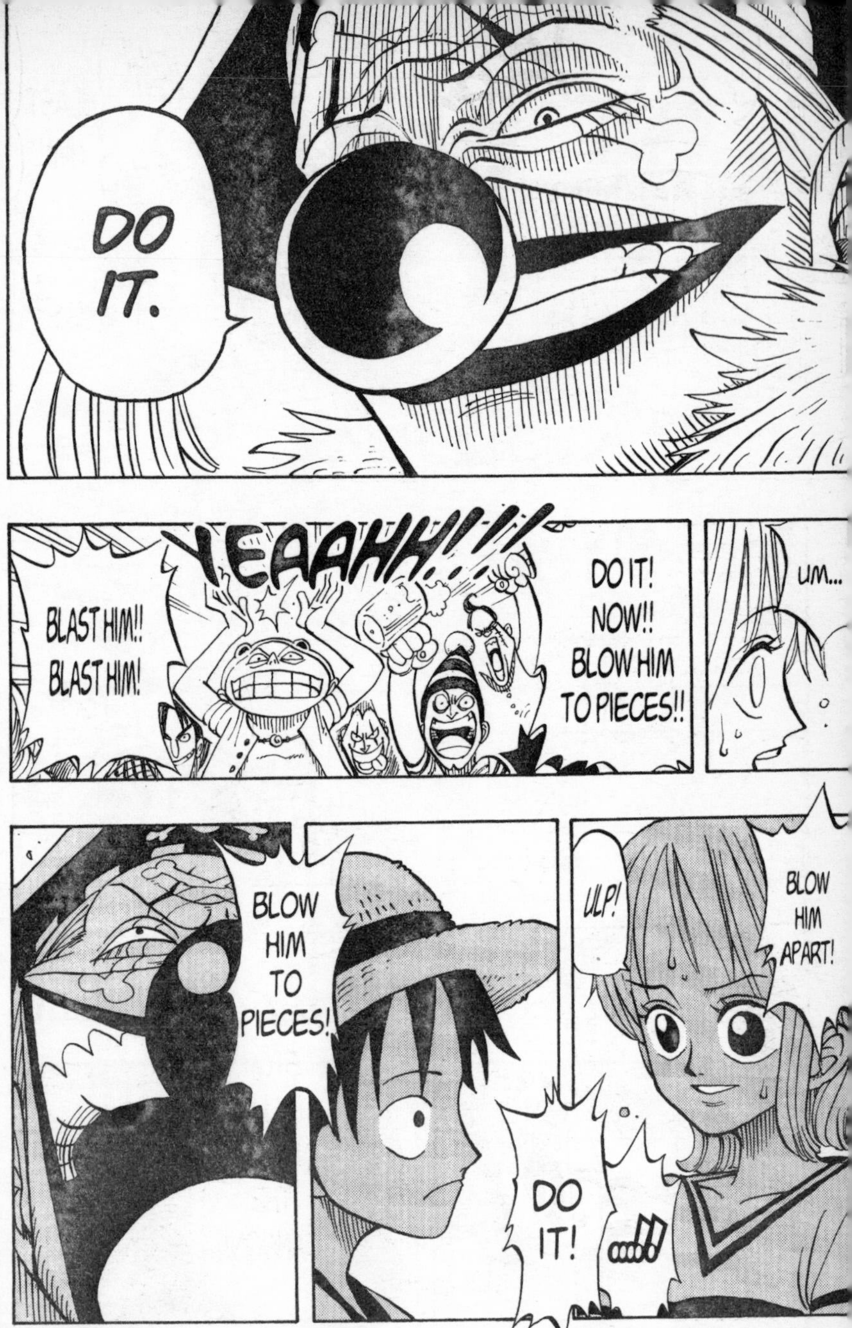
DO IT.
BLAST HIM!! BLAST HIM!
YEAAHH!!!!
DO IT! NOW!! BLOW HIM TO PIECES!!
UM...
BLOW HIM TO PIECES!
ULP!
BLOW HIM APART!
DO IT!
...!!

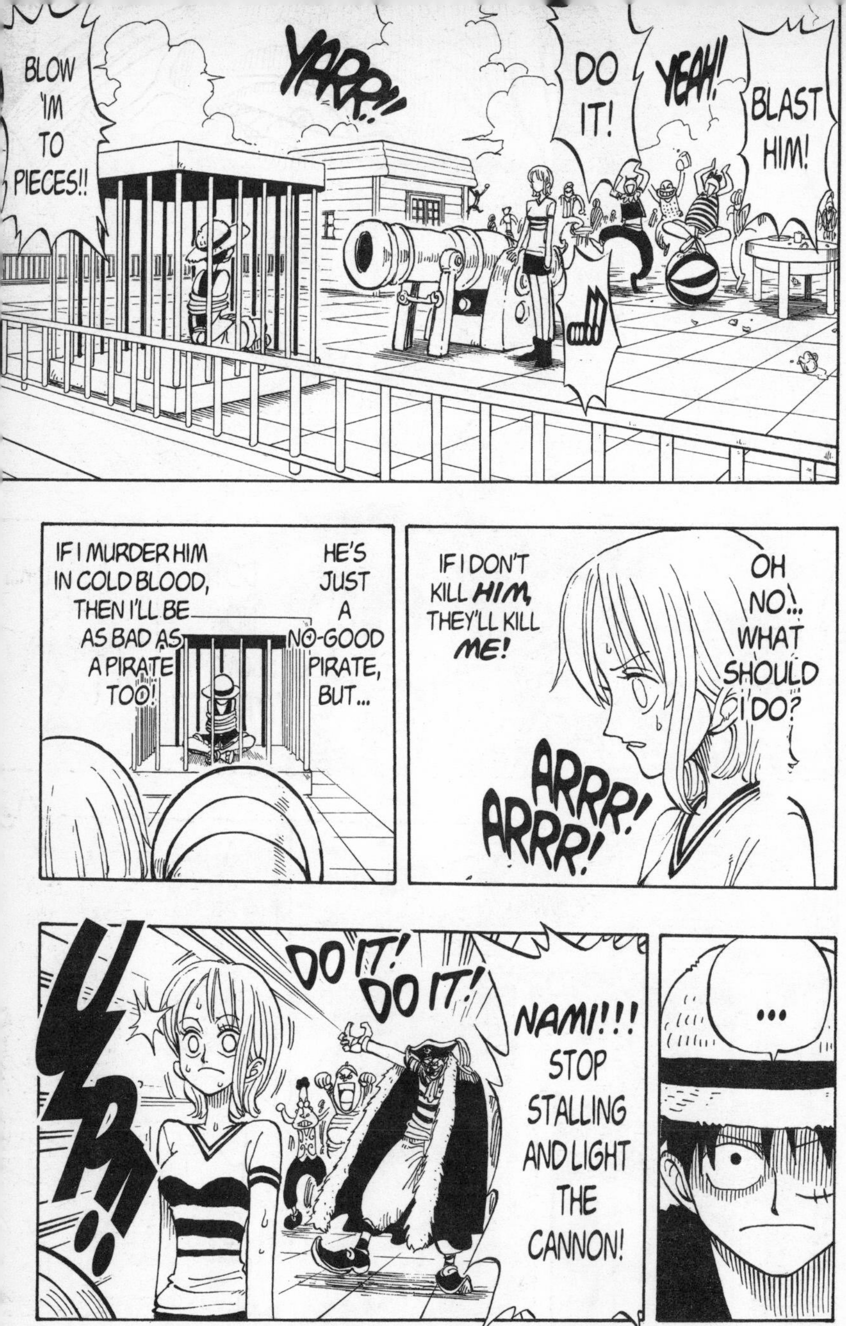
BLOW 'IM TO PIECES!!
YARR?!!
DO IT!
YEAH!
BLAST HIM!
HE'S JUST A NO-GOOD PIRATE, BUT...
IF I MURDER HIM IN COLD BLOOD, THEN I'LL BE AS BAD AS A PIRATE TOO!
IF I DON'T KILL HIM, THEY'LL KILL ME!
OH NO... WHAT SHOULD I DO?
ARRRR! ARRRR!
UH?!!
DO IT! DO IT!
NAMI!!! STOP STALLING AND LIGHT THE CANNON!
...

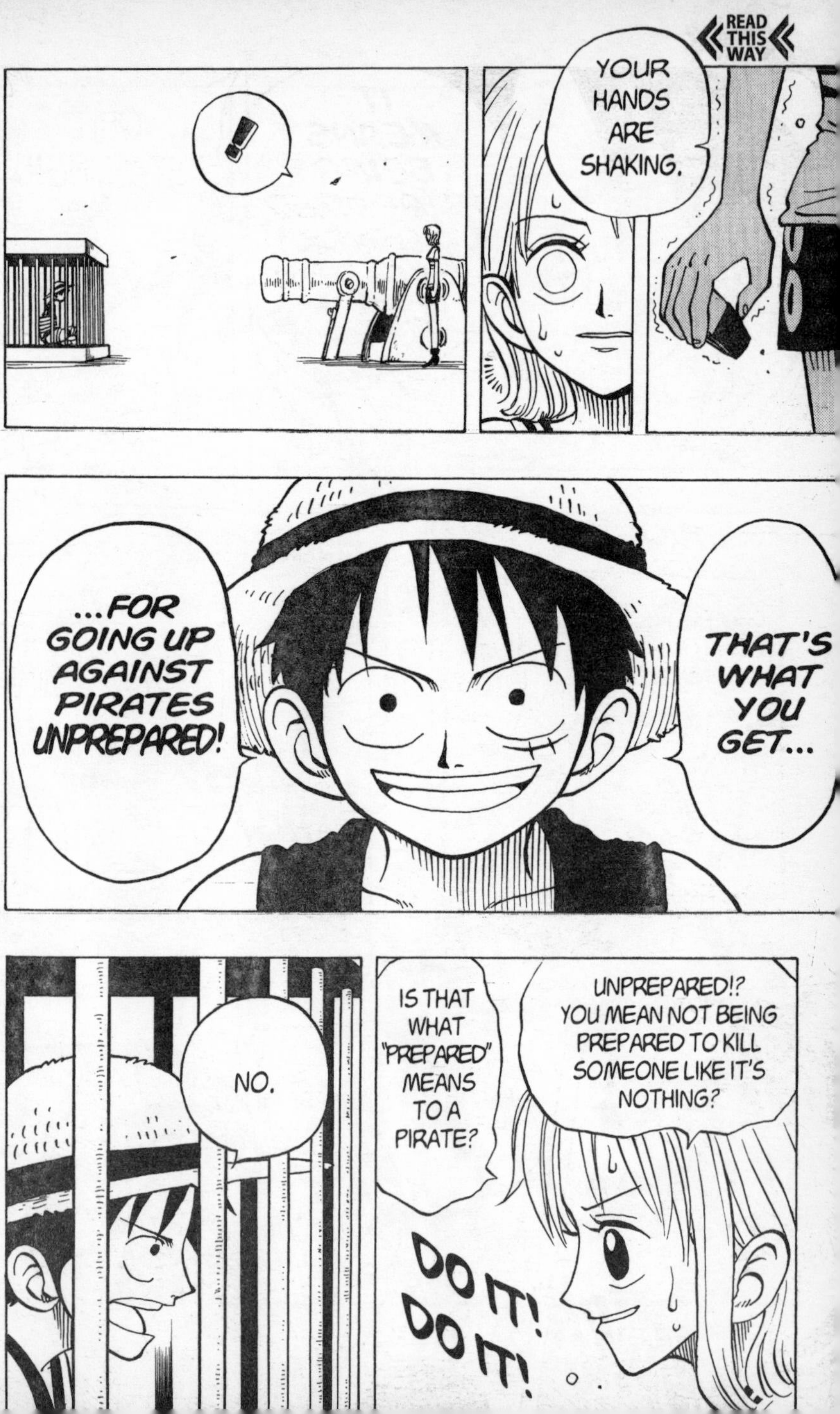
READ THIS WAY
YOUR HANDS ARE SHAKING.
!
THAT'S WHAT YOU GET...
...FOR GOING UP AGAINST PIRATES UNPREPARED!
UNPREPARED!? YOU MEAN NOT BEING PREPARED TO KILL SOMEONE LIKE IT'S NOTHING?
IS THAT WHAT "PREPARED" MEANS TO A PIRATE?
DO IT! DO IT!
NO.

READ THIS WAY

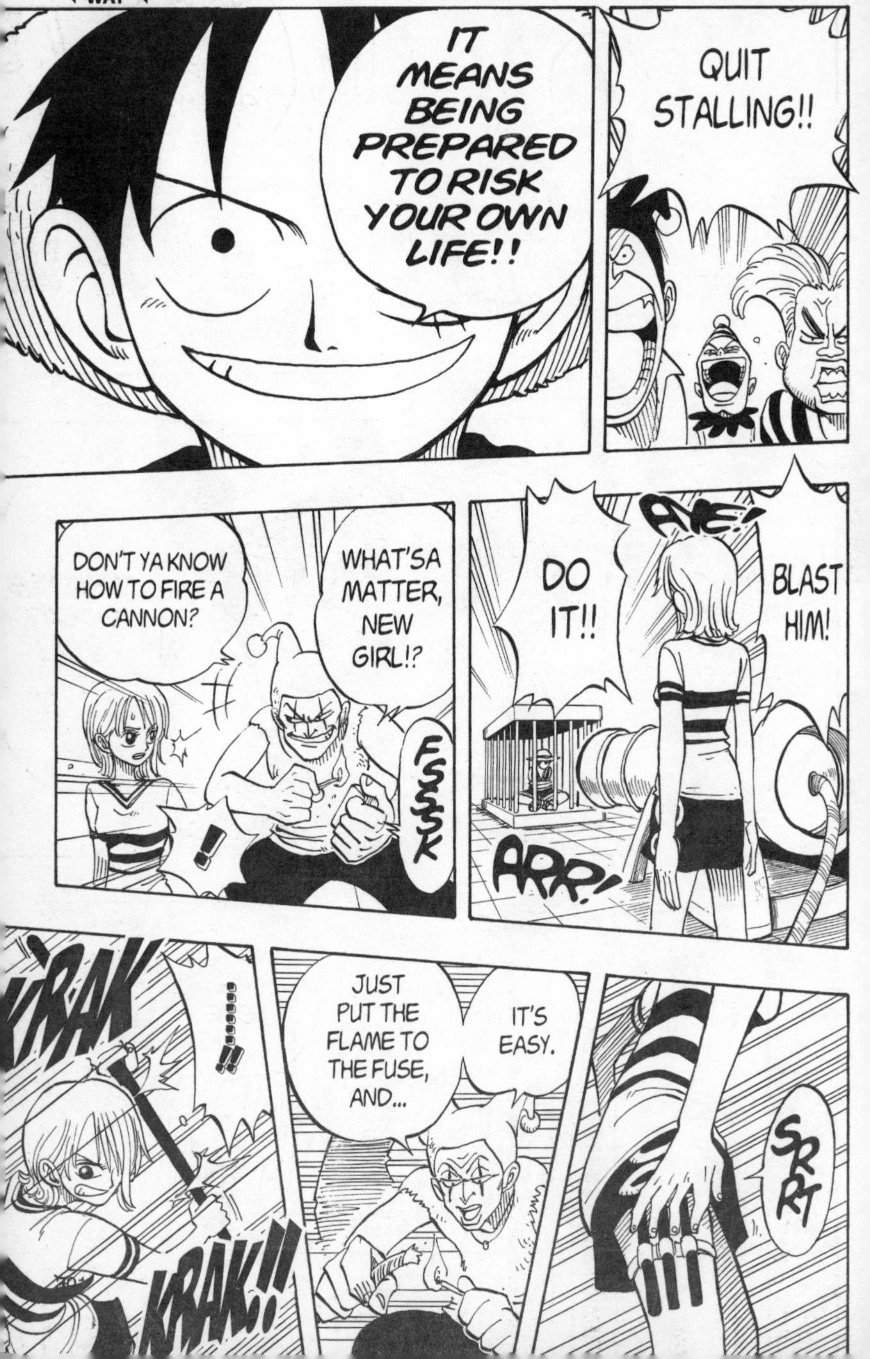
QUIT STALLING!!
IT MEANS BEING PREPARED TO RISK YOUR OWN LIFE!!
AYE!
BLAST HIM!
DO IT!!
ARR!
WHAT'SA MATTER, NEW GIRL!?
DON'T YA KNOW HOW TO FIRE A CANNON?
FSSSK
!
SRRT
IT'S EASY.
JUST PUT THE FLAME TO THE FUSE, AND...
KRAK
......!!
KRAK!!

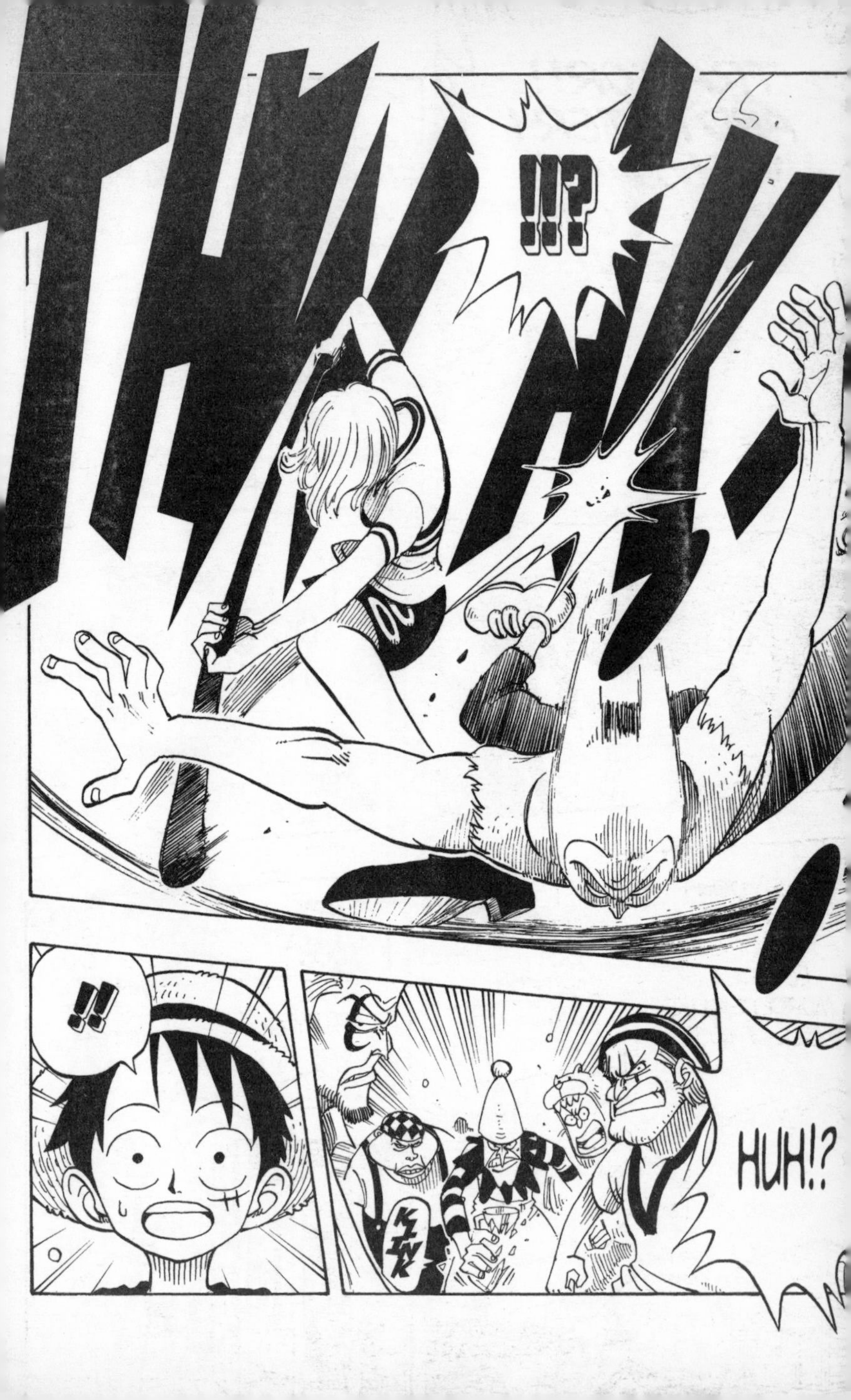
!!?
!!
HUH!?
KLINK

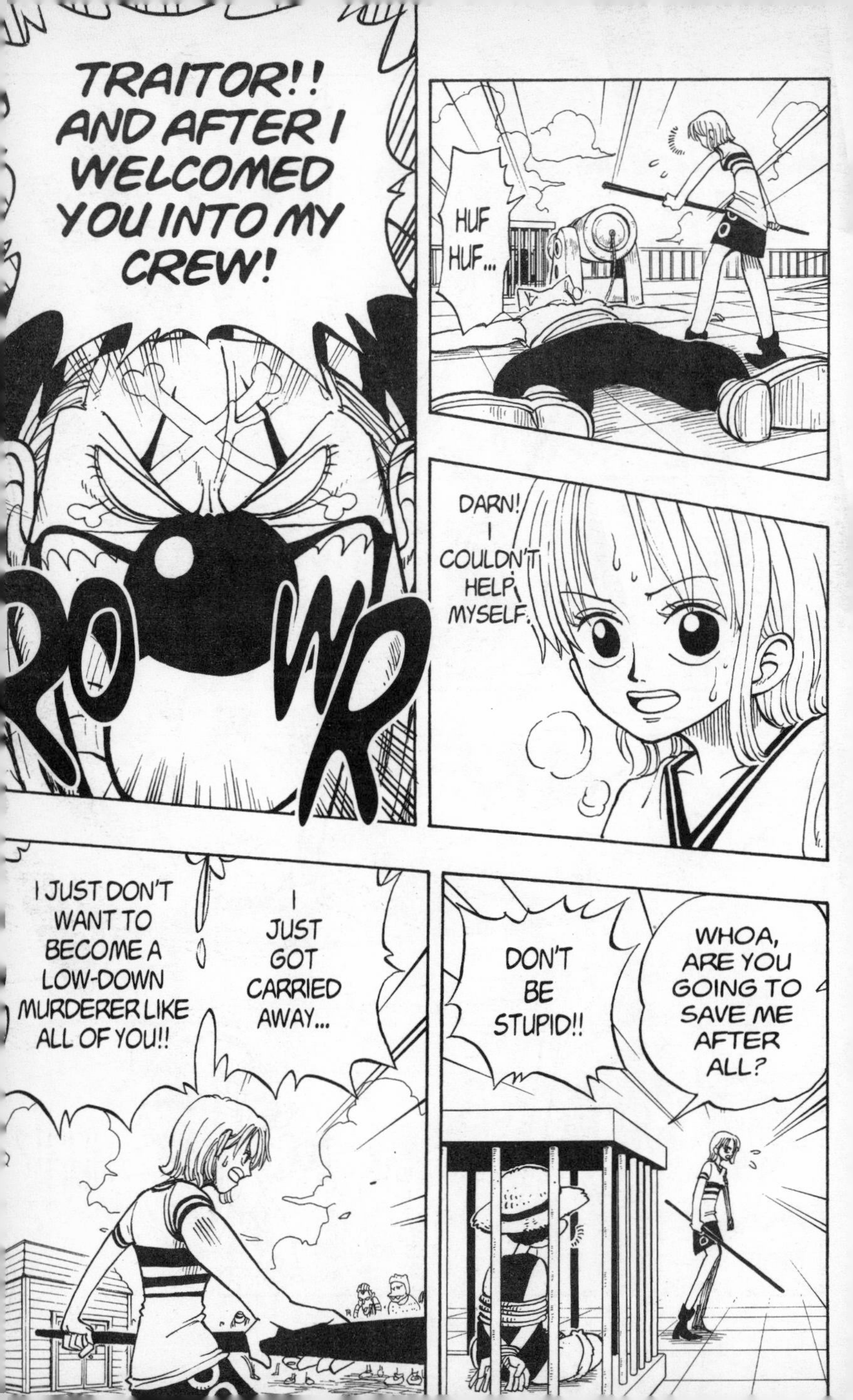
HUF
HUF...
DARN! I COULDN'T HELP MYSELF.
TRAITOR!! AND AFTER I WELCOMED YOU INTO MY CREW!
ROWR
WHOA, ARE YOU GOING TO SAVE ME AFTER ALL?
DON'T BE STUPID!!
I JUST GOT CARRIED AWAY...
I JUST DON'T WANT TO BECOME A LOW-DOWN MURDERER LIKE ALL OF YOU!!

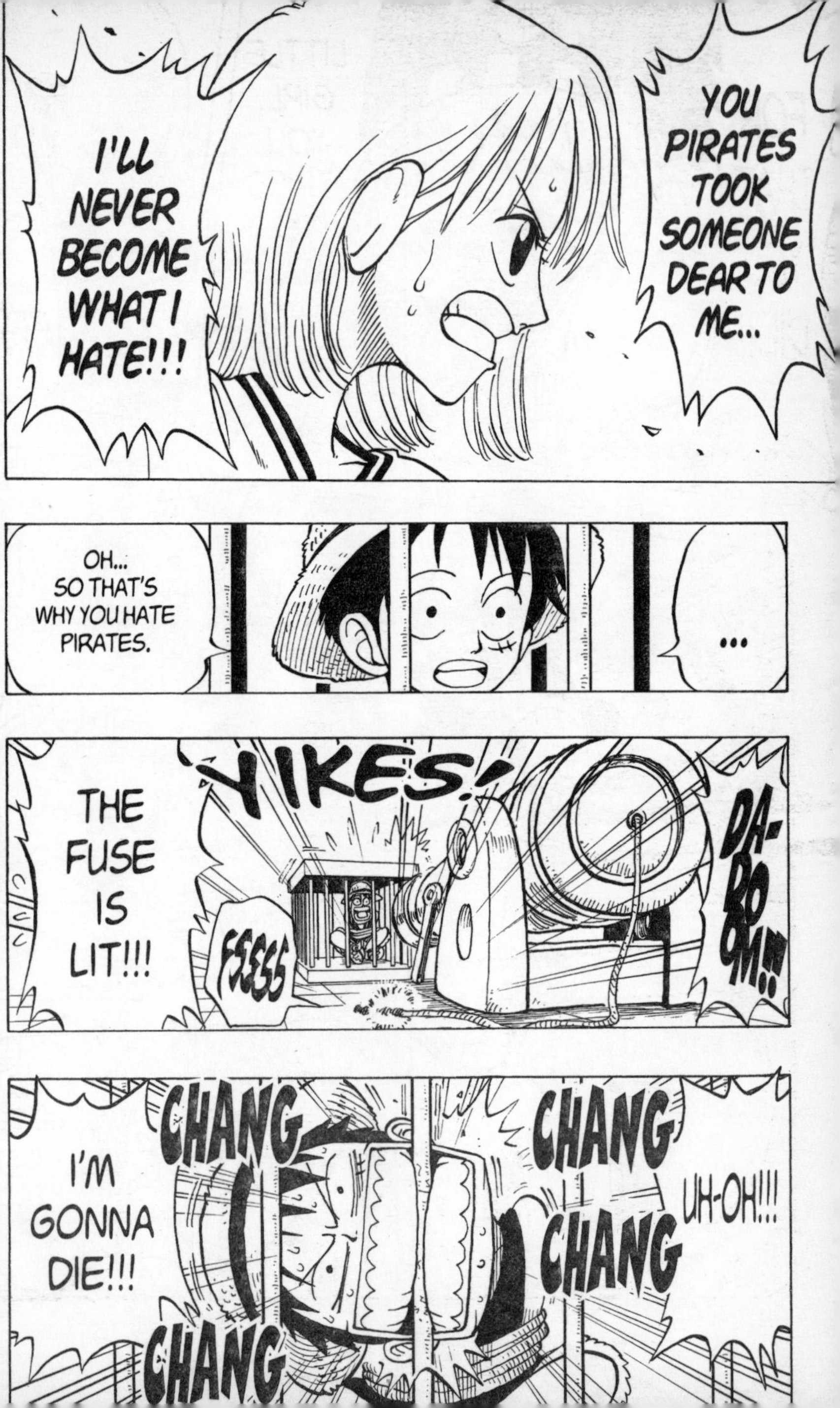
YOU PIRATES TOOK SOMEONE DEAR TO ME...
I'LL NEVER BECOME WHAT I HATE!!!
...
OH... SO THAT'S WHY YOU HATE PIRATES.
DA-DOOM!!
YIKES!
FSSSS
THE FUSE IS LIT!!!
CHANG
CHANG
UH-OH!!!
CHANG
I'M GONNA DIE!!!
CHANG

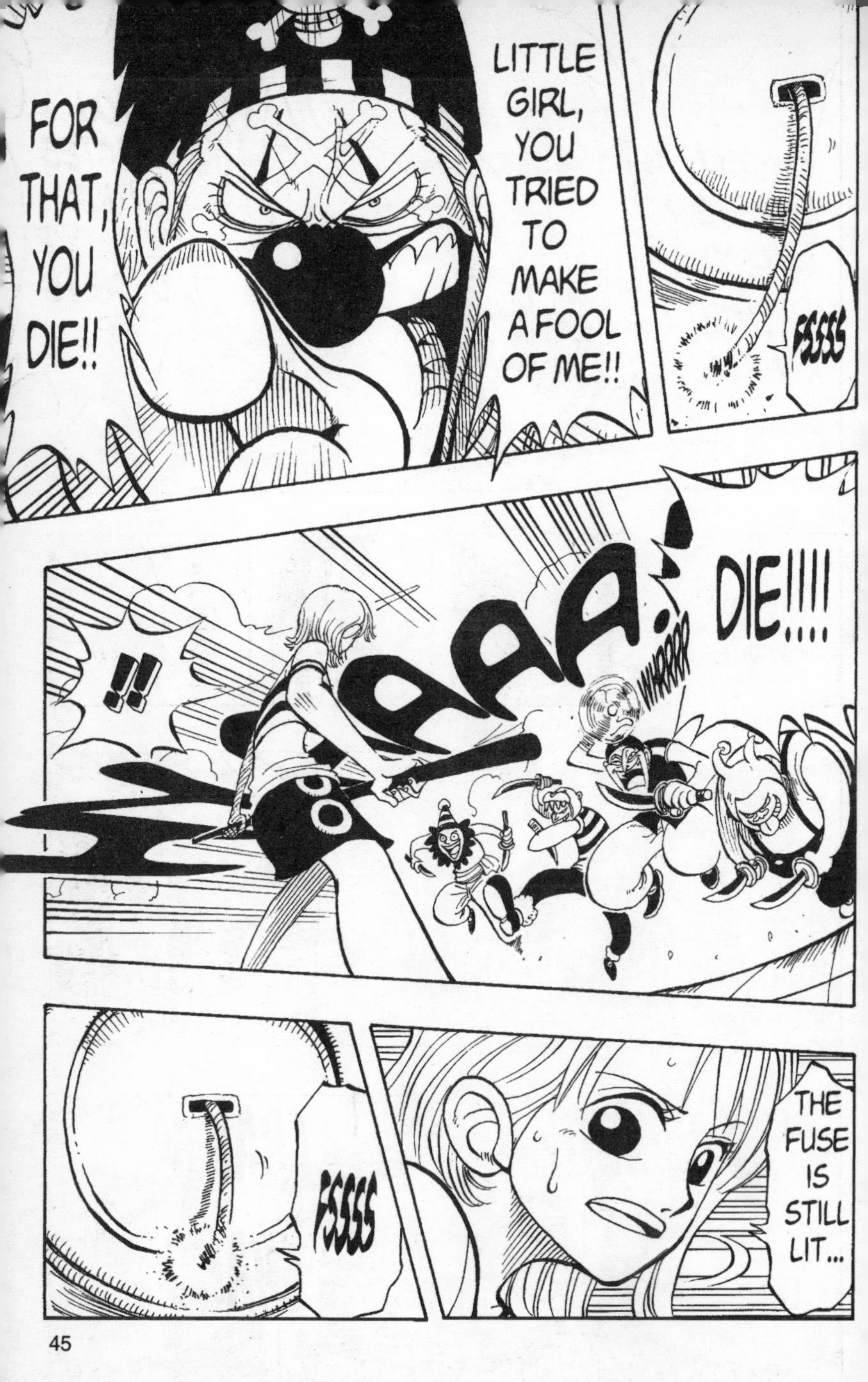

LITTLE GIRL, YOU TRIED TO MAKE A FOOL OF ME!!
FOR THAT, YOU DIE!!
FSSSSS
DIE!!!!
WAAA
WHRRRR
!!
FSSSSS
THE FUSE IS STILL LIT...

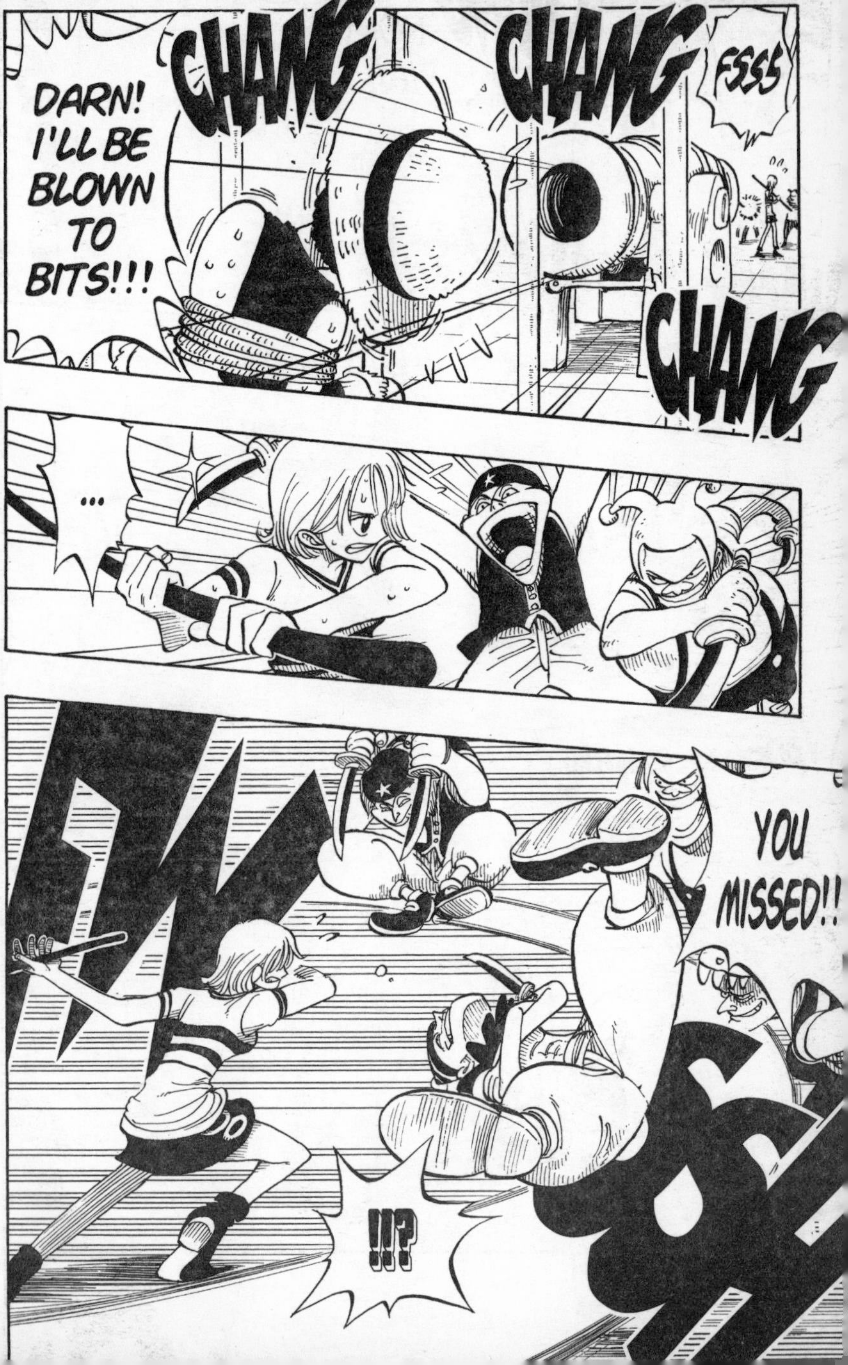
READ THIS WAY
FSSS
CHANG
CHANG
DARN! I'LL BE BLOWN TO BITS!!!
CHANG
...
YOU MISSED!!
!!?

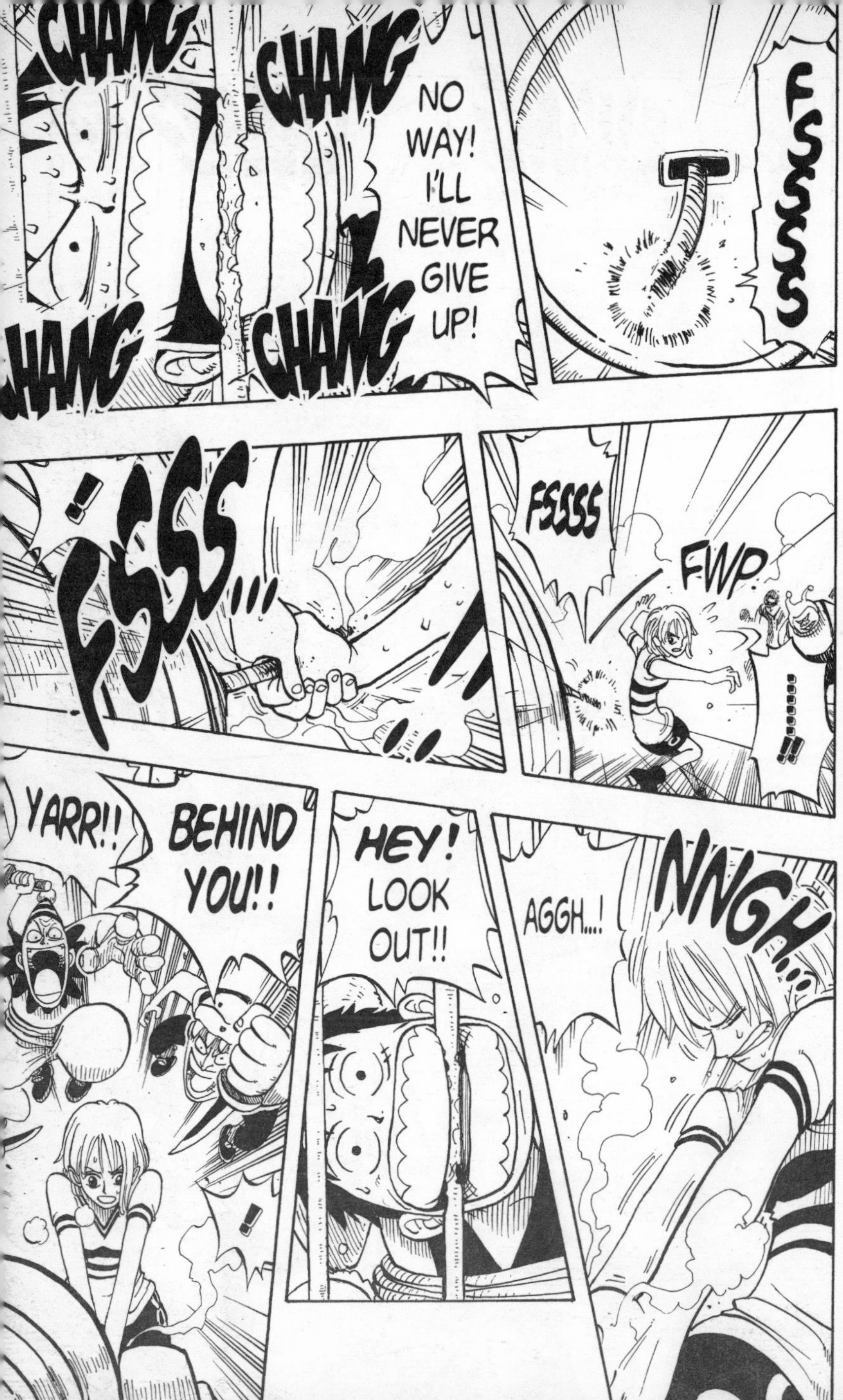
CHANG
CHANG
CHANG
CHANG
NO WAY! I'LL NEVER GIVE UP!
FSSSSS
!
FSSS...
FSSSSS
FWP
......!!
YARR!!
BEHIND YOU!!
!
HEY! LOOK OUT!!
AGGH...!
NNGH...

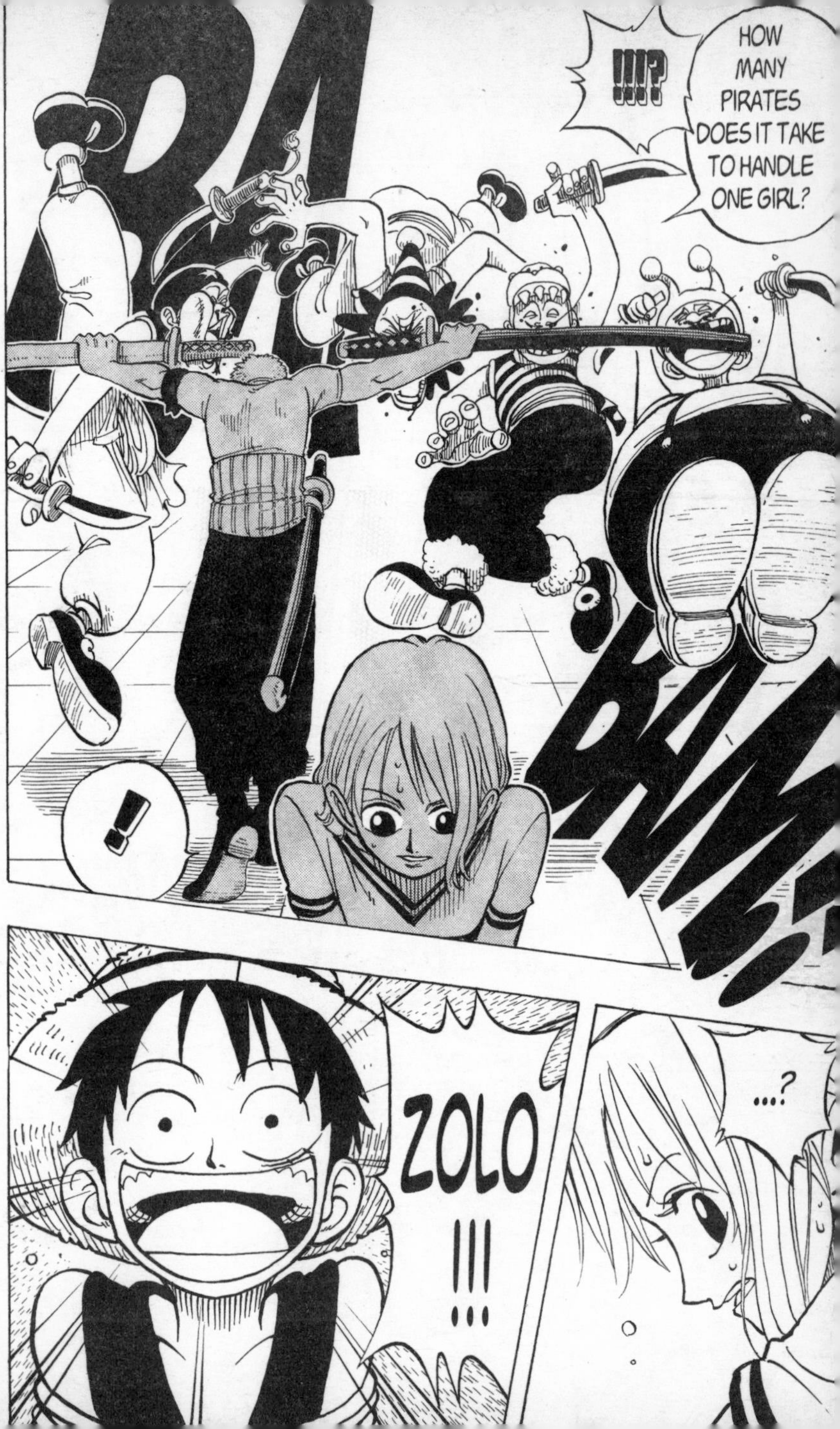

HOW MANY PIRATES DOES IT TAKE TO HANDLE ONE GIRL?
!!!?
BA
BAM
!
ZOLO !!!
...?

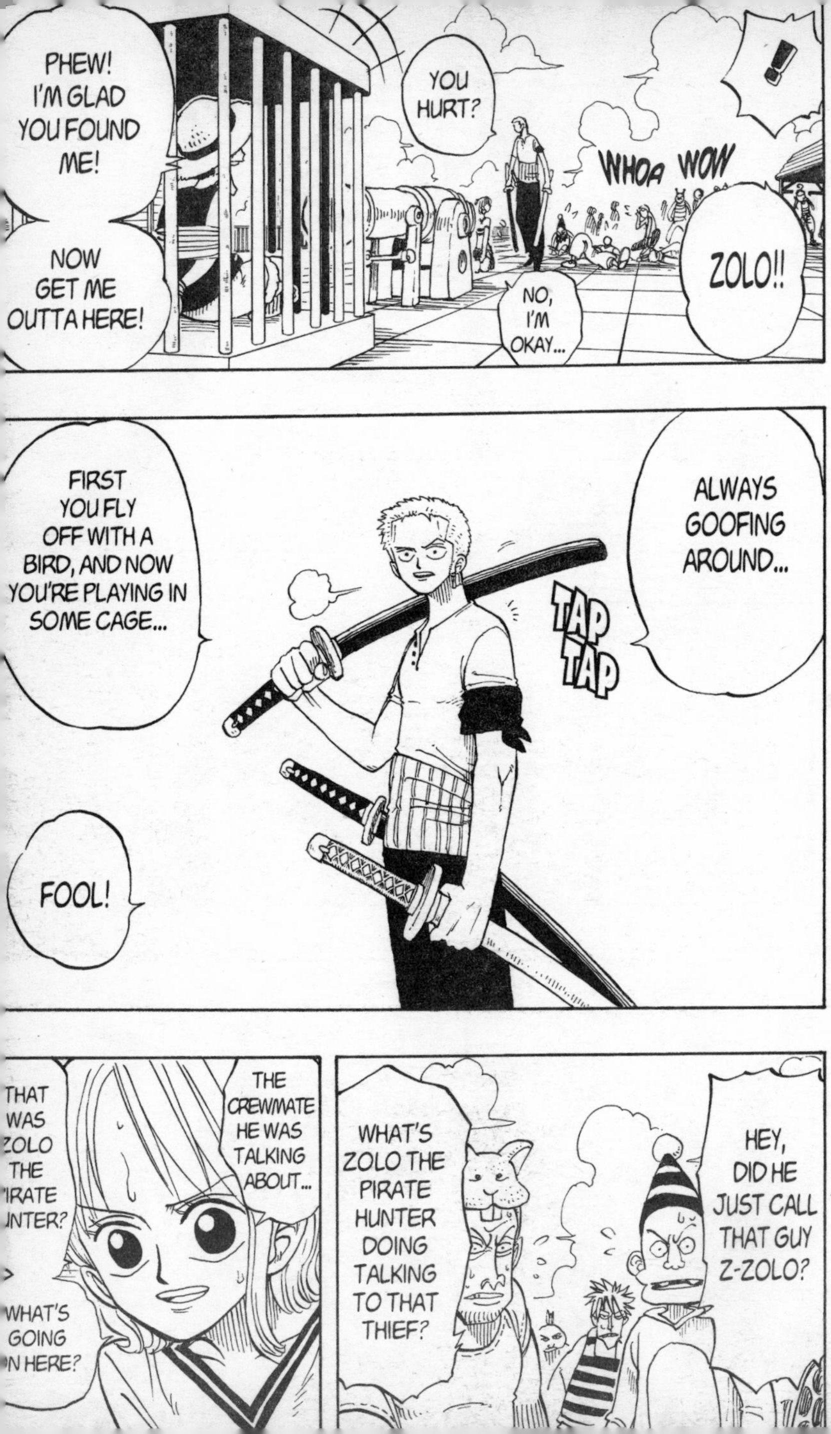
!
ZOLO!!
WHOA WOW
YOU HURT?
NO, I'M OKAY...
PHEW! I'M GLAD YOU FOUND ME!
NOW GET ME OUTTA HERE!
ALWAYS GOOFING AROUND...
TAP TAP
FIRST YOU FLY OFF WITH A BIRD, AND NOW YOU'RE PLAYING IN SOME CAGE...
FOOL!
HEY, DID HE JUST CALL THAT GUY Z-ZOLO?
WHAT'S ZOLO THE PIRATE HUNTER DOING TALKING TO THAT THIEF?
THE CREWMATE HE WAS TALKING ABOUT...
THAT WAS OLO THE IRATE NTER?
WHAT'S GOING N HERE?

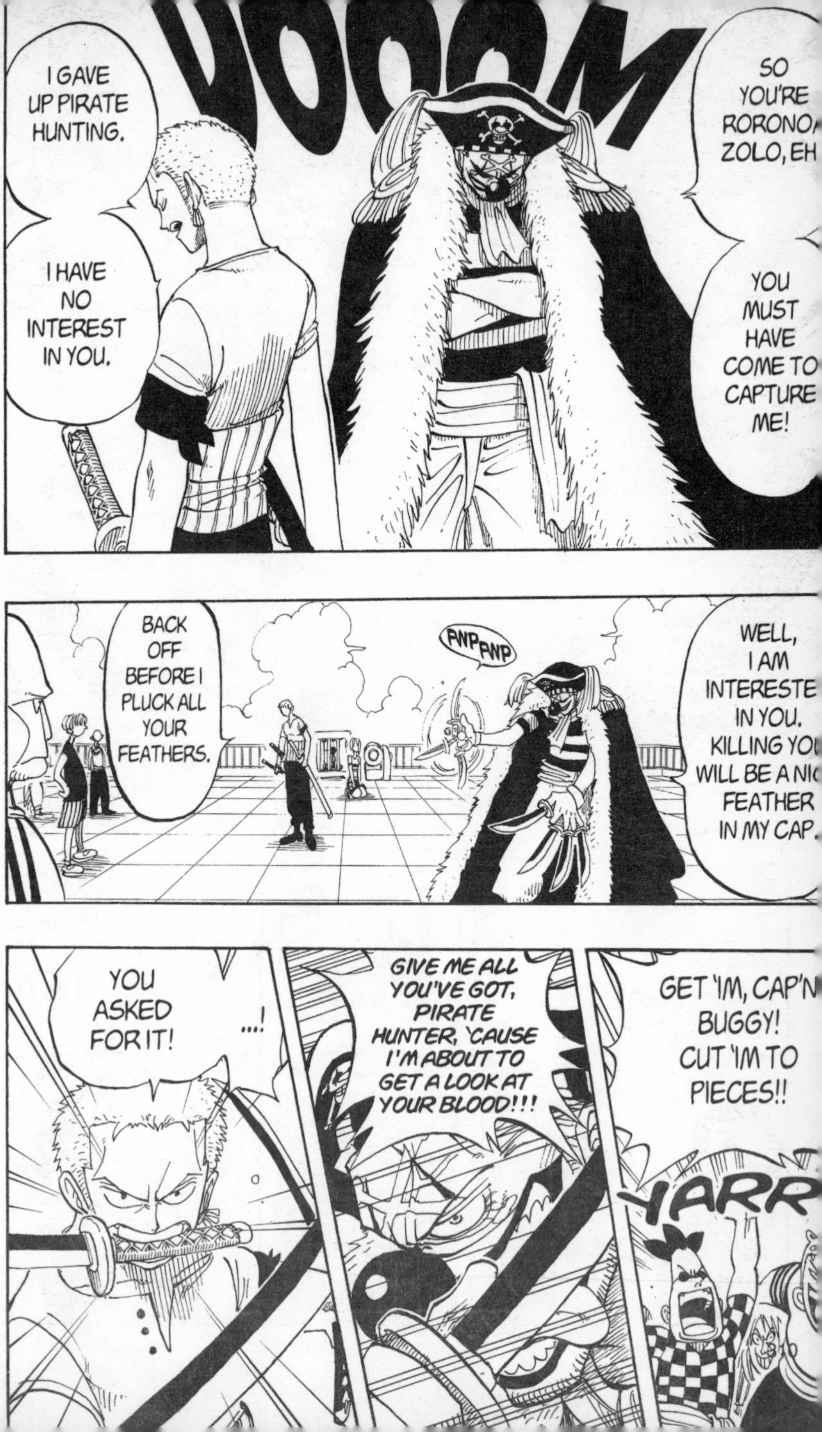
VOOOM
SO YOU'RE RORONO ZOLO, EH
YOU MUST HAVE COME TO CAPTURE ME!
I GAVE UP PIRATE HUNTING.
I HAVE NO INTEREST IN YOU.
WELL, I AM INTERESTE IN YOU. KILLING YO WILL BE A NI FEATHER IN MY CAP.
PNP PNP
BACK OFF BEFORE I PLUCK ALL YOUR FEATHERS.
GET 'IM, CAP'N BUGGY! CUT 'IM TO PIECES!!
YARR
GIVE ME ALL YOU'VE GOT, PIRATE HUNTER, 'CAUSE I'M ABOUT TO GET A LOOK AT YOUR BLOOD!!!
YOU ASKED FOR IT!
...!

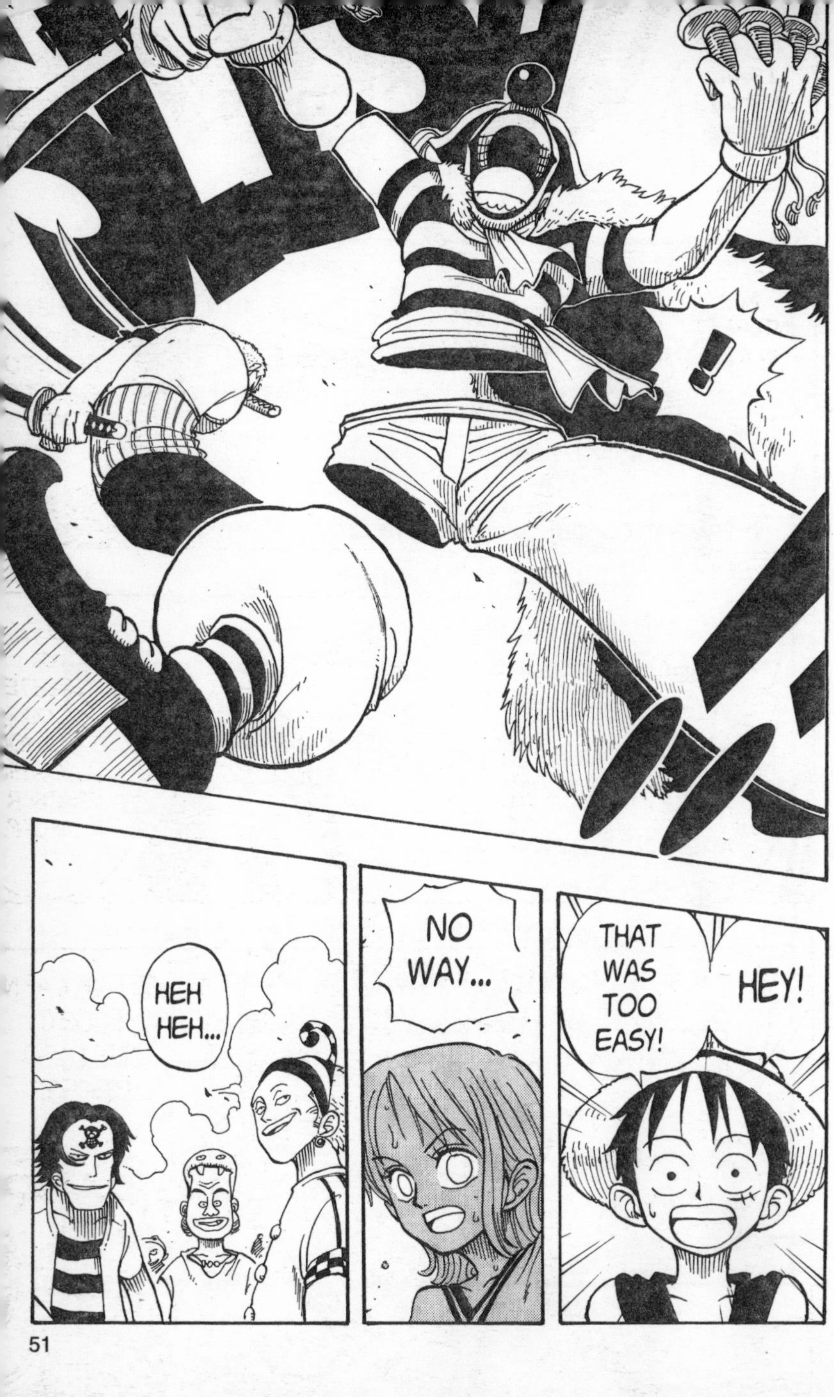
!
HEH HEH...
NO WAY...
THAT WAS TOO EASY!
HEY!

VIKINGS, PART I

- All pirates are sea-roving plunderers, but throughout history there have been many different kinds of pirates in different times and places.

- I want to talk about one of my favorite kinds of pirates: the Vikings.

- Over a thousand years ago, Viking raiders swept down from Scandinavia and ran amok through Europe.

SCANDINAVIA
<EUROPE>
AROUND HERE
ENGLAND

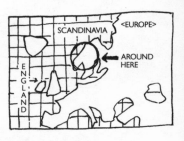

They came from the present-day countries of Norway, Sweden and Denmark. As to why they were called Vikings, well, that's easy: that's what they called themselves. Why did they call themselves Vikings? To know that, we'd have to go back a thousand years and ask them.

Chapter 11:
FLIGHT

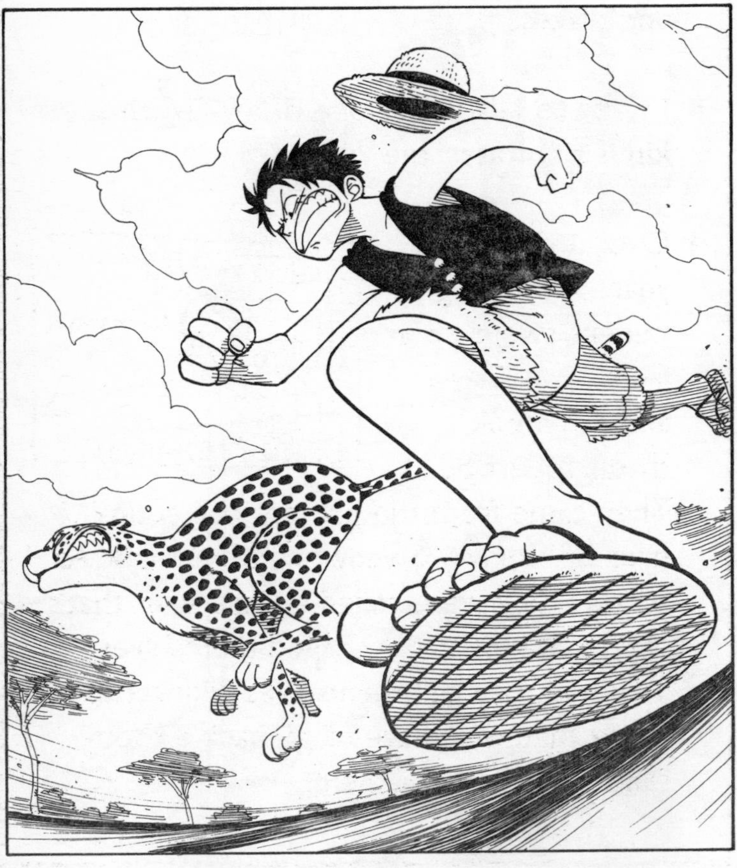

FLUMP!!!

FLUMP

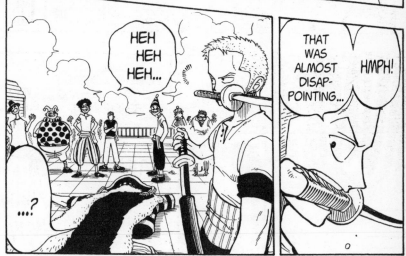

HEH HEH HEH...

....?

THAT WAS ALMOST DISAPPOINTING...

HMPH!

READ THIS WAY

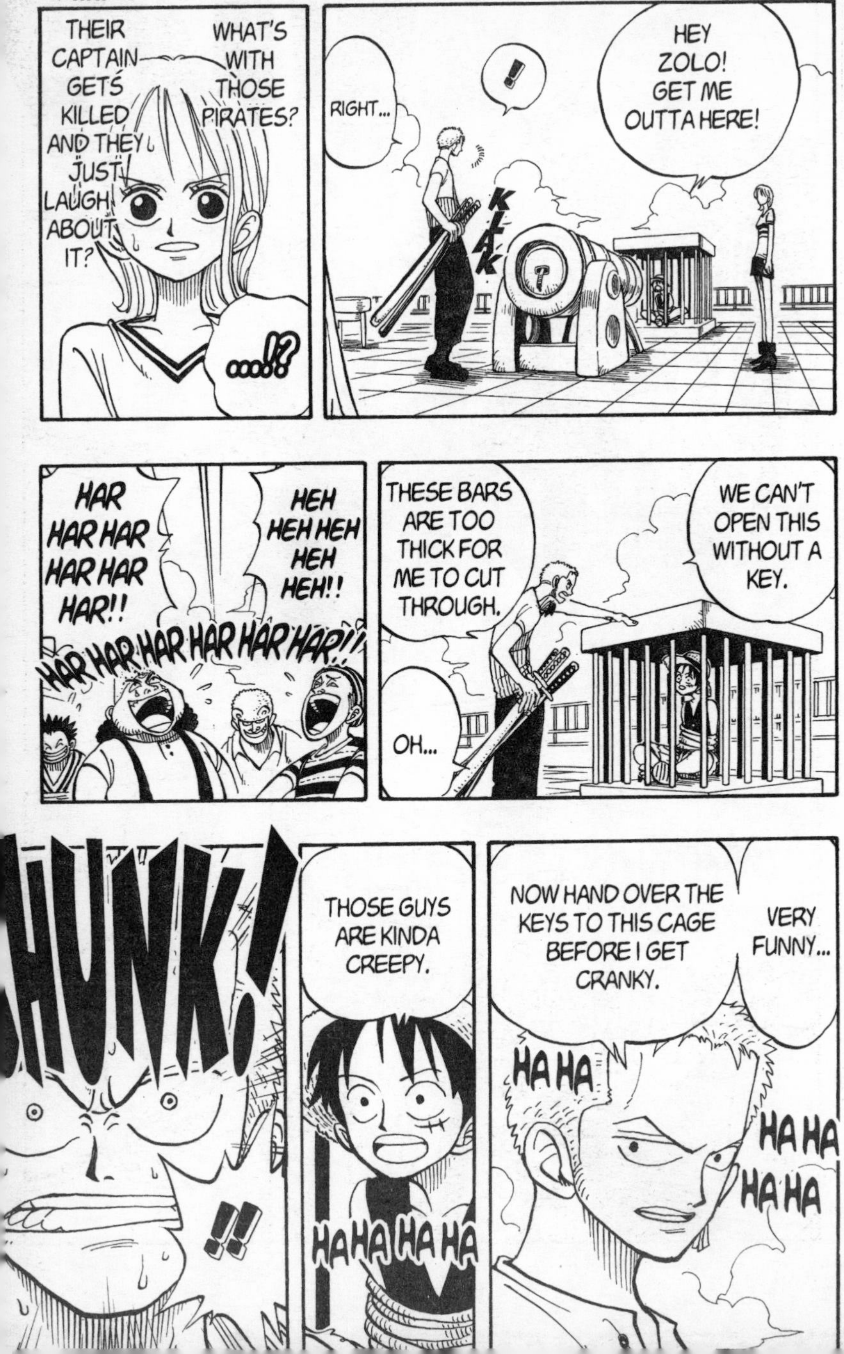
HEY ZOLO! GET ME OUTTA HERE!
!
RIGHT...
KLAK
WHAT'S WITH THOSE PIRATES?
THEIR CAPTAIN GETS KILLED AND THEY JUST LAUGH ABOUT IT?
...!!?
WE CAN'T OPEN THIS WITHOUT A KEY.
THESE BARS ARE TOO THICK FOR ME TO CUT THROUGH.
OH...
HEH HEH HEH HEH HEH!!
HAR HAR HAR HAR HAR HAR!!
HAR HAR HAR HAR HAR HAR!!
VERY FUNNY...
NOW HAND OVER THE KEYS TO THIS CAGE BEFORE I GET CRANKY.
HA HA
HA HA HA HA
THOSE GUYS ARE KINDA CREEPY.
HA HA HA HA
HUNK!
!!

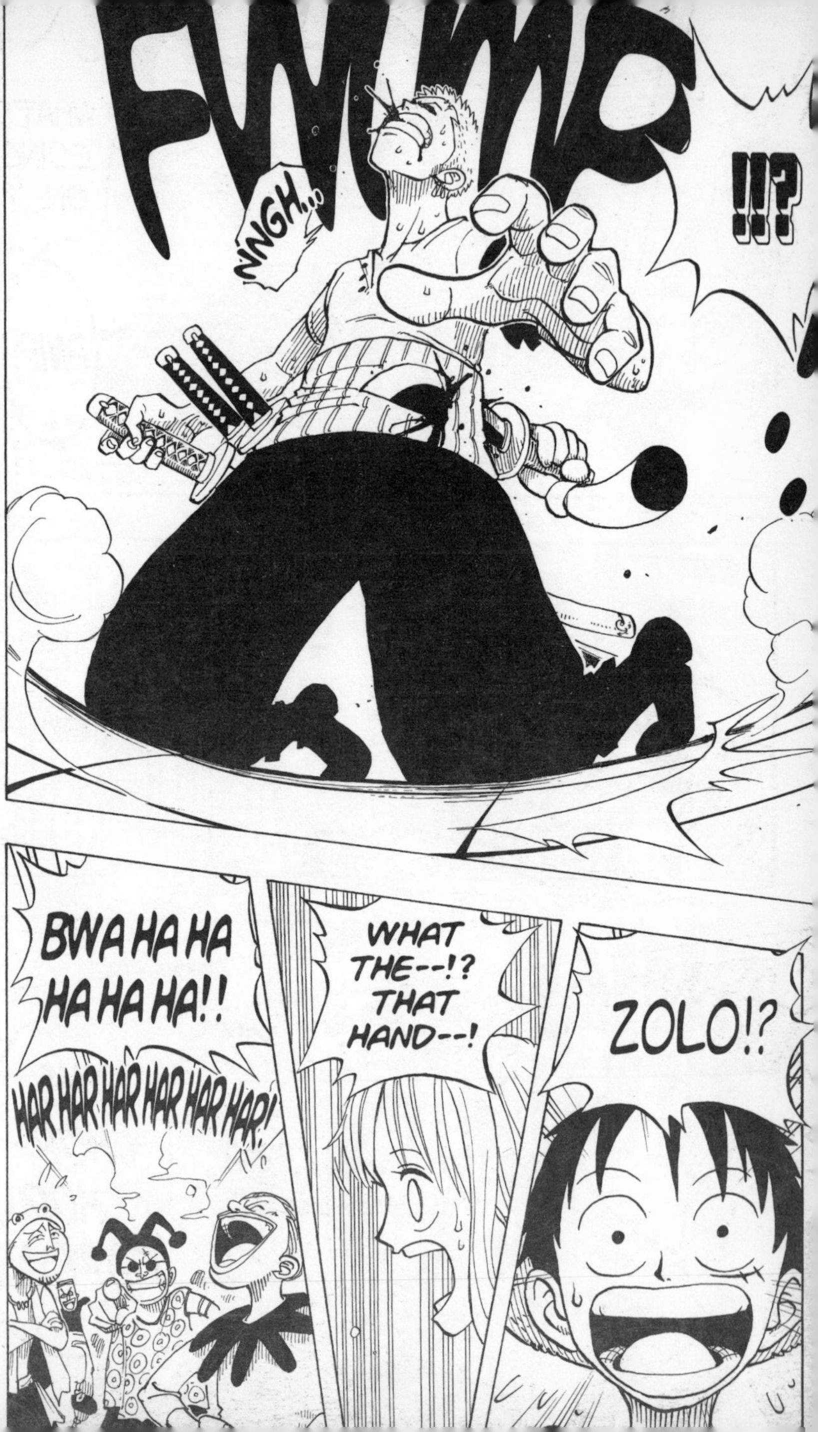
FWMP
NNGH...
!!?
BWA HA HA HA HA HA!!
HAR HAR HAR HAR HAR HAR!
WHAT THE--!? THAT HAND--!
ZOLO!?

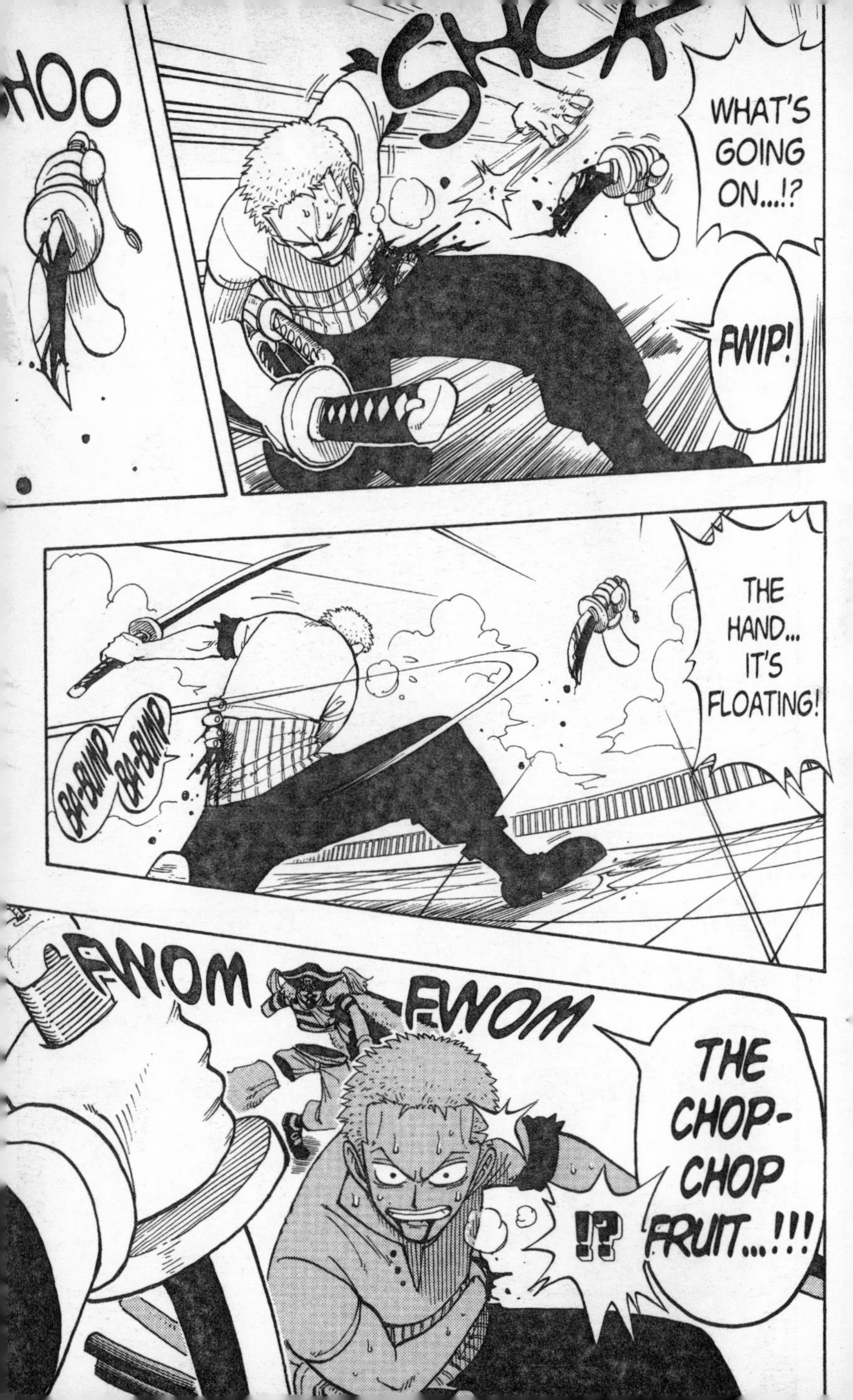
SHOO
SHCK
WHAT'S GOING ON...!?
FWIP!
THE HAND... IT'S FLOATING!
BA-BUMP
BA-BUMP
FWOM
FWOM
!?
THE CHOP-CHOP FRUIT...!!!

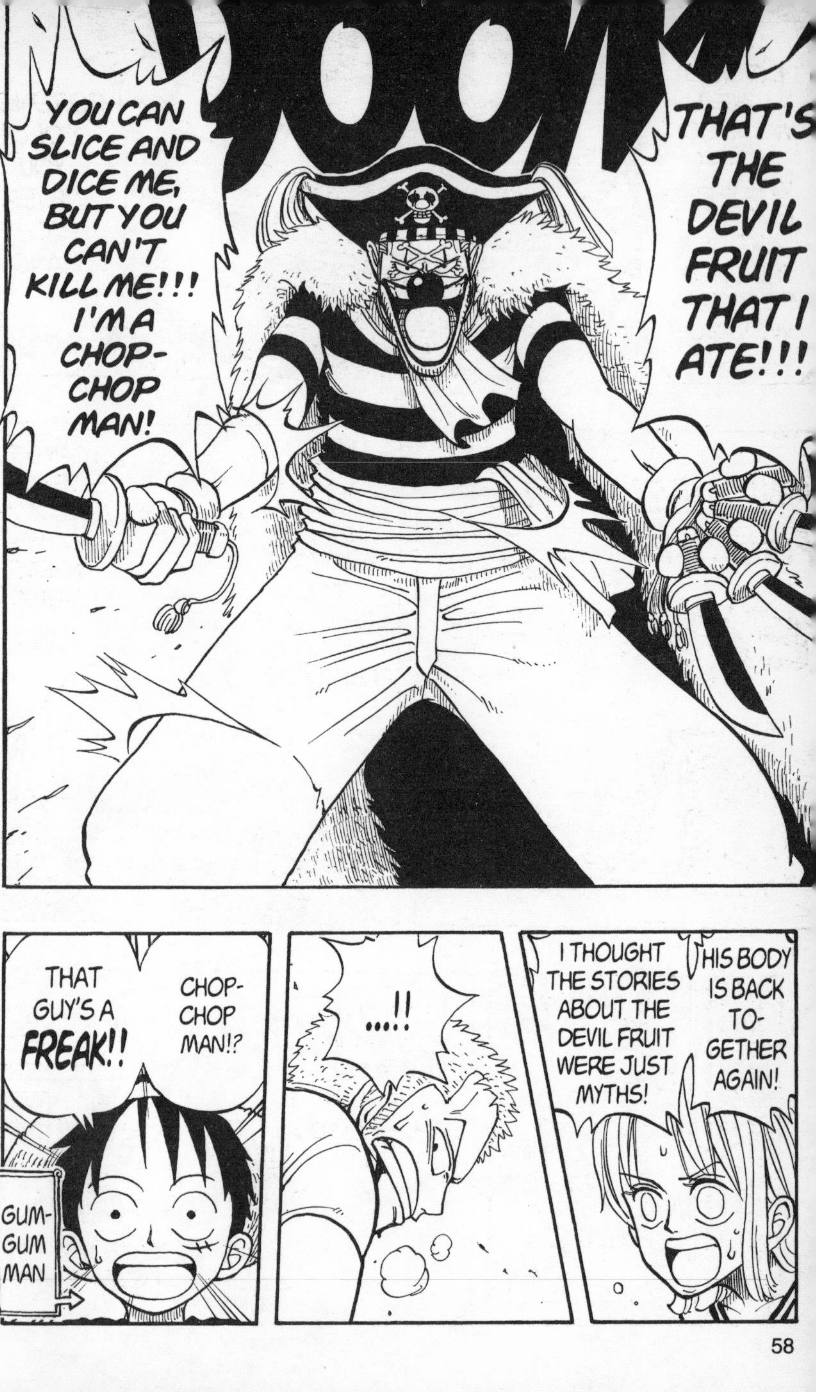
YOU CAN SLICE AND DICE ME, BUT YOU CAN'T KILL ME!!! I'M A CHOP-CHOP MAN!
THAT'S THE DEVIL FRUIT THAT I ATE!!!
THAT GUY'S A FREAK!!
CHOP-CHOP MAN!?
GUM-GUM MAN
...!!
HIS BODY IS BACK TO-GETHER AGAIN!
I THOUGHT THE STORIES ABOUT THE DEVIL FRUIT WERE JUST MYTHS!

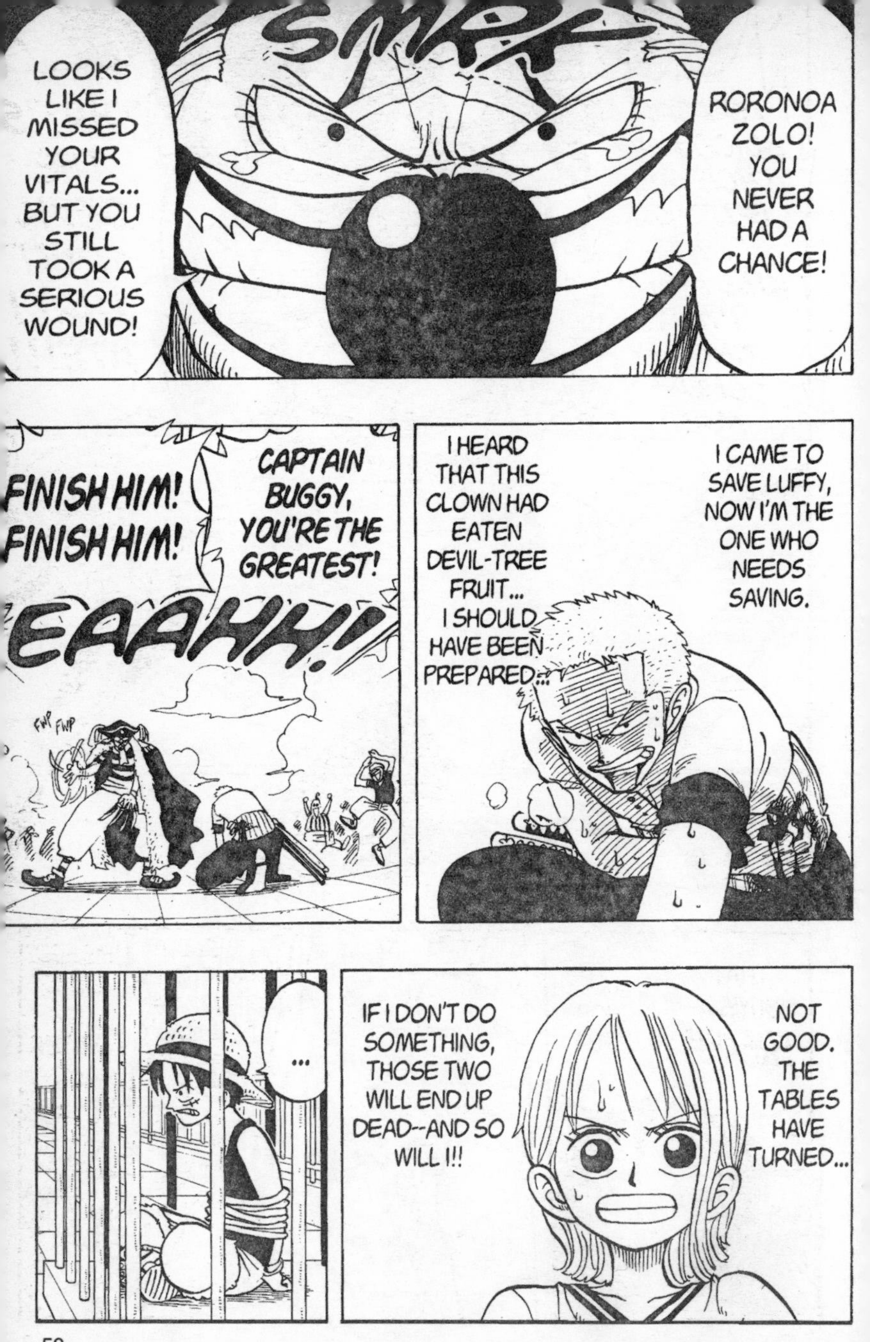
SMAK
LOOKS LIKE I MISSED YOUR VITALS... BUT YOU STILL TOOK A SERIOUS WOUND!
RORONOA ZOLO! YOU NEVER HAD A CHANCE!
FINISH HIM! FINISH HIM!
CAPTAIN BUGGY, YOU'RE THE GREATEST!
EAAHH!!
FWP FWP
I HEARD THAT THIS CLOWN HAD EATEN DEVIL-TREE FRUIT... I SHOULD HAVE BEEN PREPARED...
I CAME TO SAVE LUFFY, NOW I'M THE ONE WHO NEEDS SAVING.
...
IF I DON'T DO SOMETHING, THOSE TWO WILL END UP DEAD--AND SO WILL I!!
NOT GOOD. THE TABLES HAVE TURNED...

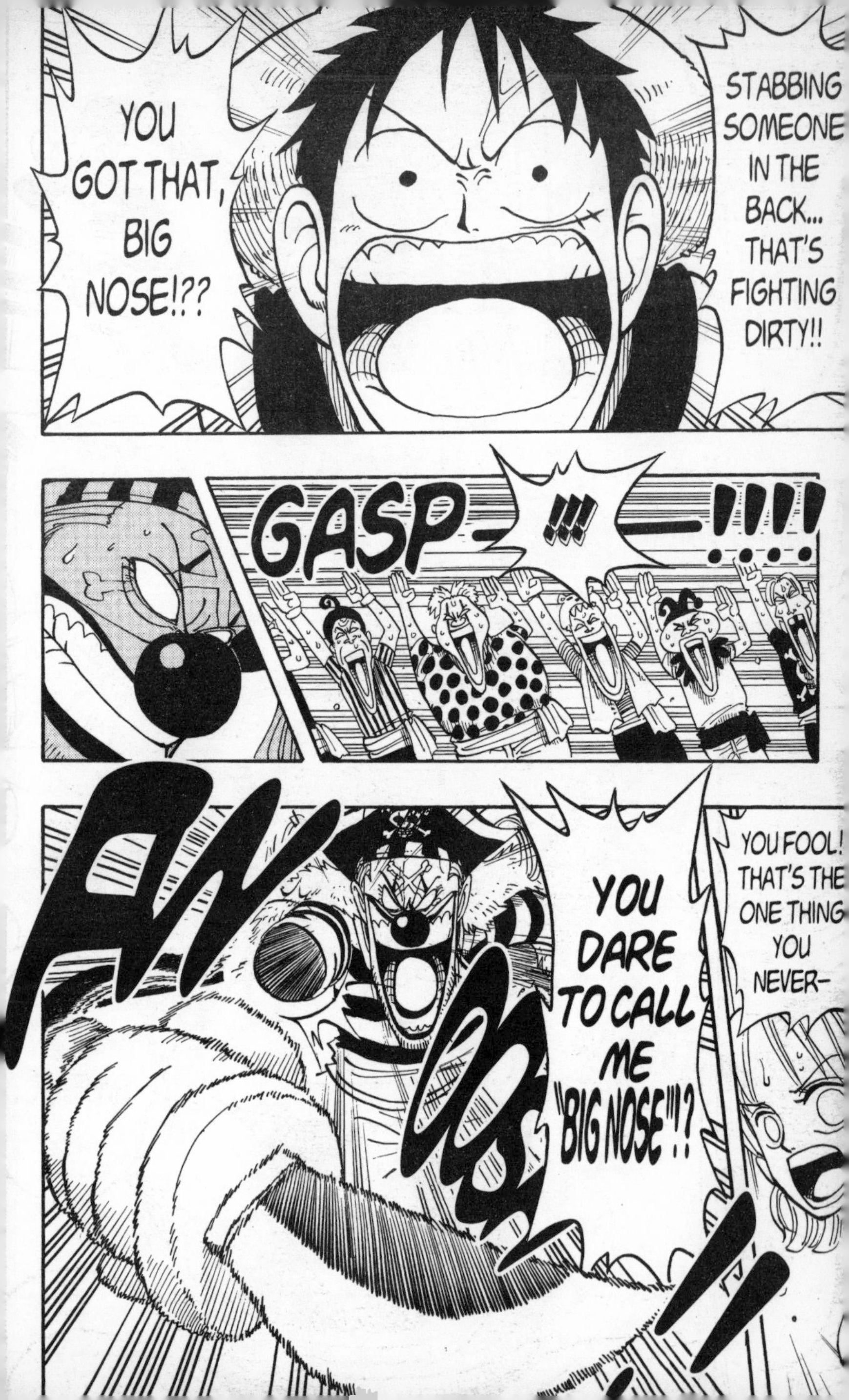
STABBING SOMEONE IN THE BACK... THAT'S FIGHTING DIRTY!!
YOU GOT THAT, BIG NOSE!??
GASP—!!! —!!!!
YOU FOOL! THAT'S THE ONE THING YOU NEVER—
YOU DARE TO CALL ME "BIG NOSE"!?

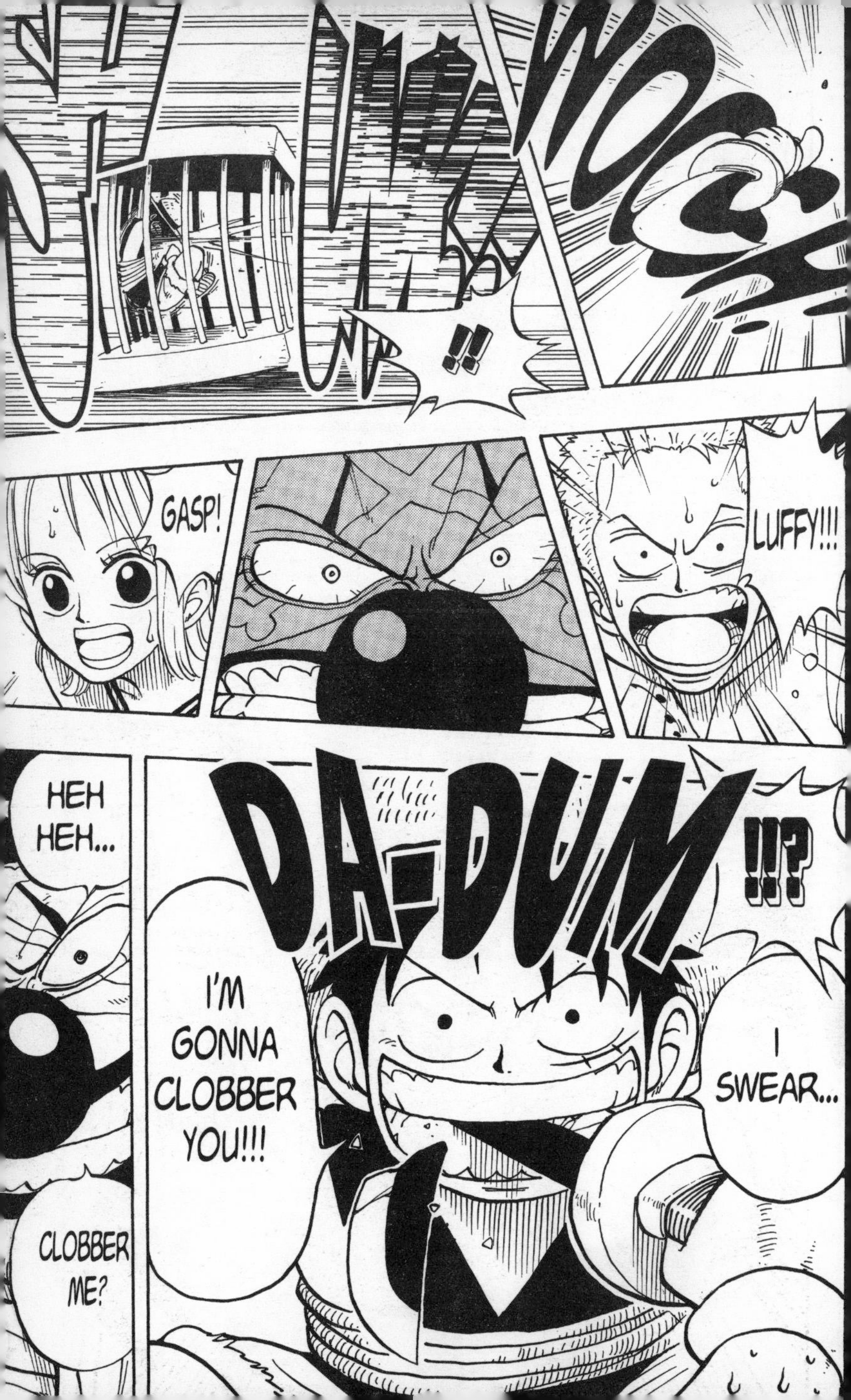

!!
GASP!
LUFFY!!!!
HEH HEH...
CLOBBER ME?
DA-DUM!!?
I SWEAR...
I'M GONNA CLOBBER YOU!!!

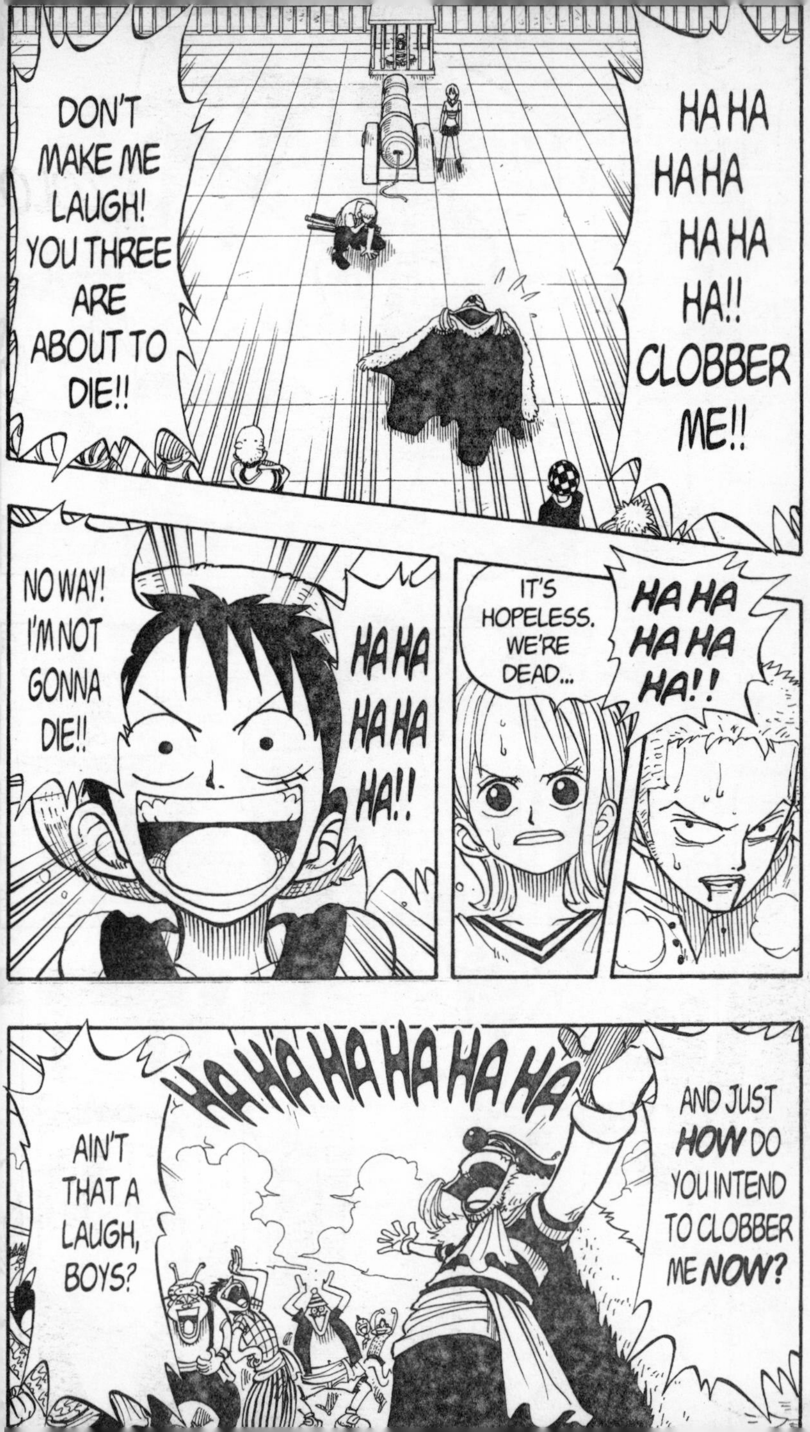
DON'T MAKE ME LAUGH! YOU THREE ARE ABOUT TO DIE!!
HA HA HA HA HA HA HA!! CLOBBER ME!!
NO WAY! I'M NOT GONNA DIE!!
HA HA HA HA HA!!
IT'S HOPELESS. WE'RE DEAD...
HA HA HA HA HA!!
HA HA HA HA HA HA HA HA HA
AIN'T THAT A LAUGH, BOYS?
AND JUST HOW DO YOU INTEND TO CLOBBER ME NOW?

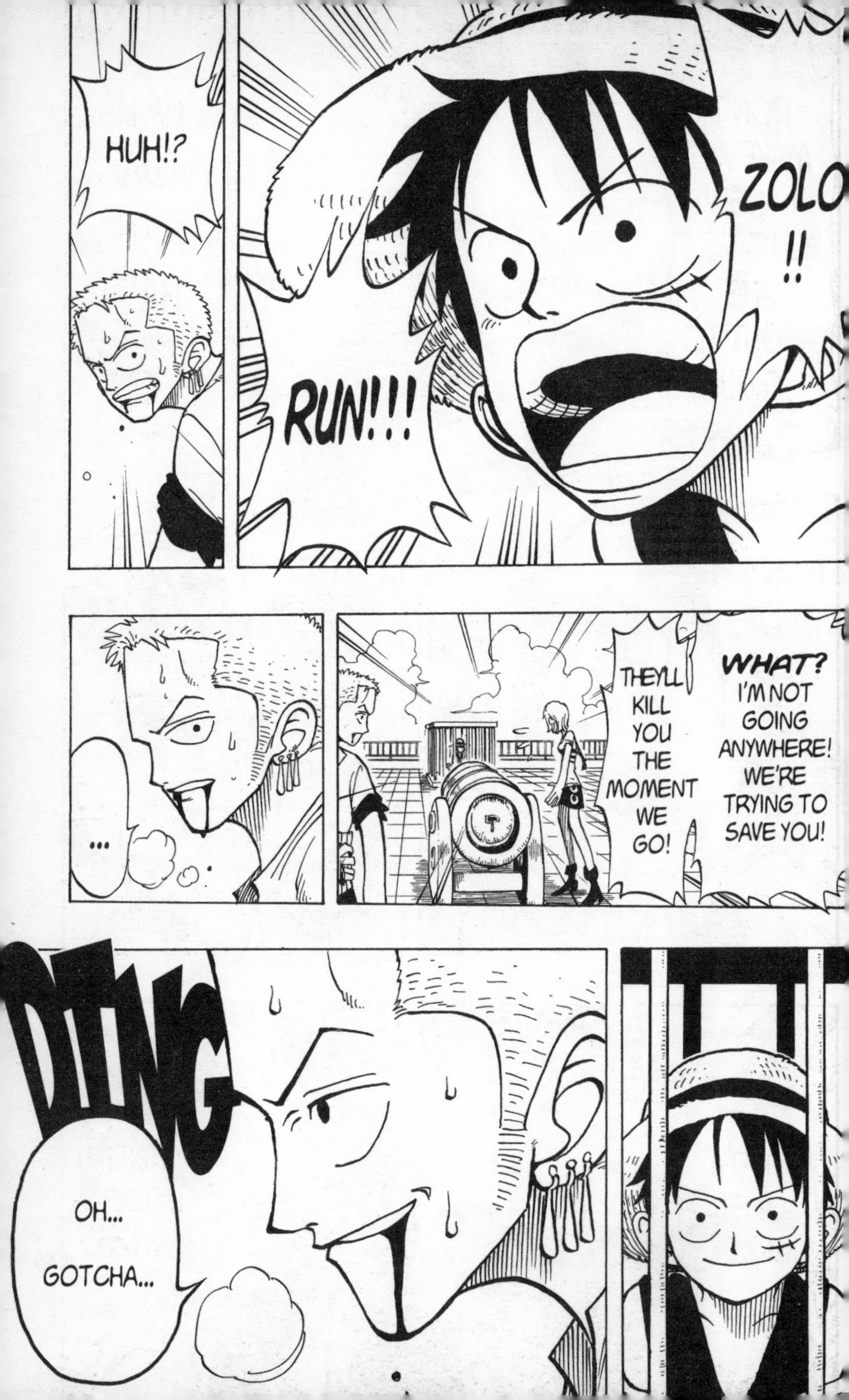
ZOLO!!
RUN!!!
HUH!?
WHAT? I'M NOT GOING ANYWHERE! WE'RE TRYING TO SAVE YOU!
THEY'LL KILL YOU THE MOMENT WE GO!
...
OH... GOTCHA...

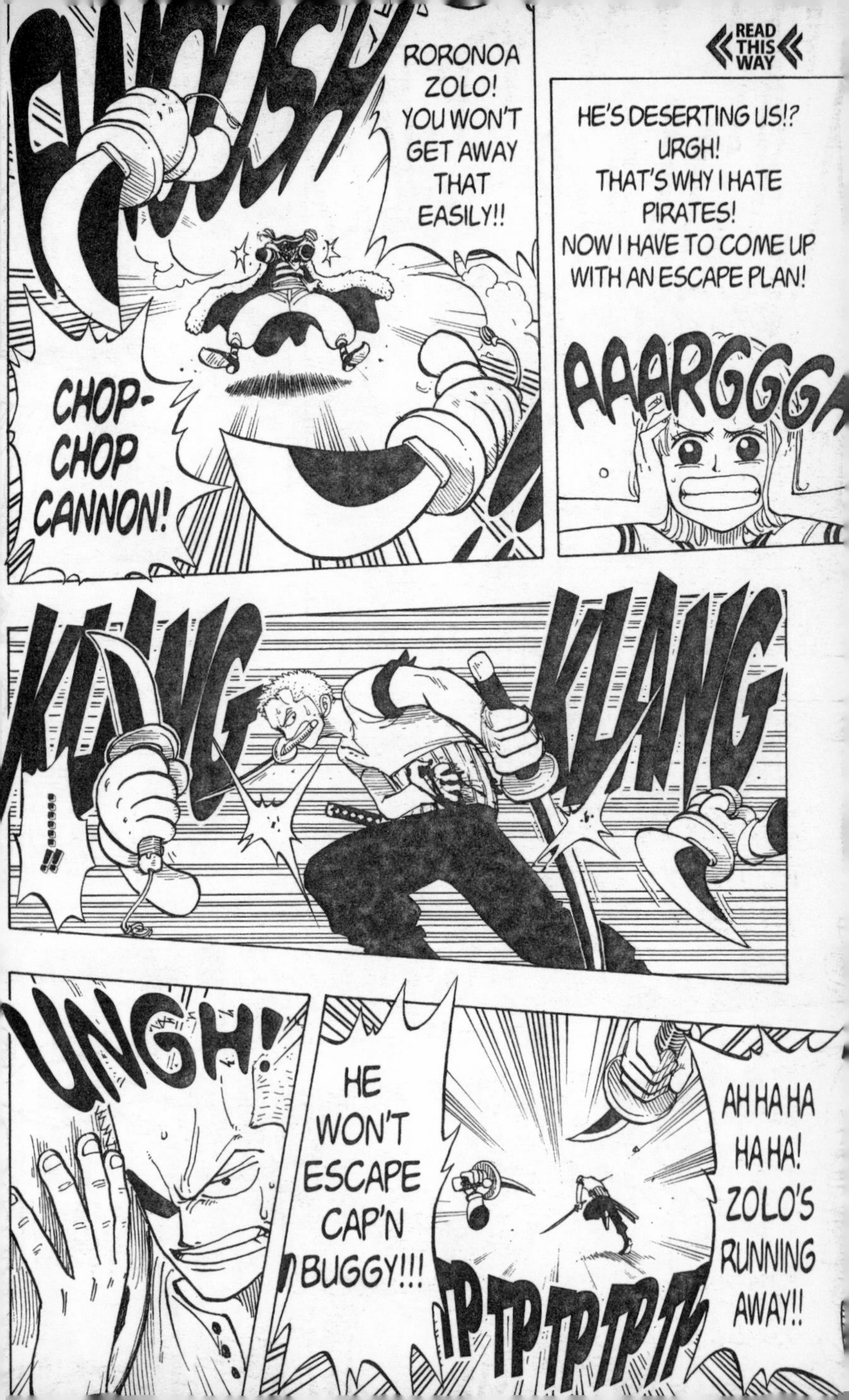
READ THIS WAY
HE'S DESERTING US!? URGH! THAT'S WHY I HATE PIRATES! NOW I HAVE TO COME UP WITH AN ESCAPE PLAN!
RORONOA ZOLO! YOU WON'T GET AWAY THAT EASILY!!
CHOP-CHOP CANNON!
KLANG
KLANG
AH HA HA HA HA! ZOLO'S RUNNING AWAY!!
TP TP TP TP TP
HE WON'T ESCAPE CAP'N BUGGY!!!
UNGH!

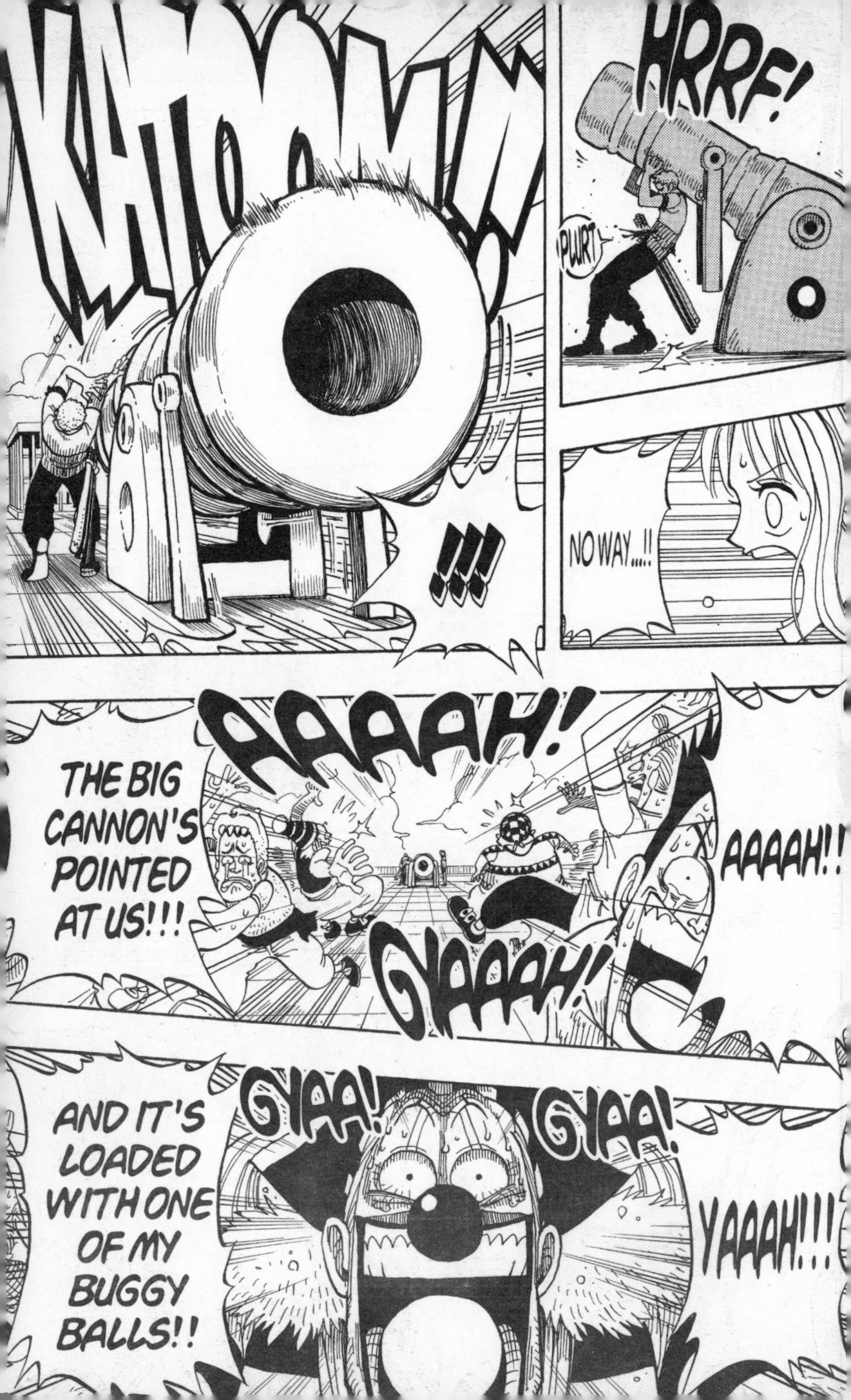
HRRF!
PWURT
NO WAY...!!
!!!
AAAAH!!
AAAAAH!
THE BIG CANNON'S POINTED AT US!!!
GYAAAH!
GYAA!
GYAA!
YAAAH!!!
AND IT'S LOADED WITH ONE OF MY BUGGY BALLS!!

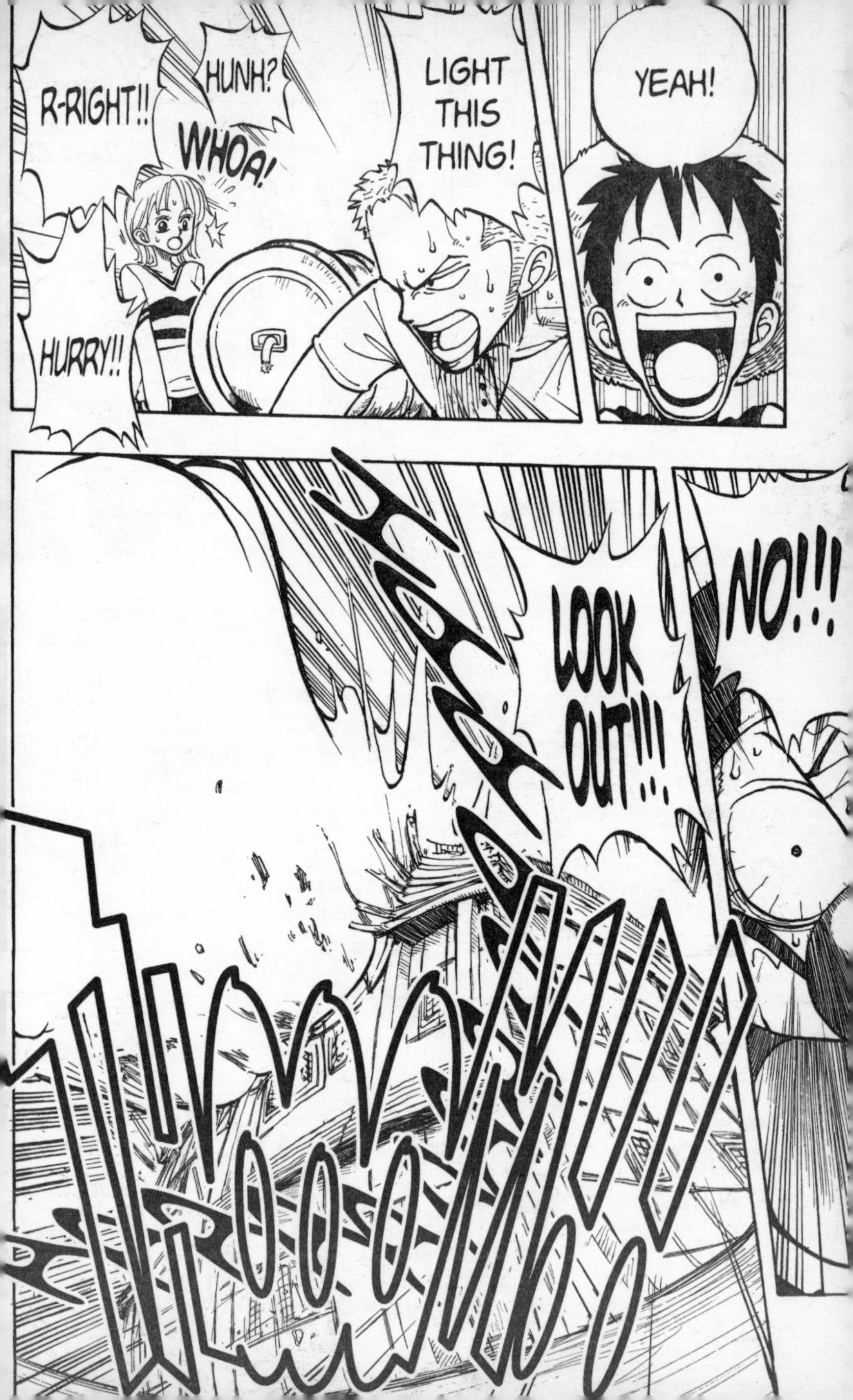
YEAH!
LIGHT THIS THING!
HUNH?
WHOA!
R-RIGHT!!
HURRY!!
NO!!!
LOOK OUT!!!

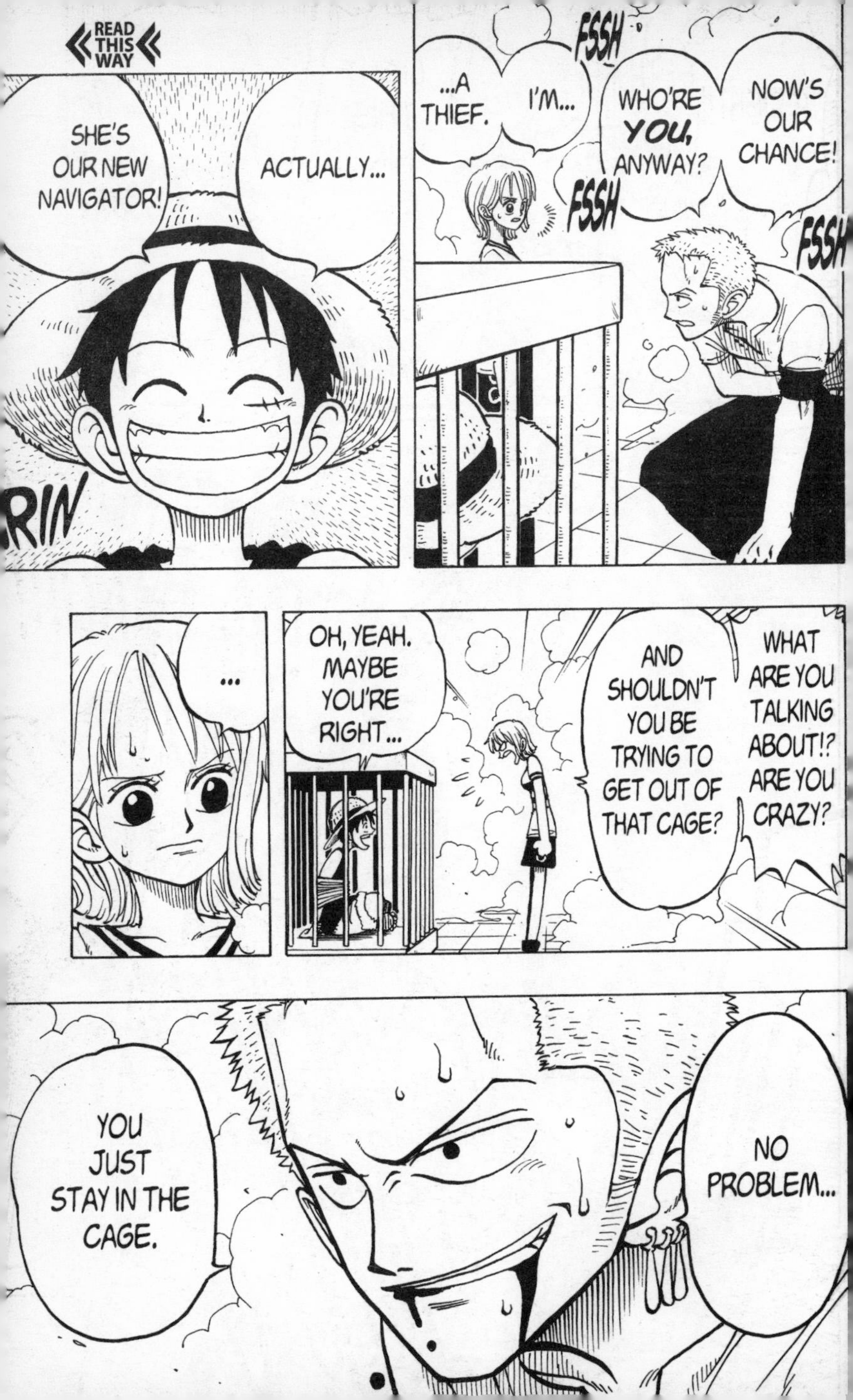
READ THIS WAY
NOW'S OUR CHANCE!
FSSH
WHO'RE *YOU,* ANYWAY?
FSSH
FSSH
I'M...
...A THIEF.
ACTUALLY...
SHE'S OUR NEW NAVIGATOR!
WHAT ARE YOU TALKING ABOUT!? ARE YOU CRAZY?
AND SHOULDN'T YOU BE TRYING TO GET OUT OF THAT CAGE?
OH, YEAH. MAYBE YOU'RE RIGHT...
...
NO PROBLEM...
YOU JUST STAY IN THE CAGE.

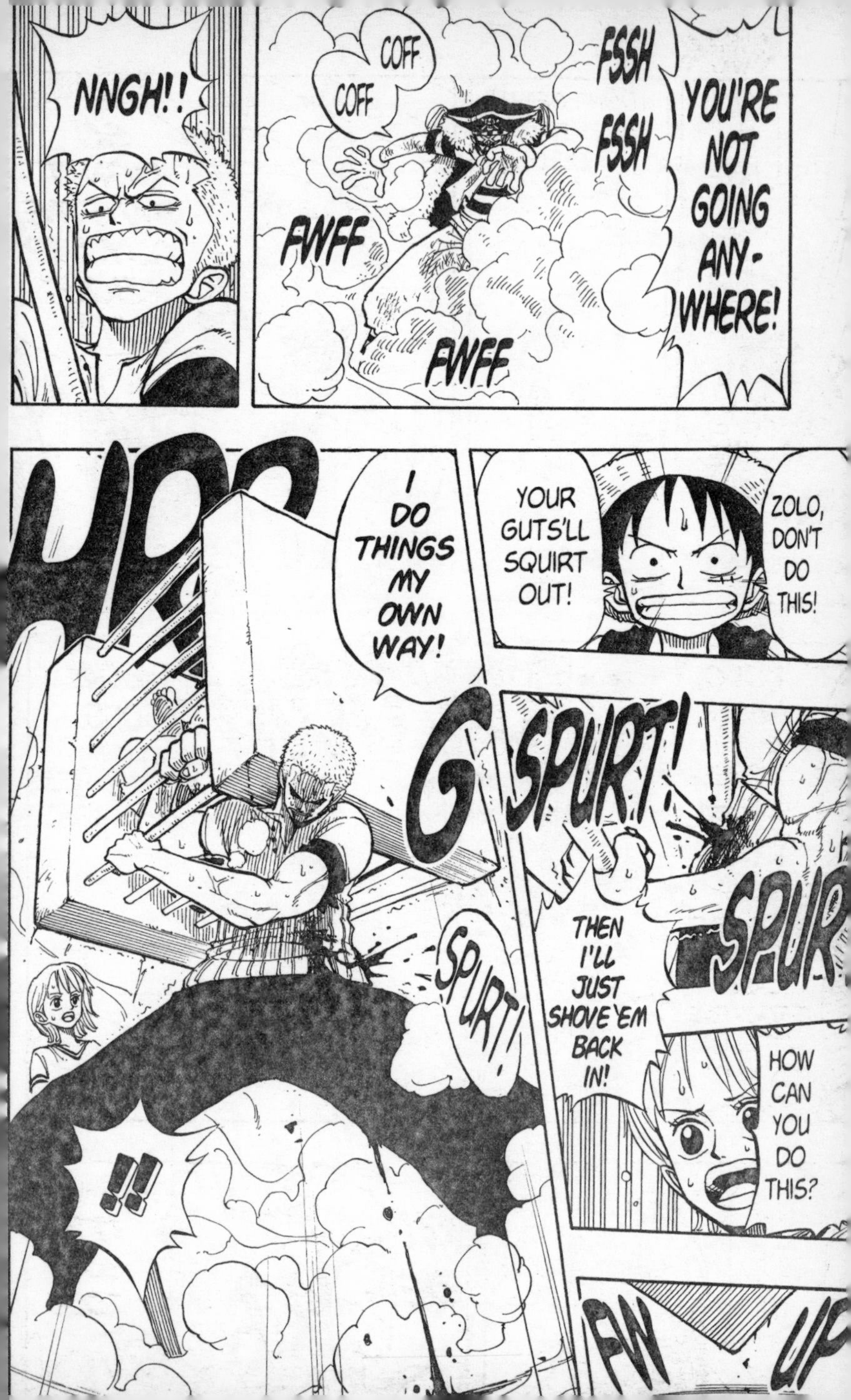
YOU'RE NOT GOING ANY-WHERE!
FSSH
FSSH
COFF
COFF
FWFF
FWFF
NNGH!!
ZOLO, DON'T DO THIS!
YOUR GUTS'LL SQUIRT OUT!
I DO THINGS MY OWN WAY!
SPURT!
G
SPUR
THEN I'LL JUST SHOVE 'EM BACK IN!
SPURT!
HOW CAN YOU DO THIS?
!!
FW
UP

PWFF PWFF

WHERE'D THEY GO!?

I DON'T GET IT! NO PIRATE WOULD SACRIFICE HIMSELF TO SAVE A FRIEND!

SO DON'T GIVE ME ANY LIP ABOUT IT!

ZOLO, NAMI... EVEN THE CAGE!

IMPOSSIBLE! IT'S AN IRON CAGE! IT TOOK FIVE OF US TO MOVE IT!

KRAKOOM

THEY'RE GONE, CAP'N!

SOME-ONE TOOK IT!

THE KEY TO THE CAGE...

WHAT'S GONE!?

OH NO!! IT'S GONE TOO!!

READ THIS WAY

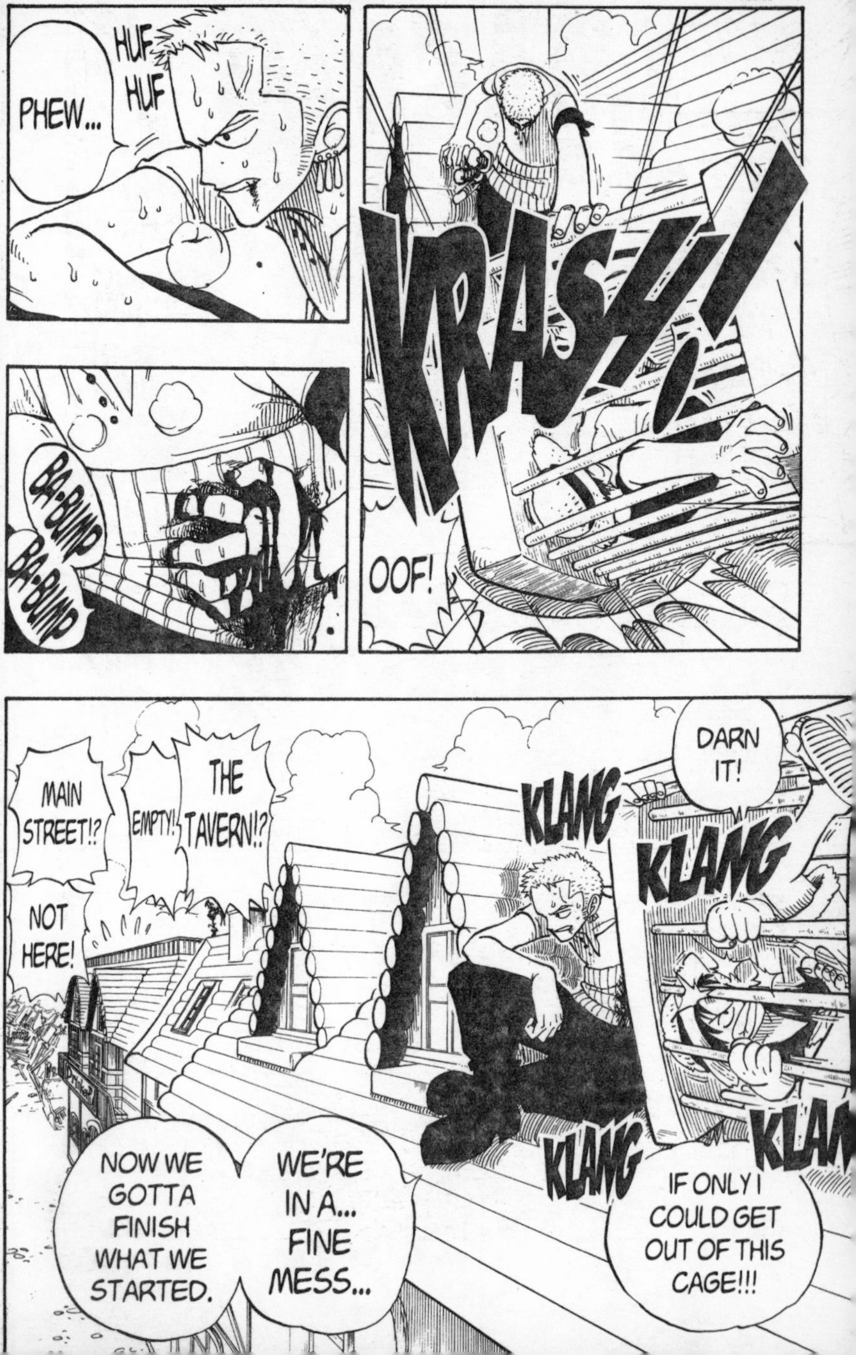
KRASH!
OOF!
HUF HUF
PHEW...
BA-BUMP BA-BUMP
DARN IT!
KLANG
KLANG
THE TAVERN!?
EMPTY!
MAIN STREET!?
NOT HERE!
KLANG
KLAN
IF ONLY I COULD GET OUT OF THIS CAGE!!!
WE'RE IN A... FINE MESS...
NOW WE GOTTA FINISH WHAT WE STARTED.

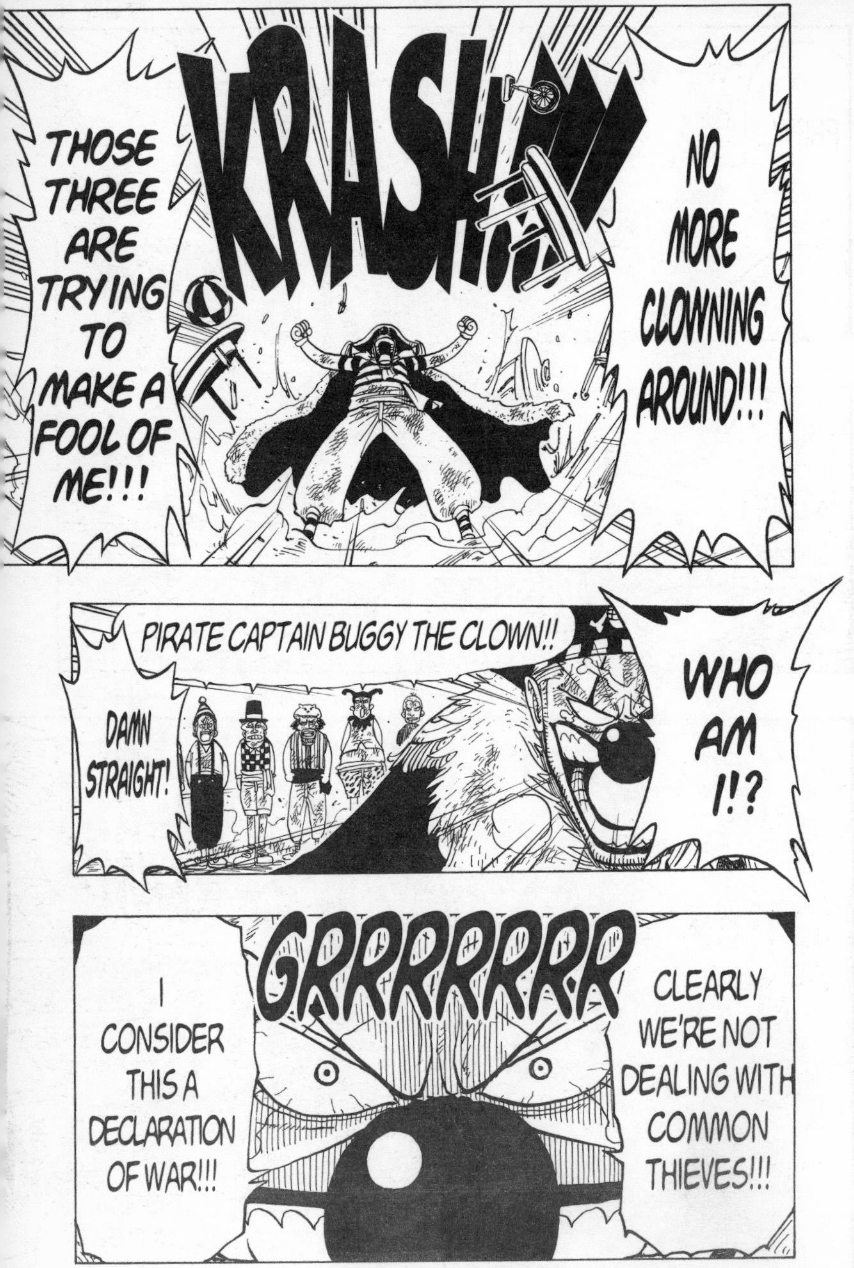
KRASH!!!
NO MORE CLOWNING AROUND!!!
THOSE THREE ARE TRYING TO MAKE A FOOL OF ME!!!
WHO AM I!?
PIRATE CAPTAIN BUGGY THE CLOWN!!
DAMN STRAIGHT!
GRRRRRRRR
CLEARLY WE'RE NOT DEALING WITH COMMON THIEVES!!!
I CONSIDER THIS A DECLARATION OF WAR!!!

One Piece Rough Sketch!

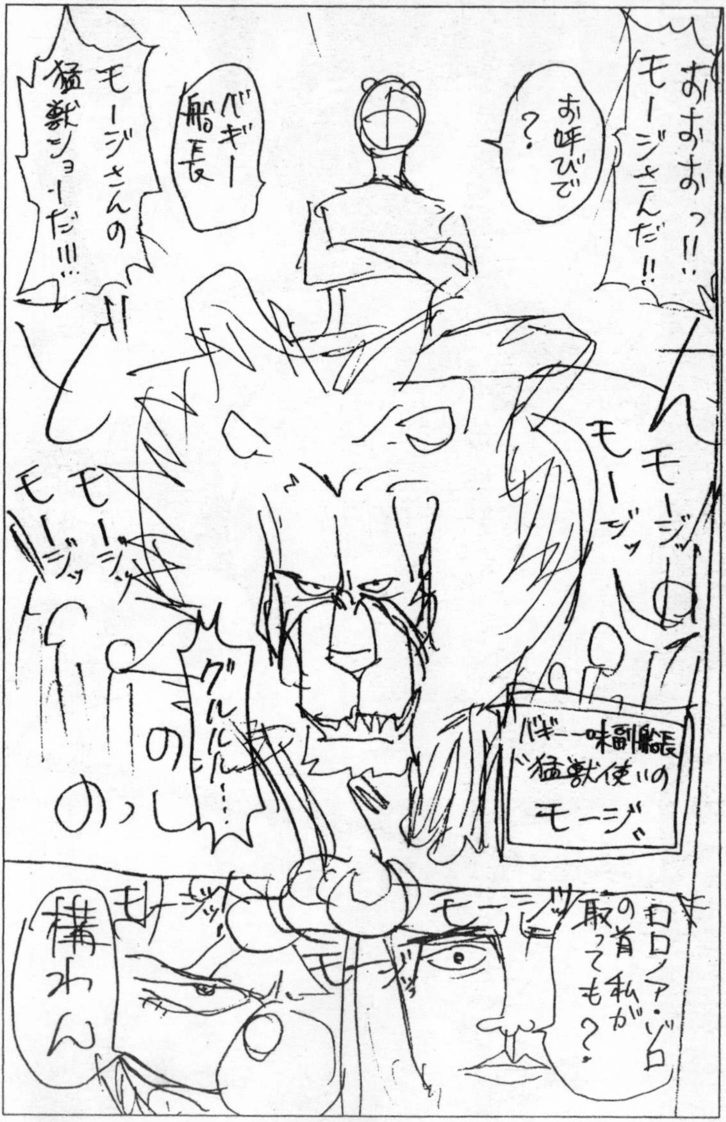

おおおっ!! モージさんだ!!
お呼びで？
バギー船長
モージさんの猛獣ショーだ!!!
バギー一味副船長 猛獣使いのモージ
グルルル…
ロロノア・ゾロの首 私が取っても？
構わん

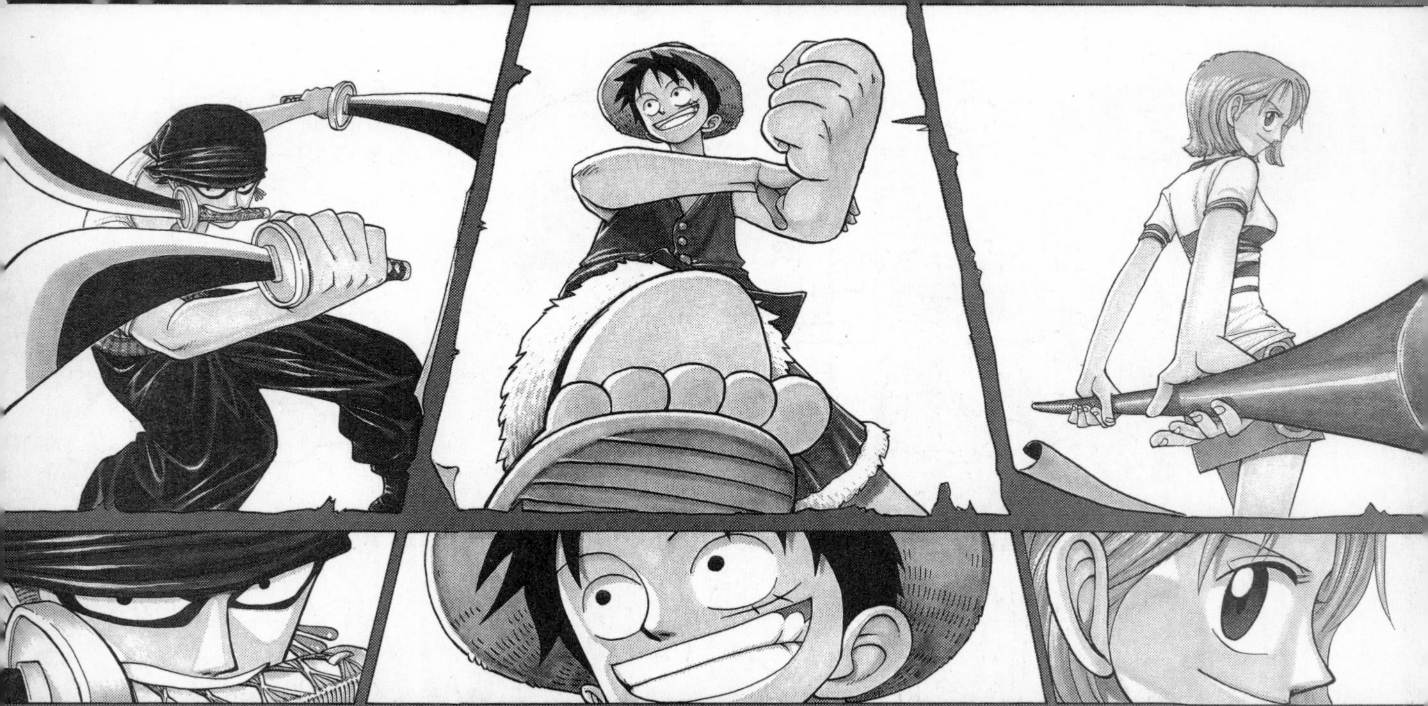

Chapter 12: DOG

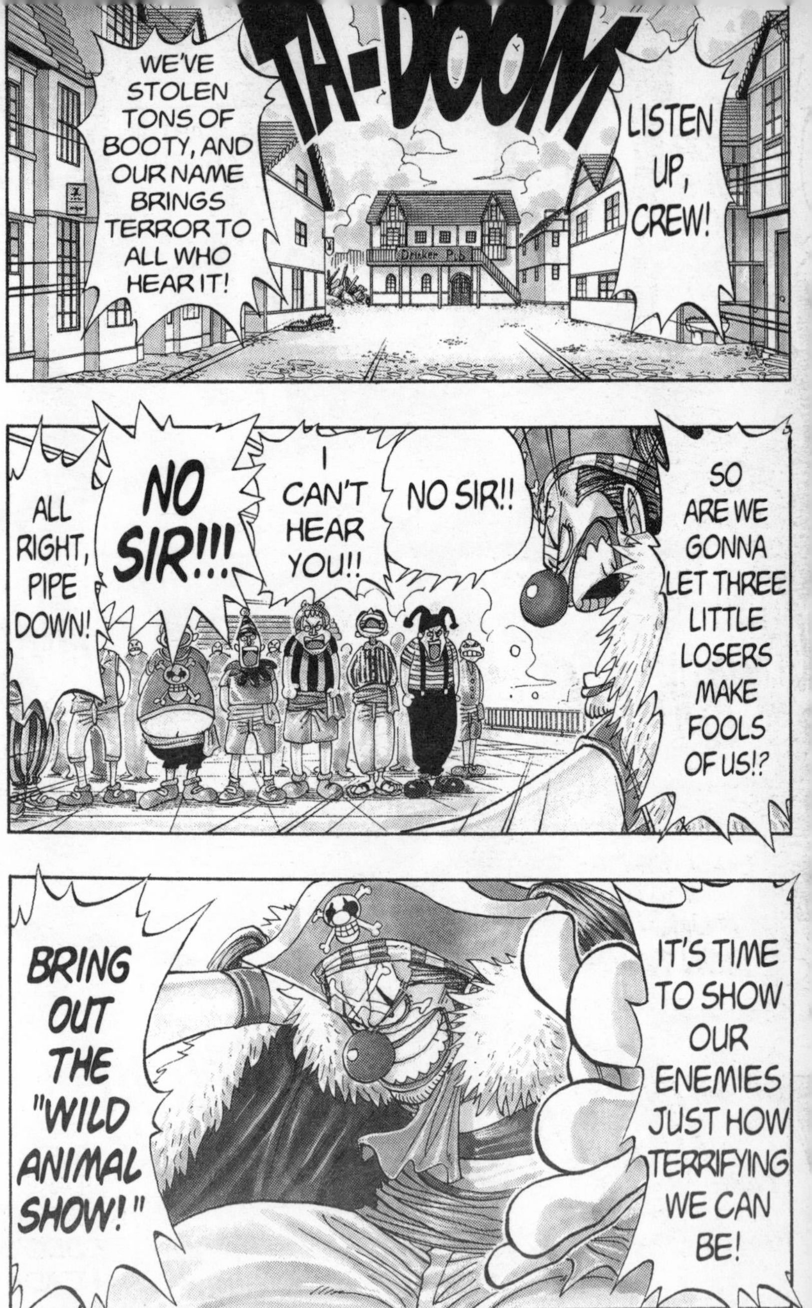
WE'VE STOLEN TONS OF BOOTY, AND OUR NAME BRINGS TERROR TO ALL WHO HEAR IT!
TA-DOOM
LISTEN UP, CREW!
SO ARE WE GONNA LET THREE LITTLE LOSERS MAKE FOOLS OF US!?
NO SIR!!
I CAN'T HEAR YOU!!
NO SIR!!!
ALL RIGHT, PIPE DOWN!
BRING OUT THE "WILD ANIMAL SHOW!"
IT'S TIME TO SHOW OUR ENEMIES JUST HOW TERRIFYING WE CAN BE!

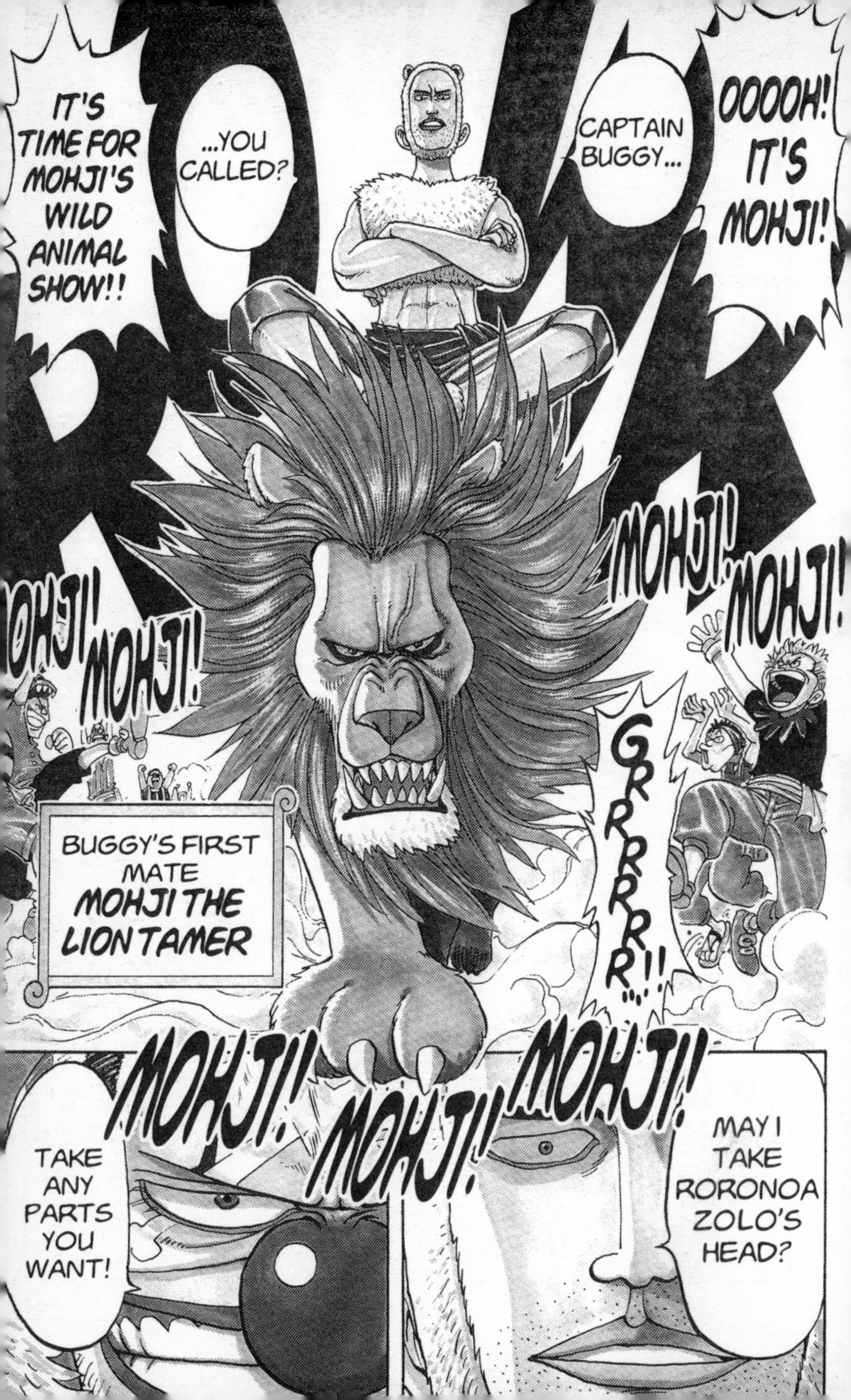
OOOOH! IT'S MOHJI!
CAPTAIN BUGGY...
...YOU CALLED?
IT'S TIME FOR MOHJI'S WILD ANIMAL SHOW!!
MOHJI! MOHJI!
OHJI! MOHJI!
GRRRRR...!!
BUGGY'S FIRST MATE MOHJI THE LION TAMER
MOHJI! MOHJI! MOHJI!
MAY I TAKE RORONOA ZOLO'S HEAD?
TAKE ANY PARTS YOU WANT!

READ THIS WAY

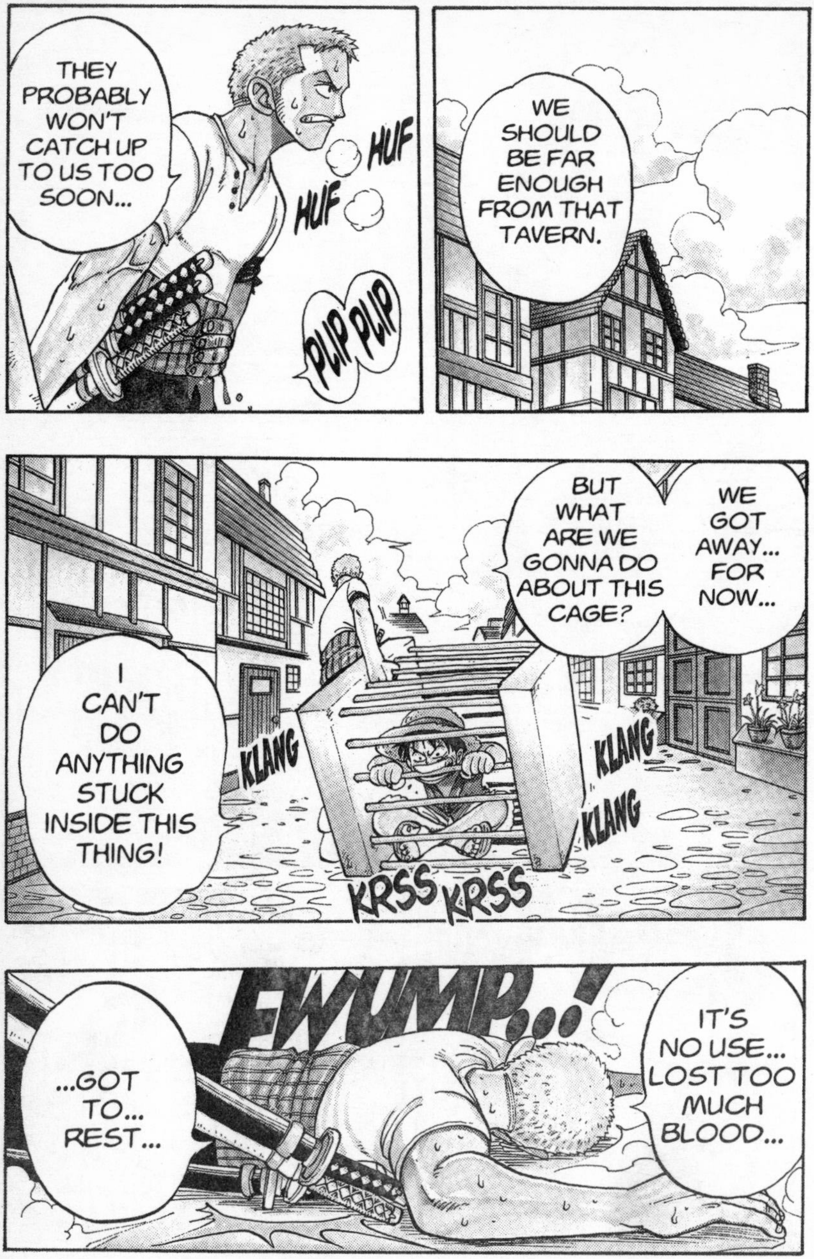

WE SHOULD BE FAR ENOUGH FROM THAT TAVERN.
THEY PROBABLY WON'T CATCH UP TO US TOO SOON...
HUF
HUF
PLIP PLIP
WE GOT AWAY... FOR NOW...
BUT WHAT ARE WE GONNA DO ABOUT THIS CAGE?
KLANG
KLANG
KLANG
I CAN'T DO ANYTHING STUCK INSIDE THIS THING!
KRSS KRSS
IT'S NO USE... LOST TOO MUCH BLOOD...
FWUMP...!
...GOT TO... REST...

READ THIS WAY

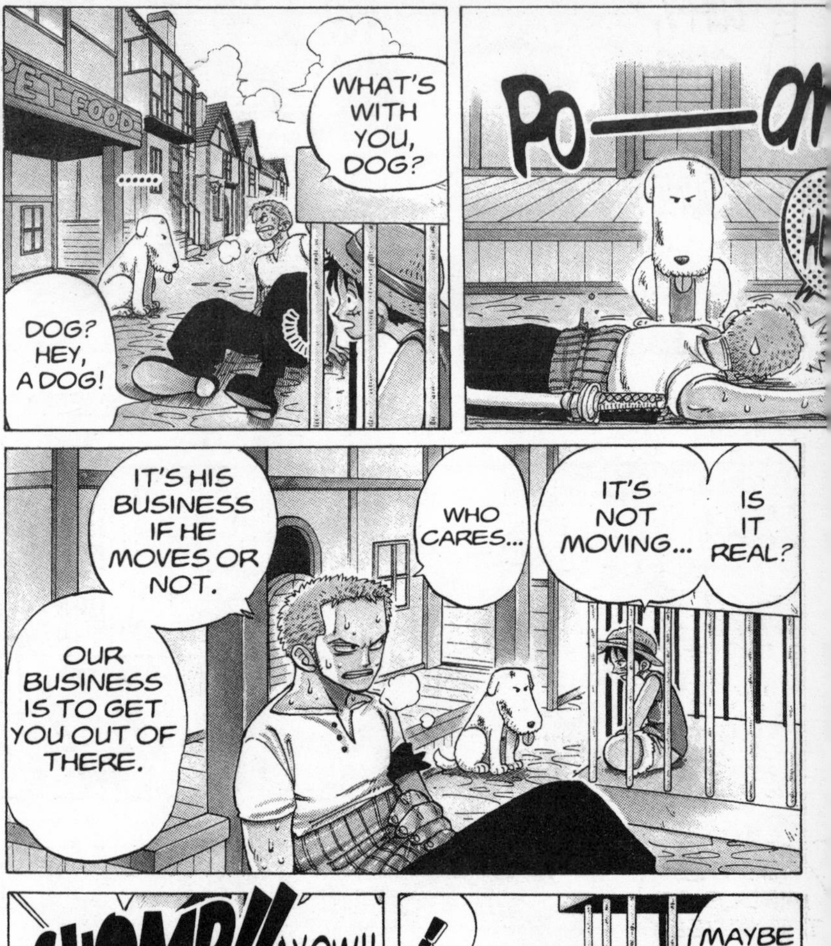
PO——
WHAT'S WITH YOU, DOG?
......
DOG? HEY, A DOG!
IS IT REAL?
IT'S NOT MOVING...
WHO CARES...
IT'S HIS BUSINESS IF HE MOVES OR NOT.
OUR BUSINESS IS TO GET YOU OUT OF THERE.
MAYBE IT'S DEAD.
DOINK
!
YOW!!
CHOMP!!

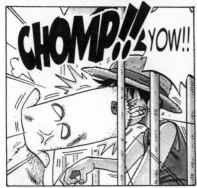

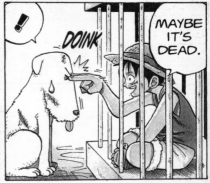

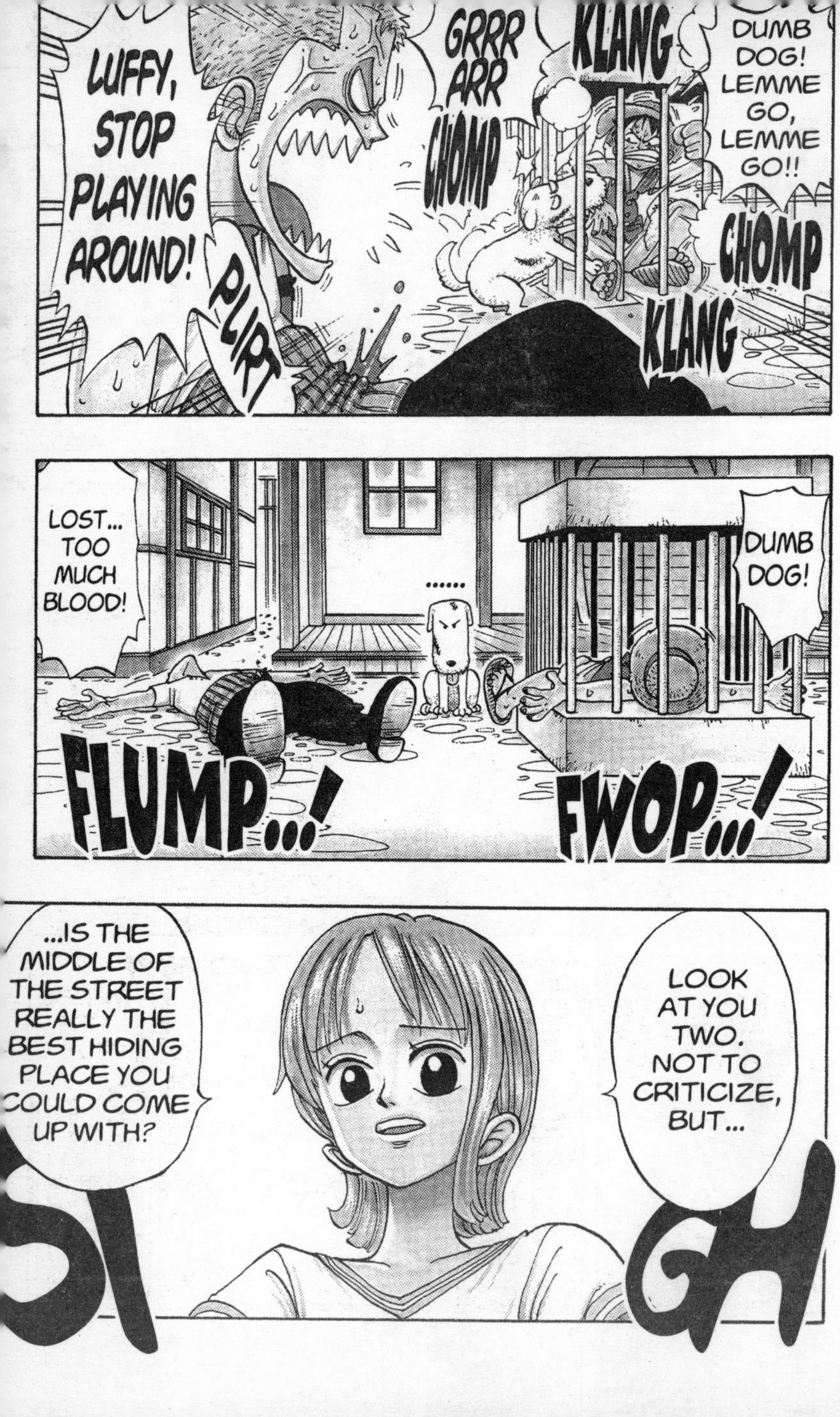
DUMB DOG! LEMME GO, LEMME GO!!
KLANG
CHOMP
KLANG
GRRR ARR
CHOMP
LUFFY, STOP PLAYING AROUND!
PLIRT
DUMB DOG!
......
LOST... TOO MUCH BLOOD!
FWOP...!
FLUMP...!
LOOK AT YOU TWO. NOT TO CRITICIZE, BUT...
...IS THE MIDDLE OF THE STREET REALLY THE BEST HIDING PLACE YOU COULD COME UP WITH?
SIGH

READ THIS WAY

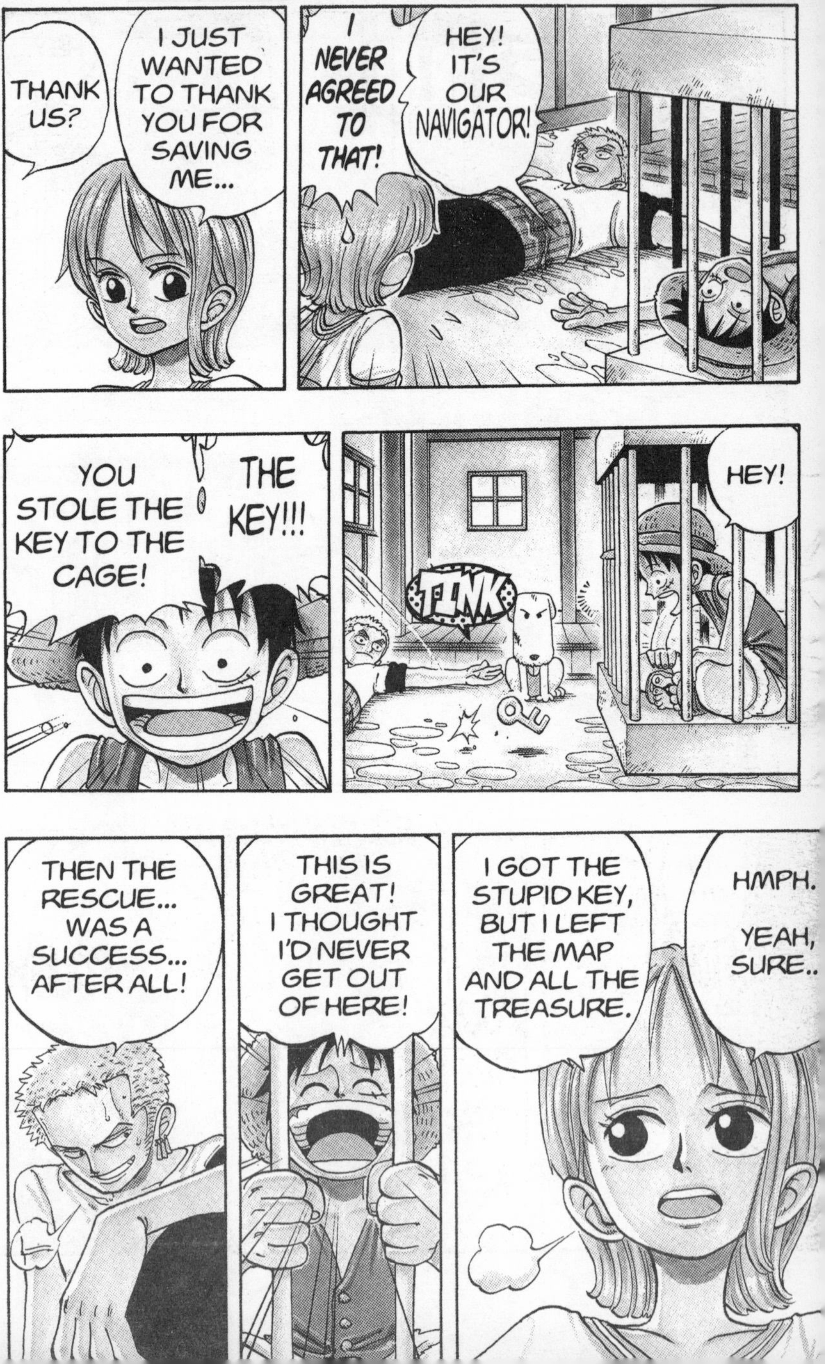
HEY! IT'S OUR NAVIGATOR!
I NEVER AGREED TO THAT!
I JUST WANTED TO THANK YOU FOR SAVING ME...
THANK US?
HEY!
TINK
THE KEY!!!
YOU STOLE THE KEY TO THE CAGE!
HMPH. YEAH, SURE..
I GOT THE STUPID KEY, BUT I LEFT THE MAP AND ALL THE TREASURE.
THIS IS GREAT! I THOUGHT I'D NEVER GET OUT OF HERE!
THEN THE RESCUE... WAS A SUCCESS... AFTER ALL!

READ THIS WAY

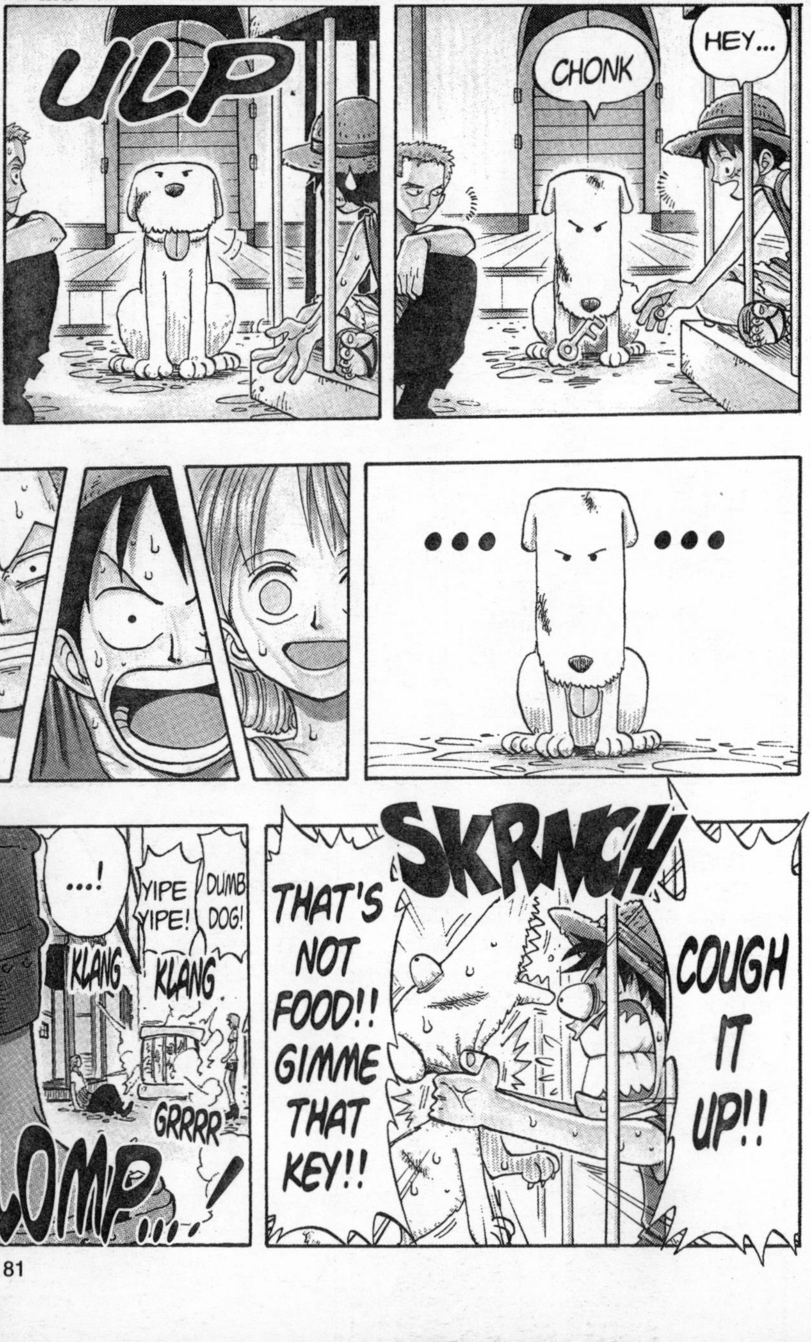
HEY...
CHONK
ULP
... ...
SKRNCH
COUGH IT UP!!
THAT'S NOT FOOD!! GIMME THAT KEY!!
...!
DUMB DOG!
YIPE YIPE!
KLANG
KLANG
GRRRR
LOMP...!

READ THIS WAY

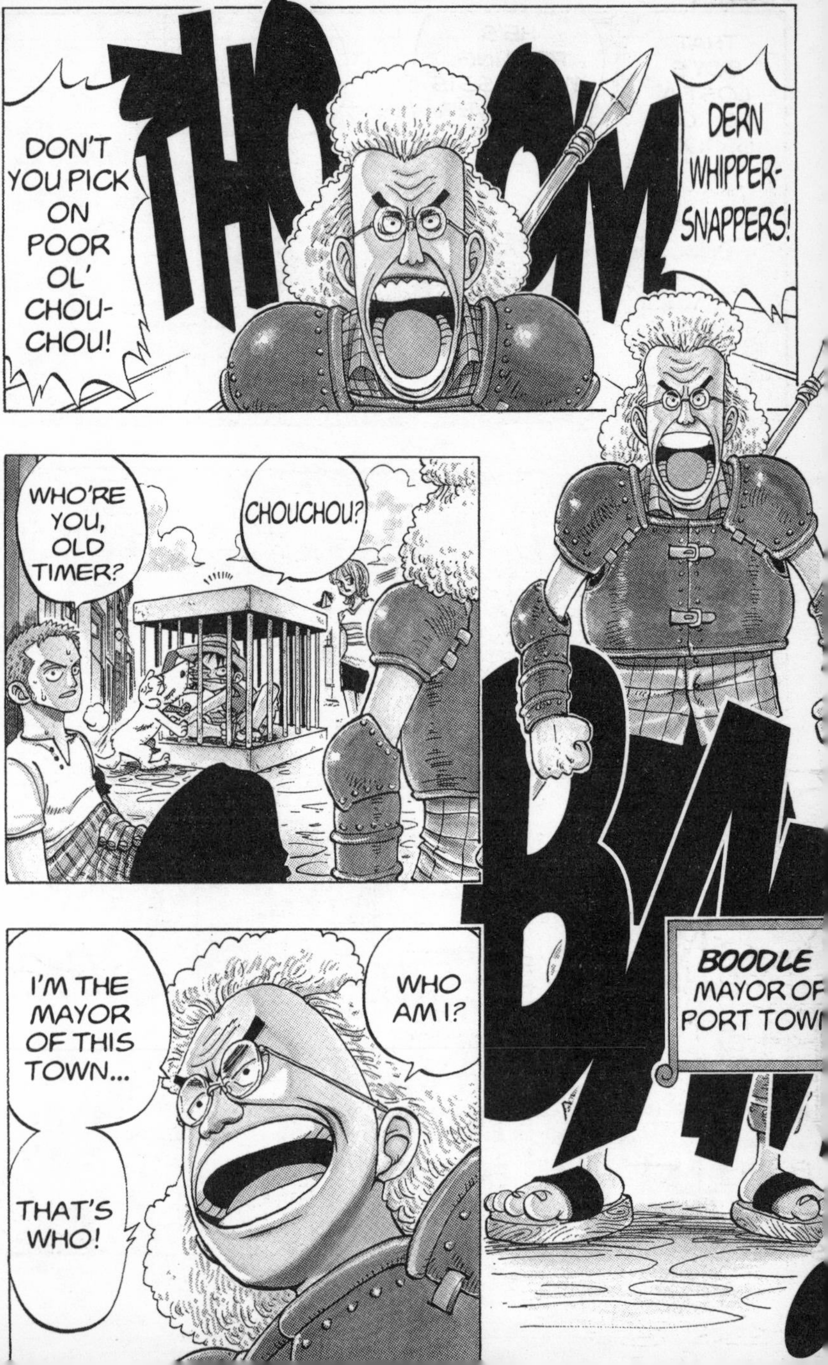
THOOM
DERN WHIPPER-SNAPPERS!
DON'T YOU PICK ON POOR OL' CHOU-CHOU!
BAM
BOODLE
MAYOR OF
PORT TOW
CHOUCHOU?
WHO'RE YOU, OLD TIMER?
WHO AM I?
I'M THE MAYOR OF THIS TOWN...
THAT'S WHO!

READ THIS WAY

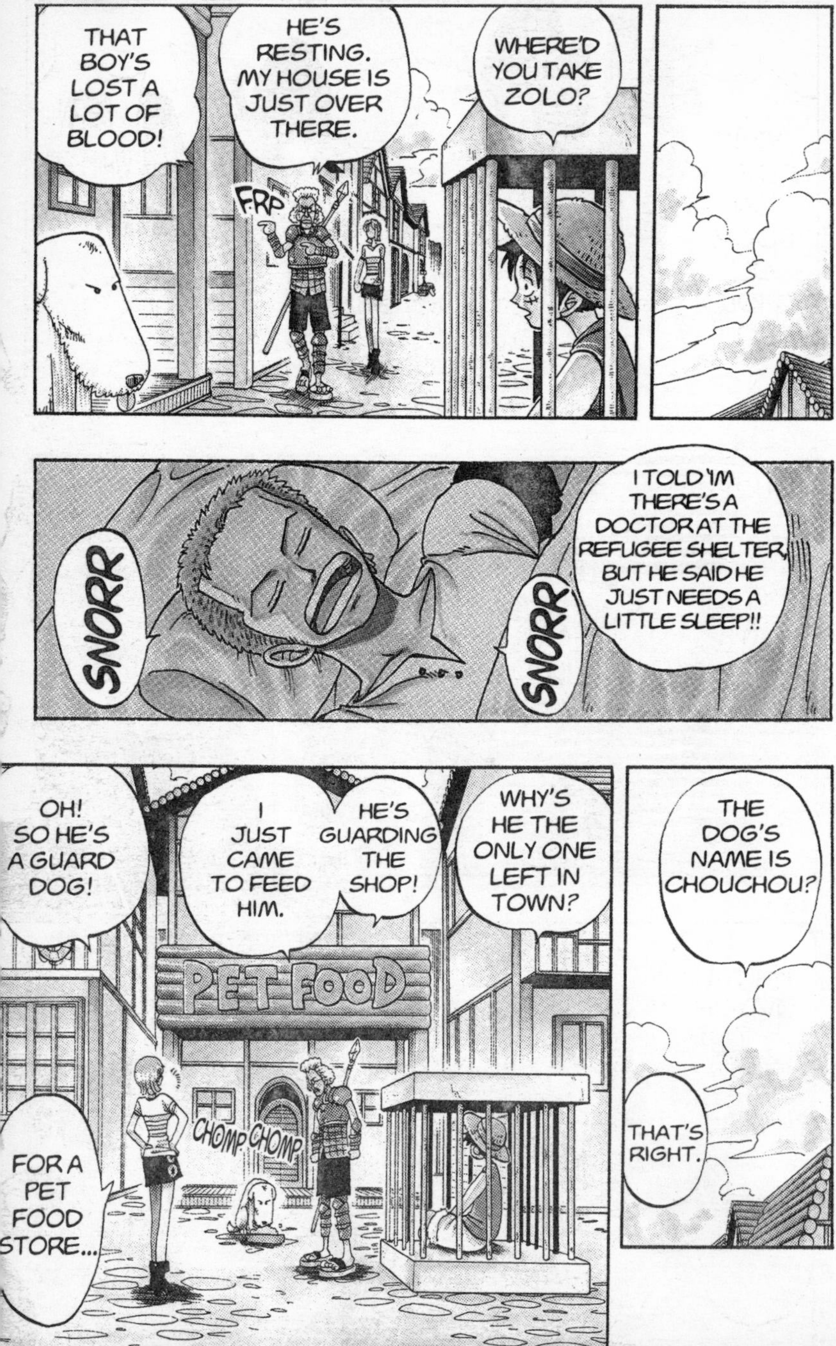

WHERE'D YOU TAKE ZOLO?
HE'S RESTING. MY HOUSE IS JUST OVER THERE.
FRP
THAT BOY'S LOST A LOT OF BLOOD!
I TOLD 'IM THERE'S A DOCTOR AT THE REFUGEE SHELTER, BUT HE SAID HE JUST NEEDS A LITTLE SLEEP!!
SNORR
SNORR
THE DOG'S NAME IS CHOUCHOU?
THAT'S RIGHT.
WHY'S HE THE ONLY ONE LEFT IN TOWN?
HE'S GUARDING THE SHOP!
I JUST CAME TO FEED HIM.
OH! SO HE'S A GUARD DOG!
PET FOOD
CHOMP CHOMP
FOR A PET FOOD STORE...

READ THIS WAY

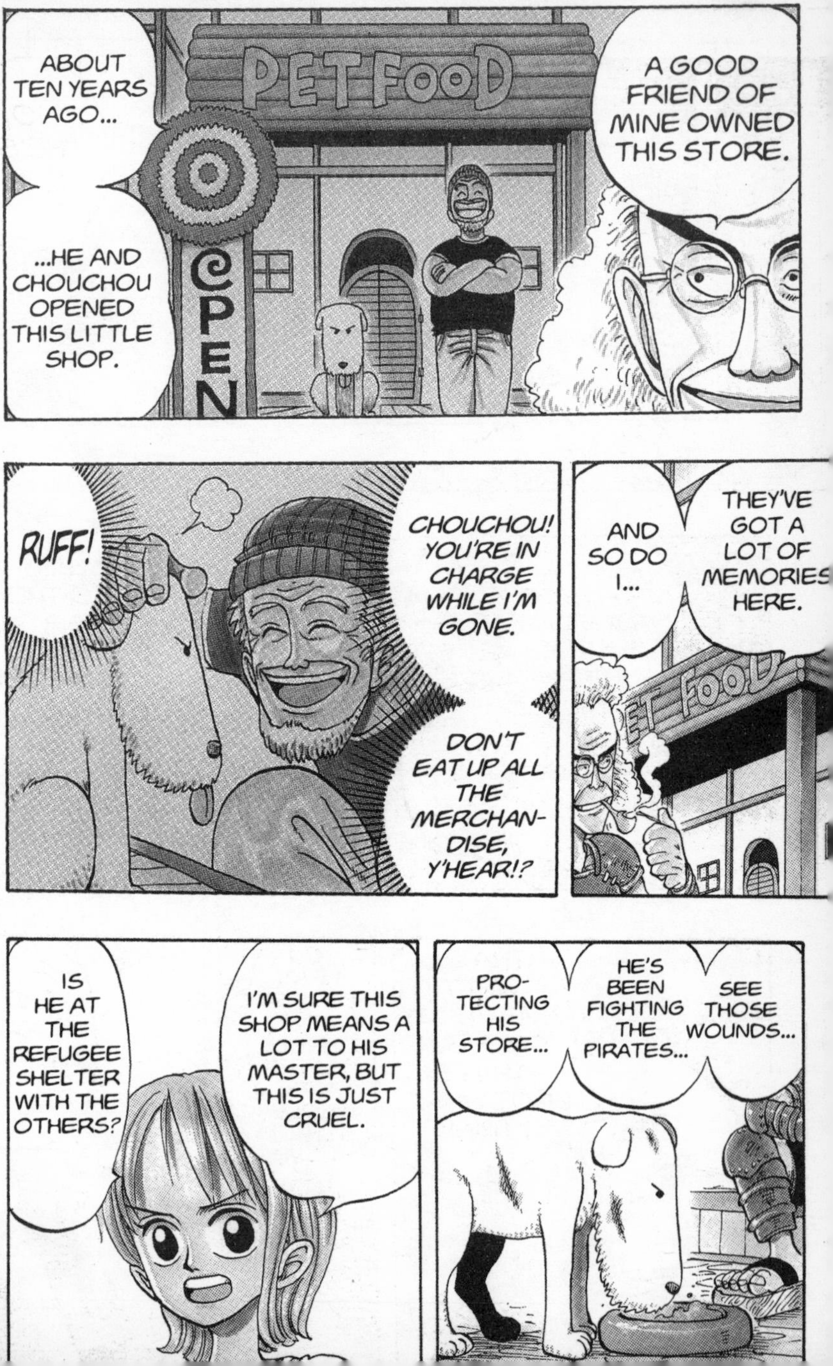
PET FOOD
A GOOD FRIEND OF MINE OWNED THIS STORE.
ABOUT TEN YEARS AGO...
...HE AND CHOUCHOU OPENED THIS LITTLE SHOP.
OPEN
THEY'VE GOT A LOT OF MEMORIES HERE.
AND SO DO I...
CHOUCHOU! YOU'RE IN CHARGE WHILE I'M GONE.
DON'T EAT UP ALL THE MERCHANDISE, Y'HEAR!?
RUFF!
SEE THOSE WOUNDS...
HE'S BEEN FIGHTING THE PIRATES...
PROTECTING HIS STORE...
I'M SURE THIS SHOP MEANS A LOT TO HIS MASTER, BUT THIS IS JUST CRUEL.
IS HE AT THE REFUGEE SHELTER WITH THE OTHERS?

READ THIS WAY

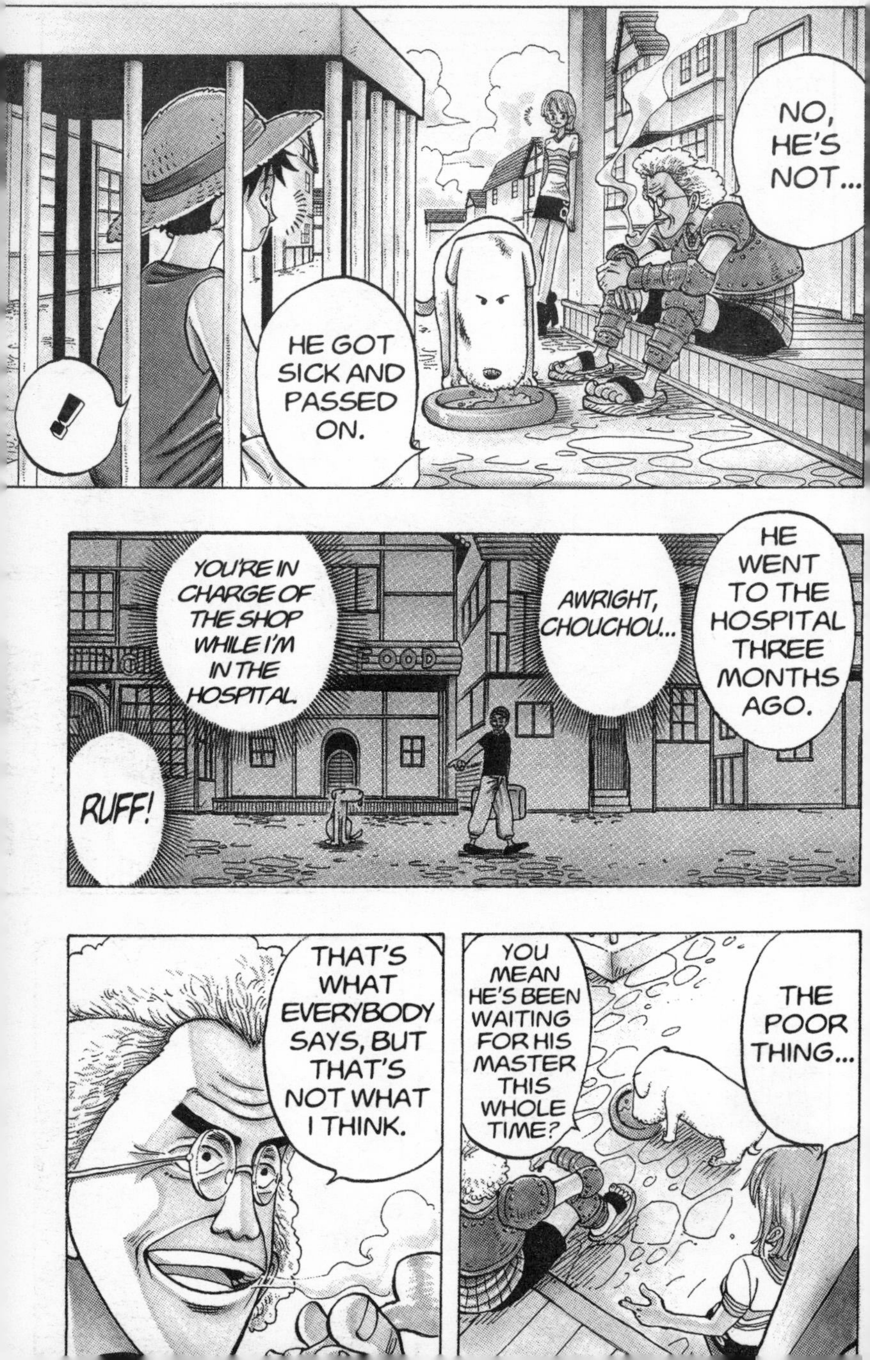

NO, HE'S NOT...
HE GOT SICK AND PASSED ON.
!
HE WENT TO THE HOSPITAL THREE MONTHS AGO.
AWRIGHT, CHOUCHOU...
YOU'RE IN CHARGE OF THE SHOP WHILE I'M IN THE HOSPITAL.
FOOD
RUFF!
THE POOR THING...
YOU MEAN HE'S BEEN WAITING FOR HIS MASTER THIS WHOLE TIME?
THAT'S WHAT EVERYBODY SAYS, BUT THAT'S NOT WHAT I THINK.

READ THIS WAY

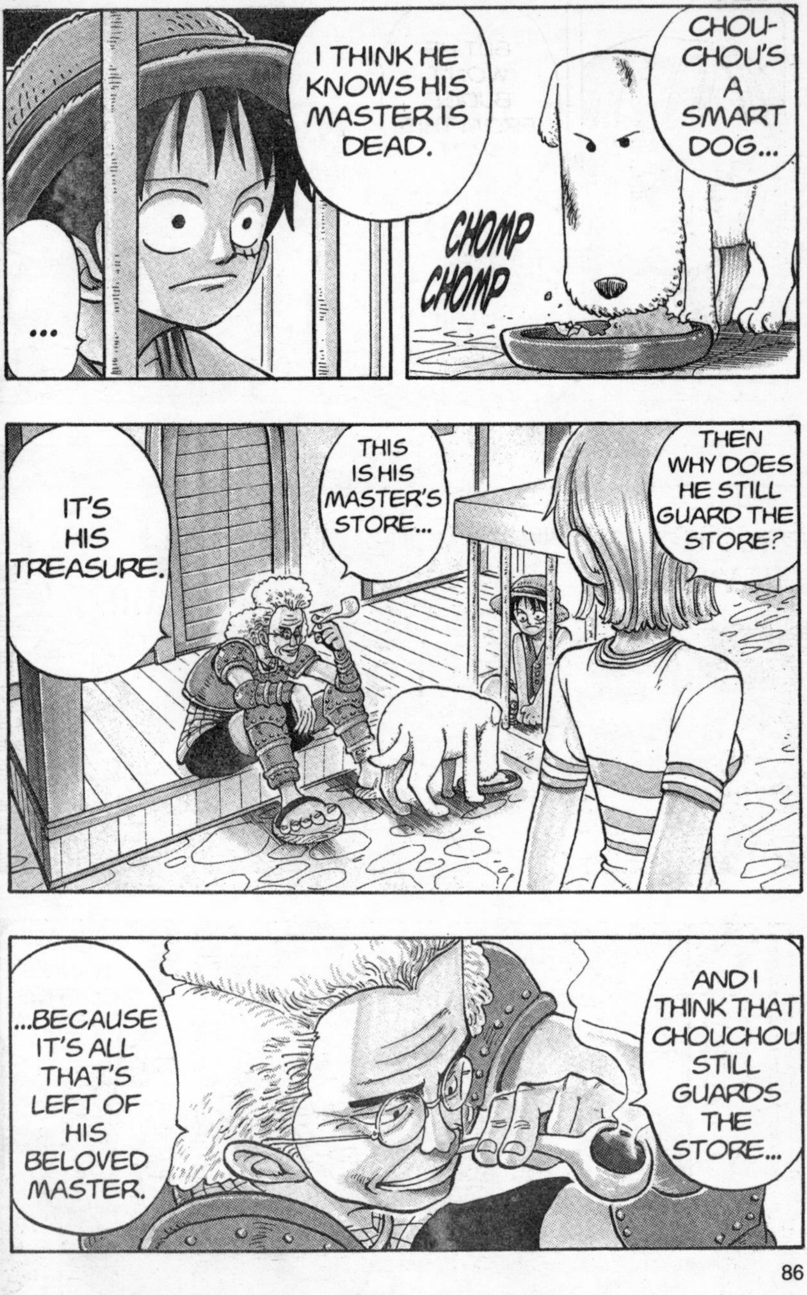
CHOU-CHOU'S A SMART DOG...
CHOMP CHOMP
I THINK HE KNOWS HIS MASTER IS DEAD.
...
THEN WHY DOES HE STILL GUARD THE STORE?
THIS IS HIS MASTER'S STORE...
IT'S HIS TREASURE.
AND I THINK THAT CHOUCHOU STILL GUARDS THE STORE...
...BECAUSE IT'S ALL THAT'S LEFT OF HIS BELOVED MASTER.

BUT HE WON'T BUDGE FROM THIS SPOT.

HE'D RATHER STARVE TO DEATH THAN LEAVE HIS POST.

I'VE BEEN TRYING TO GET HIM TO THE SHELTER...

PHEW

LAP LAP

...

I-IT MUST BE MOHJI, THE LION TAMER!!

WHAT'S THAT HORRIBLE ROAR!?

ROWRR

ROOWWRR...!!!

GASP!!

HUH!!

RUN!!!

TP TP TP TP TP TP

SIGH

WURF!

GIVE ME THAT KEY, DOG!

SOMETHING'S COMING THIS WAY!

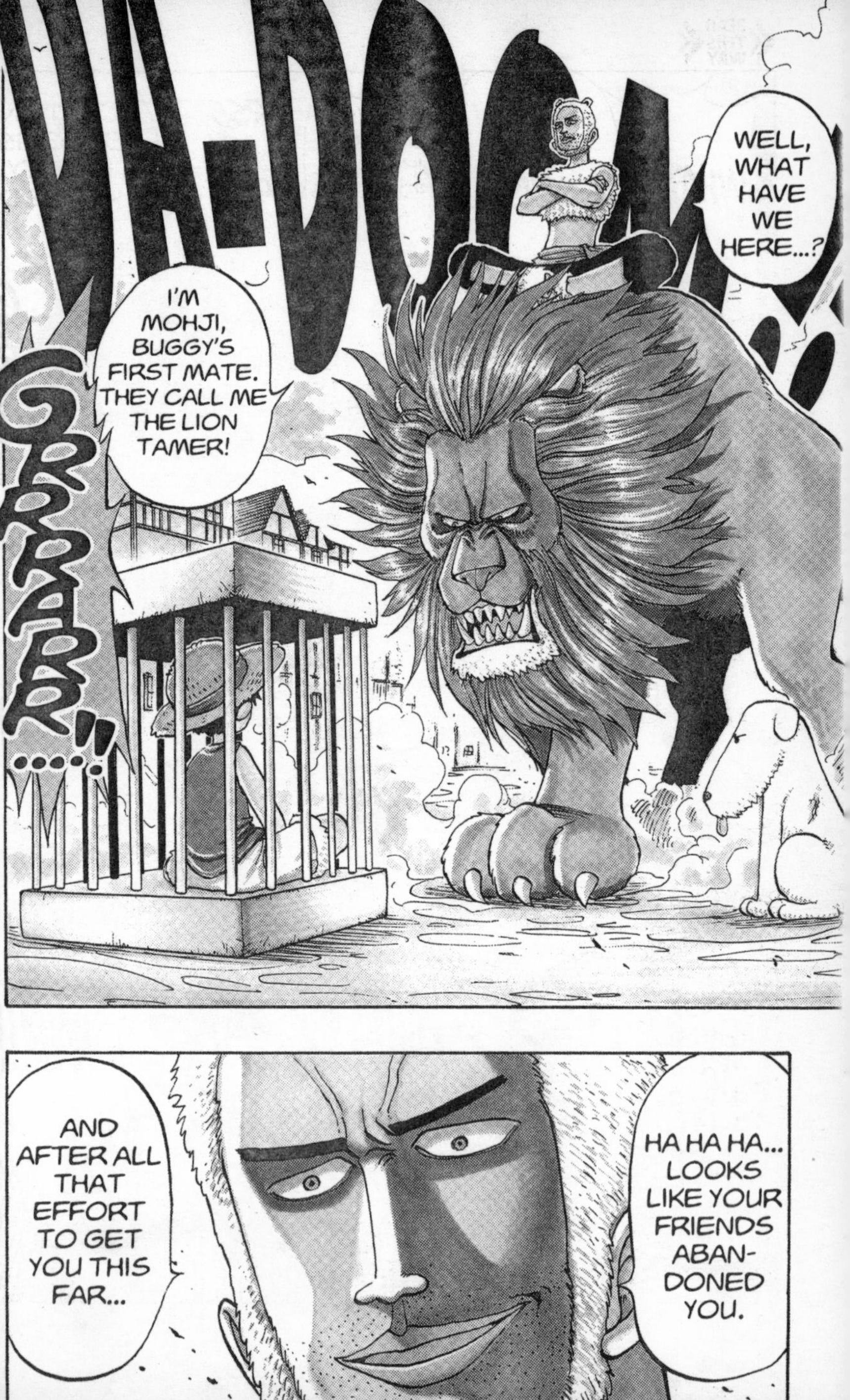
WELL, WHAT HAVE WE HERE...?
I'M MOHJI, BUGGY'S FIRST MATE. THEY CALL ME THE LION TAMER!
HA HA HA... LOOKS LIKE YOUR FRIENDS ABAN-DONED YOU.
AND AFTER ALL THAT EFFORT TO GET YOU THIS FAR...

HEY, WHAT'S WITH THE WEIRD COSTUME?

WHAT!!?

YOU GUYS STIRRED UP A REAL HORNET'S NEST.

KRSS
KRSS

CAPTAIN BUGGY IS PRETTY WORKED UP...

GRRRRR...

GRRRRR...

SHUT UP!

THAT JUST MAKES IT WEIRDER.

COSTUME!? THIS IS MY HAIR!!!

IF SO, THEN YOU REALLY DON'T KNOW WHO I AM...

MAYBE YOU THINK YOU'RE SAFE IN THAT CAGE...

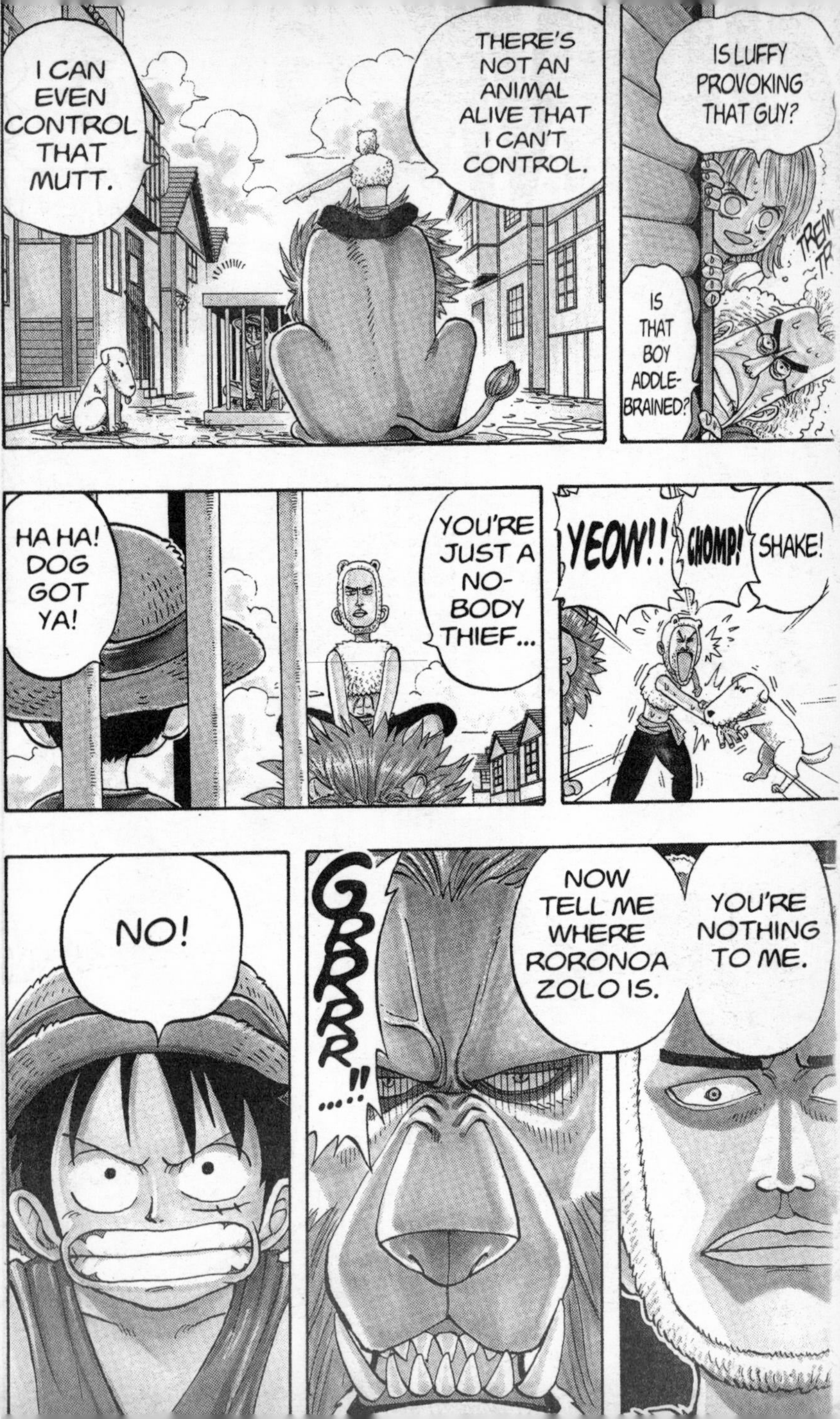
I CAN EVEN CONTROL THAT MUTT.
THERE'S NOT AN ANIMAL ALIVE THAT I CAN'T CONTROL.
IS LUFFY PROVOKING THAT GUY?
IS THAT BOY ADDLE-BRAINED?
HA HA! DOG GOT YA!
YOU'RE JUST A NO-BODY THIEF...
YEOW!!
CHOMP!
SHAKE!
NO!
GRRRR...!!
NOW TELL ME WHERE RORONOA ZOLO IS.
YOU'RE NOTHING TO ME.

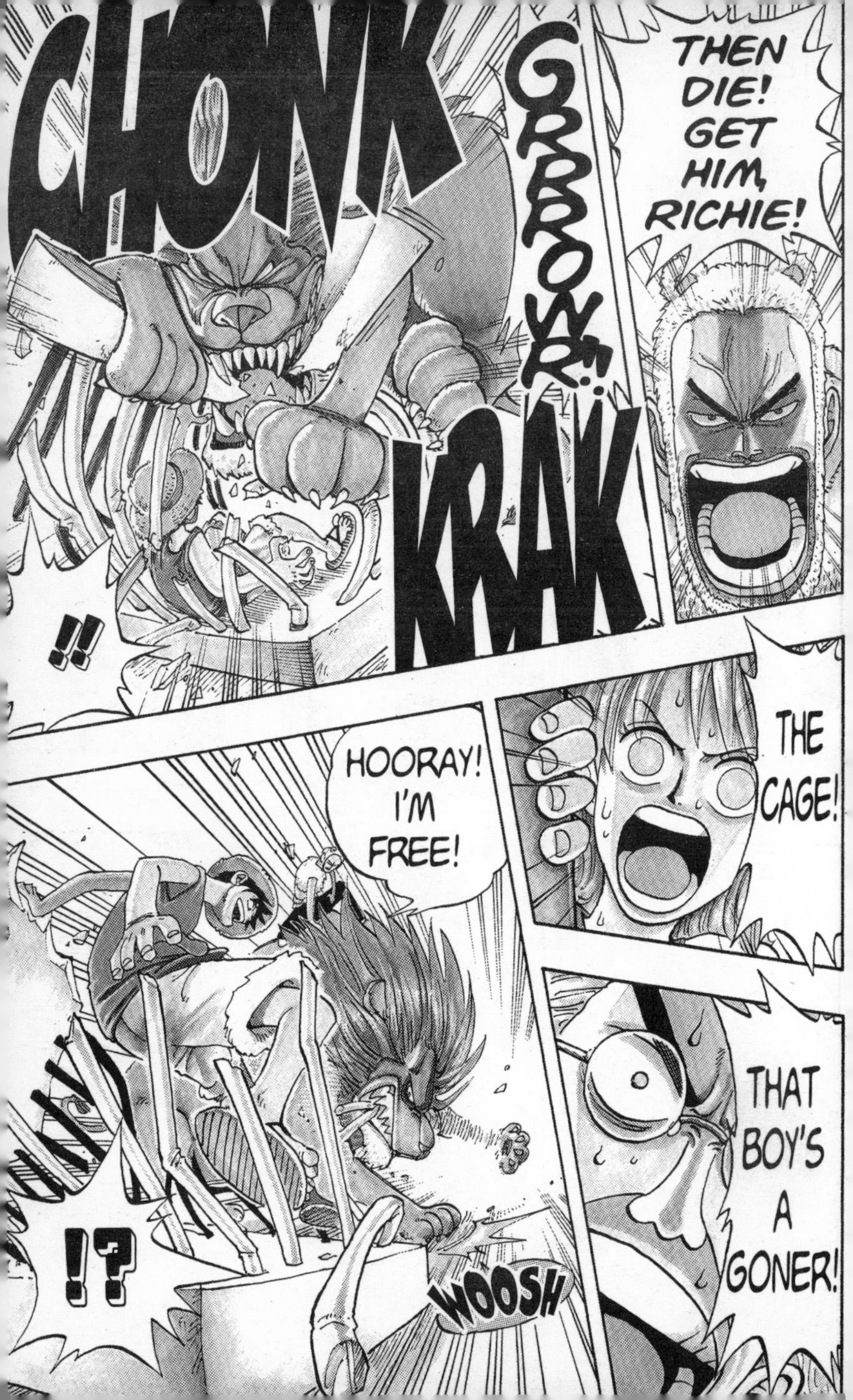
THEN DIE! GET HIM, RICHIE!
GRRROWR!!
CHONK
KRAK
!!
THE CAGE!
HOORAY! I'M FREE!
THAT BOY'S A GONER!
WOOSH
!?

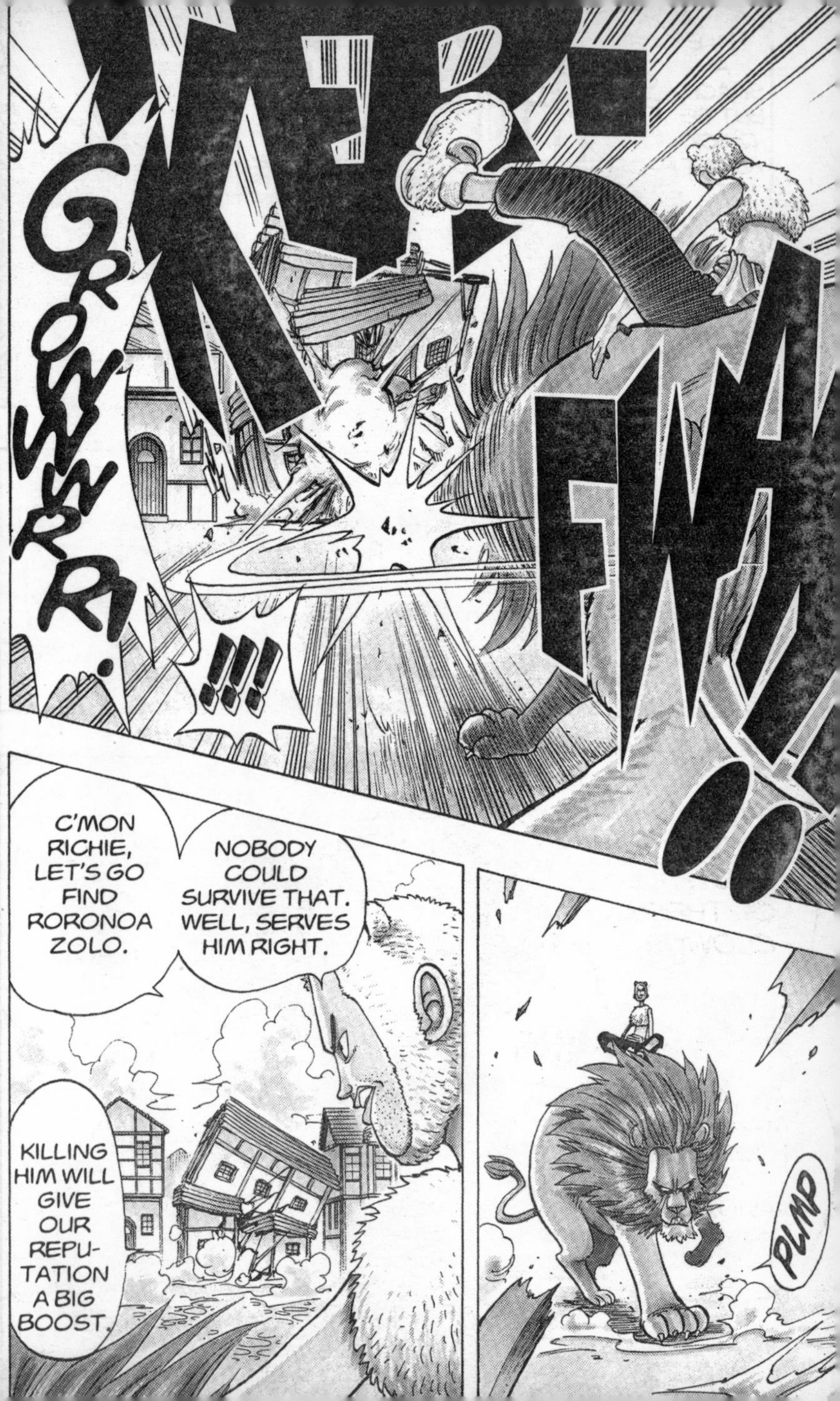

GROWWRR!
!!!
NOBODY COULD SURVIVE THAT. WELL, SERVES HIM RIGHT.
C'MON RICHIE, LET'S GO FIND RORONOA ZOLO.
KILLING HIM WILL GIVE OUR REPU-TATION A BIG BOOST.
PLMP

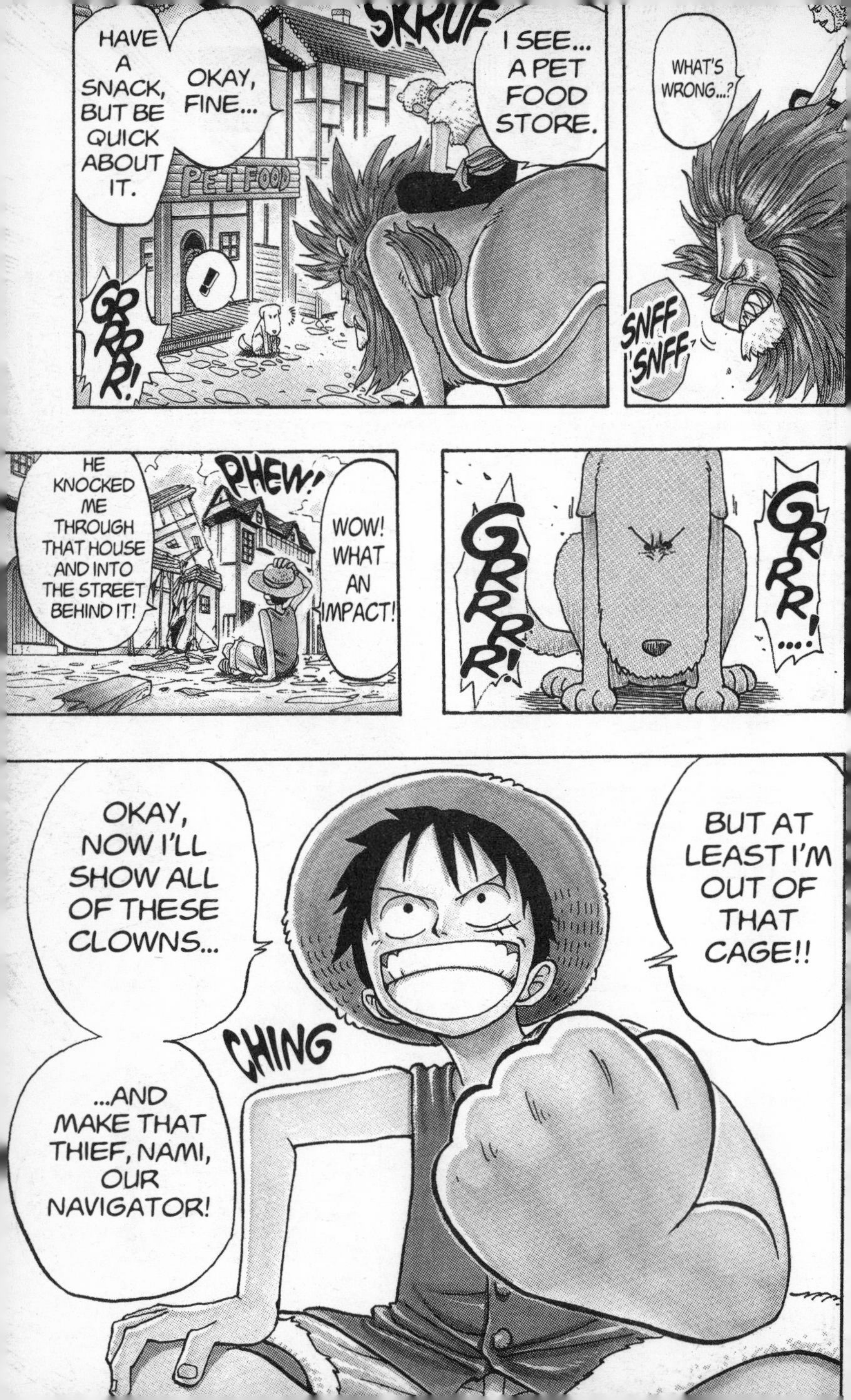
HAVE A SNACK, BUT BE QUICK ABOUT IT.
OKAY, FINE...
SKRUF
I SEE... A PET FOOD STORE.
PET FOOD
!
GRRRR!
WHAT'S WRONG...?
SNFF SNFF
HE KNOCKED ME THROUGH THAT HOUSE AND INTO THE STREET BEHIND IT!
PHEW!
WOW! WHAT AN IMPACT!
GRRRR!
GRRR...!
OKAY, NOW I'LL SHOW ALL OF THESE CLOWNS...
BUT AT LEAST I'M OUT OF THAT CAGE!!
CHING
...AND MAKE THAT THIEF, NAMI, OUR NAVIGATOR!

VIKINGS, PART 2

✢ These guys were really scary. How scary were
they? Well, they'd sweep out of an inlet, attack
ships or villages, and slaughter everyone, even
the local priests. They stole food and anything of
value, and when they were done they set fire to
everything they didn't want. They were unbeliev-
able villians.

✢ But from their perspective, they were
just trying to make a living. They
brought the spoils of their piracy home to better their villages. This was "men's
work." These people con-
sidered a lifetime of pillage and battle to be a
good career.

✢

Some say the word
Viking comes from
"vik," meaning "creek"
or "inlet"—meaning
the people who
attack from the
inlets.

Chapter 13:
TREASURE

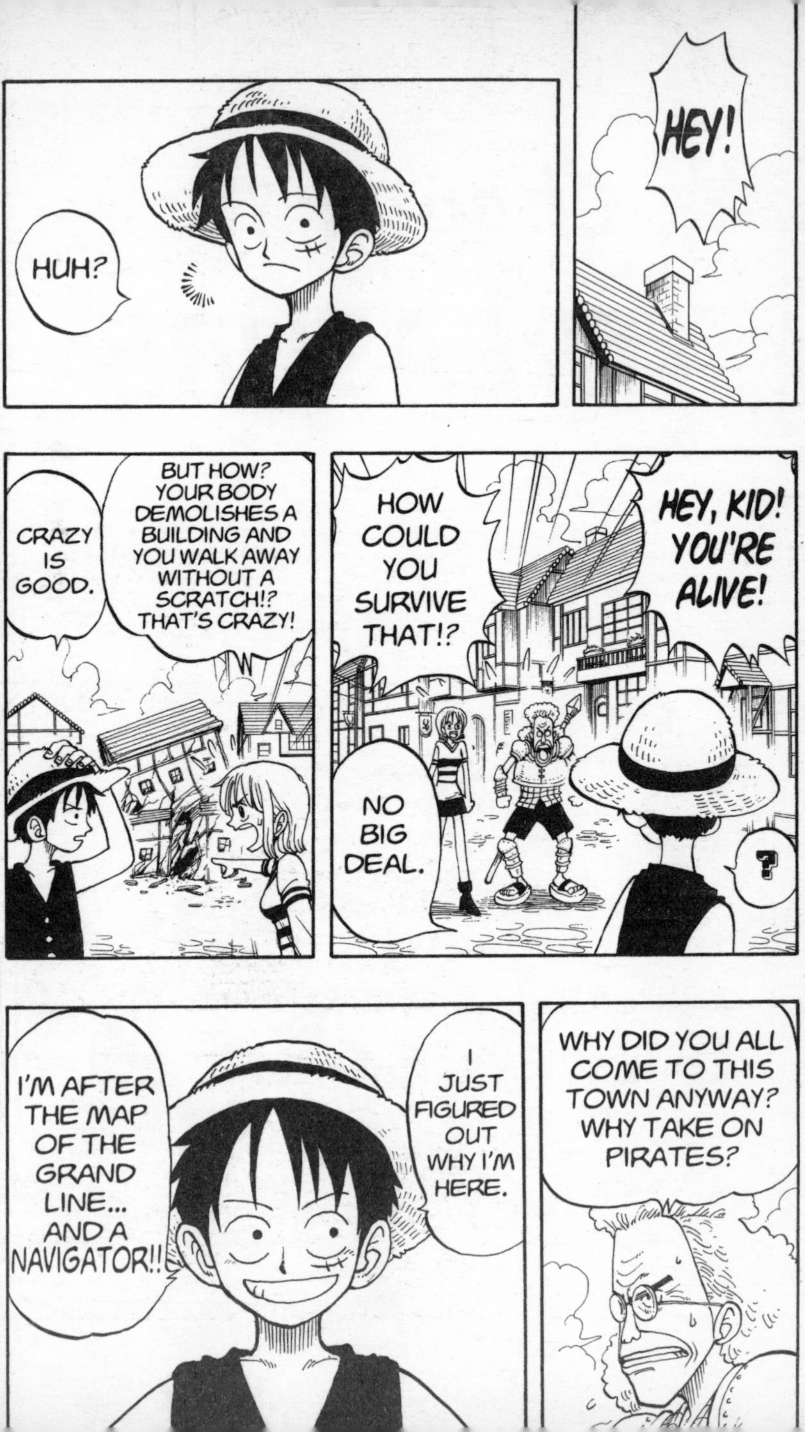
HEY!
HUH?
HEY, KID! YOU'RE ALIVE!
HOW COULD YOU SURVIVE THAT!?
?
NO BIG DEAL.
BUT HOW? YOUR BODY DEMOLISHES A BUILDING AND YOU WALK AWAY WITHOUT A SCRATCH!? THAT'S CRAZY!
CRAZY IS GOOD.
WHY DID YOU ALL COME TO THIS TOWN ANYWAY? WHY TAKE ON PIRATES?
I JUST FIGURED OUT WHY I'M HERE.
I'M AFTER THE MAP OF THE GRAND LINE... AND A NAVIGATOR!!

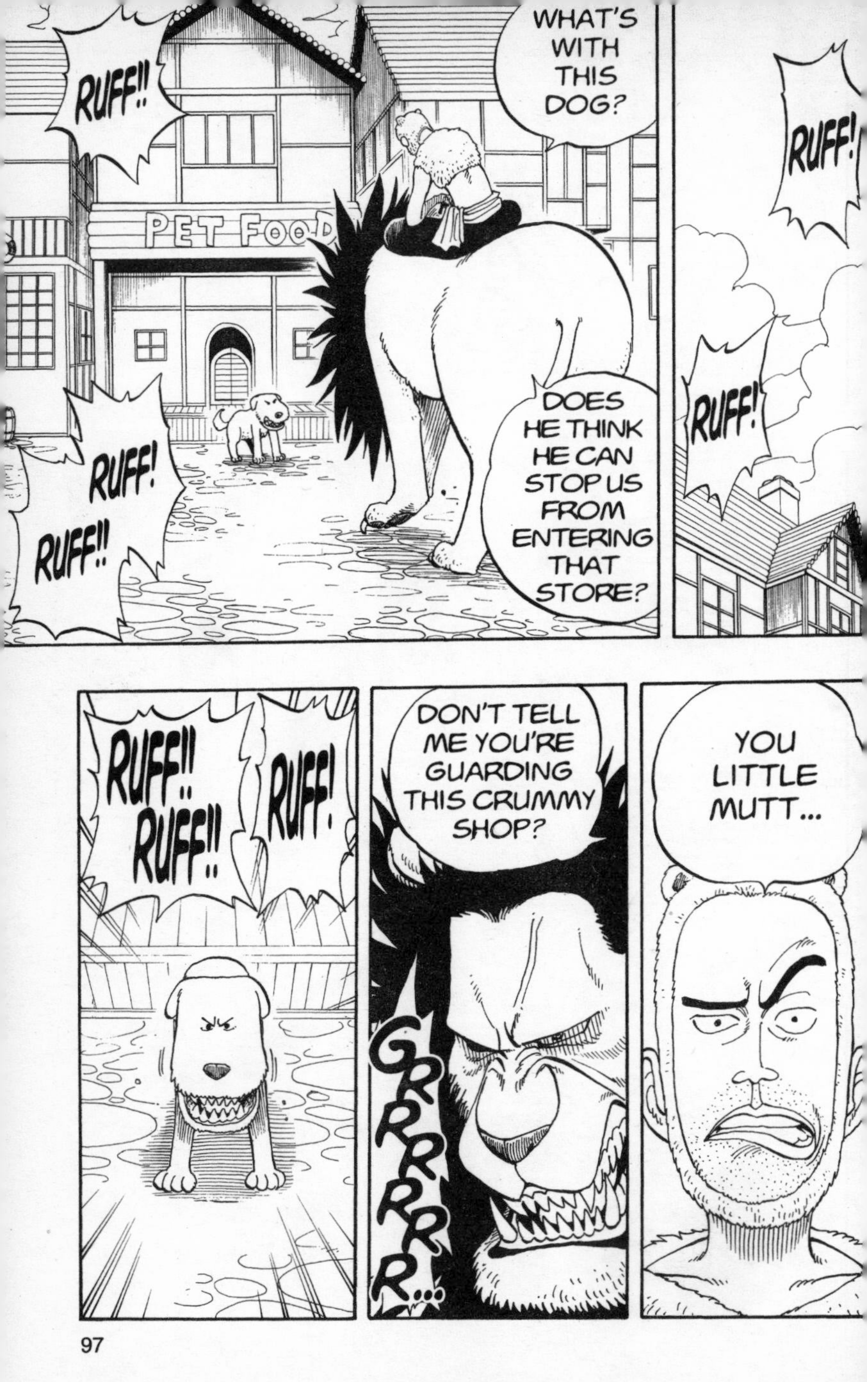
RUFF!!
WHAT'S WITH THIS DOG?
RUFF!
RUFF!!
DOES HE THINK HE CAN STOP US FROM ENTERING THAT STORE?
RUFF!
RUFF!
RUFF!! RUFF!!
RUFF!
DON'T TELL ME YOU'RE GUARDING THIS CRUMMY SHOP?
GRRRRR...
YOU LITTLE MUTT...

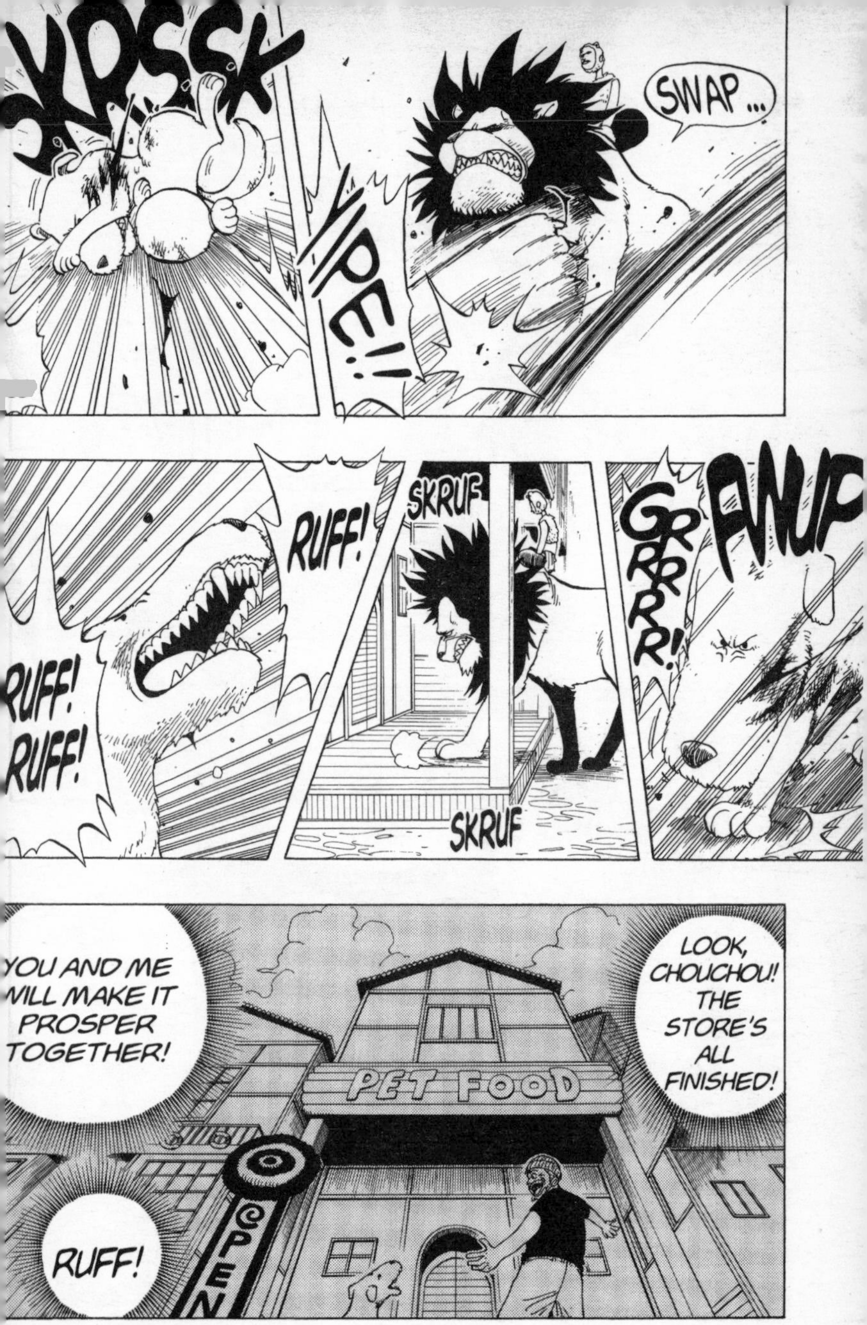

SKRSSK
YIPE!!
SWAP...
RUFF!
RUFF!
RUFF!
SKRUF
SKRUF
GRRRRR!
FWUP
YOU AND ME WILL MAKE IT PROSPER TOGETHER!
LOOK, CHOUCHOU! THE STORE'S ALL FINISHED!
PET FOOD
OPEN
RUFF!

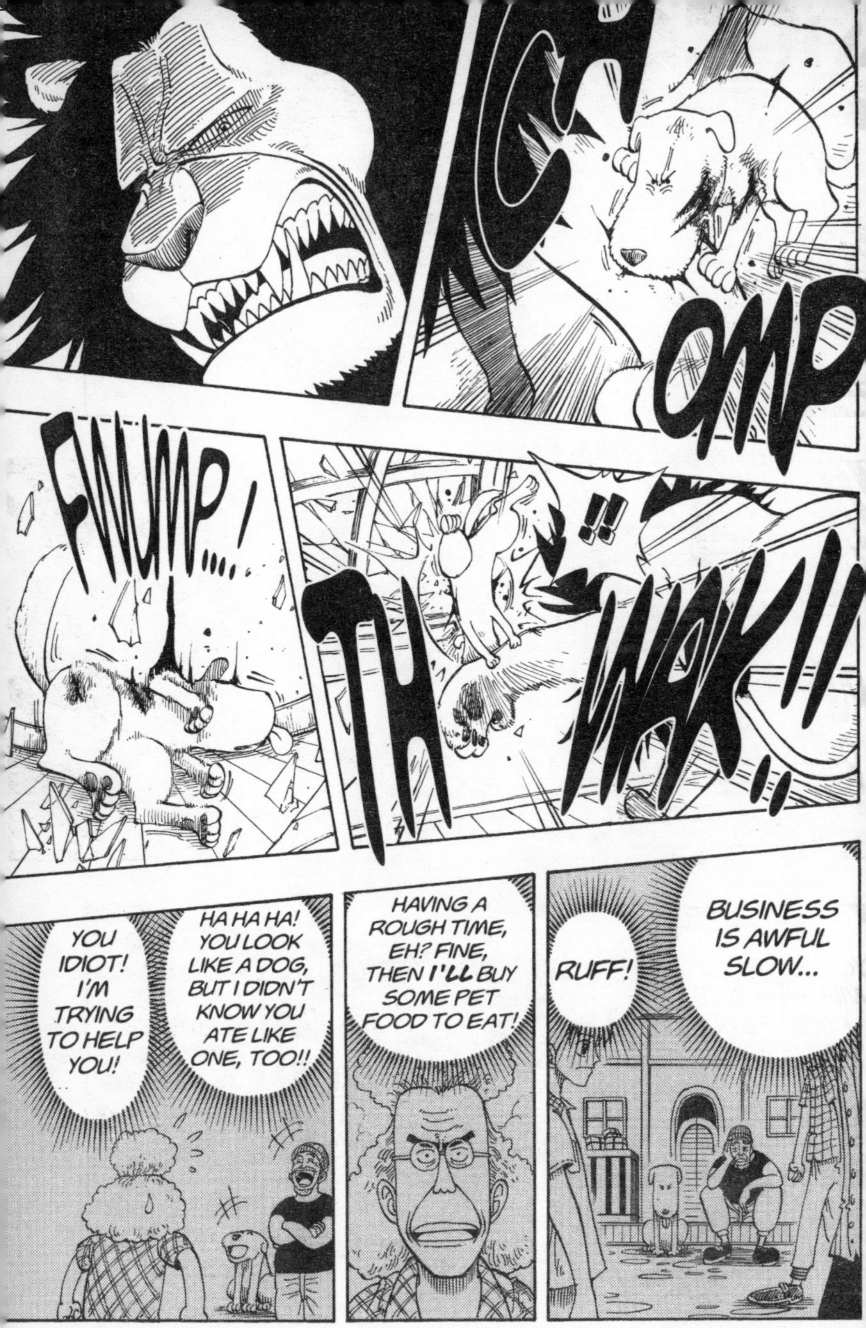
CHOMP
!!
THWAK!!
FWUMP...!
BUSINESS IS AWFUL SLOW...
RUFF!
HAVING A ROUGH TIME, EH? FINE, THEN I'LL BUY SOME PET FOOD TO EAT!
HA HA HA! YOU LOOK LIKE A DOG, BUT I DIDN'T KNOW YOU ATE LIKE ONE, TOO!!
YOU IDIOT! I'M TRYING TO HELP YOU!

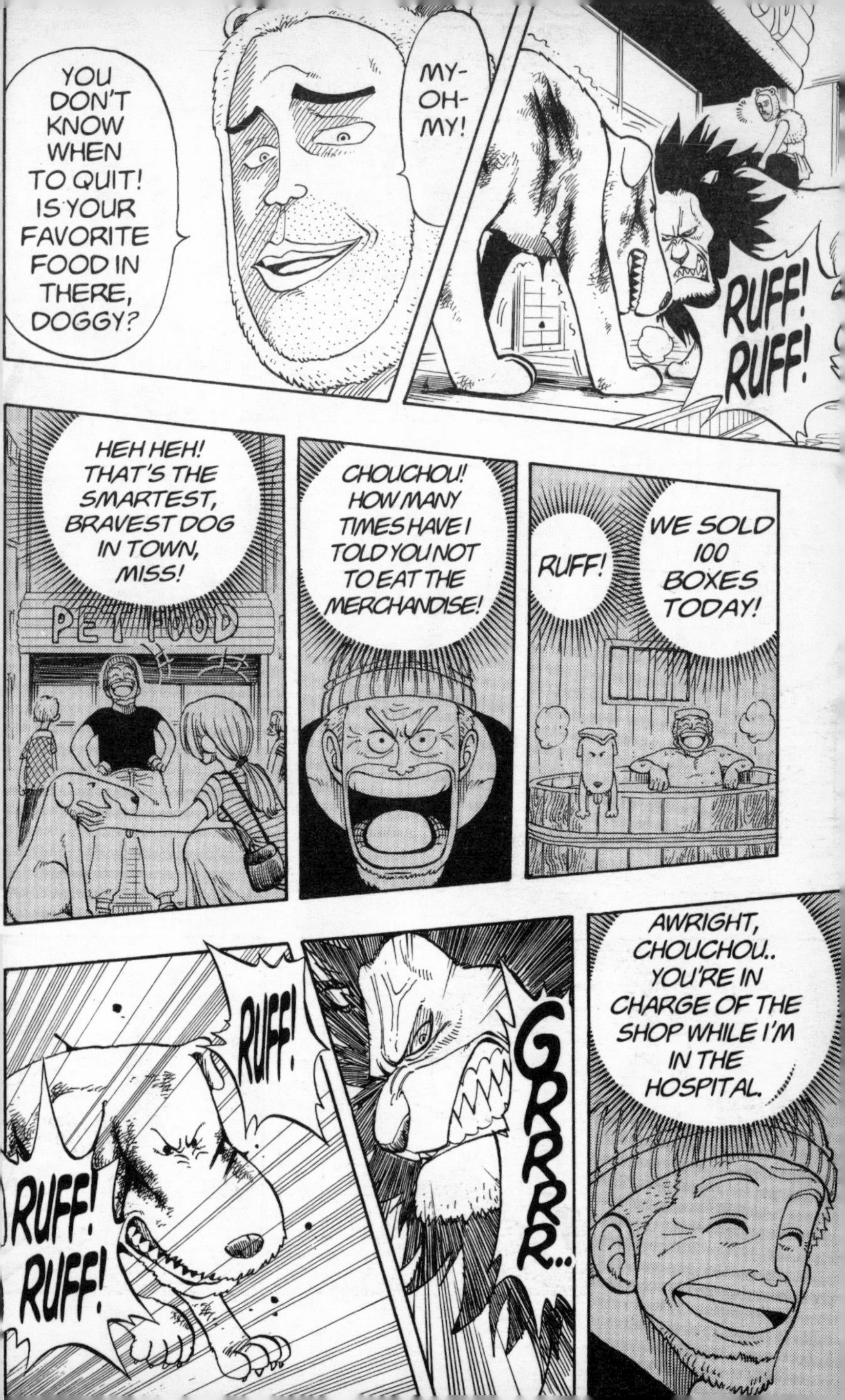
YOU DON'T KNOW WHEN TO QUIT! IS YOUR FAVORITE FOOD IN THERE, DOGGY?
MY- OH- MY!
RUFF! RUFF!
HEH HEH! THAT'S THE SMARTEST, BRAVEST DOG IN TOWN, MISS!
PET FOOD
CHOUCHOU! HOW MANY TIMES HAVE I TOLD YOU NOT TO EAT THE MERCHANDISE!
RUFF!
WE SOLD 100 BOXES TODAY!
RUFF!
RUFF! RUFF!
GRRRR..
AWRIGHT, CHOUCHOU.. YOU'RE IN CHARGE OF THE SHOP WHILE I'M IN THE HOSPITAL.

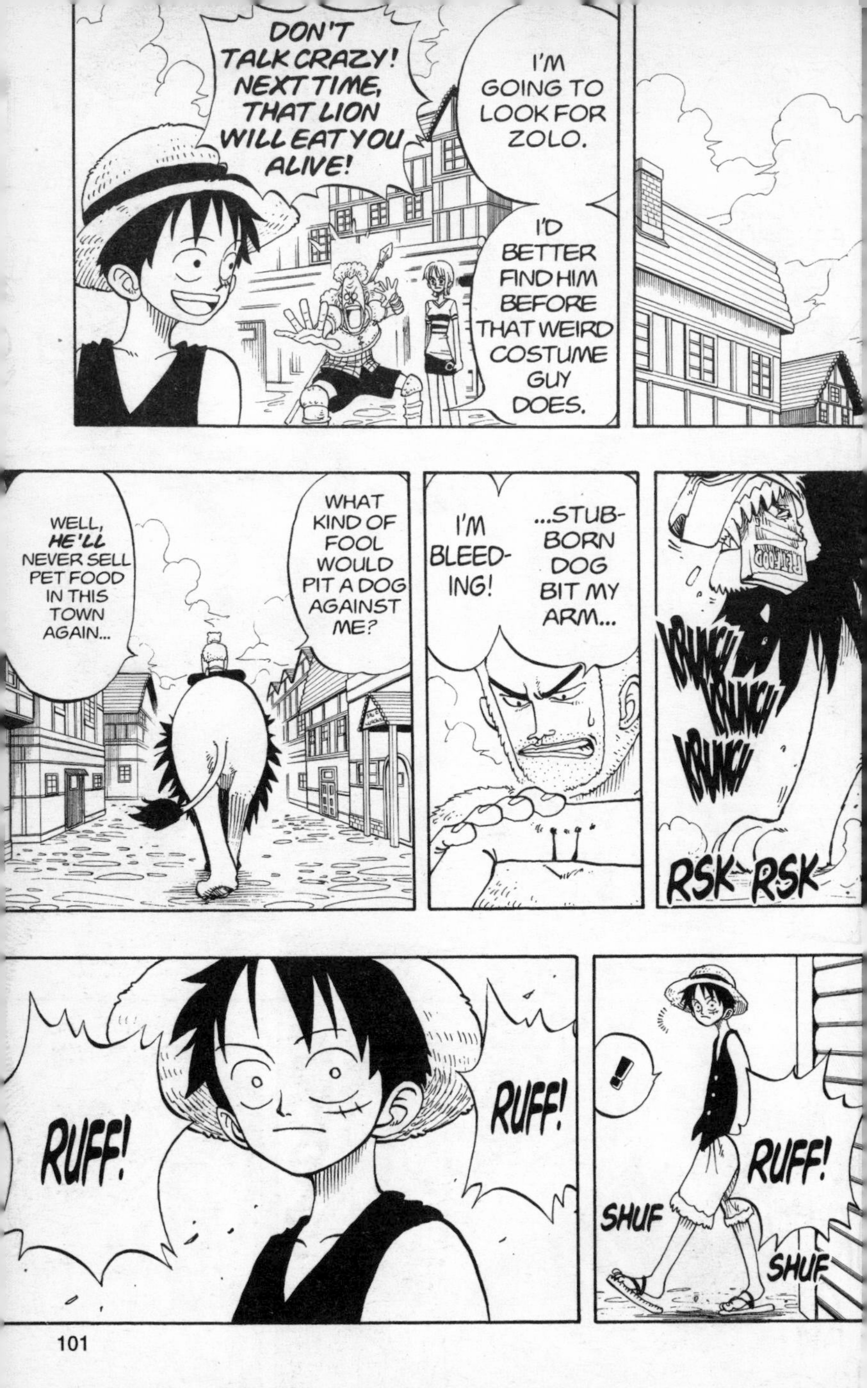
DON'T TALK CRAZY! NEXT TIME, THAT LION WILL EAT YOU ALIVE!
I'M GOING TO LOOK FOR ZOLO.
I'D BETTER FIND HIM BEFORE THAT WEIRD COSTUME GUY DOES.
WHAT KIND OF FOOL WOULD PIT A DOG AGAINST ME?
WELL, HE'LL NEVER SELL PET FOOD IN THIS TOWN AGAIN...
...STUBBORN DOG BIT MY ARM...
I'M BLEEDING!
KRUNCH KRUNCH KRUNCH
RSK RSK
RUFF!
RUFF!
!
RUFF!
SHUF
SHUF

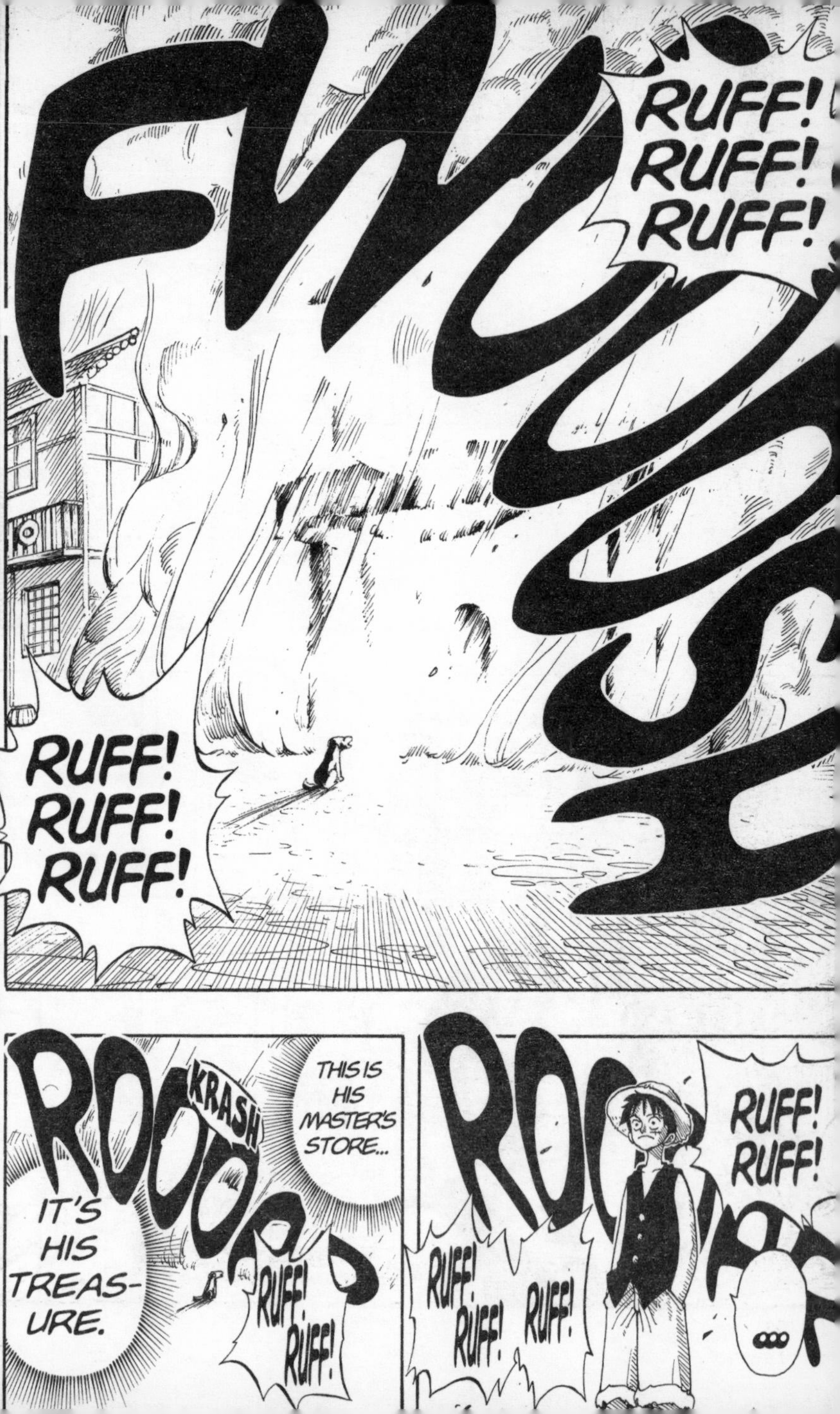
FWOOSH
RUFF! RUFF! RUFF!
RUFF! RUFF! RUFF!
KRASH
THIS IS HIS MASTER'S STORE...
IT'S HIS TREAS-URE.
RUFF! RUFF!
RUFF! RUFF! RUFF!
RUFF! RUFF!
...

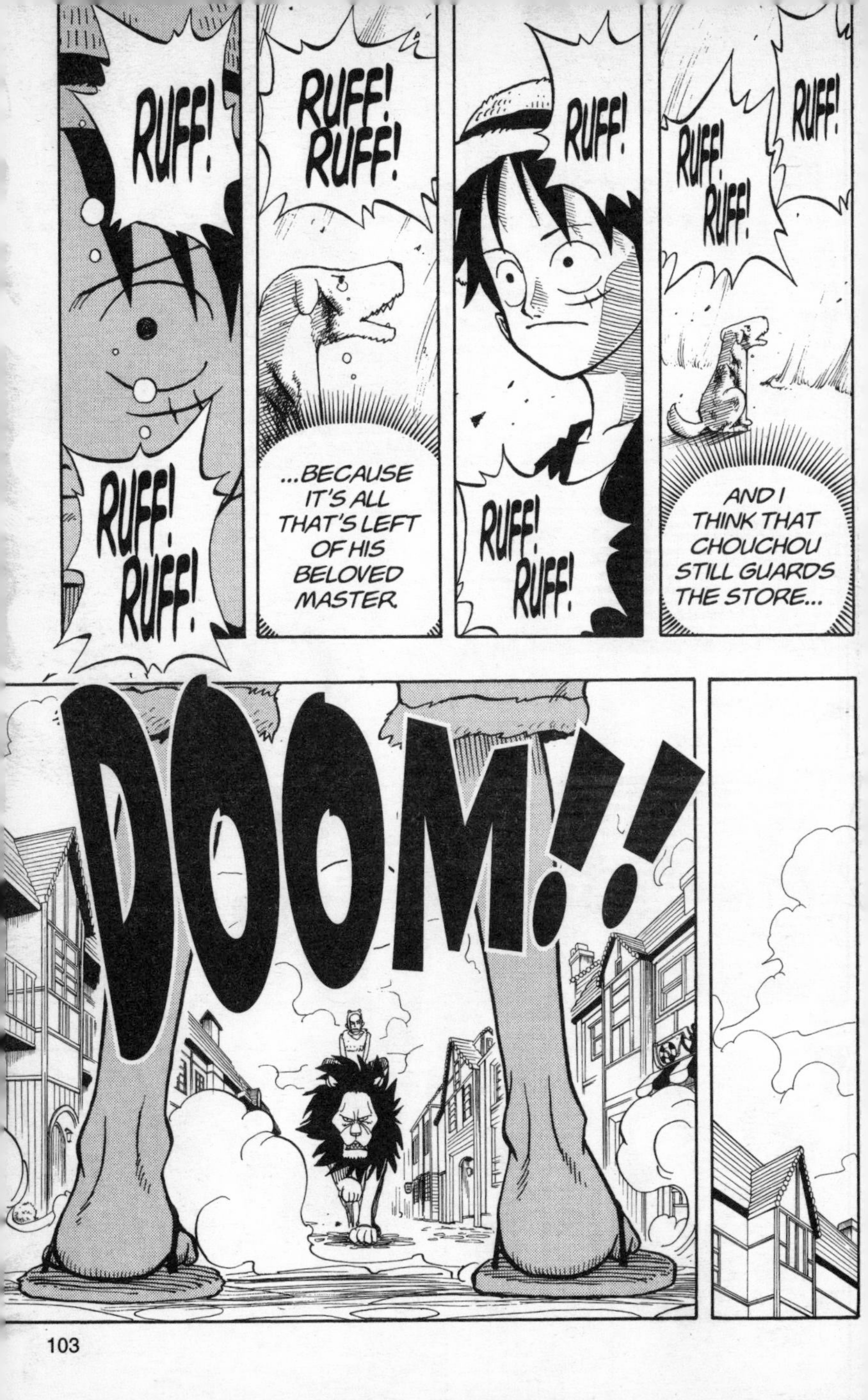
RUFF!
RUFF! RUFF!
RUFF!
RUFF! RUFF!
RUFF! RUFF!
RUFF!
...BECAUSE IT'S ALL THAT'S LEFT OF HIS BELOVED MASTER.
RUFF! RUFF!
RUFF! RUFF!
AND I THINK THAT CHOUCHOU STILL GUARDS THE STORE...
DOOM!!

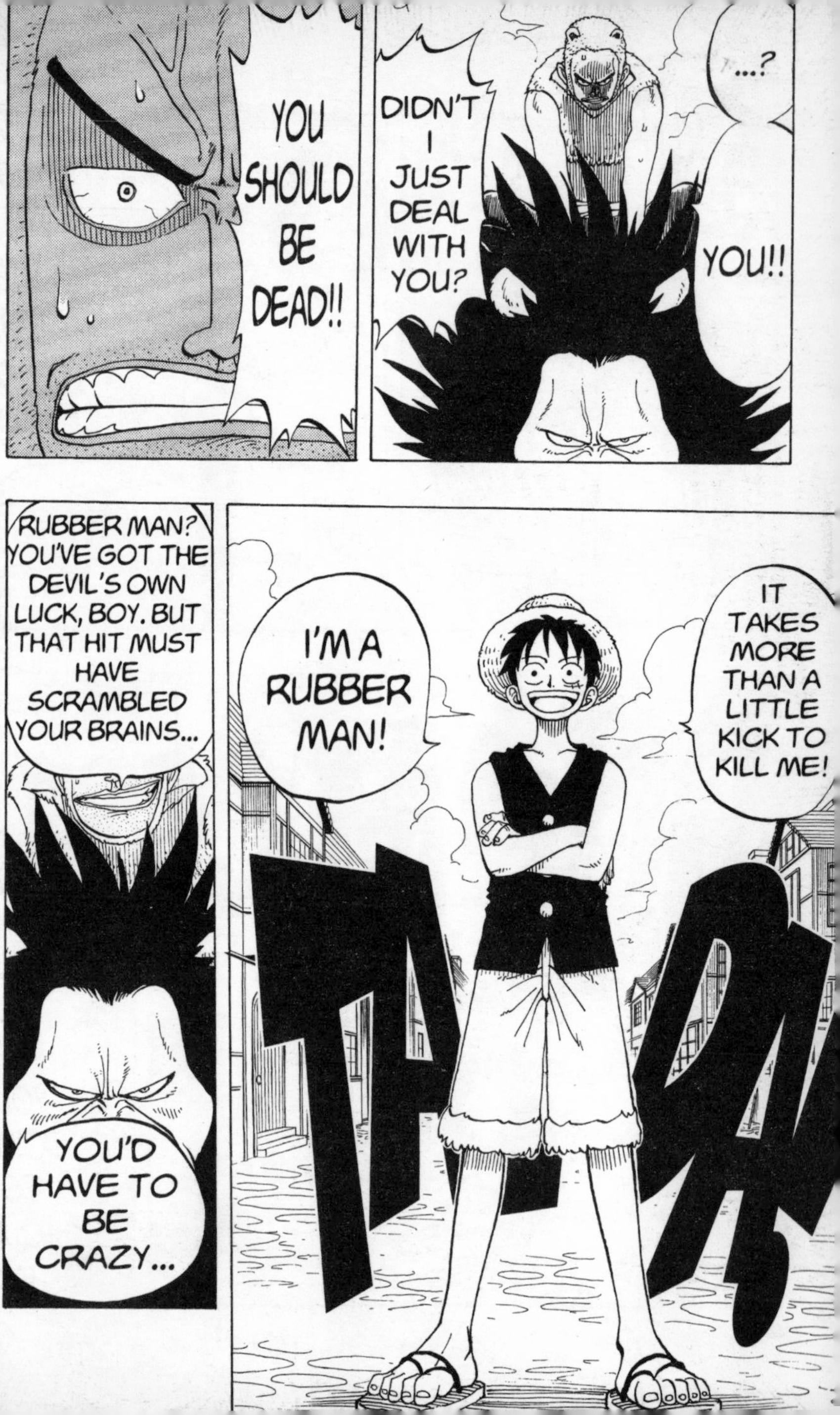
...?
YOU!!
DIDN'T I JUST DEAL WITH YOU?
YOU SHOULD BE DEAD!!
IT TAKES MORE THAN A LITTLE KICK TO KILL ME!
I'M A RUBBER MAN!
RUBBER MAN? YOU'VE GOT THE DEVIL'S OWN LUCK, BOY. BUT THAT HIT MUST HAVE SCRAMBLED YOUR BRAINS...
YOU'D HAVE TO BE CRAZY...

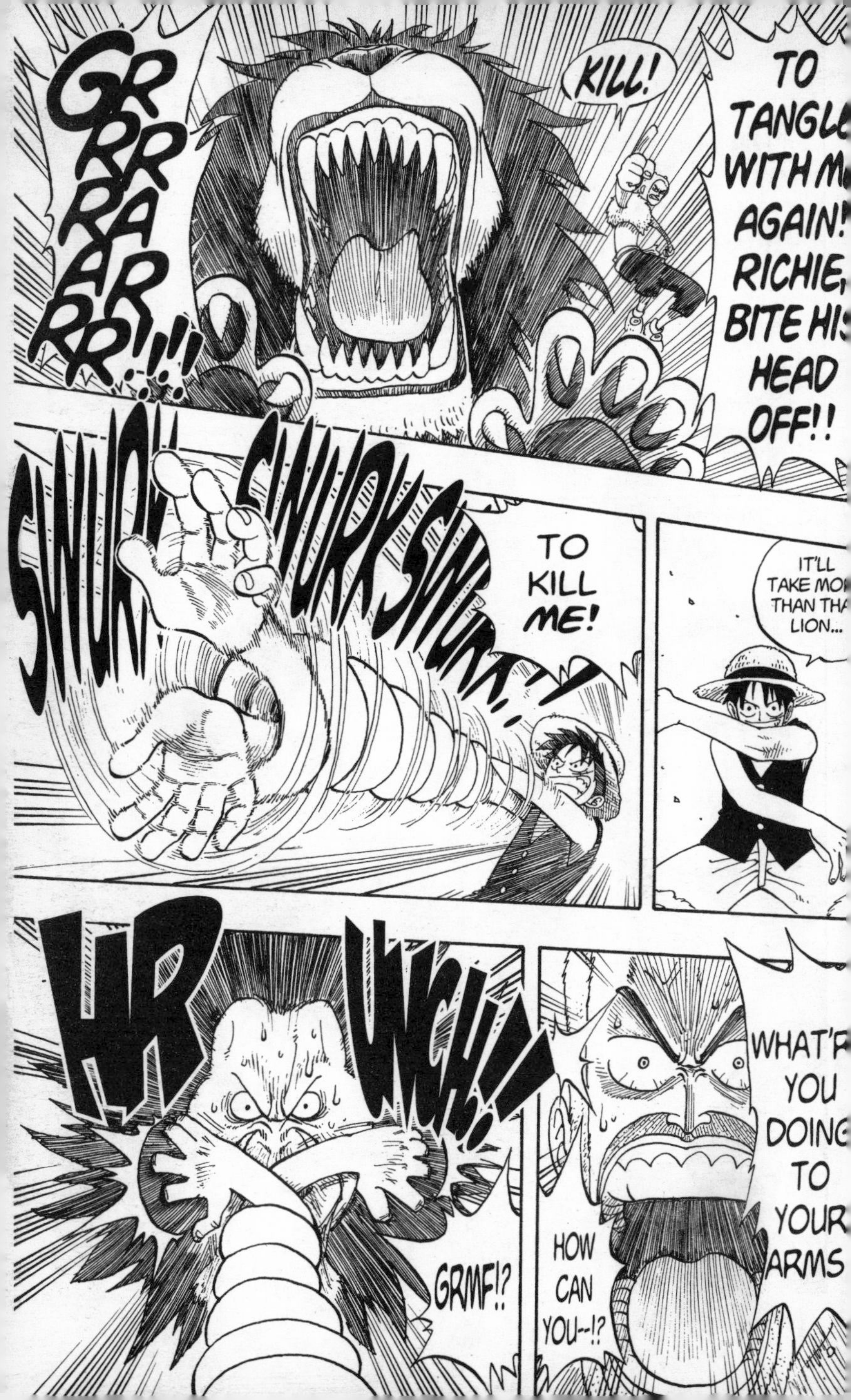
TO TANGLE WITH ME AGAIN! RICHIE, BITE HIS HEAD OFF!!
KILL!
GRRRARRARRR!!!
IT'LL TAKE MORE THAN THAT LION...
TO KILL ME!
SWURK SWURK SWURK!!
WHAT'RE YOU DOING TO YOUR ARMS
HOW CAN YOU--!?
GRMF!?

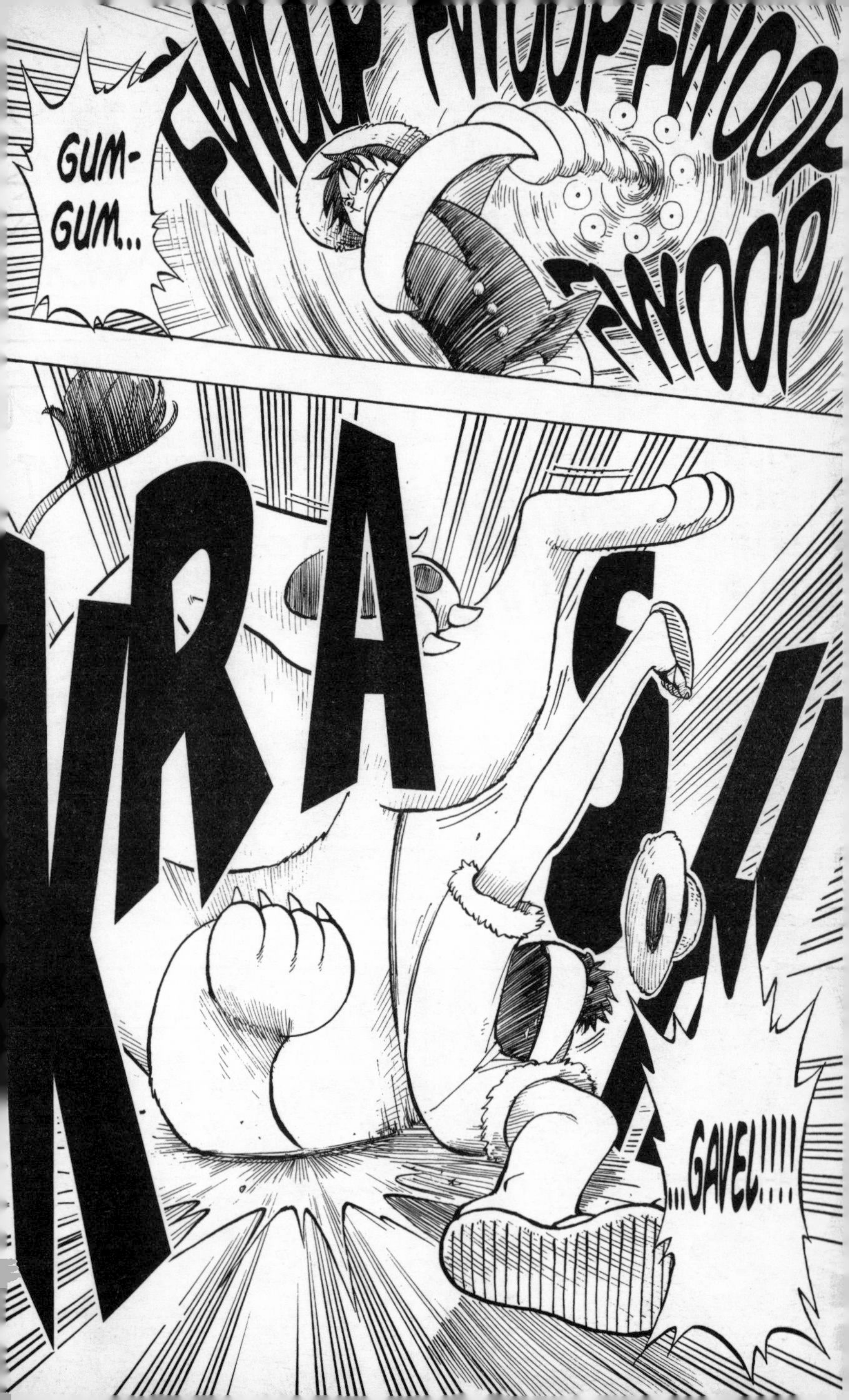
FWOOP FWOOP FWOOP FWOOP
GUM-GUM...
KRASH
...GAVEL!!!!

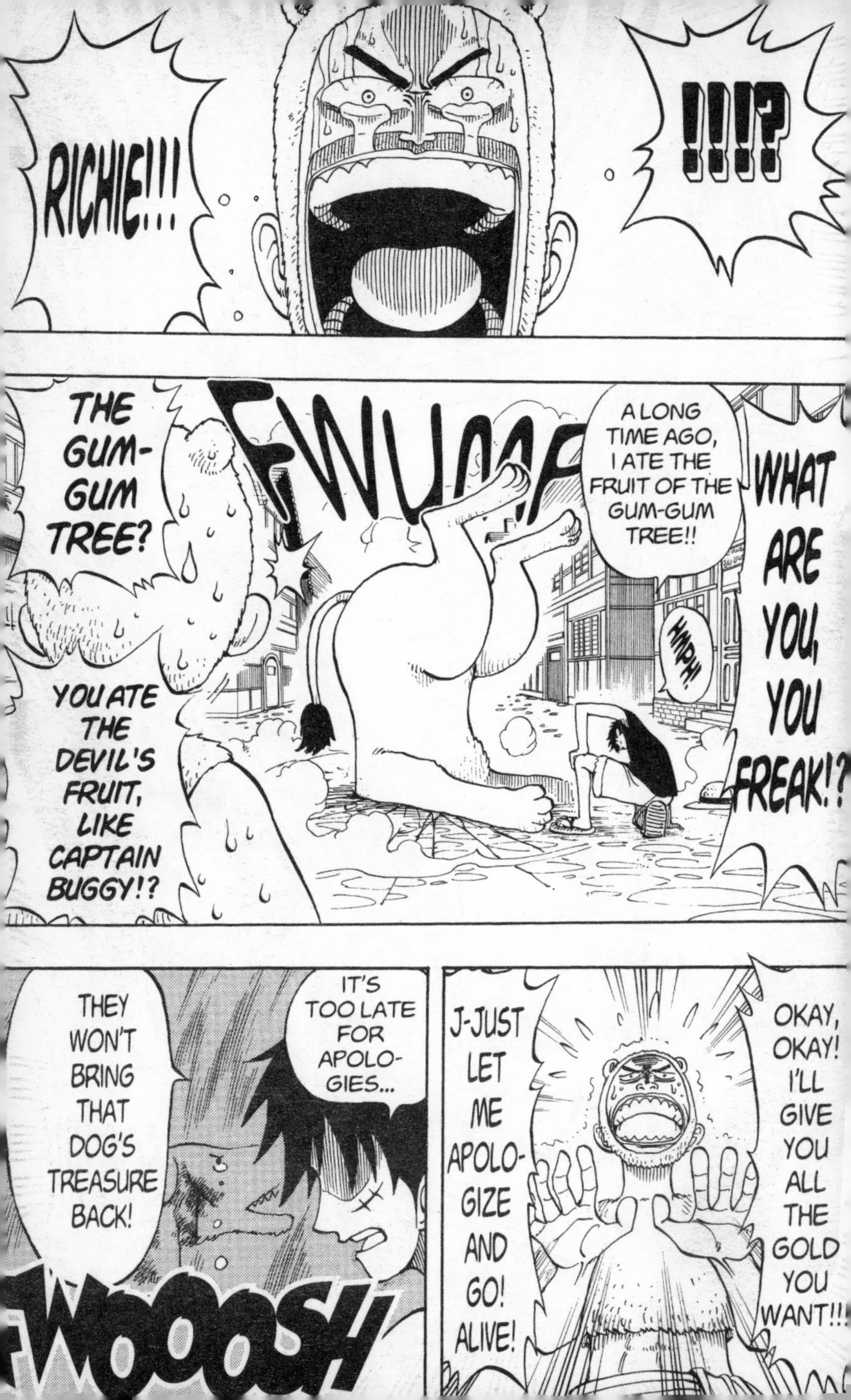
!!!?
RICHIE!!!
WHAT ARE YOU, YOU FREAK!?
HMPH!
A LONG TIME AGO, I ATE THE FRUIT OF THE GUM-GUM TREE!!
FWUMP
THE GUM-GUM TREE?
YOU ATE THE DEVIL'S FRUIT, LIKE CAPTAIN BUGGY!?
OKAY, OKAY! I'LL GIVE YOU ALL THE GOLD YOU WANT!!!
J-JUST LET ME APOLOGIZE AND GO! ALIVE!
IT'S TOO LATE FOR APOLOGIES...
THEY WON'T BRING THAT DOG'S TREASURE BACK!
WOOOSH

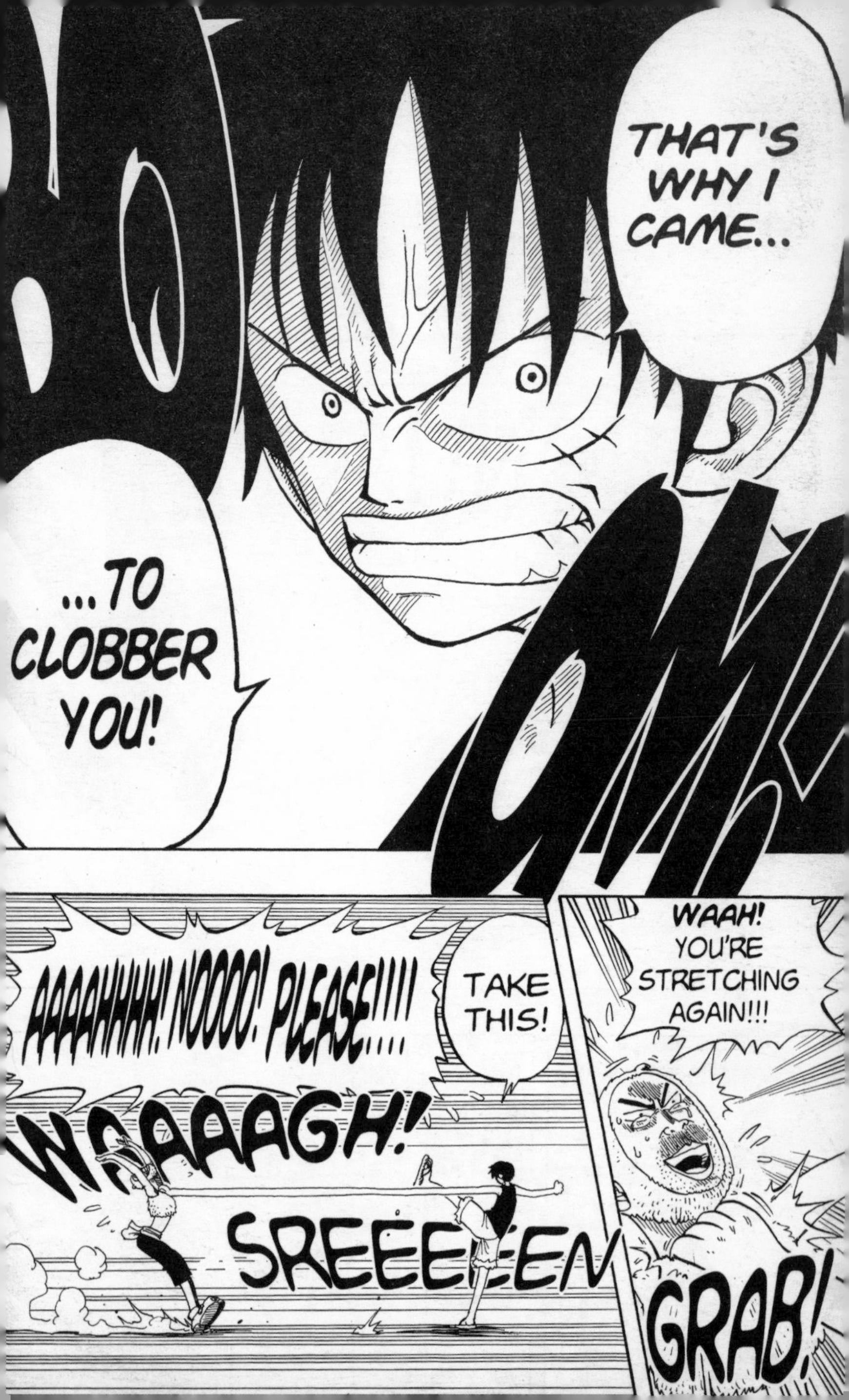
THAT'S WHY I CAME...
...TO CLOBBER YOU!
WAAH! YOU'RE STRETCHING AGAIN!!!
GRAB!
TAKE THIS!
AAAAHHHH! NOOOO! PLEASE!!!!!
WAAAAAGH!
SREEEEEEN

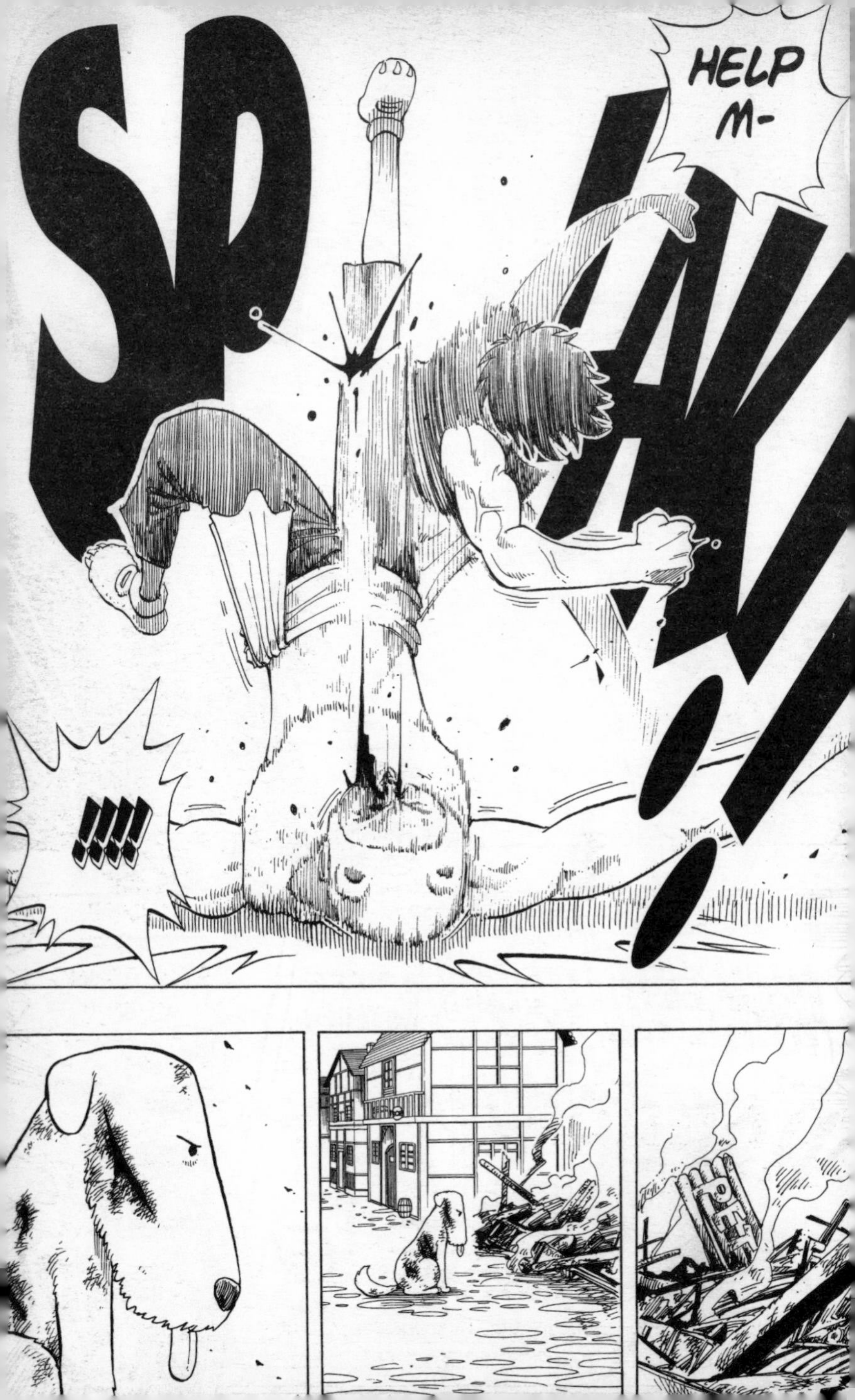
HELP M-
!!!!

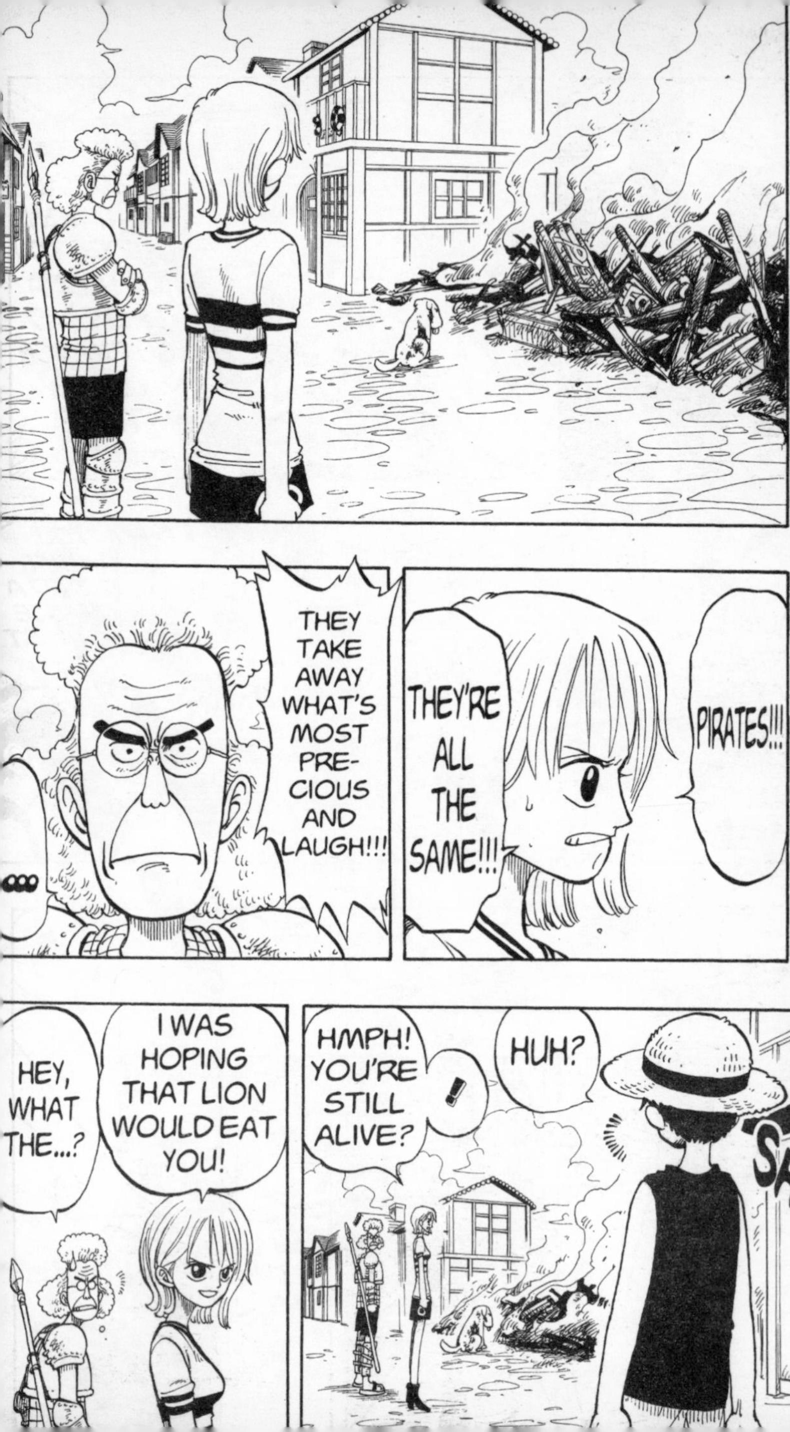

THEY TAKE AWAY WHAT'S MOST PRE-CIOUS AND LAUGH!!!
THEY'RE ALL THE SAME!!!
PIRATES!!!
HEY, WHAT THE...?
I WAS HOPING THAT LION WOULD EAT YOU!
HMPH! YOU'RE STILL ALIVE?
!
HUH?
SHUF

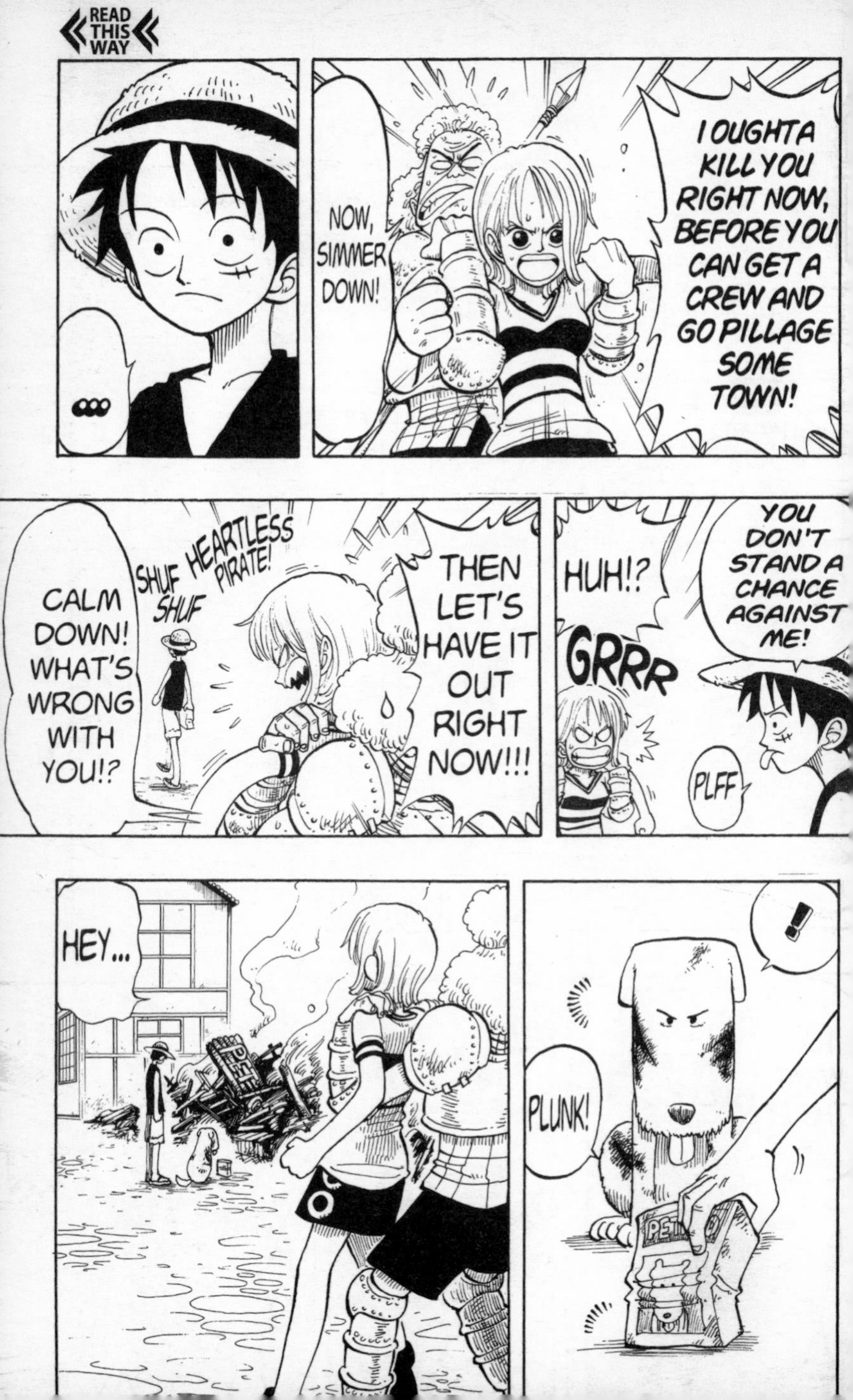
READ THIS WAY
I OUGHTA KILL YOU RIGHT NOW, BEFORE YOU CAN GET A CREW AND GO PILLAGE SOME TOWN!
NOW, SIMMER DOWN!
...
YOU DON'T STAND A CHANCE AGAINST ME!
PLFF
HUH!?
GRRR
THEN LET'S HAVE IT OUT RIGHT NOW!!!
HEARTLESS PIRATE!
SHUF SHUF
CALM DOWN! WHAT'S WRONG WITH YOU!?
!
PLUNK!
HEY...

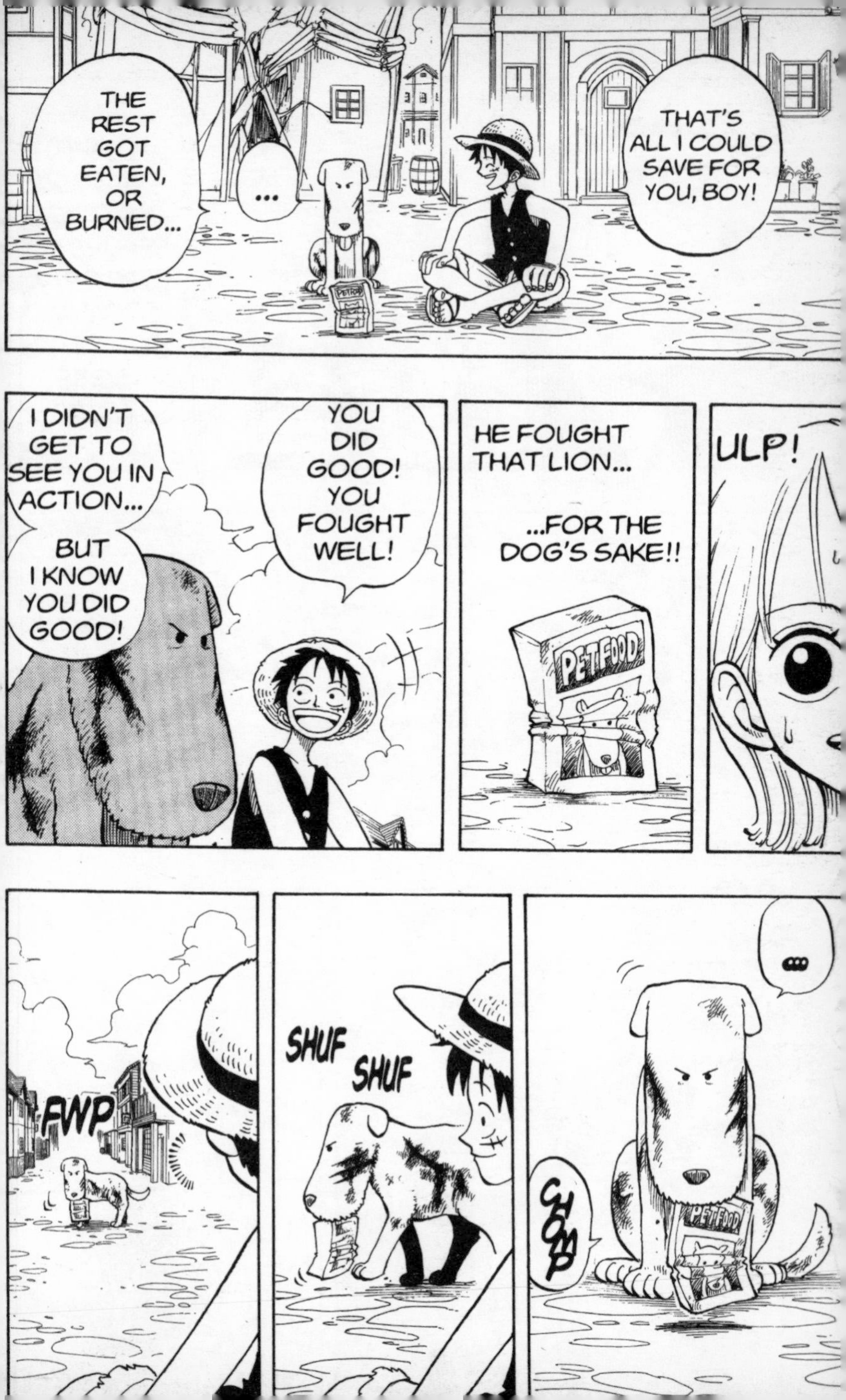
THE REST GOT EATEN, OR BURNED...
...
THAT'S ALL I COULD SAVE FOR YOU, BOY!
I DIDN'T GET TO SEE YOU IN ACTION...
BUT I KNOW YOU DID GOOD!
YOU DID GOOD! YOU FOUGHT WELL!
HE FOUGHT THAT LION...
...FOR THE DOG'S SAKE!!
PETFOOD
ULP!
FWP
SHUF
SHUF
CHOMP
PETFOOD
...

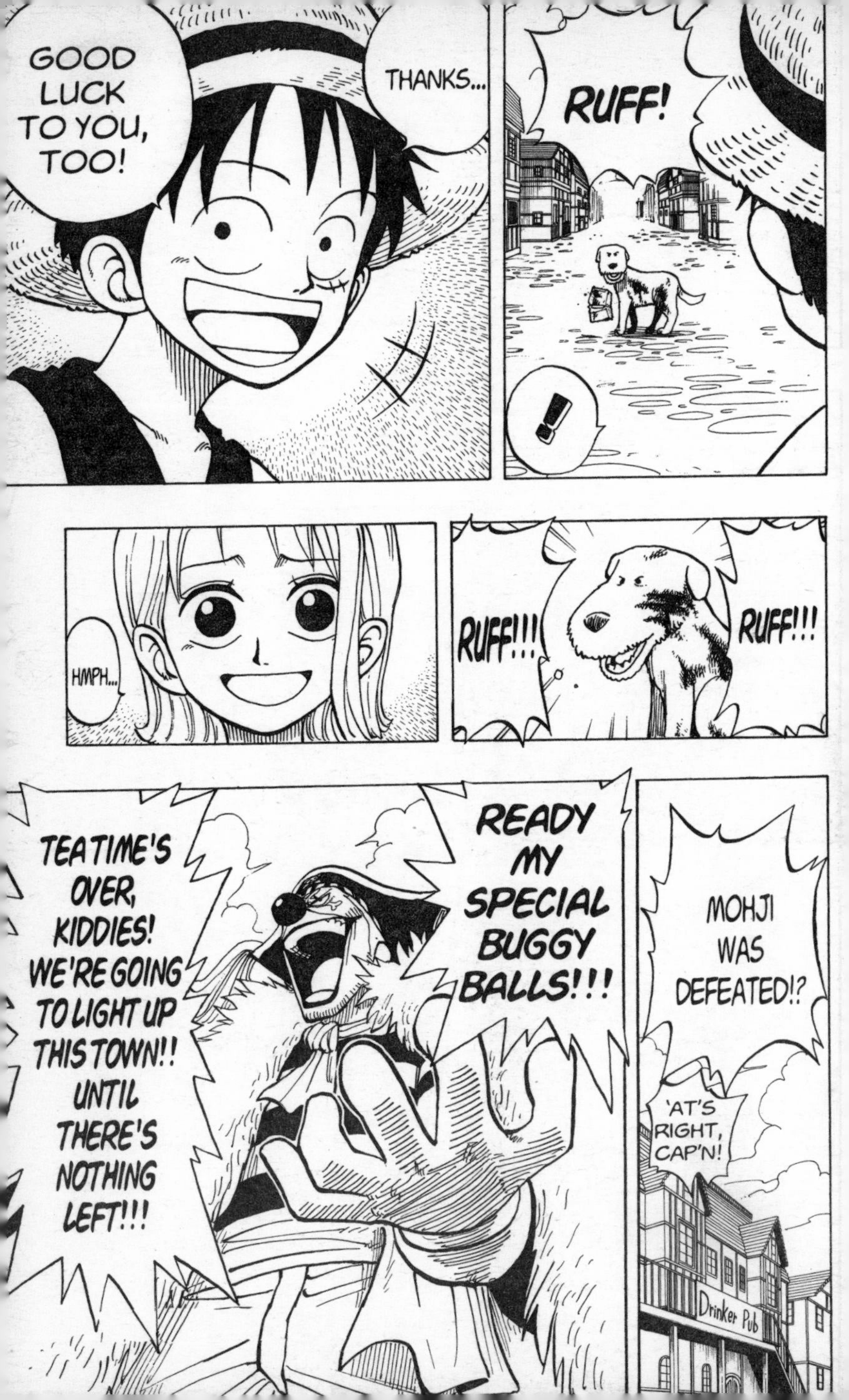
RUFF!
!
THANKS...
GOOD LUCK TO YOU, TOO!
RUFF!!!
RUFF!!!
HMPH...
MOHJI WAS DEFEATED!?
'AT'S RIGHT, CAP'N!
Drinker Pub
TEA TIME'S OVER, KIDDIES! WE'RE GOING TO LIGHT UP THIS TOWN!! UNTIL THERE'S NOTHING LEFT!!!
READY MY SPECIAL BUGGY BALLS!!!

One Piece Rough Sketch!

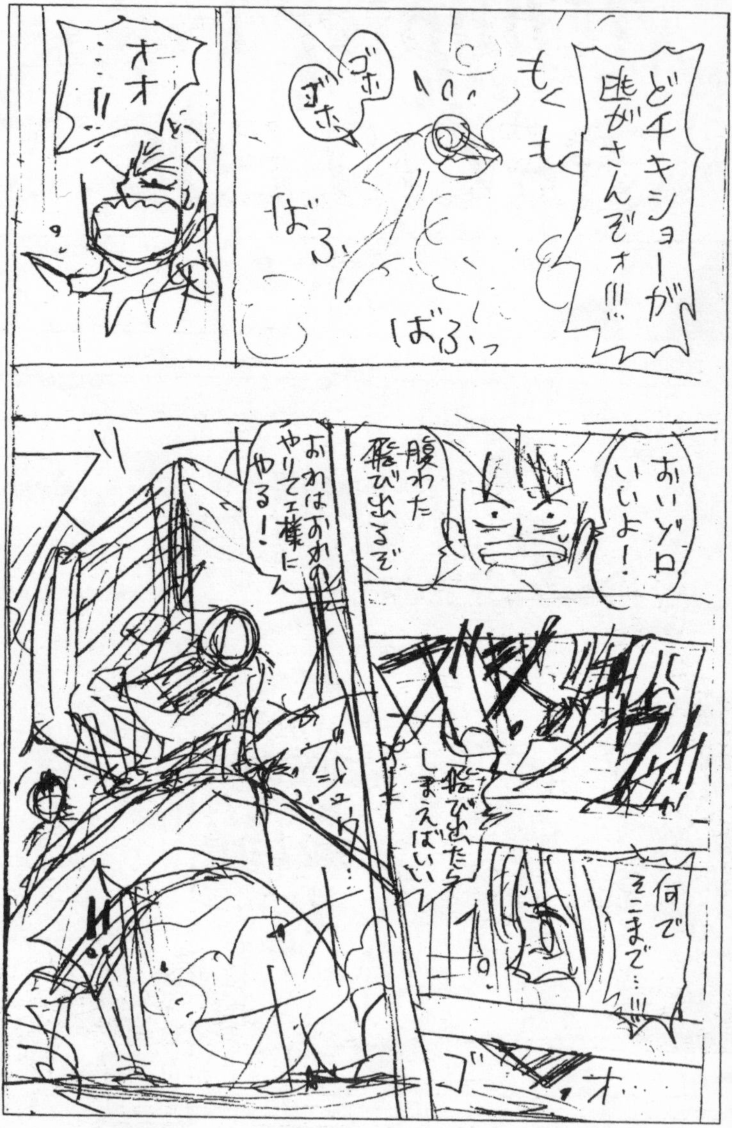

どチキショーが
逃がさんぞォ!!!
もく
もく
ばふ
ばふっ
オオ…!!
おいゾロ
いいよ!
腹わた
飛び出るぞ
おれはおれの
やりてェ様に
やる!
飛び出たら
しまえばいい
何で
そこまで…!!!
ゴォ…

Chapter 14: RECKLESS

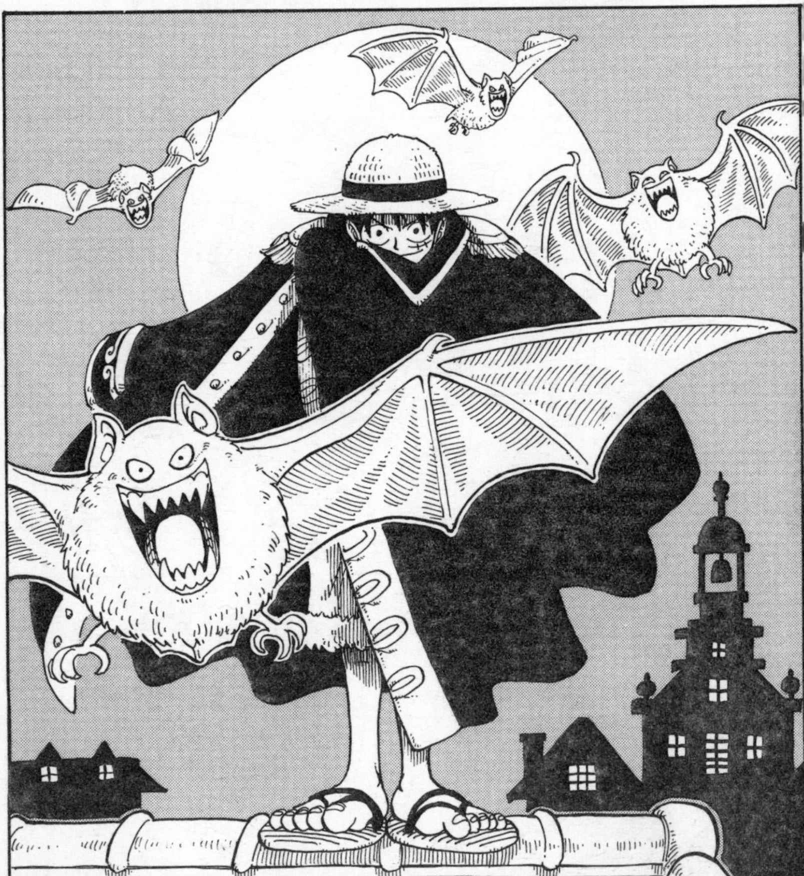

READ THIS WAY

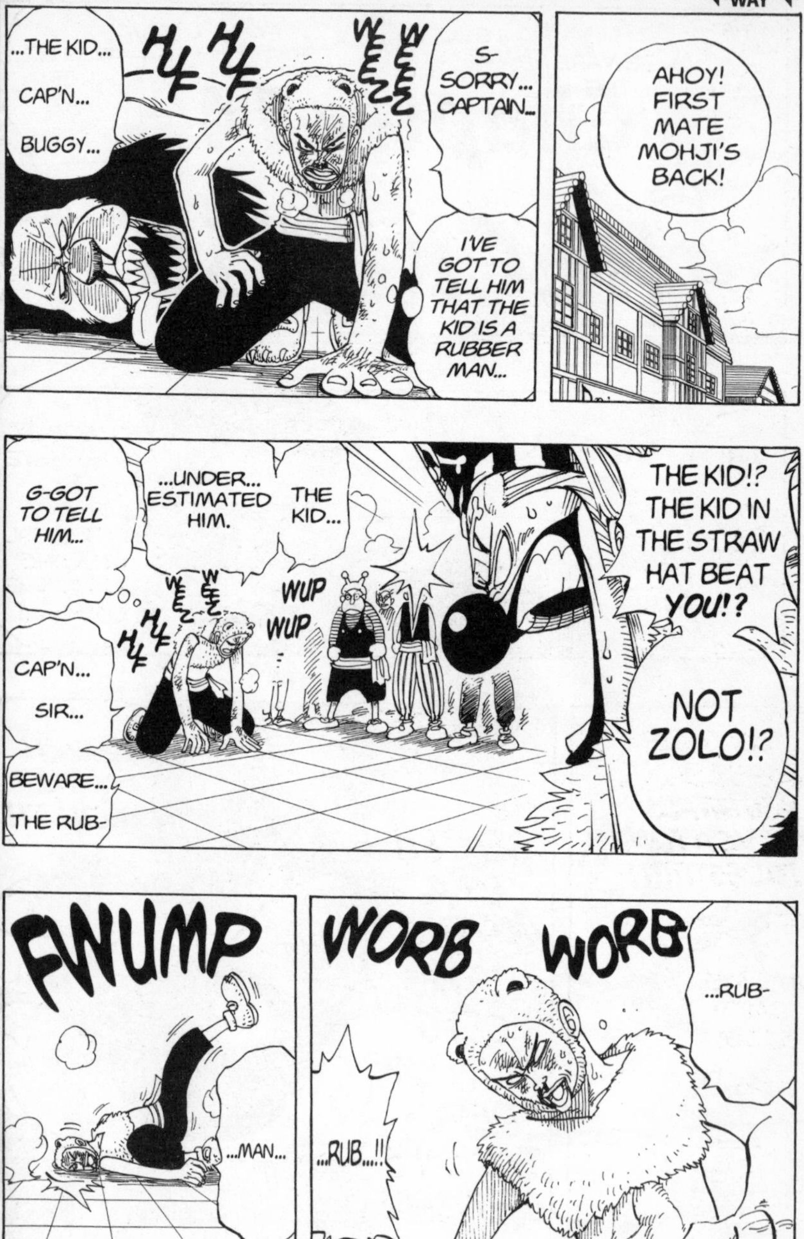
AHOY! FIRST MATE MOHJI'S BACK!
S-SORRY... CAPTAIN...
WEEZE WEEZE
HUF HUF
...THE KID...
CAP'N...
BUGGY...
I'VE GOT TO TELL HIM THAT THE KID IS A RUBBER MAN...
THE KID!? THE KID IN THE STRAW HAT BEAT YOU!?
NOT ZOLO!?
THE KID...
...UNDER... ESTIMATED HIM.
G-GOT TO TELL HIM...
WUP WUP
WEEZE
HUF HUF
CAP'N...
SIR...
BEWARE...
THE RUB-
WORB WORB
...RUB-
...RUB...!!
FWUMP
...MAN...

READ THIS WAY

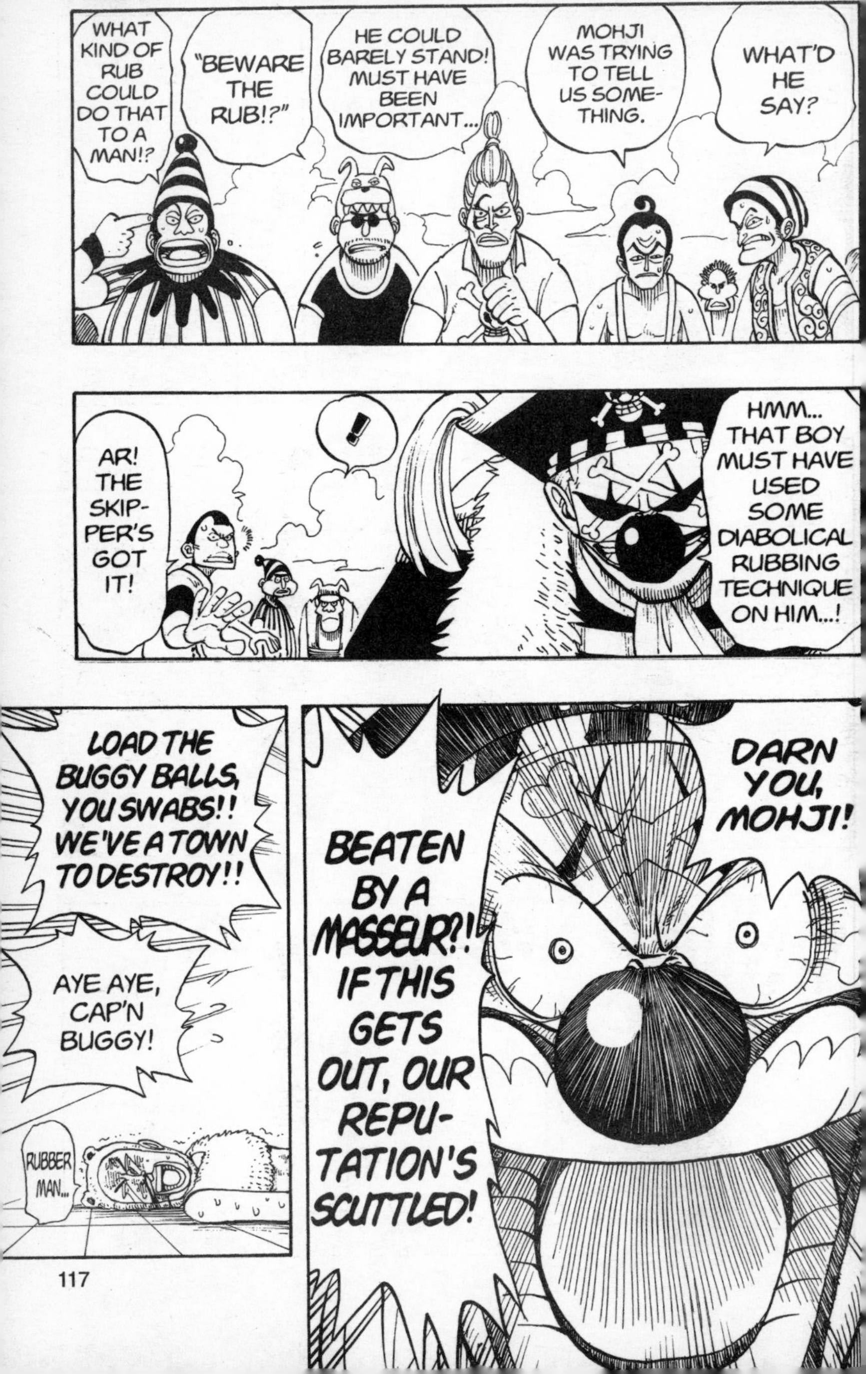

WHAT'D HE SAY?
MOHJI WAS TRYING TO TELL US SOME-THING.
HE COULD BARELY STAND! MUST HAVE BEEN IMPORTANT...
"BEWARE THE RUB!?"
WHAT KIND OF RUB COULD DO THAT TO A MAN!?
HMM... THAT BOY MUST HAVE USED SOME DIABOLICAL RUBBING TECHNIQUE ON HIM...!
!
AR! THE SKIP-PER'S GOT IT!
DARN YOU, MOHJI!
BEATEN BY A MASSEUR?! IF THIS GETS OUT, OUR REPU-TATION'S SCUTTLED!
LOAD THE BUGGY BALLS, YOU SWABS!! WE'VE A TOWN TO DESTROY!!
AYE AYE, CAP'N BUGGY!
RUBBER MAN...

HEY! IT'S CHOUCHOU FROM THE PETFOOD SHOP!

WHAT'S THAT!?

THE REFUGE OF THE TOWNSPEOPLE

TMP
TMP
TMP
TMP
TMP

HE'S HURT BAD. DAMN PIRATES!

IT'S CHOUCHOU!

WE'RE GLAD YOU'RE OKAY, BOY! WE WERE WORRIED ABOUT YOU.

LET'S TAKE CARE OF HIS WOUNDS.

THAT'S RIGHT...! MAYOR BOODLE WENT TO FEED CHOUCHOU.

BUT WHERE'S THE MAYOR?

MURMUR *MURMUR*

WHAT'S CHOUCHOU DOING HERE WITHOUT HIM?

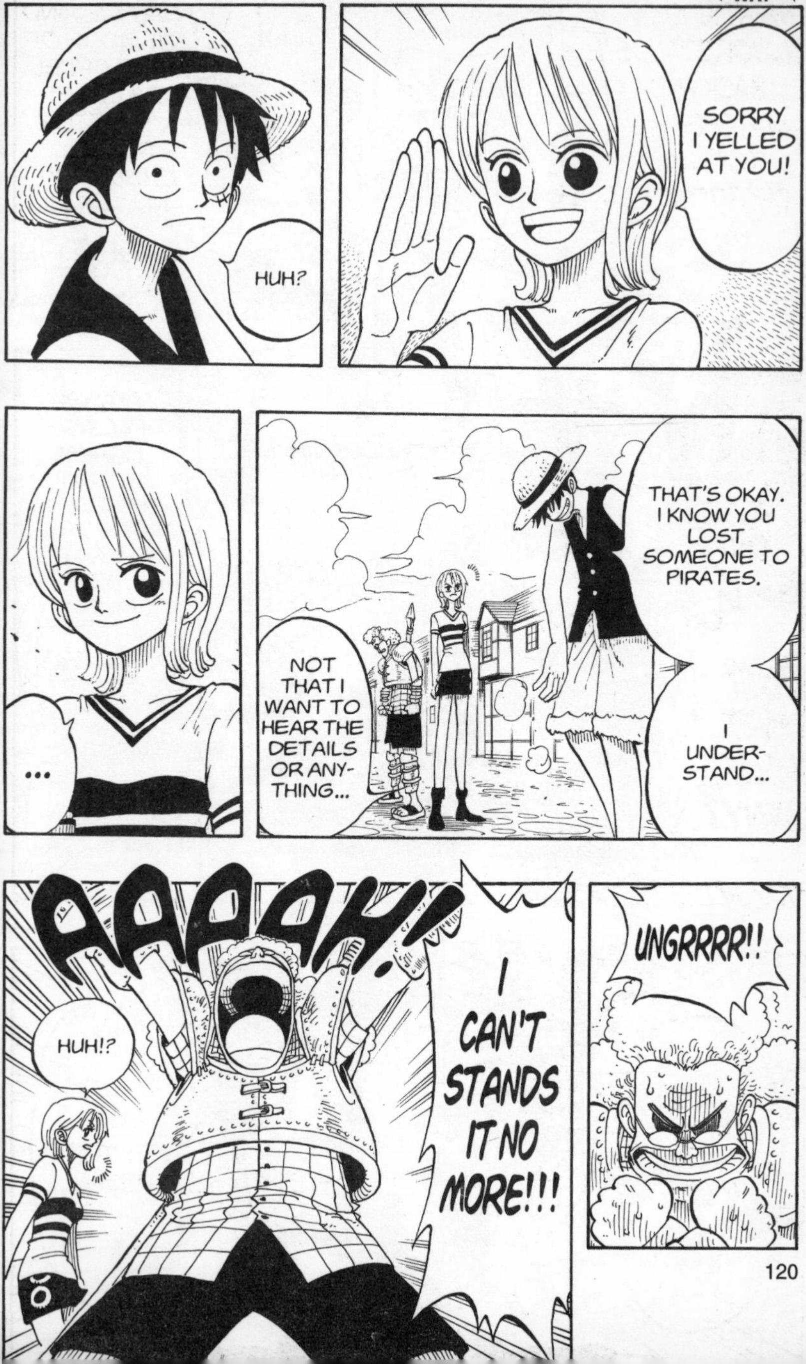
SORRY I YELLED AT YOU!
HUH?
THAT'S OKAY. I KNOW YOU LOST SOMEONE TO PIRATES.
I UNDERSTAND...
NOT THAT I WANT TO HEAR THE DETAILS OR ANYTHING...
...
UNGRRRR!!
AAAAAH!!
I CAN'T STANDS IT NO MORE!!!
HUH!?

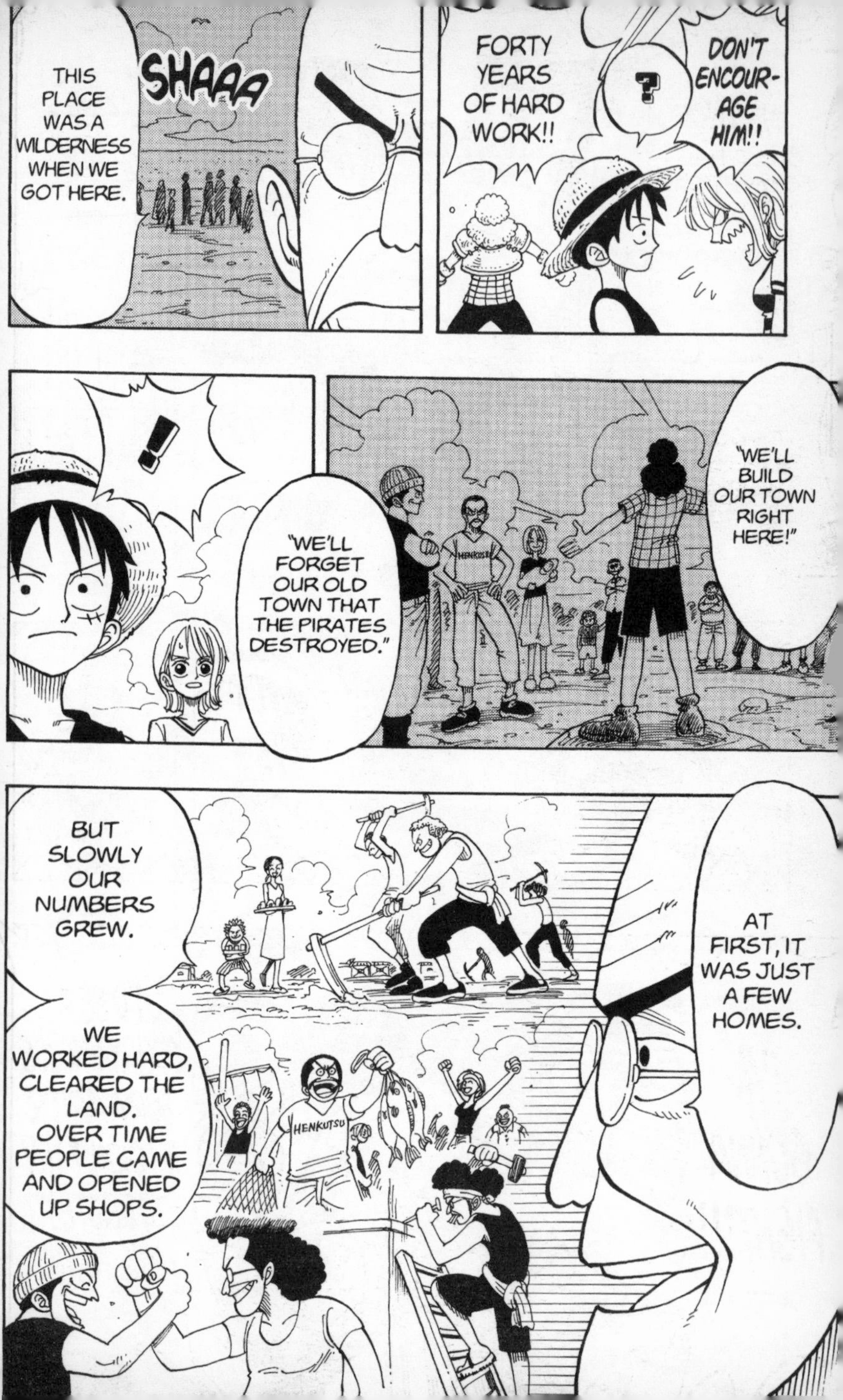
FORTY YEARS OF HARD WORK!!
?
DON'T ENCOURAGE HIM!!
THIS PLACE WAS A WILDERNESS WHEN WE GOT HERE.
SHAAA
"WE'LL BUILD OUR TOWN RIGHT HERE!"
"WE'LL FORGET OUR OLD TOWN THAT THE PIRATES DESTROYED."
HENKUTSU
!
AT FIRST, IT WAS JUST A FEW HOMES.
BUT SLOWLY OUR NUMBERS GREW.
WE WORKED HARD, CLEARED THE LAND. OVER TIME PEOPLE CAME AND OPENED UP SHOPS.
HENKUTSU

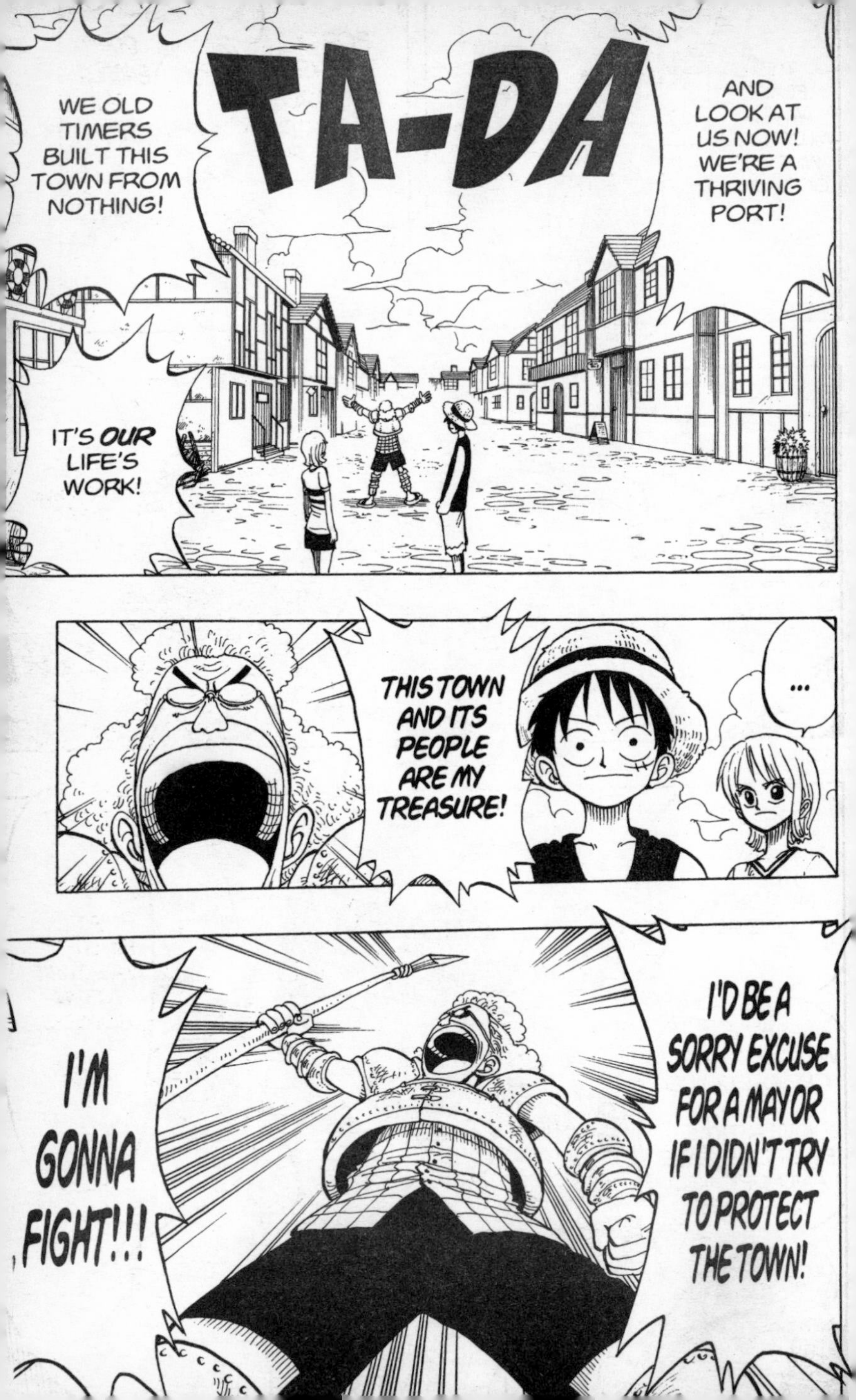
TA-DA
AND LOOK AT US NOW! WE'RE A THRIVING PORT!
WE OLD TIMERS BUILT THIS TOWN FROM NOTHING!
IT'S OUR LIFE'S WORK!
...
THIS TOWN AND ITS PEOPLE ARE MY TREASURE!
I'D BE A SORRY EXCUSE FOR A MAYOR IF I DIDN'T TRY TO PROTECT THE TOWN!
I'M GONNA FIGHT!!!

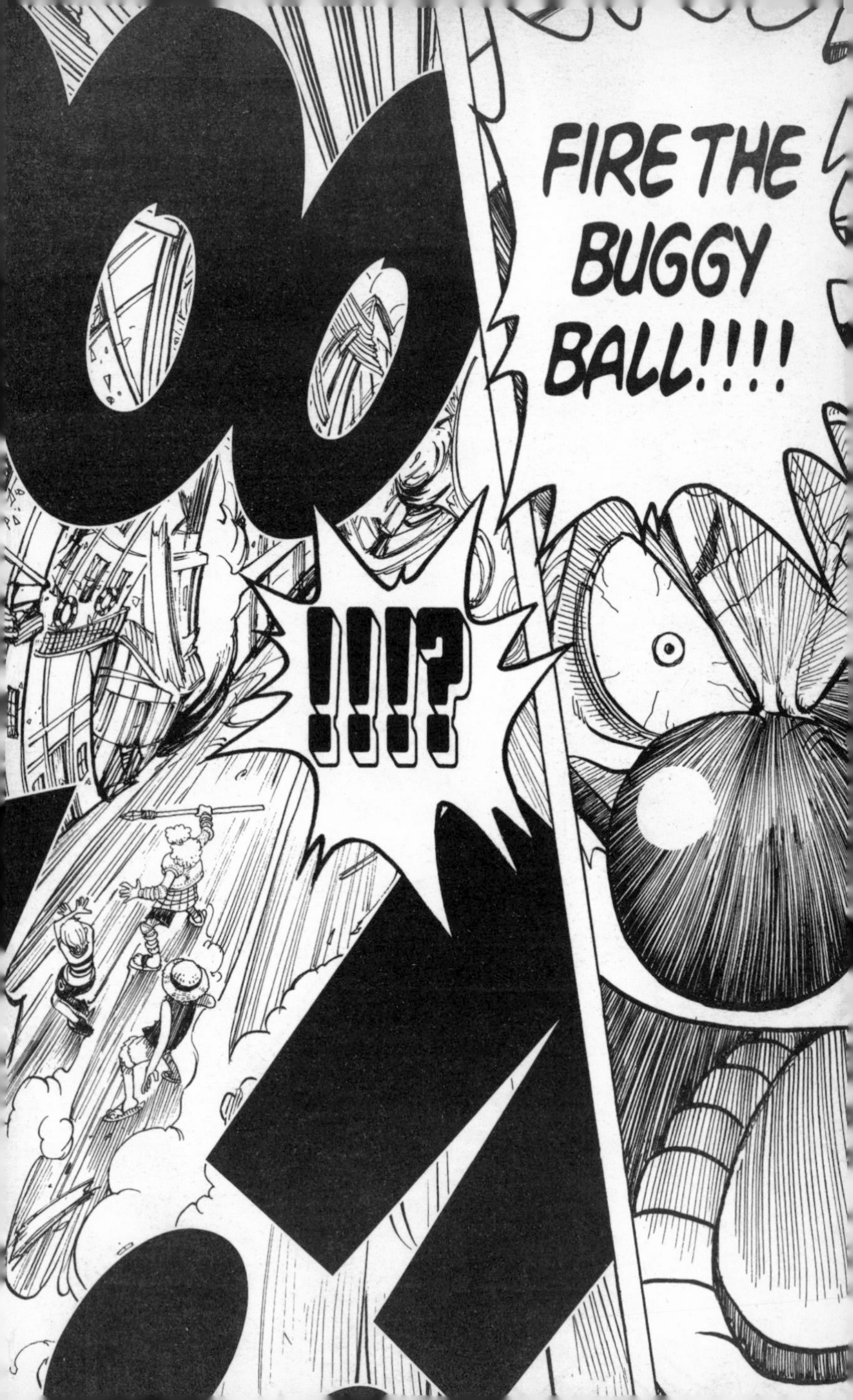
FIRE THE BUGGY BALL!!!!
!!!?

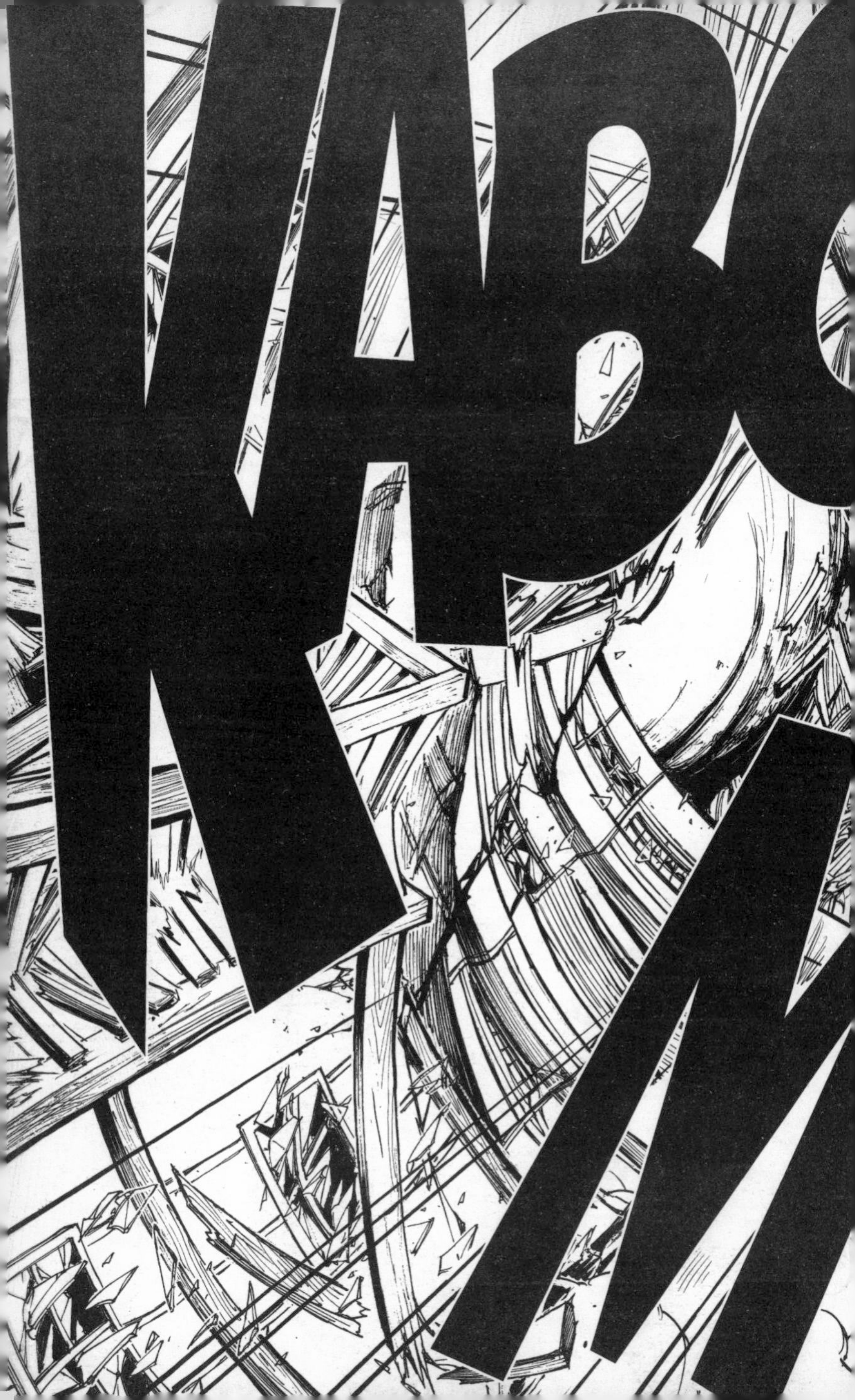

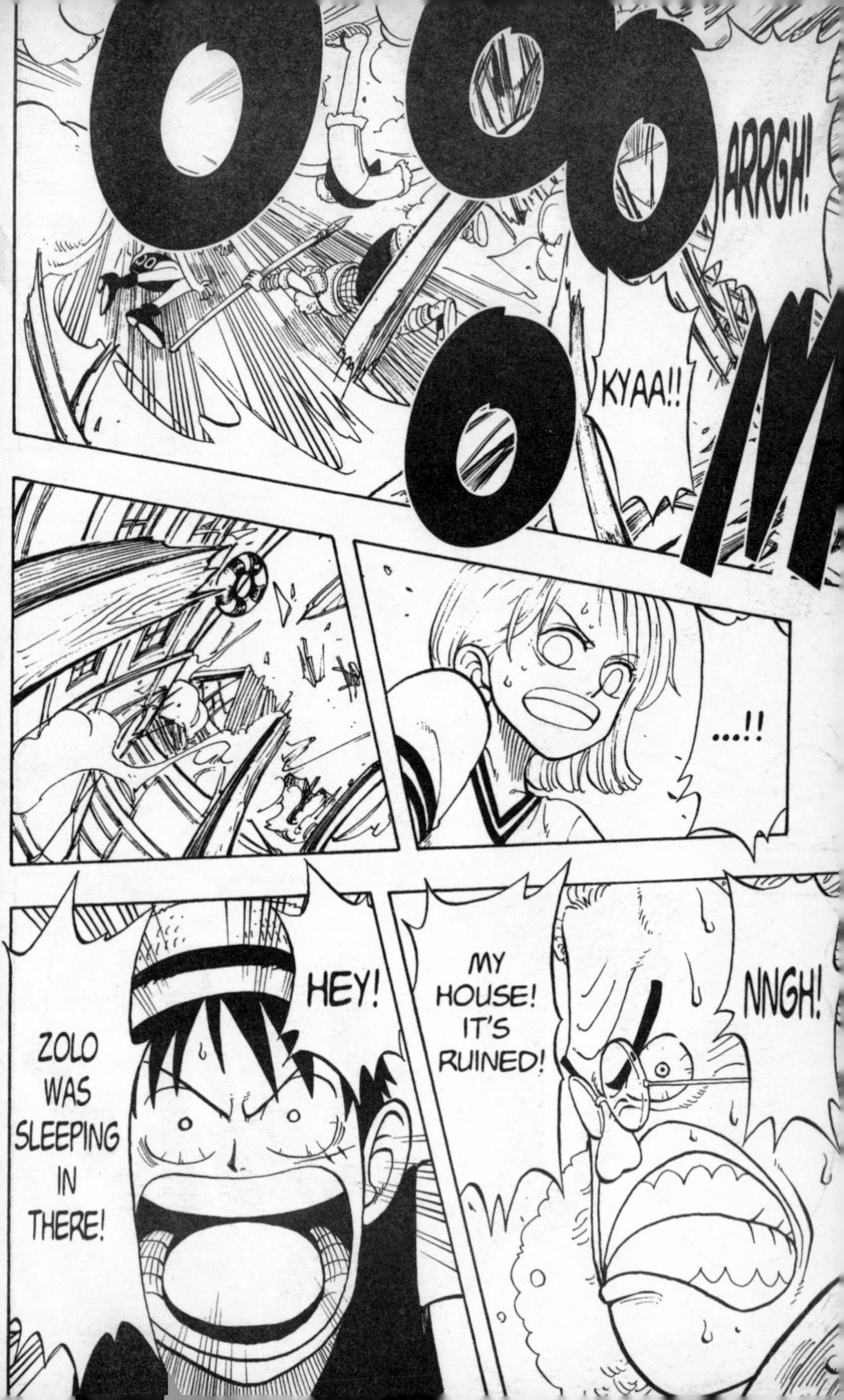
ARRGH!
KYAA!!
OOOOM
...!!
NNGH!
MY HOUSE! IT'S RUINED!
HEY!
ZOLO WAS SLEEPING IN THERE!

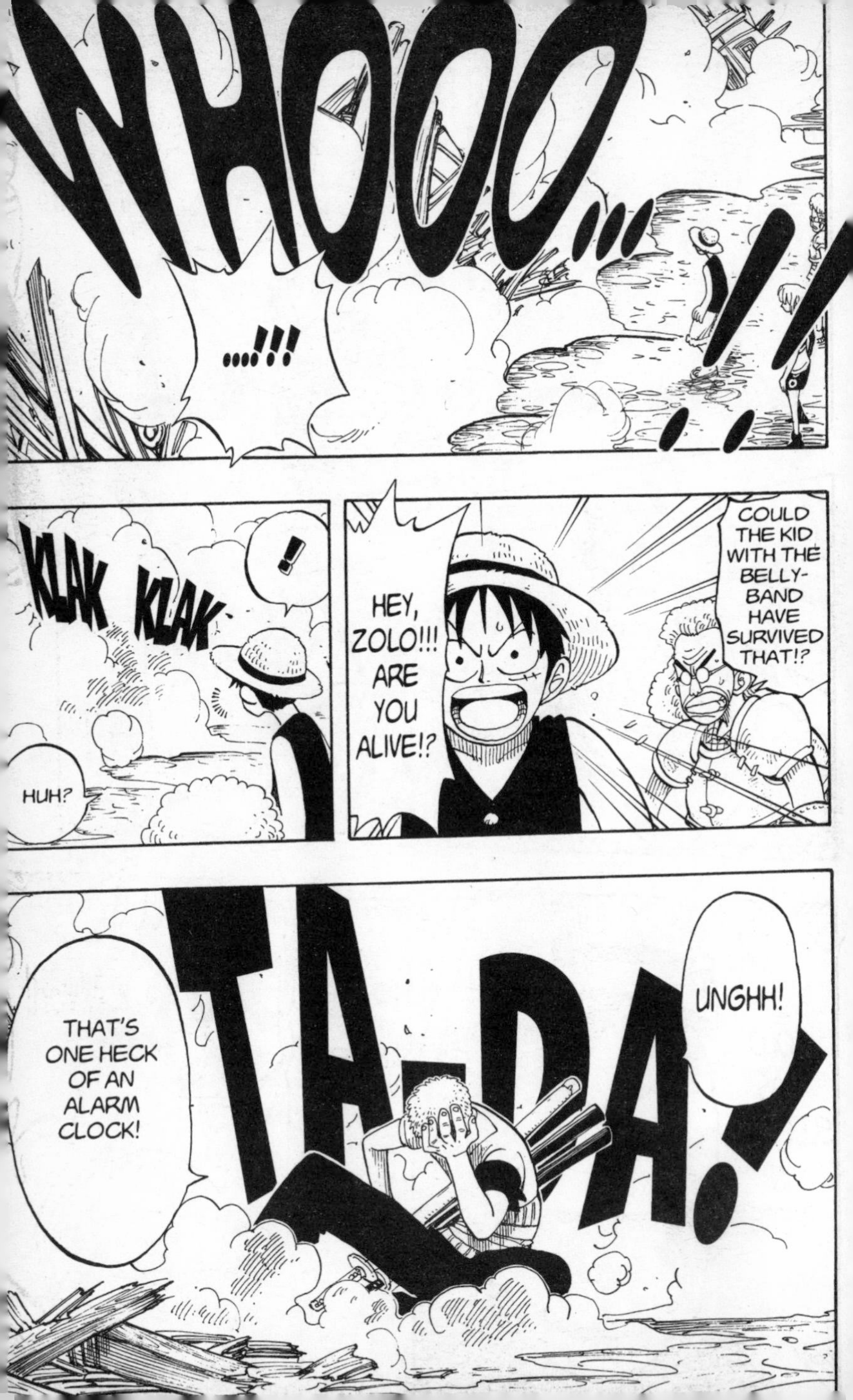
WHOOO...!!
...!!!
KLAK KLAK
!
HUH?
HEY, ZOLO!!! ARE YOU ALIVE!?
COULD THE KID WITH THE BELLY-BAND HAVE SURVIVED THAT!?
TA-DA!
THAT'S ONE HECK OF AN ALARM CLOCK!
UNGHH!

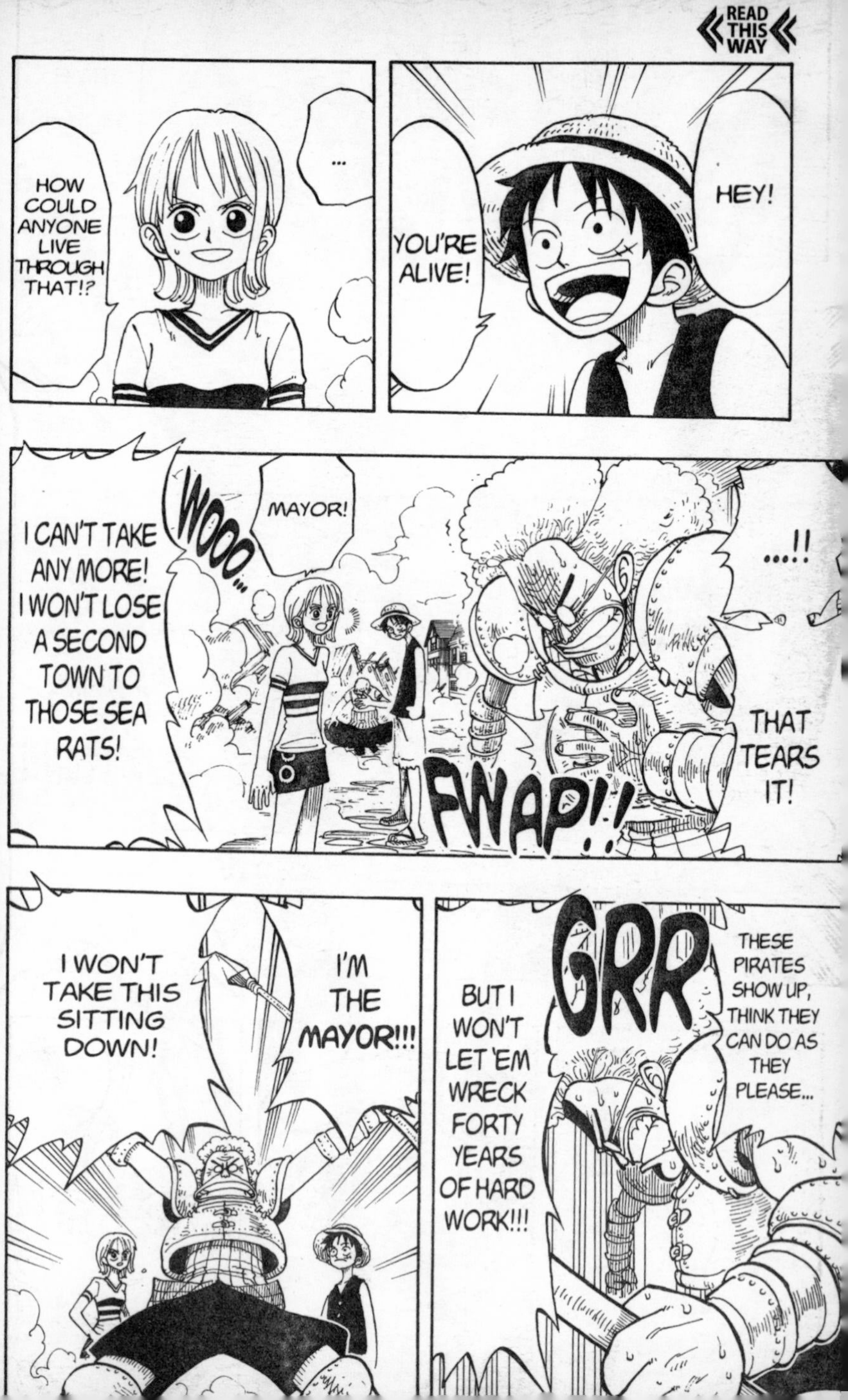
READ THIS WAY
HEY!
YOU'RE ALIVE!
...
HOW COULD ANYONE LIVE THROUGH THAT!?
...!!
THAT TEARS IT!
FWAP!!
MAYOR!
WOOO...
I CAN'T TAKE ANY MORE! I WON'T LOSE A SECOND TOWN TO THOSE SEA RATS!
GRR
THESE PIRATES SHOW UP, THINK THEY CAN DO AS THEY PLEASE...
BUT I WON'T LET 'EM WRECK FORTY YEARS OF HARD WORK!!!
I'M THE MAYOR!!!
I WON'T TAKE THIS SITTING DOWN!

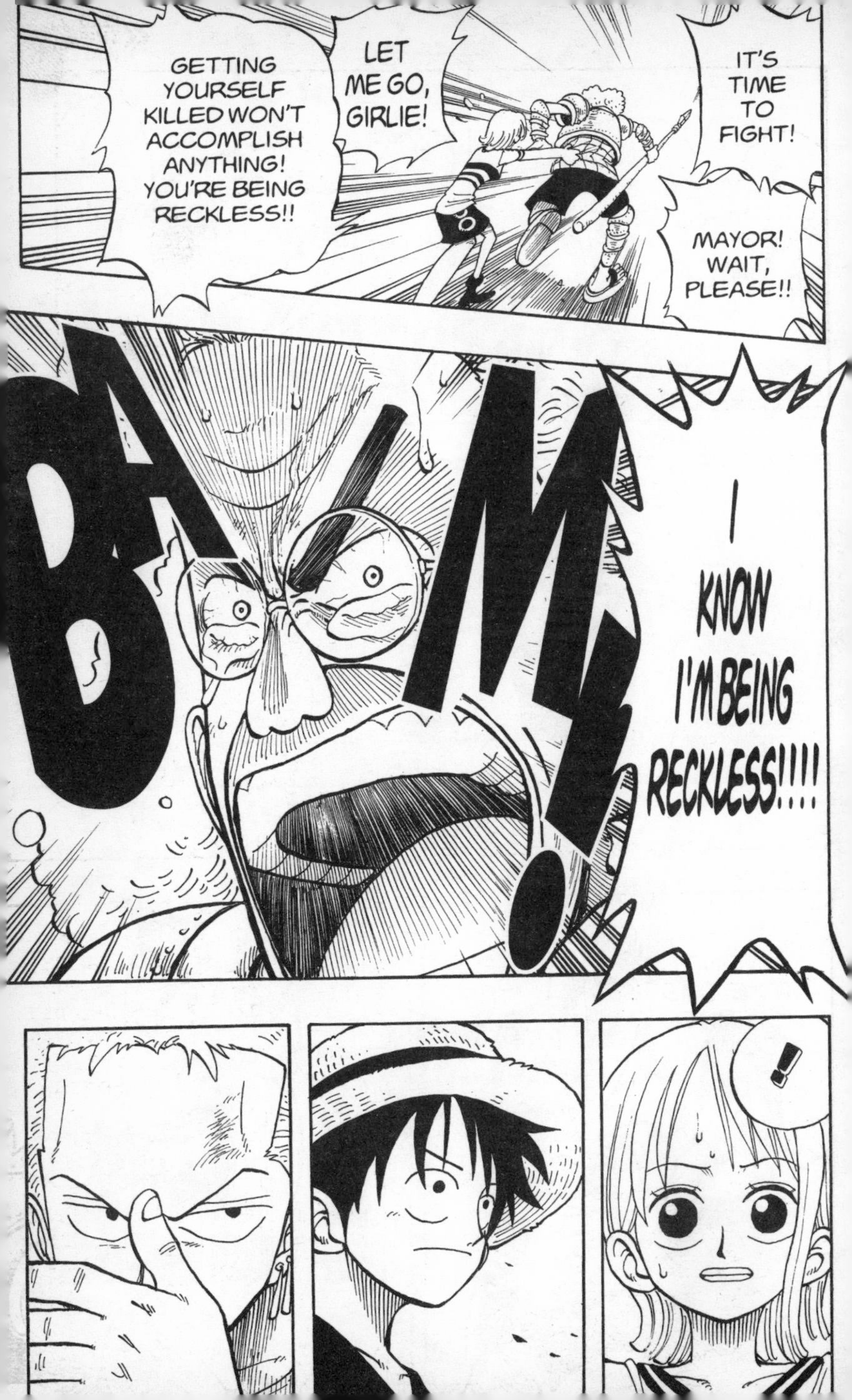
GETTING YOURSELF KILLED WON'T ACCOMPLISH ANYTHING! YOU'RE BEING RECKLESS!!
LET ME GO, GIRLIE!
IT'S TIME TO FIGHT!
MAYOR! WAIT, PLEASE!!
BAM
I KNOW I'M BEING RECKLESS!!!!
!

ARGHHH!

PREPARE TO FACE THE MAYOR!

BUGGY THE CLOWN!!

TMP TMP TMP TMP TM... TMP

IT DIDN'T LOOK THAT WAY TO ME!

THE MAYOR...

...HE WAS CRYING!!

I WON'T LET HIM GET KILLED!

DON'T WORRY, I LIKE THAT OLD MAN!

THIS IS NO LAUGHING MATTER!

HA HA HA! YEAH!

THINGS ARE FINALLY GONNA GET FUN!

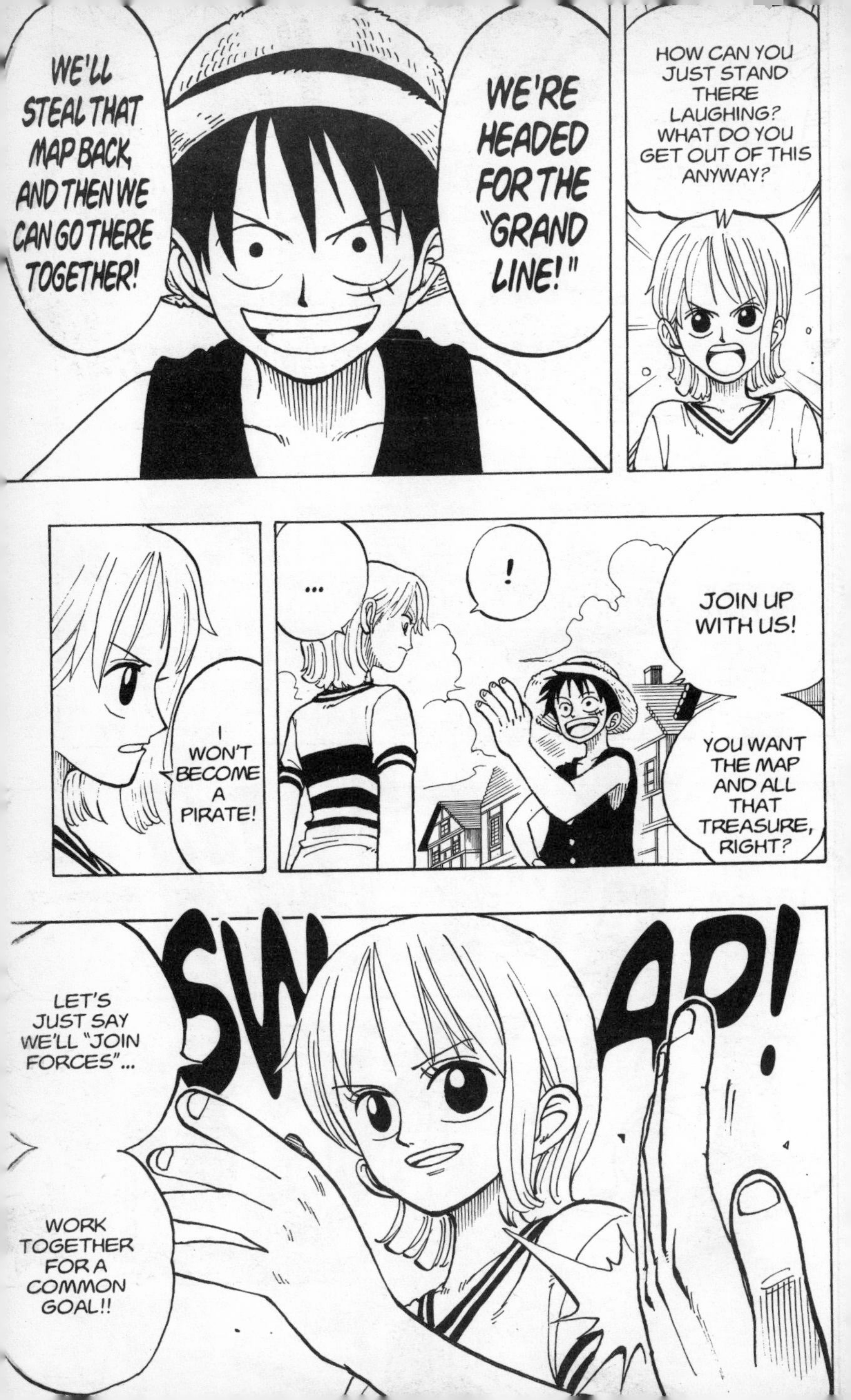
WE'RE HEADED FOR THE "GRAND LINE!"
WE'LL STEAL THAT MAP BACK, AND THEN WE CAN GO THERE TOGETHER!
HOW CAN YOU JUST STAND THERE LAUGHING? WHAT DO YOU GET OUT OF THIS ANYWAY?
JOIN UP WITH US!
YOU WANT THE MAP AND ALL THAT TREASURE, RIGHT?
!
...
I WON'T BECOME A PIRATE!
LET'S JUST SAY WE'LL "JOIN FORCES"...
WORK TOGETHER FOR A COMMON GOAL!!
SW
AP!

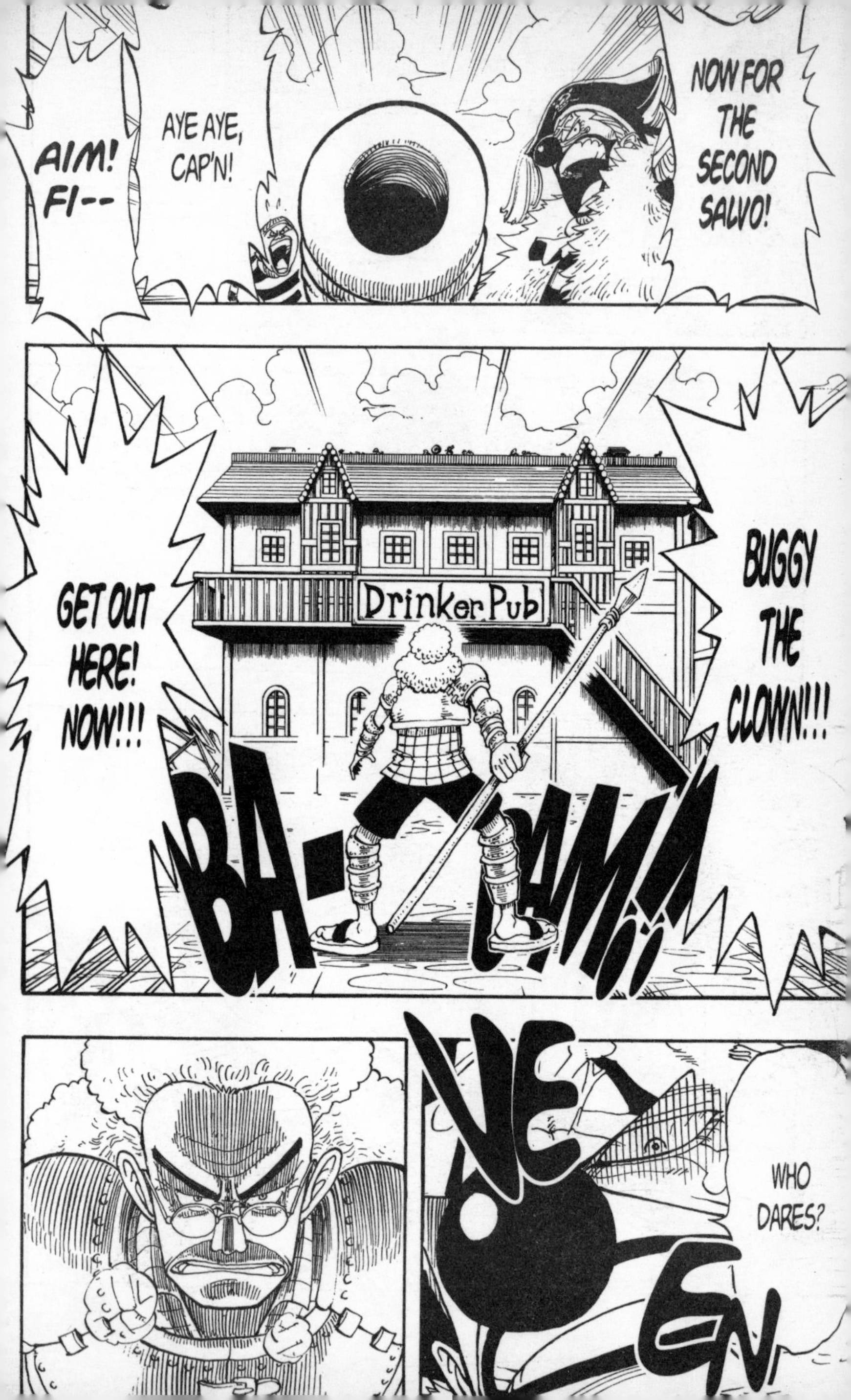
NOW FOR THE SECOND SALVO!
AYE AYE, CAP'N!
AIM! FI--
BUGGY THE CLOWN!!!
GET OUT HERE! NOW!!!
Drinker Pub
WHO DARES?

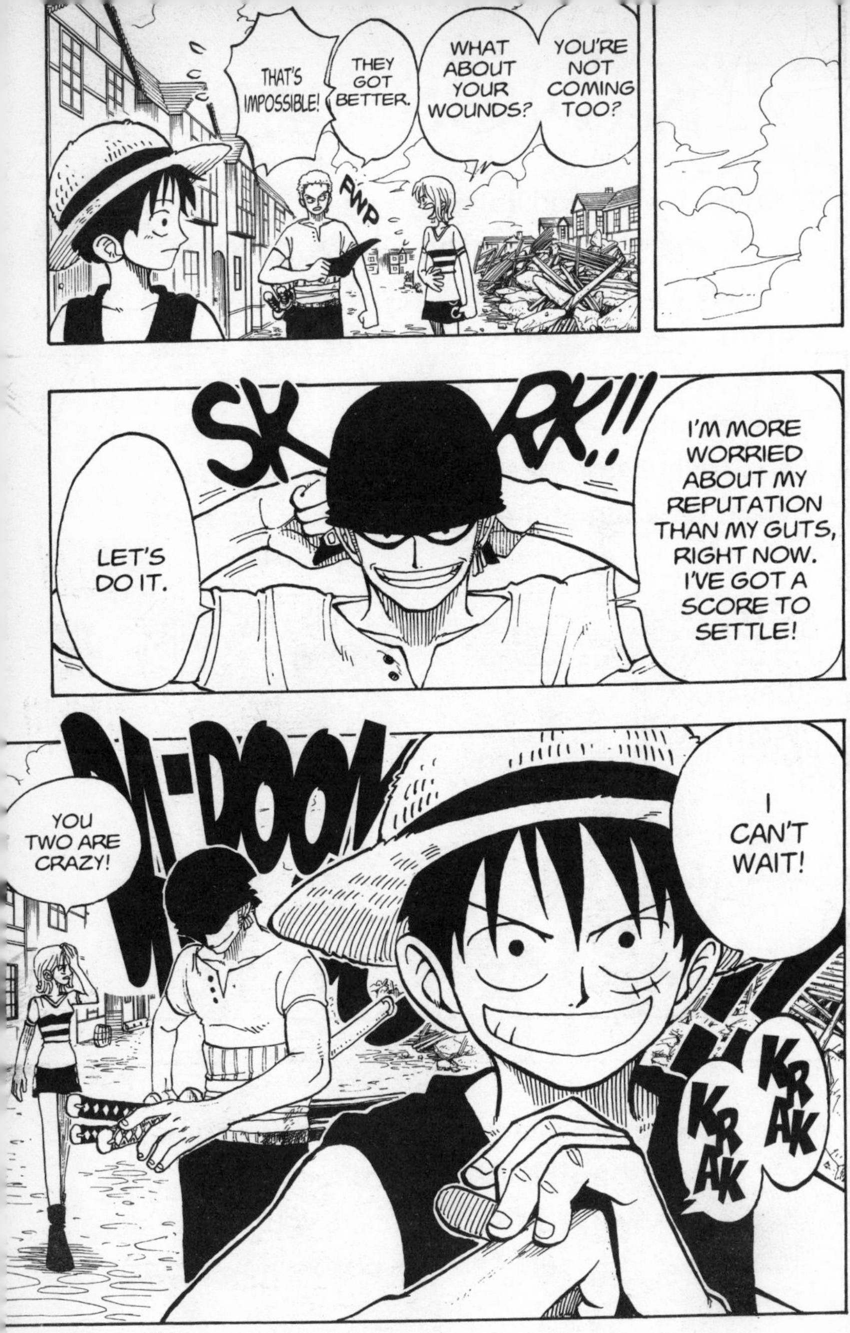

YOU'RE NOT COMING TOO?
WHAT ABOUT YOUR WOUNDS?
THEY GOT BETTER.
THAT'S IMPOSSIBLE!
FWP
SK RK!!
I'M MORE WORRIED ABOUT MY REPUTATION THAN MY GUTS, RIGHT NOW. I'VE GOT A SCORE TO SETTLE!
LET'S DO IT.
I CAN'T WAIT!
KRAK KRAK KRAK
YOU TWO ARE CRAZY!

VIKINGS, PART 3

✤ When I was a kid, I used to enjoy watching an animated TV series called **Chiisa na Viking Bikke** ("Little Viking Vic"). The show was about the adventures of a Viking boy named Vic, who wasn't very strong, but was very clever, and a group of Vikings who were very strong, but not so smart. Their adventures were very fun and entertaining.

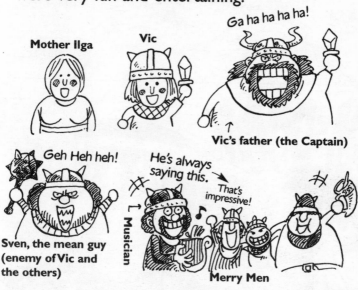

Ga ha ha ha ha!
Mother Ilga
Vic
Vic's father (the Captain)
Geh Heh heh!
He's always saying this.
That's impressive!
Musician
Sven, the mean guy (enemy of Vic and the others)
Merry Men

✤ It aired over 15 years ago, so a lot of people of my generation (I'm 28) remember it from childhood. If it ever gets rebroadcast, you should definitely check it out! That's probably how I started liking pirates.

Chapter 15:
GONG

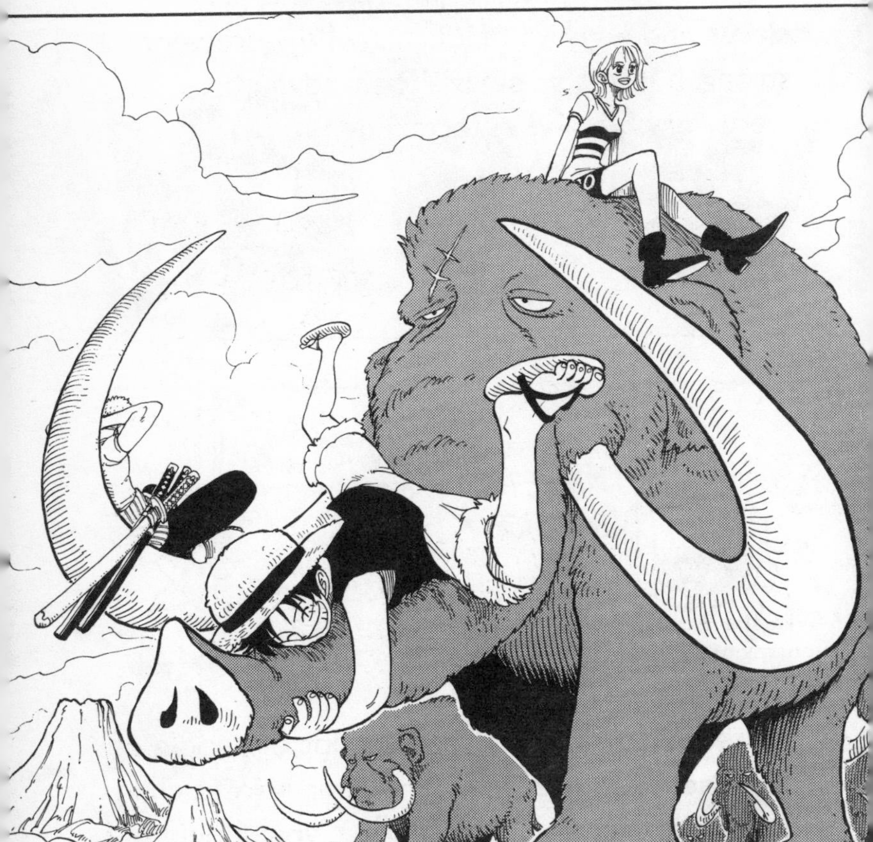

READ THIS WAY

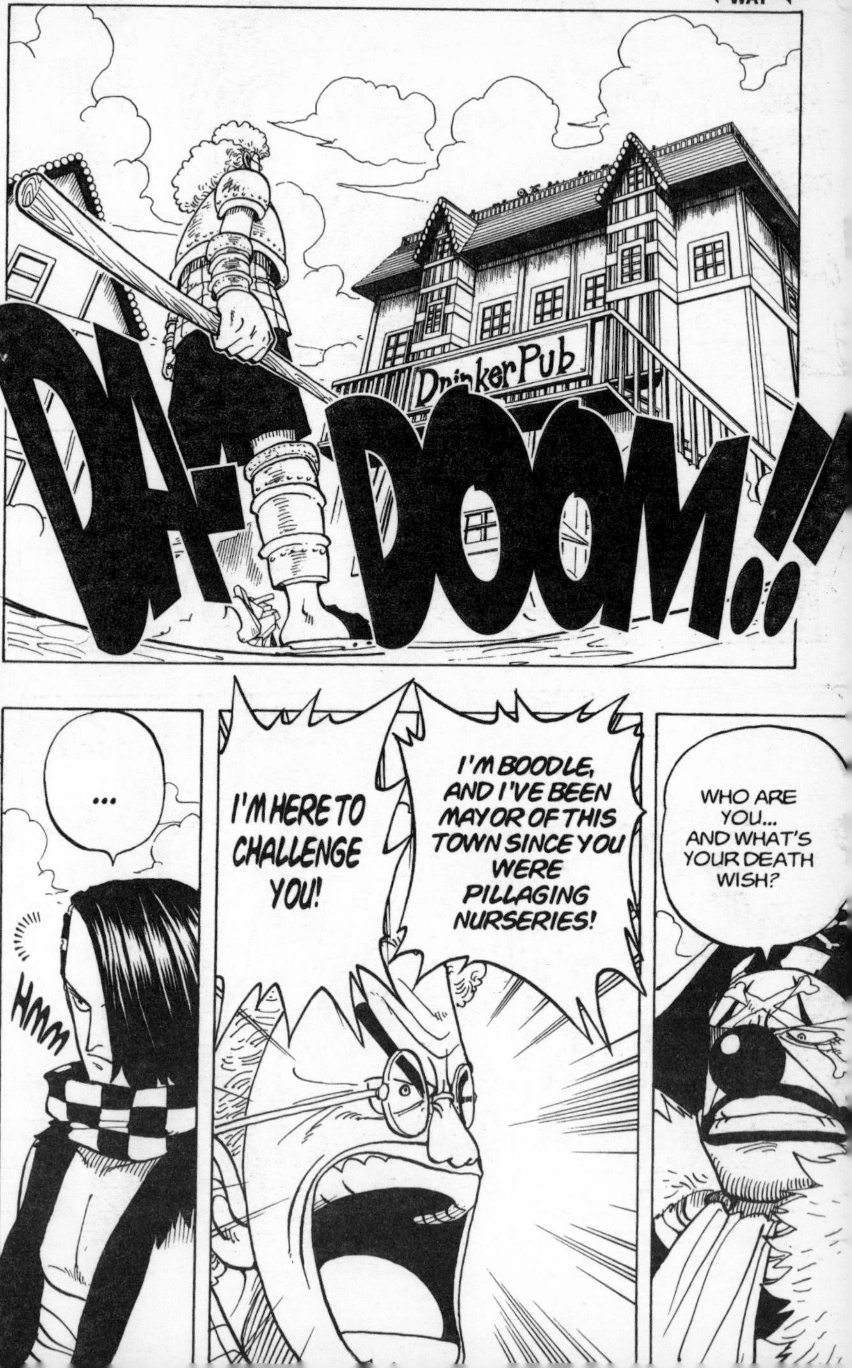
Drinker Pub
DA-DOOM!!
WHO ARE YOU... AND WHAT'S YOUR DEATH WISH?
I'M BOODLE, AND I'VE BEEN MAYOR OF THIS TOWN SINCE YOU WERE PILLAGING NURSERIES!
I'M HERE TO CHALLENGE YOU!
...
HMM

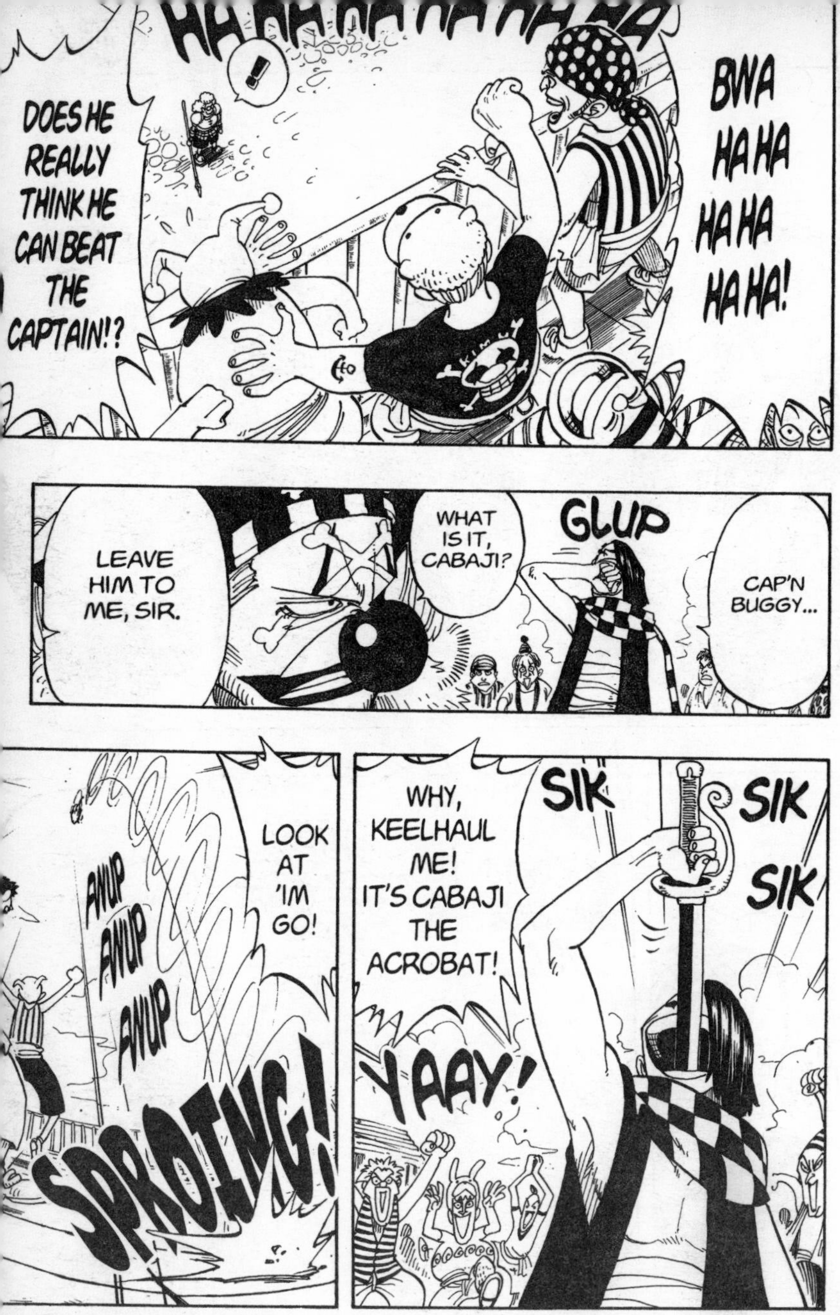
BWA HA HA HA HA HA HA!
HA HA HA HA HA HA HA
!
DOES HE REALLY THINK HE CAN BEAT THE CAPTAIN!?
CAP'N BUGGY...
GLUP
WHAT IS IT, CABAJI?
LEAVE HIM TO ME, SIR.
SIK SIK SIK
WHY, KEELHAUL ME! IT'S CABAJI THE ACROBAT!
YAAY!
LOOK AT 'IM GO!
FWUP FWUP FWUP
SPROING!

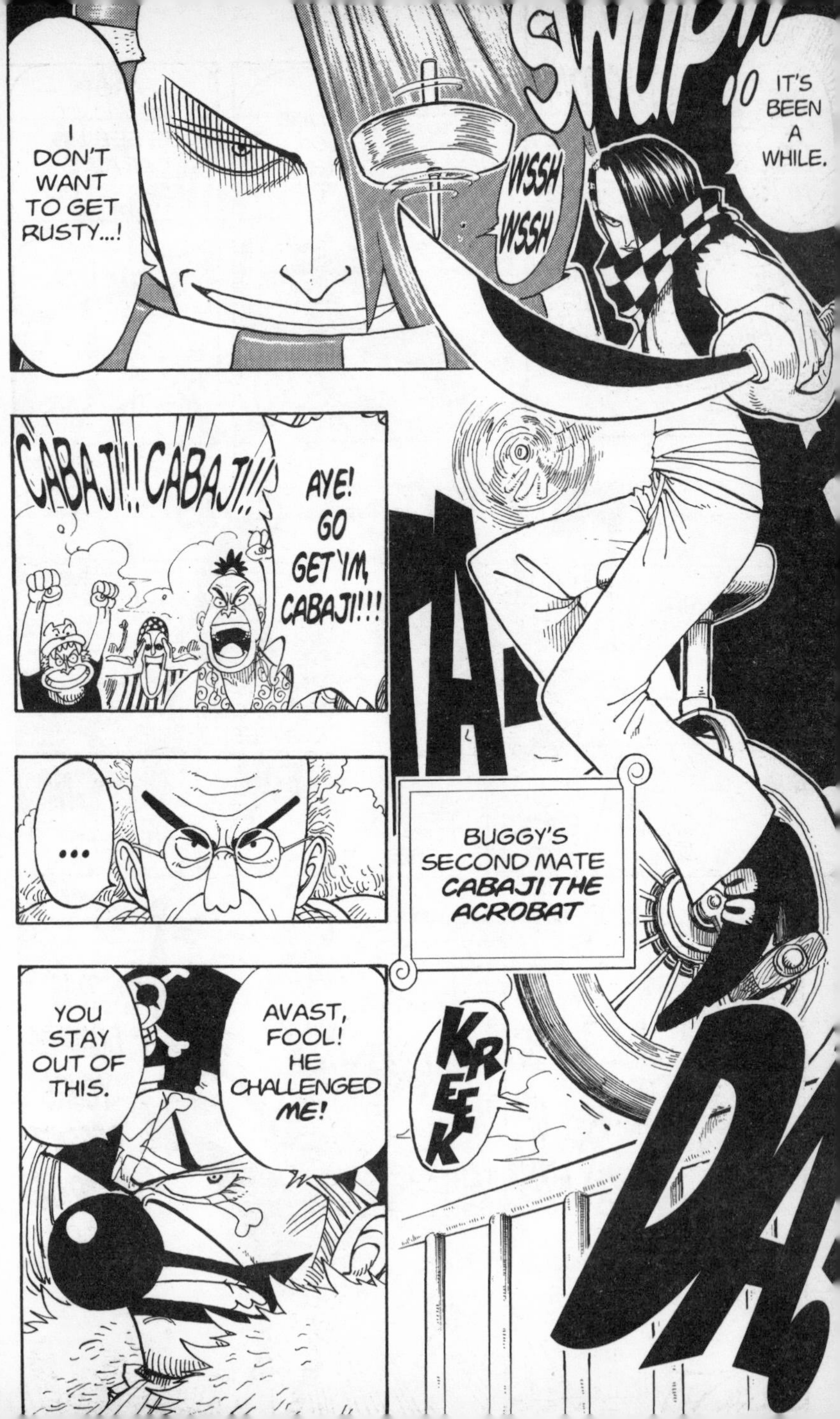

SWUP!!
IT'S BEEN A WHILE.
WSSH WSSH
I DON'T WANT TO GET RUSTY...!
TA-DA
BUGGY'S SECOND MATE *CABAJI THE ACROBAT*
KREEK
AYE! GO GET 'IM, CABAJI!!!
CABAJI!! CABAJI!!!
...
AVAST, FOOL! HE CHALLENGED *ME!*
YOU STAY OUT OF THIS.

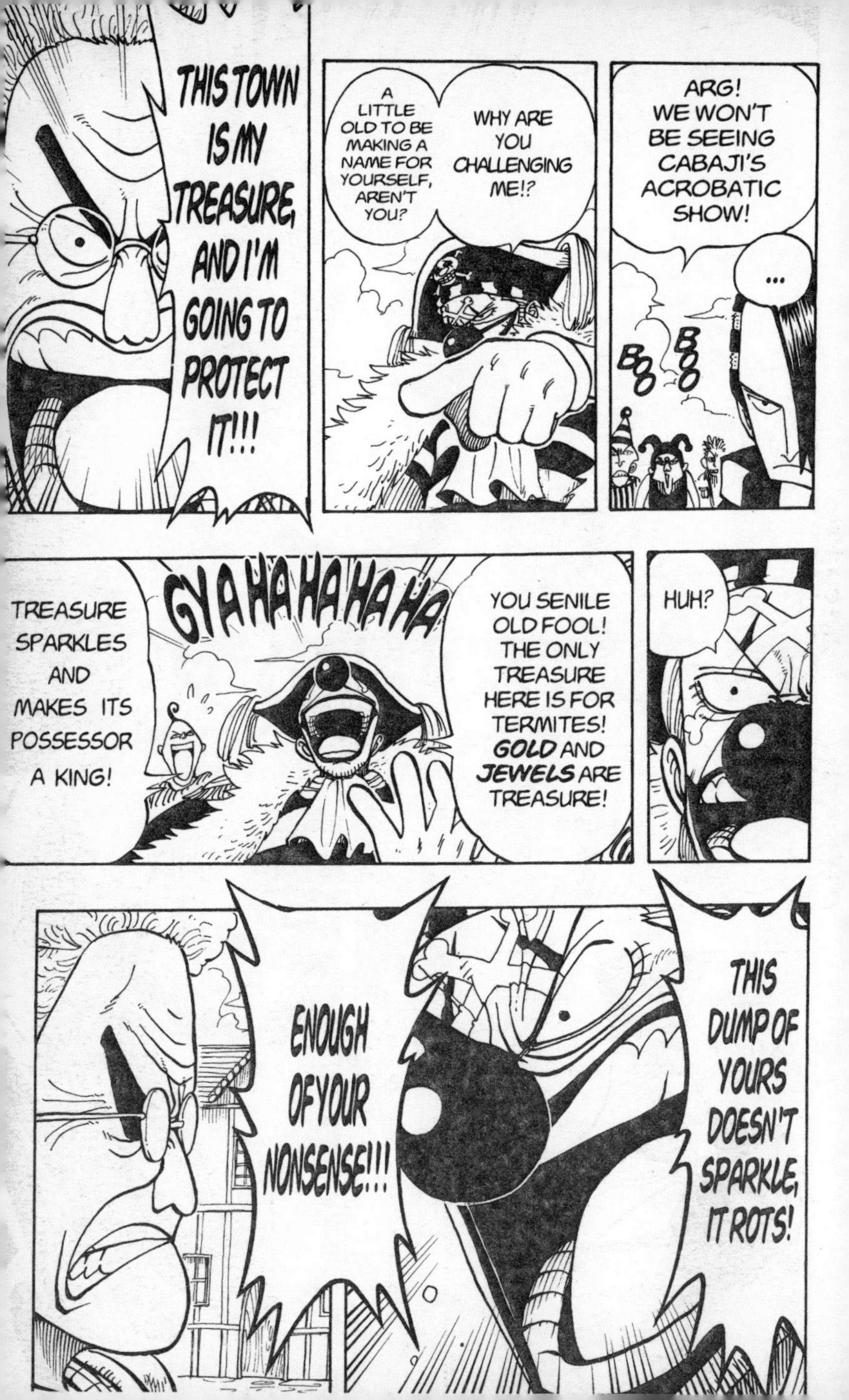
THIS TOWN IS MY TREASURE, AND I'M GOING TO PROTECT IT!!!
A LITTLE OLD TO BE MAKING A NAME FOR YOURSELF, AREN'T YOU?
WHY ARE YOU CHALLENGING ME!?
ARG! WE WON'T BE SEEING CABAJI'S ACROBATIC SHOW!
BOO
BOO
...
TREASURE SPARKLES AND MAKES ITS POSSESSOR A KING!
GYAHAHAHAHAHA
YOU SENILE OLD FOOL! THE ONLY TREASURE HERE IS FOR TERMITES! GOLD AND JEWELS ARE TREASURE!
HUH?
ENOUGH OF YOUR NONSENSE!!!
THIS DUMP OF YOURS DOESN'T SPARKLE, IT ROTS!

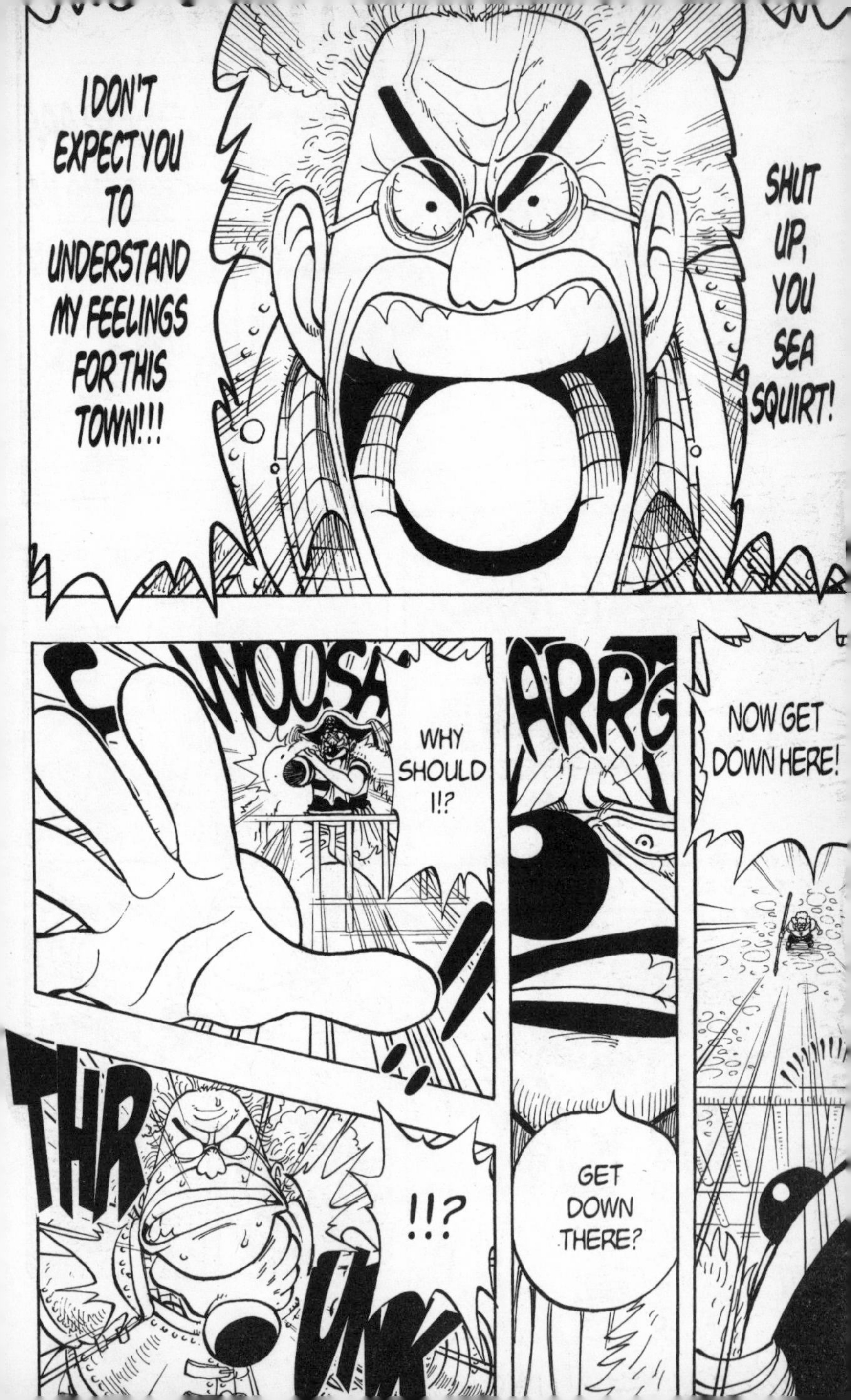
SHUT UP, YOU SEA SQUIRT!
I DON'T EXPECT YOU TO UNDERSTAND MY FEELINGS FOR THIS TOWN!!!
NOW GET DOWN HERE!
ARRG
GET DOWN THERE?
WOOSH
WHY SHOULD I!?
THR
UNK
!!?

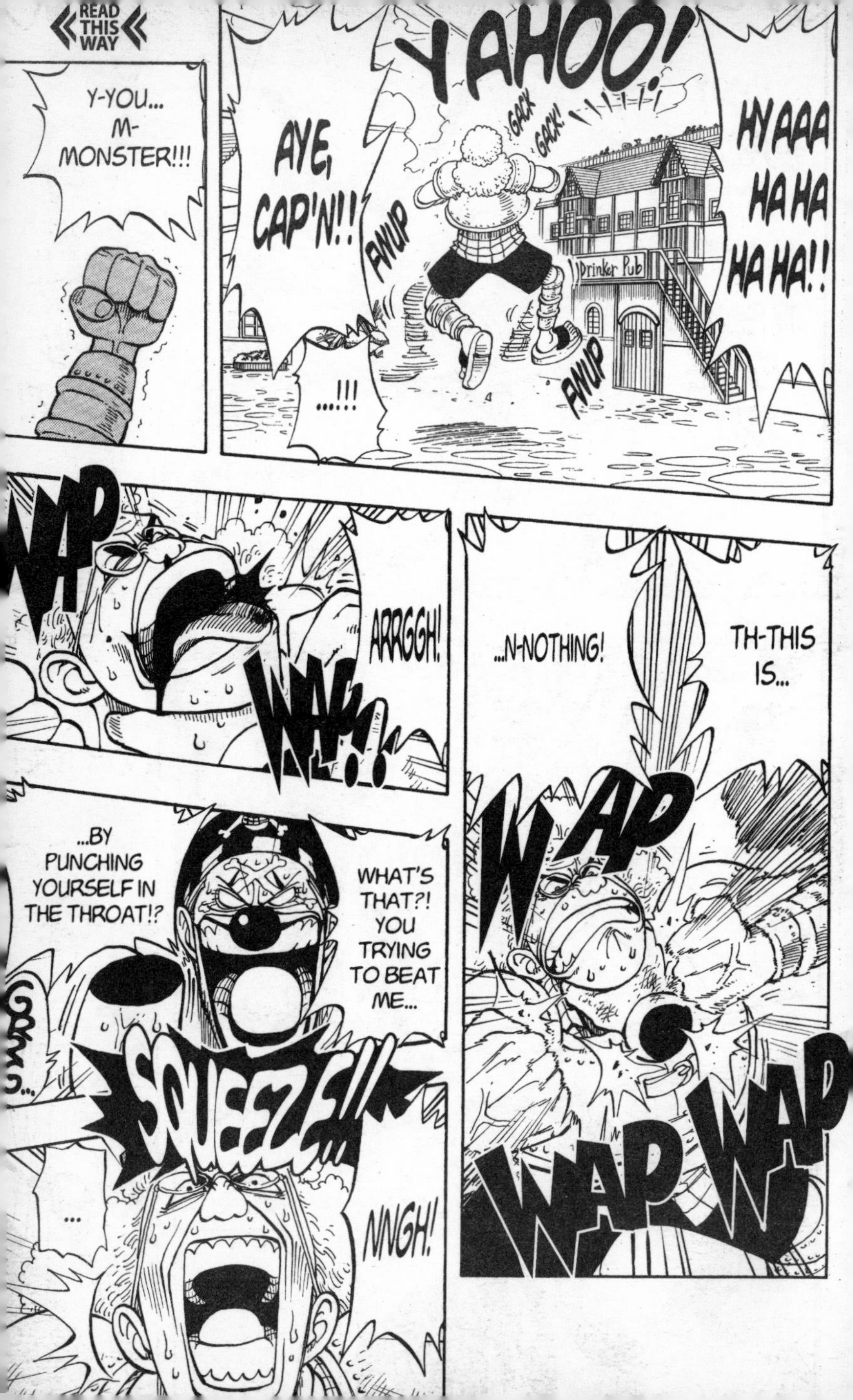
READ THIS WAY
YAHOO!
HYAAA HA HA HA HA!!
GACK GACK!
AYE, CAP'N!!
FWUP
FWUP
...!!!
Y-YOU... M-MONSTER!!!
TH-THIS IS...
...N-NOTHING!
WAP
WAP
ARRGGH!
WAP!!
WAP WAP
WHAT'S THAT?! YOU TRYING TO BEAT ME...
...BY PUNCHING YOURSELF IN THE THROAT!?
SQUEEZE!!
NNGH!
...

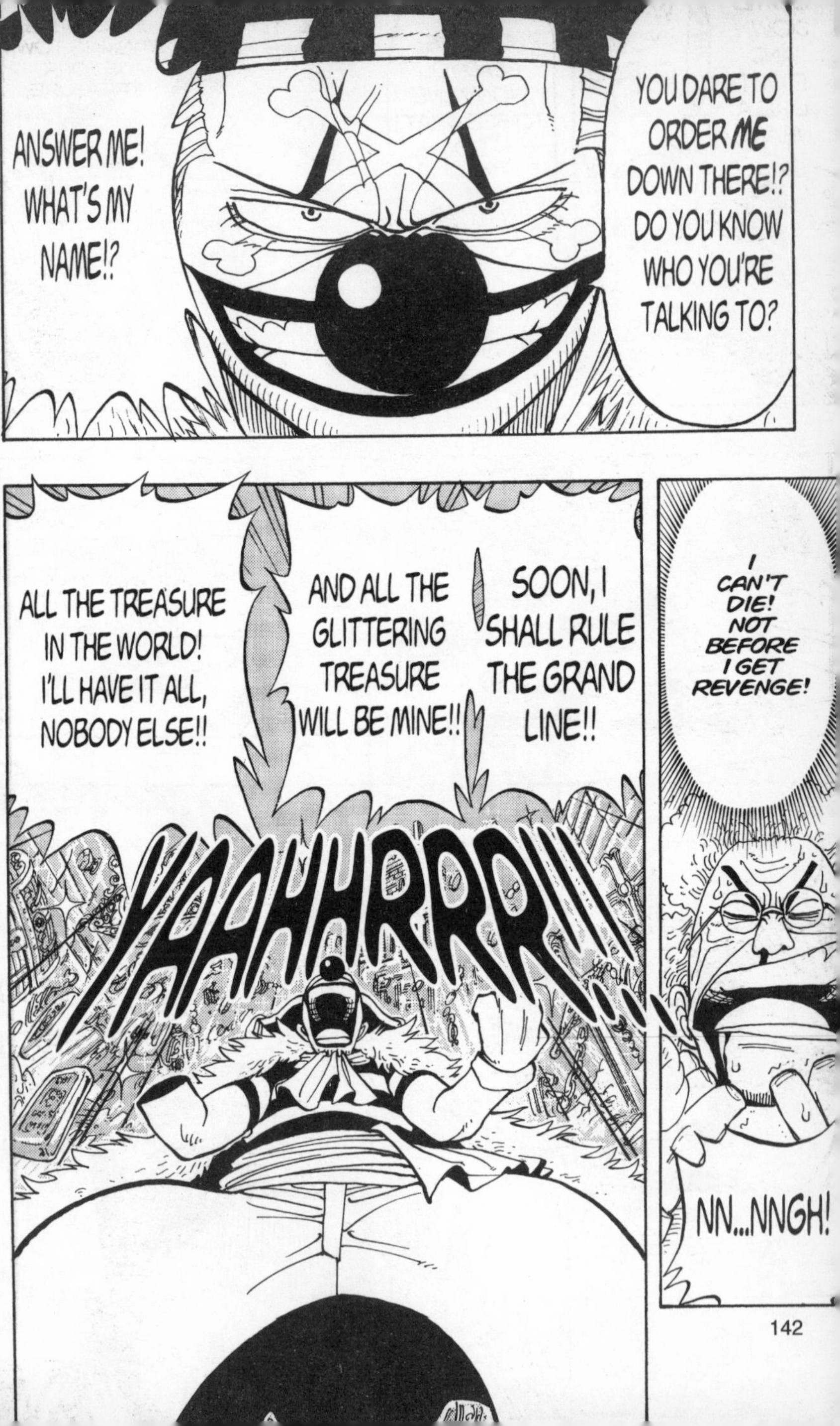
YOU DARE TO ORDER ME DOWN THERE!? DO YOU KNOW WHO YOU'RE TALKING TO?
ANSWER ME! WHAT'S MY NAME!?
I CAN'T DIE! NOT BEFORE I GET REVENGE!
SOON, I SHALL RULE THE GRAND LINE!!
AND ALL THE GLITTERING TREASURE WILL BE MINE!!
ALL THE TREASURE IN THE WORLD! I'LL HAVE IT ALL, NOBODY ELSE!!
YAAHHRRRR!!!...
NN...NNGH!

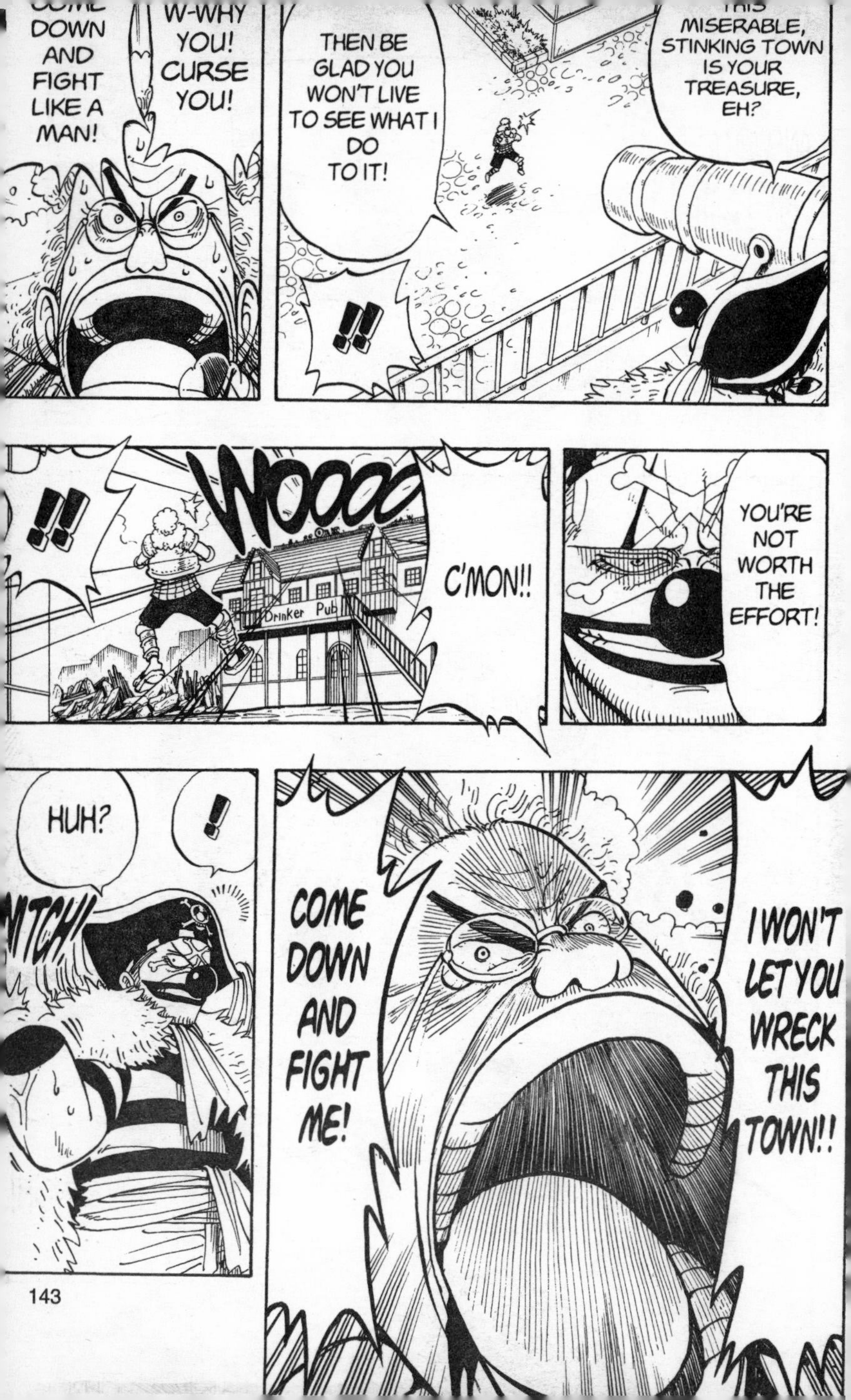
MISERABLE, STINKING TOWN IS YOUR TREASURE, EH?
!!
THEN BE GLAD YOU WON'T LIVE TO SEE WHAT I DO TO IT!
W-WHY YOU! CURSE YOU!
DOWN AND FIGHT LIKE A MAN!
YOU'RE NOT WORTH THE EFFORT!
C'MON!!
WOOOO
!!
I WON'T LET YOU WRECK THIS TOWN!!
COME DOWN AND FIGHT ME!
!
HUH?

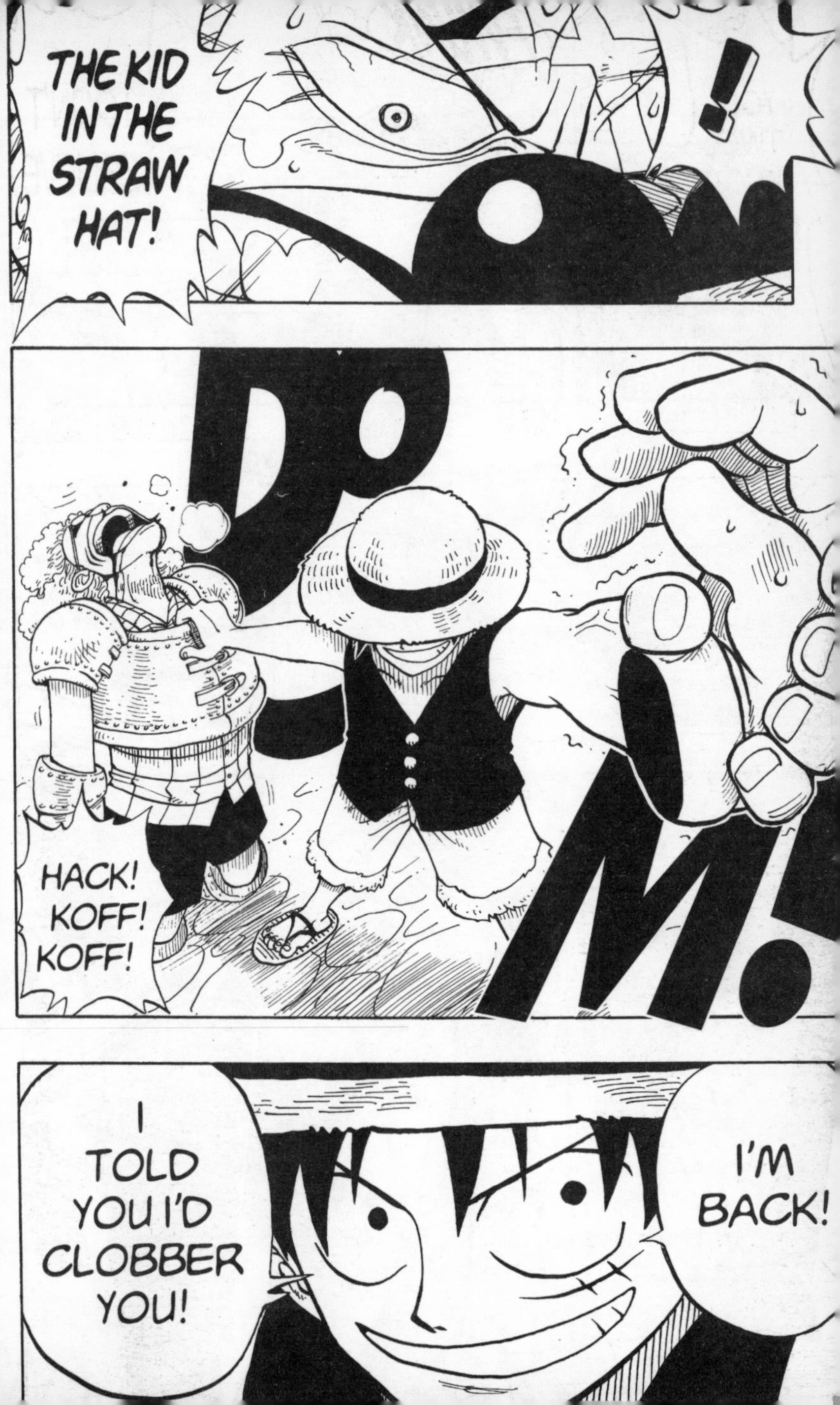
THE KID IN THE STRAW HAT!
!
DOOM!
HACK! KOFF! KOFF!
I'M BACK!
I TOLD YOU I'D CLOBBER YOU!

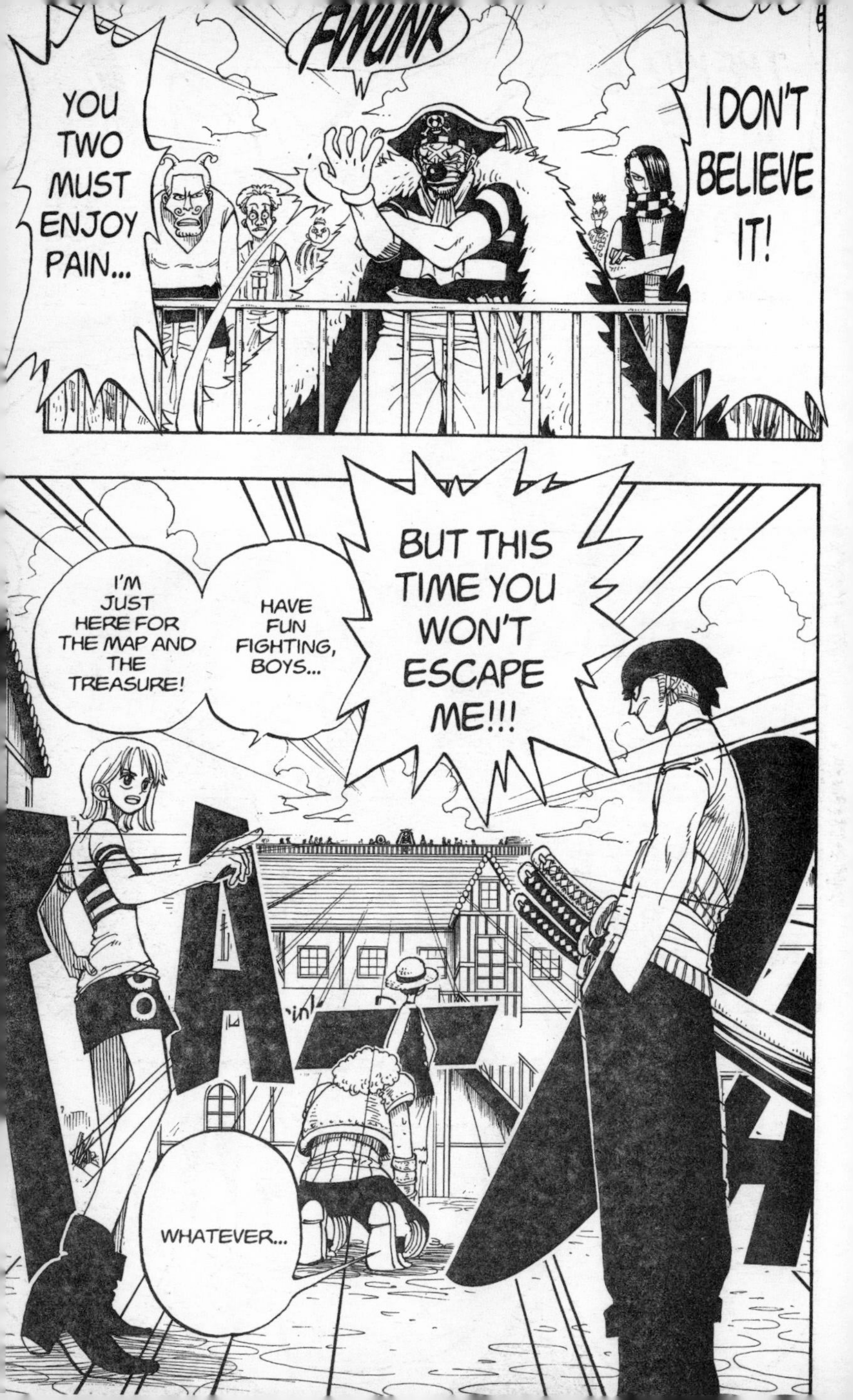
FWUNK
YOU TWO MUST ENJOY PAIN...
I DON'T BELIEVE IT!
BUT THIS TIME YOU WON'T ESCAPE ME!!!
I'M JUST HERE FOR THE MAP AND THE TREASURE!
HAVE FUN FIGHTING, BOYS...
WHATEVER...

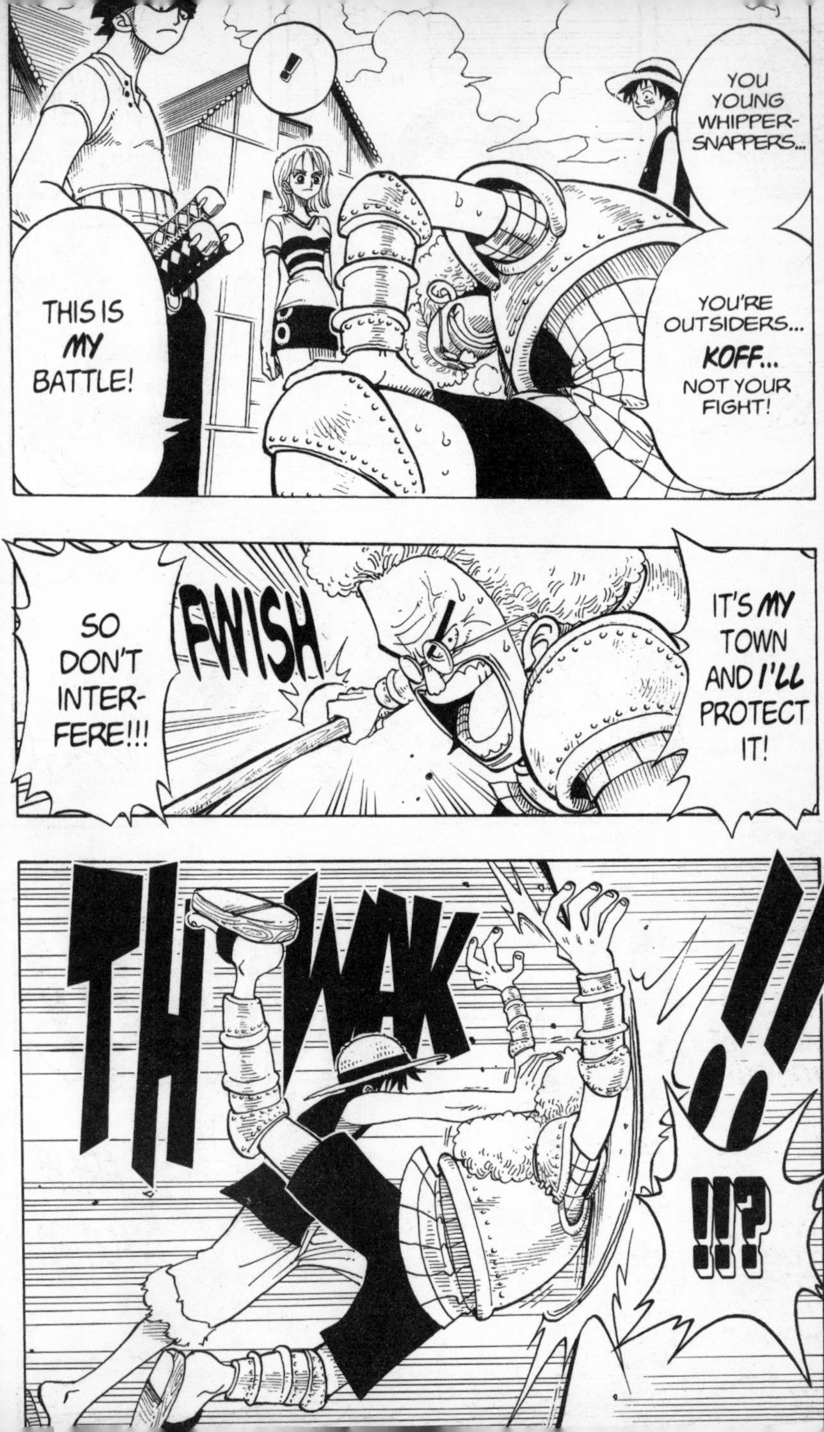
YOU YOUNG WHIPPER-SNAPPERS...
YOU'RE OUTSIDERS... KOFF... NOT YOUR FIGHT!
!
THIS IS MY BATTLE!
IT'S MY TOWN AND I'LL PROTECT IT!
FWISH
SO DON'T INTER-FERE!!!
!!?
THWAK!!

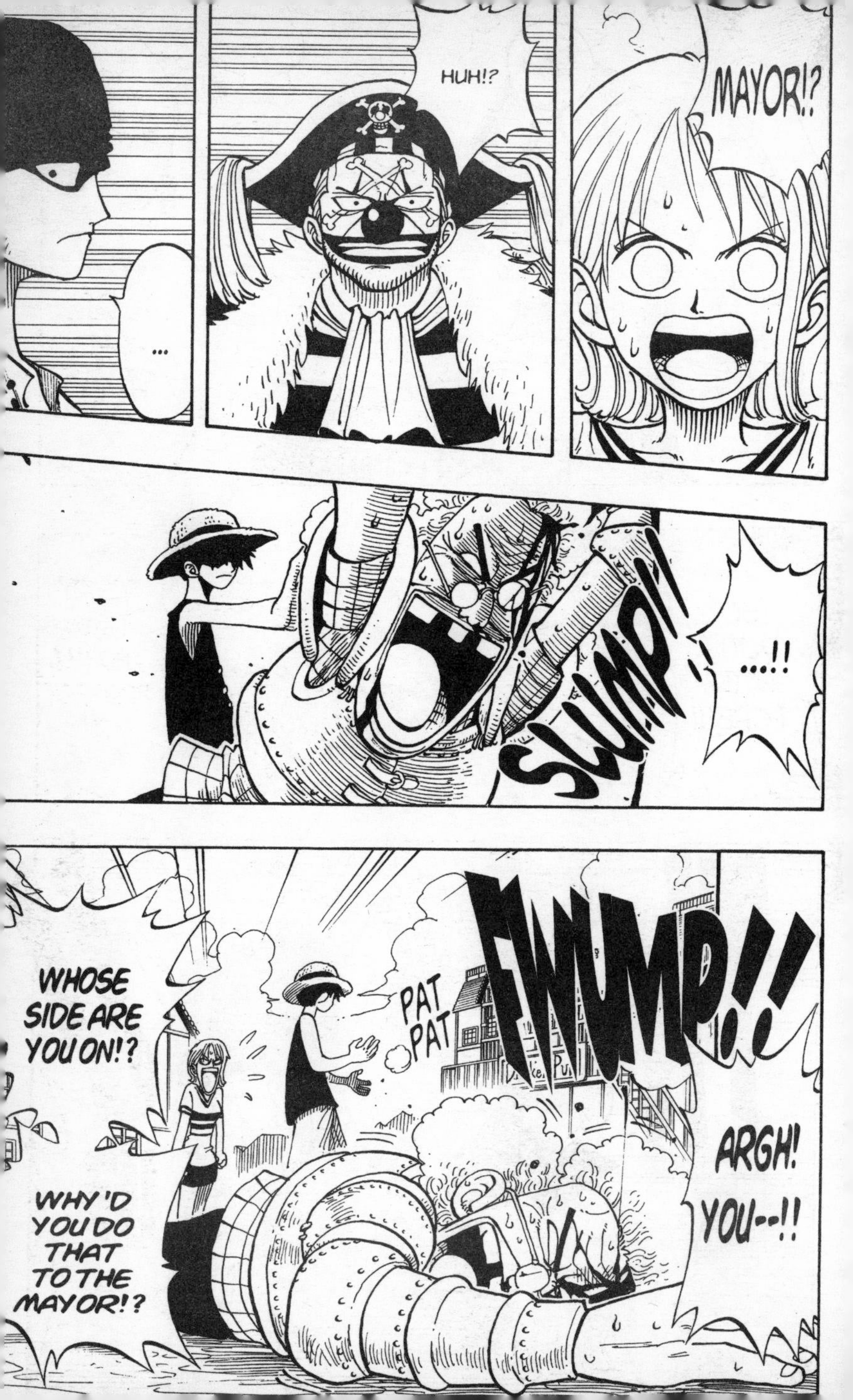
MAYOR!?
HUH!?
...
...!!
SLUMP!!
WHOSE SIDE ARE YOU ON!?
WHY'D YOU DO THAT TO THE MAYOR!?
FWUMP!!
PAT PAT
ARGH!
YOU--!!

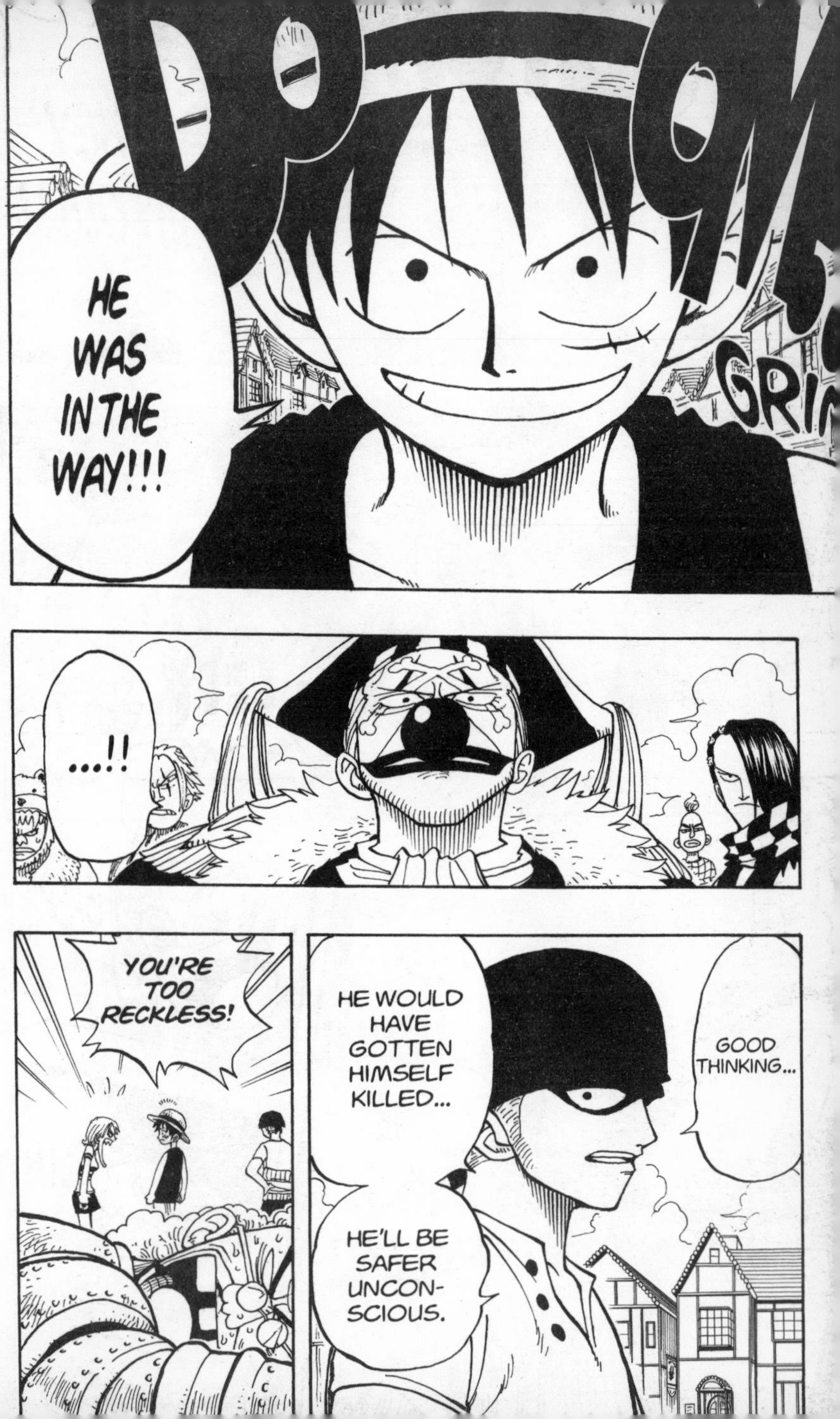
HE WAS IN THE WAY!!!
...!!
GOOD THINKING...
HE WOULD HAVE GOTTEN HIMSELF KILLED...
HE'LL BE SAFER UNCONSCIOUS.
YOU'RE TOO RECKLESS!

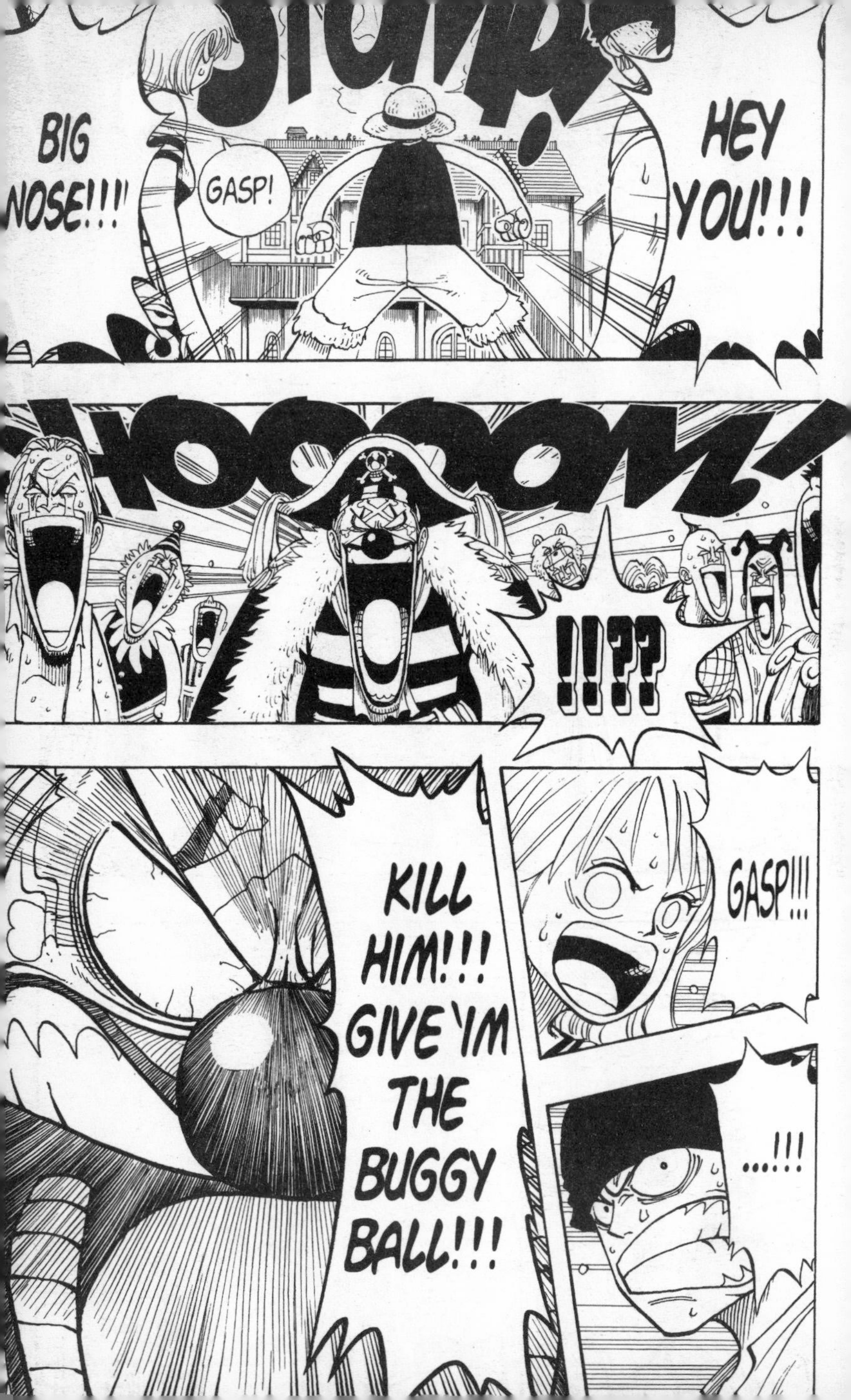

HEY YOU!!!
GASP!
BIG NOSE!!!!
!!??
KILL HIM!!! GIVE 'IM THE BUGGY BALL!!!
GASP!!!
...!!!

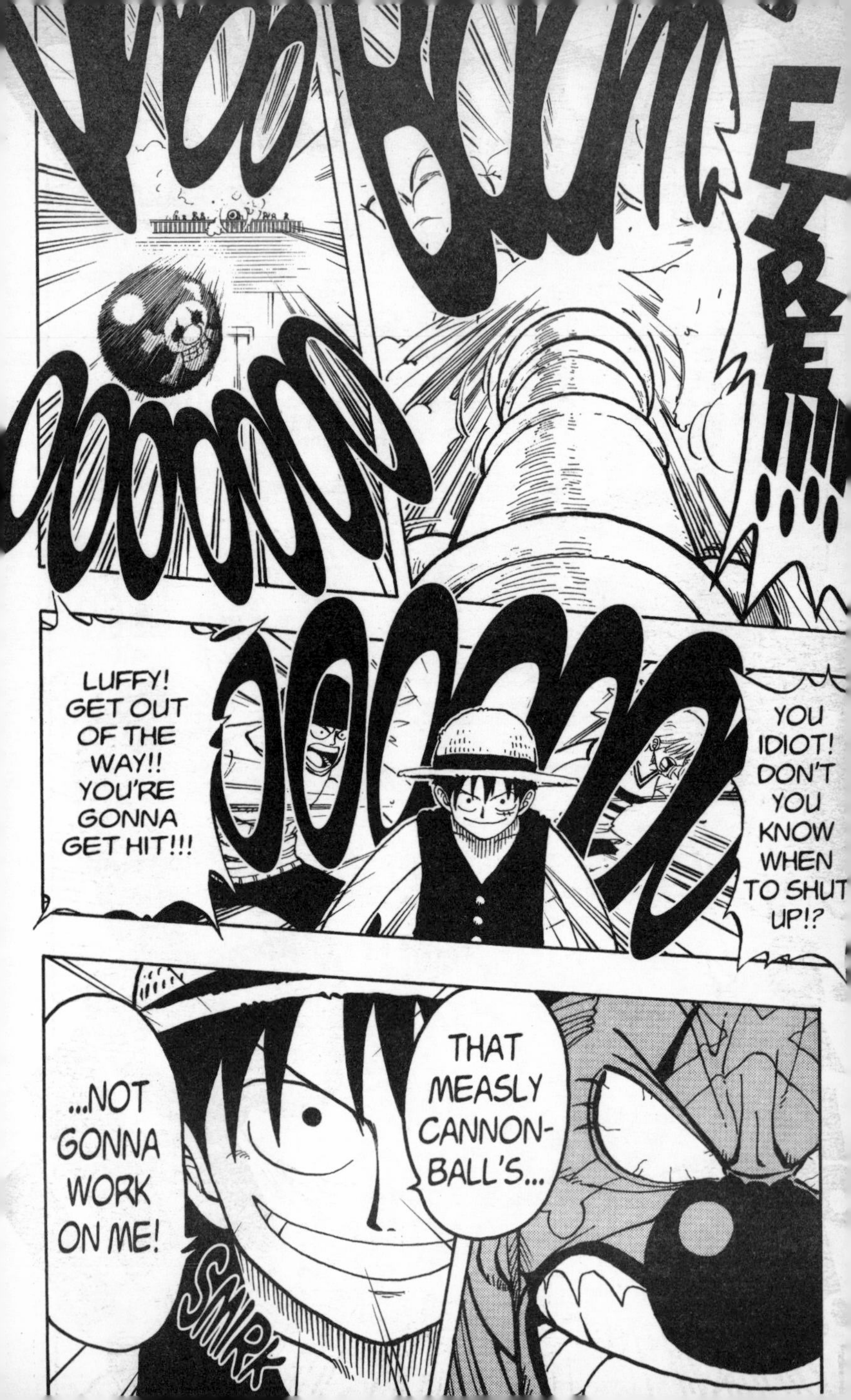
FIRE!!!
YOU IDIOT! DON'T YOU KNOW WHEN TO SHUT UP!?
LUFFY! GET OUT OF THE WAY!! YOU'RE GONNA GET HIT!!!
THAT MEASLY CANNON-BALL'S...
...NOT GONNA WORK ON ME!
SNIRK

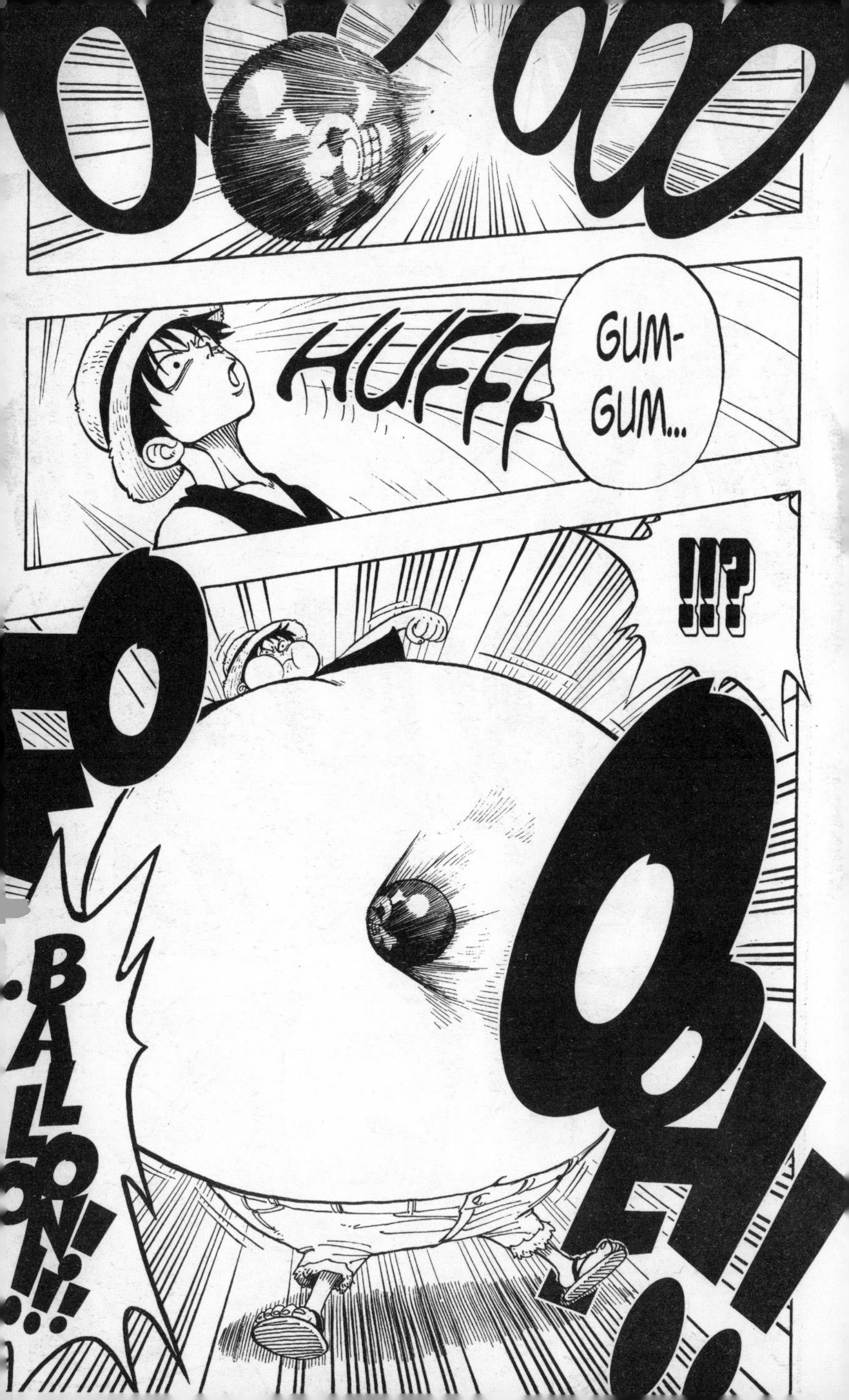
HUFF
GUM-GUM...
!!?
...BALLOON!!...

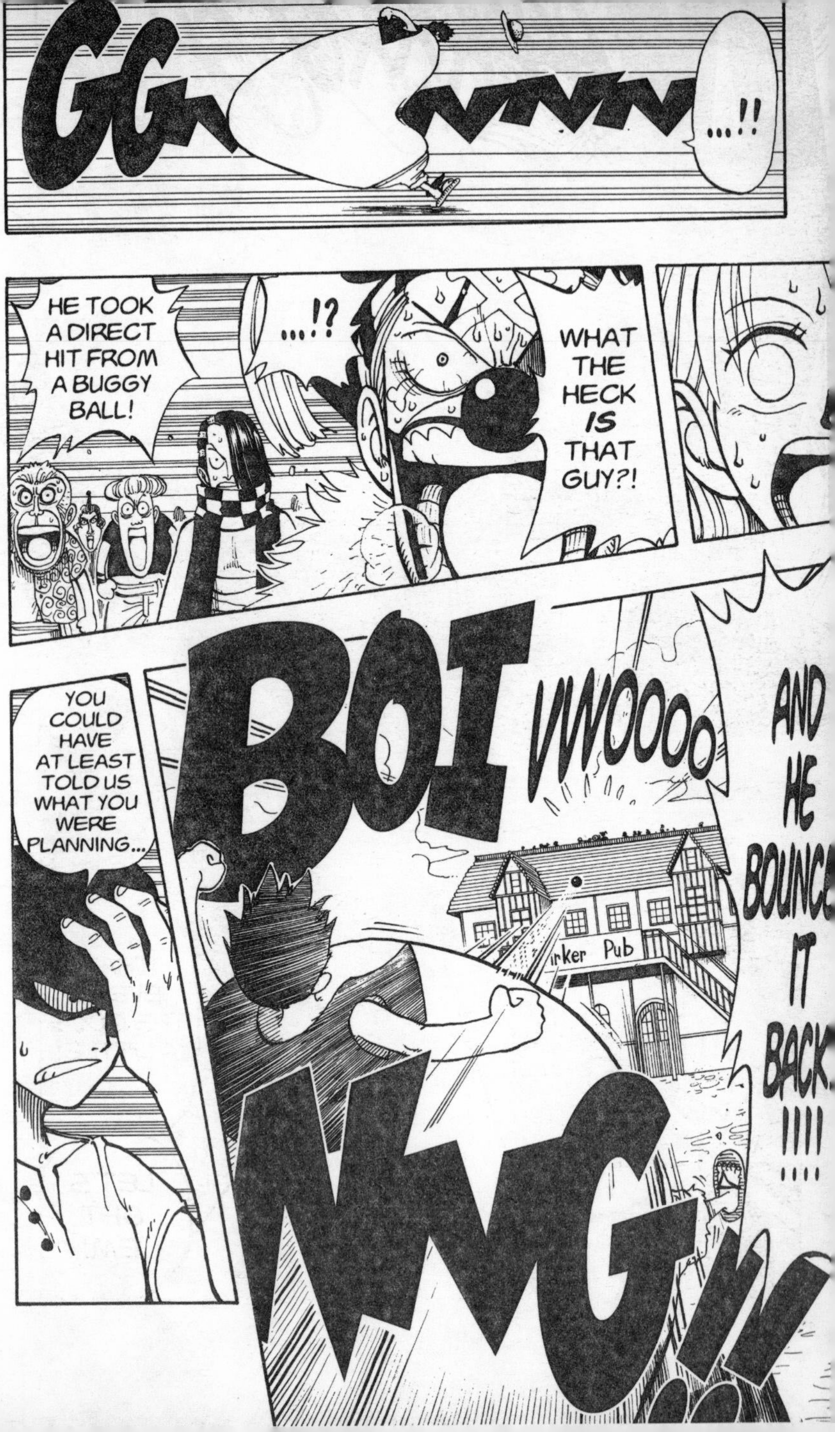
GGGNNNNN
...!!
HE TOOK A DIRECT HIT FROM A BUGGY BALL!
...!?
WHAT THE HECK IS THAT GUY?!
YOU COULD HAVE AT LEAST TOLD US WHAT YOU WERE PLANNING...
BOI
VWOOOO
AND HE BOUNCE IT BACK!!!!
NNG
rker Pub

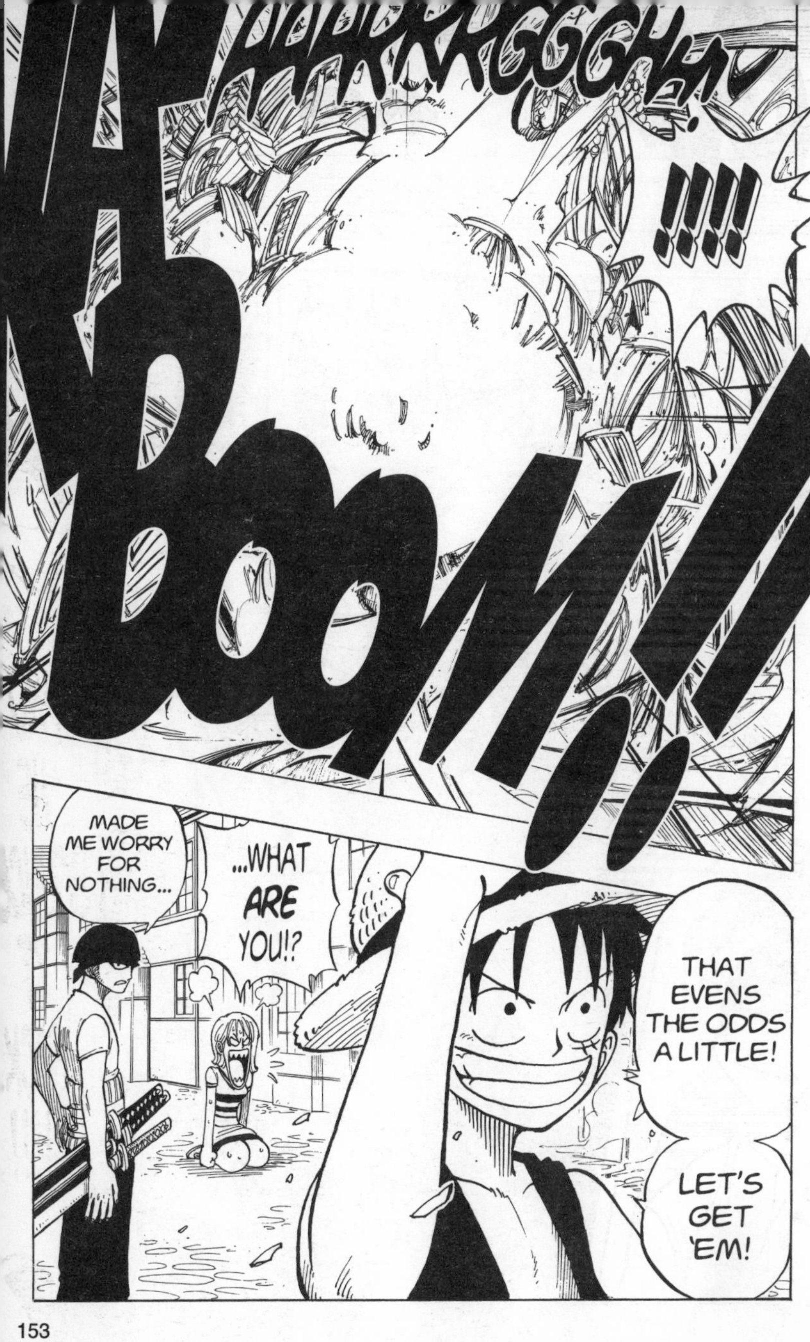
BOOM!!
THAT EVENS THE ODDS A LITTLE!
LET'S GET 'EM!
...WHAT ARE YOU!?
MADE ME WORRY FOR NOTHING...

One Piece Rough Sketch!

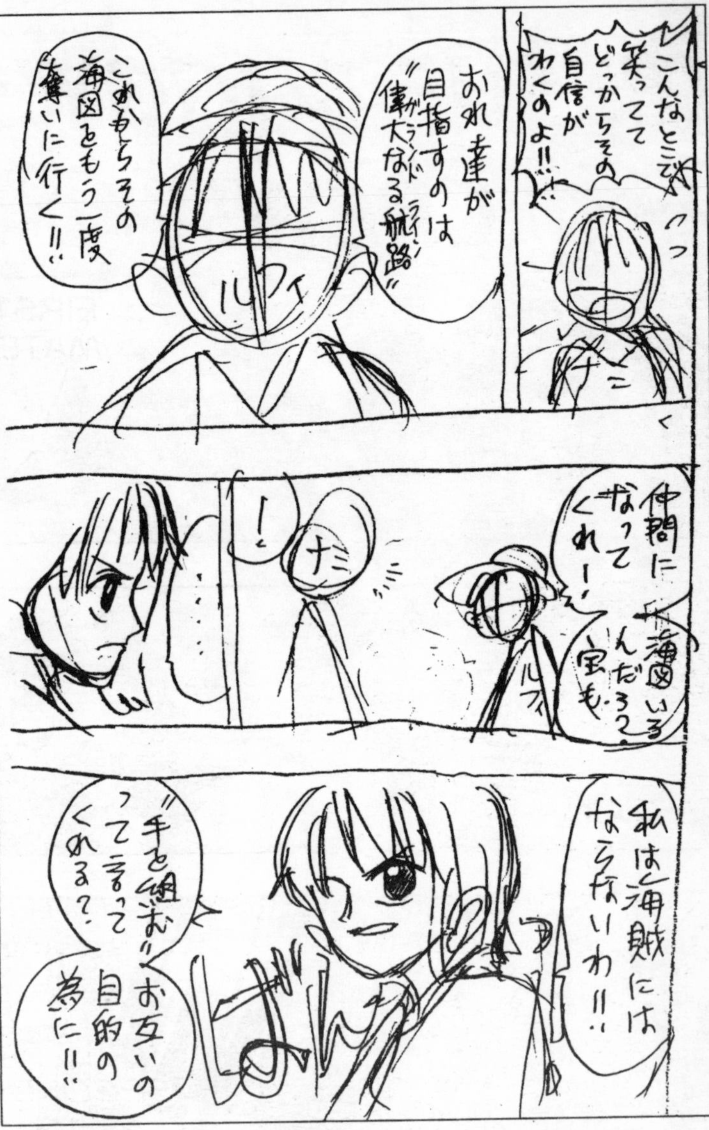
こんなとこで笑っててどっからその自信がわくのよ!!
ナミ
おれ達が目指すのは"偉大なる航路(グランドライン)"
ルフィ
これからその海図をもう一度奪いに行く!!
仲間になってくれー!
海図いるんだろ? 宝も
ルフィ
ナミ
!
……
私は海賊にはならないわ!!
"手を組む"って言ってくれる?
お互いの目的の為に!!

Chapter 16:
VERSUS BUGGY'S CREW!

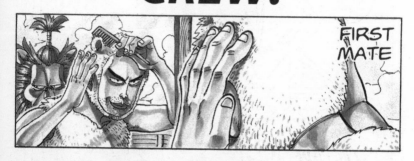

FIRST MATE

CAPTAIN

SECOND MATE

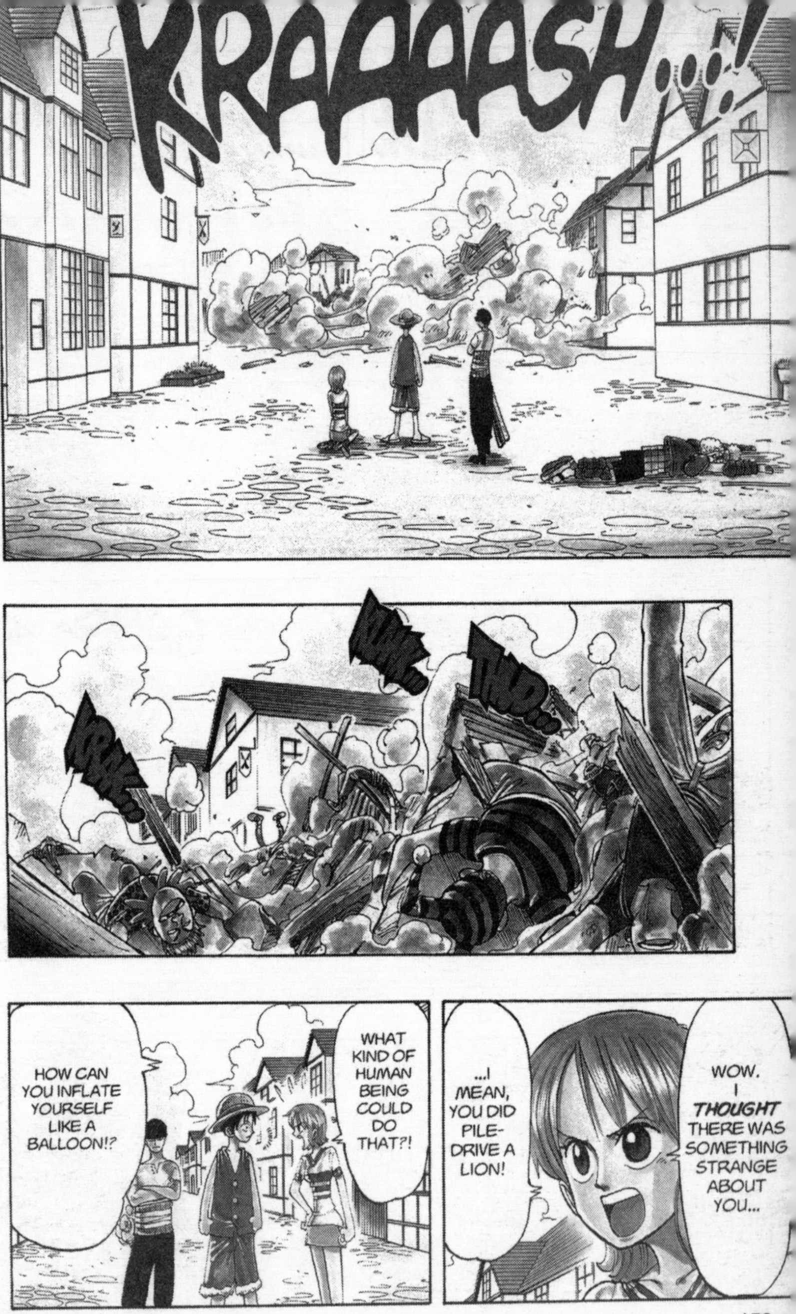
KRAAAASH...!!
KRAK...
THUD...
HOW CAN YOU INFLATE YOURSELF LIKE A BALLOON!?
WHAT KIND OF HUMAN BEING COULD DO THAT?!
WOW. I *THOUGHT* THERE WAS SOMETHING STRANGE ABOUT YOU...
...I MEAN, YOU DID PILE-DRIVE A LION!

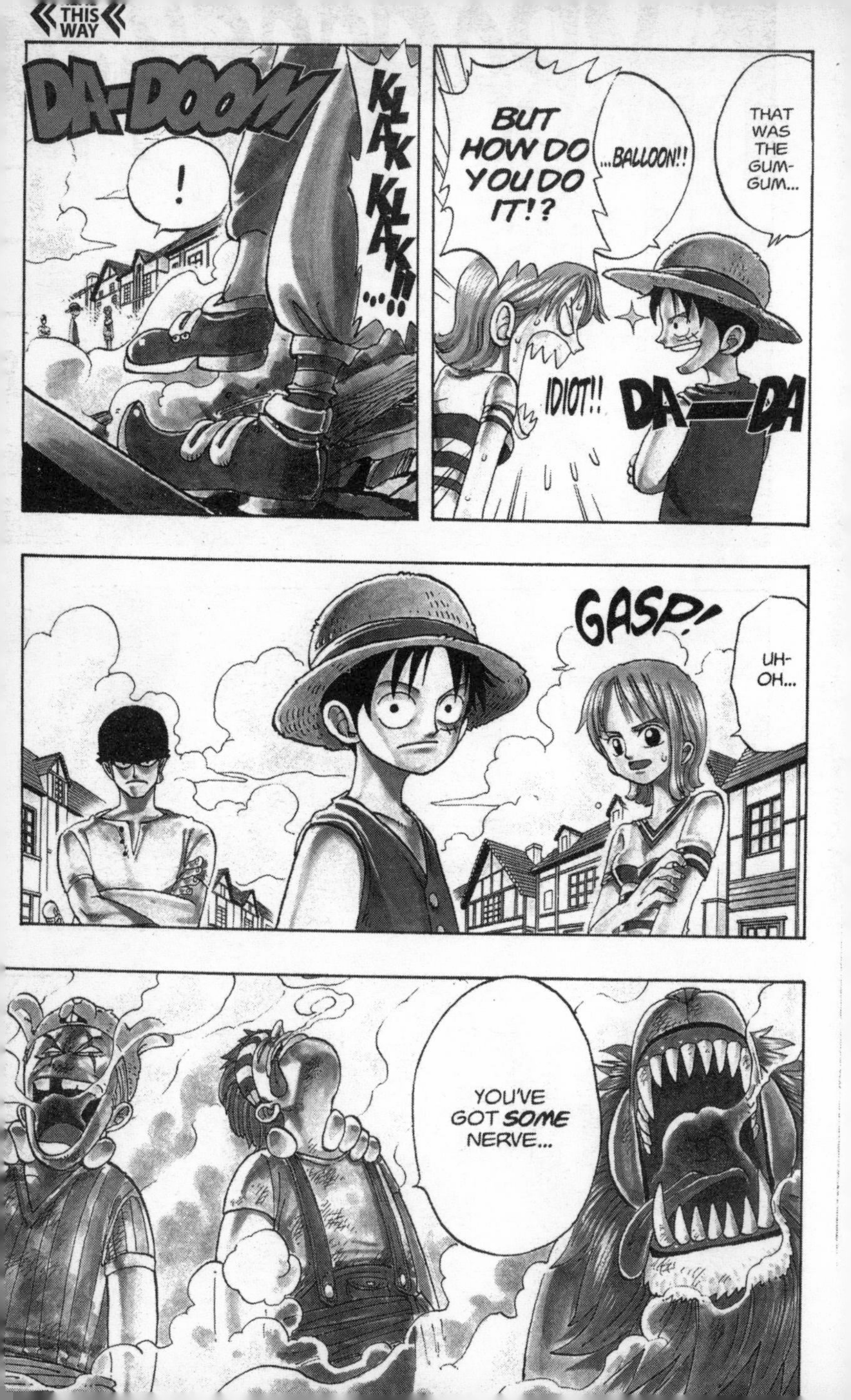
THIS WAY
THAT WAS THE GUM-GUM...
...BALLOON!!
BUT HOW DO YOU DO IT!?
IDIOT!!
DA—DA
DA-DOOM
KLLAK KLLAK!! ...!!
!
UH-OH...
GASP!
YOU'VE GOT SOME NERVE...

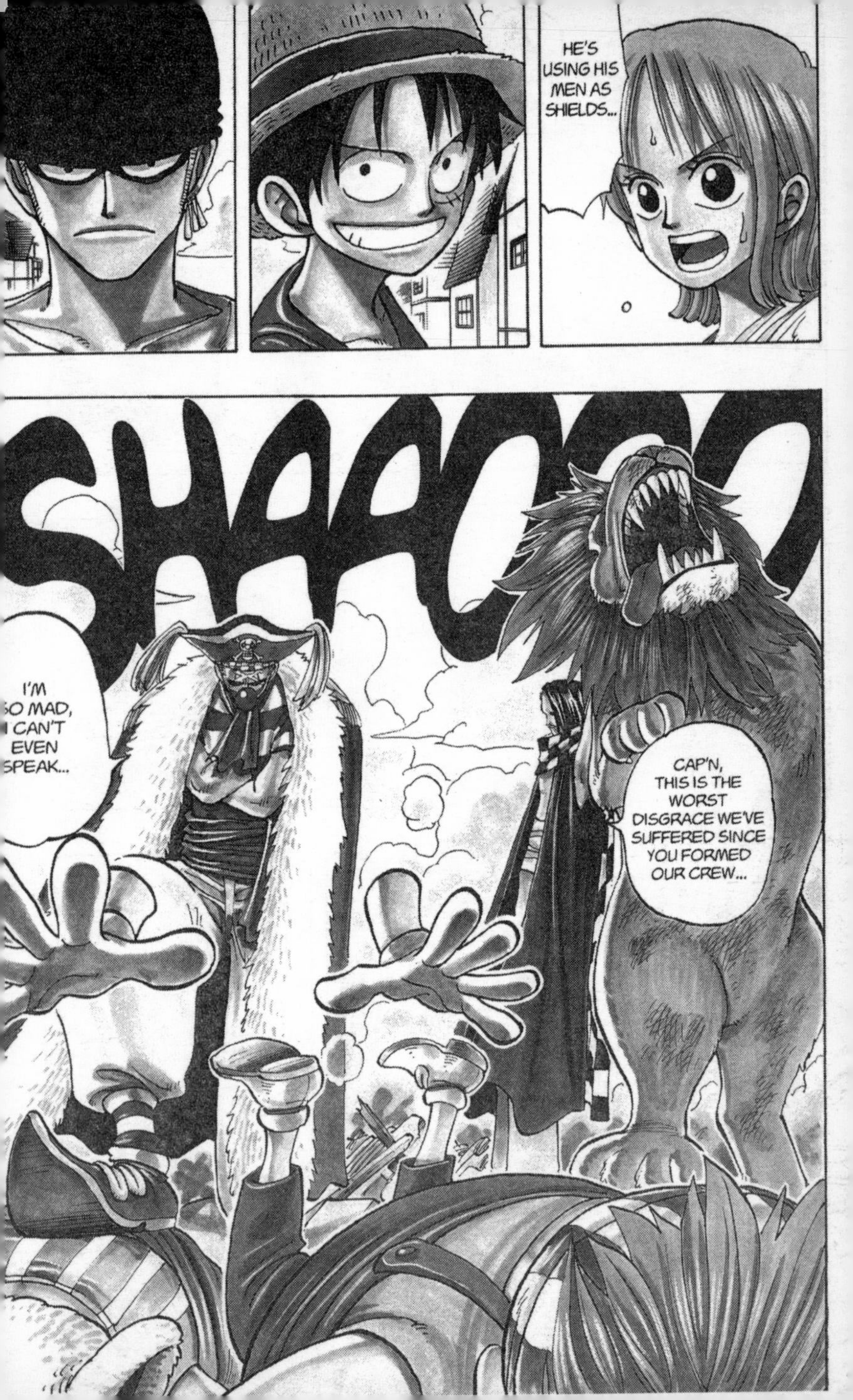

HE'S USING HIS MEN AS SHIELDS...
CAP'N, THIS IS THE WORST DISGRACE WE'VE SUFFERED SINCE YOU FORMED OUR CREW...
I'M SO MAD, I CAN'T EVEN SPEAK...

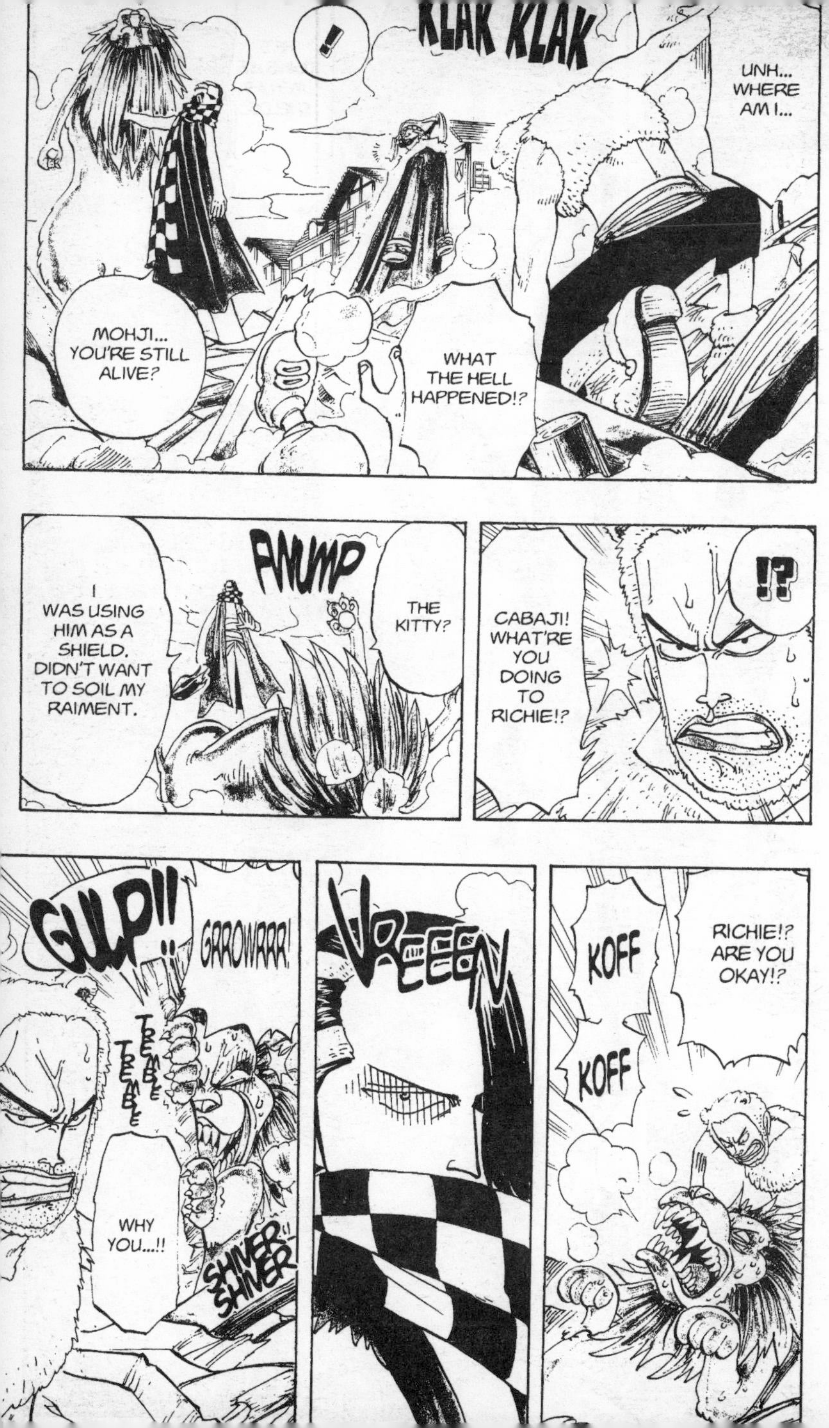
KLAK KLAK
!
UNH... WHERE AM I...
WHAT THE HELL HAPPENED!?
MOHJI... YOU'RE STILL ALIVE?
!?
CABAJI! WHAT'RE YOU DOING TO RICHIE!?
THE KITTY?
FWUMP
I WAS USING HIM AS A SHIELD. DIDN'T WANT TO SOIL MY RAIMENT.
RICHIE!? ARE YOU OKAY!?
KOFF
KOFF
GULP!!
GRROWARRR!
TREMBLE TREMBLE
WHY YOU...!!
SHIVER SHIVER

GASP! IT'S THE KID IN THE STRAW HAT!! CAP'N BUGGY, WATCH OUT FOR HIM!!

HE'S GOT SPECIAL POWERS FROM EATING THE DEVIL FRUIT-- JUST LIKE YOU!!! HE'S A RUBBER MAN!!!

MOHJI, IF YOU **KNEW** THAT...

HAH...

GRAB

THAT'S WHY MY BUGGY BALL BOUNCED OFF OF HIM!

THE DEVIL FRUIT!!!

YEP... SEE?

RUBBER MAN!?

WOING

I TRIED TO!

WOING

WHY DIDN'T YOU TELL ME!?

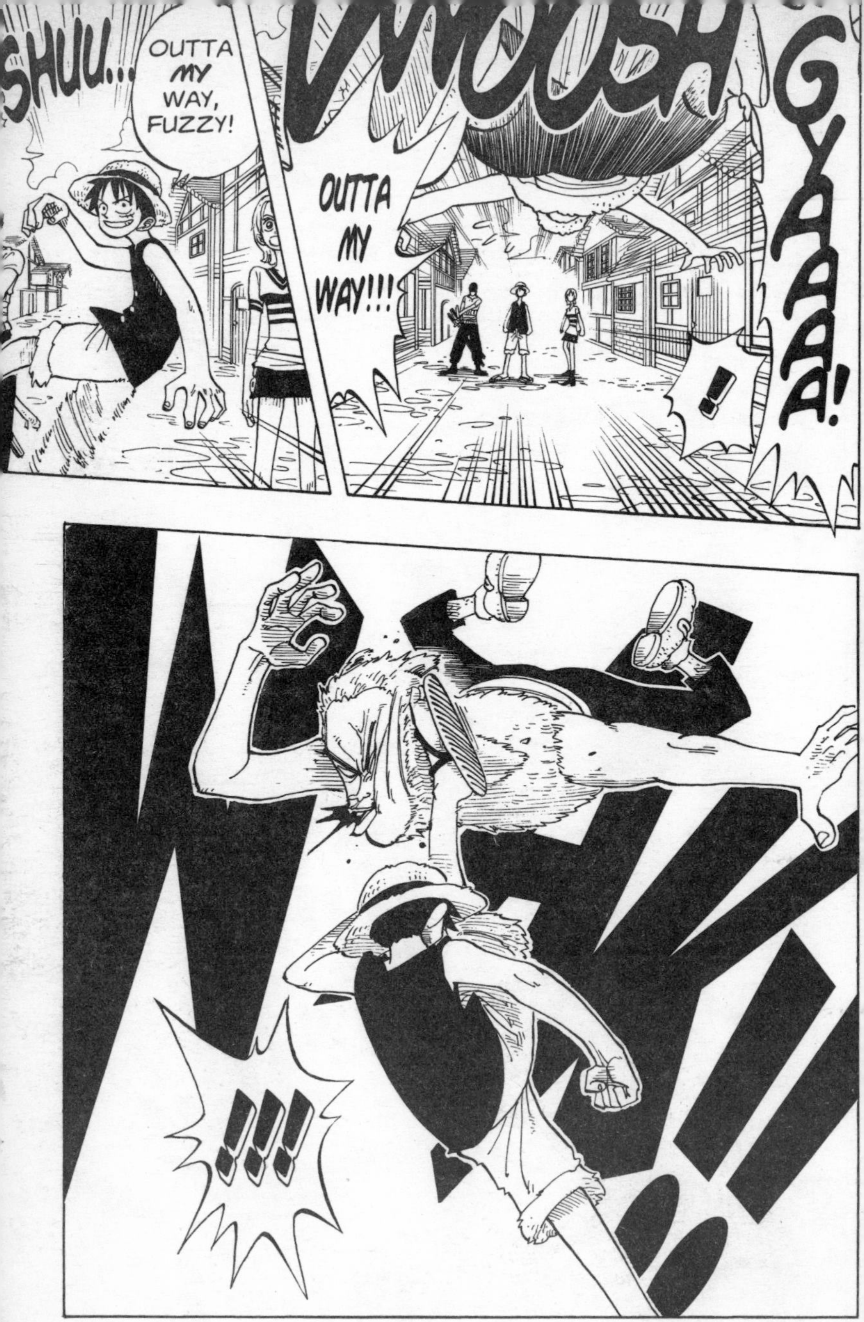
WHOOSH
GYAAAA!
OUTTA MY WAY!!!
!
SHUU...
OUTTA MY WAY, FUZZY!
!!!

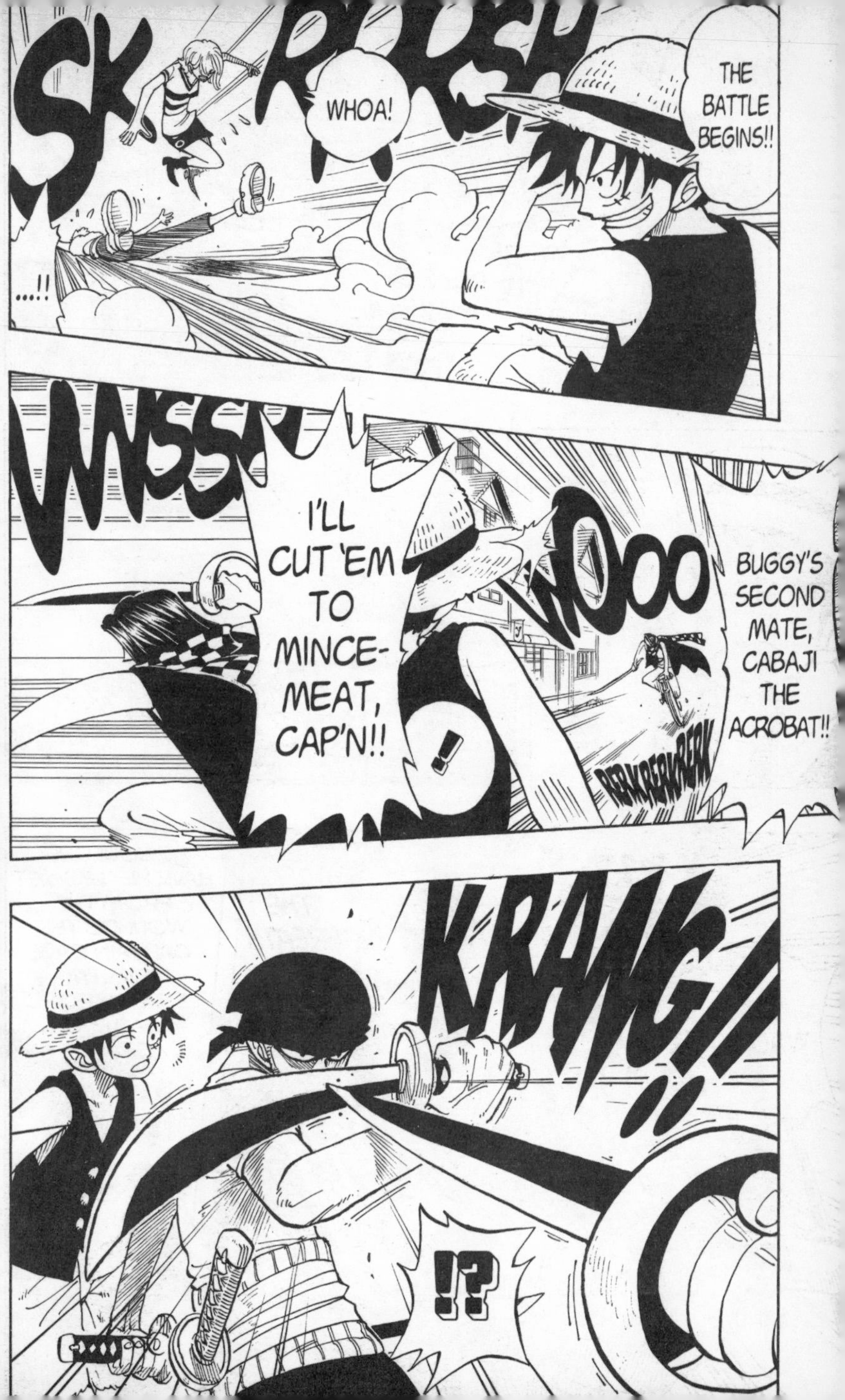
WHOA!
THE BATTLE BEGINS!!
...!!
I'LL CUT 'EM TO MINCE-MEAT, CAP'N!!
WOOO
!
BUGGY'S SECOND MATE, CABAJI THE ACROBAT!!
RERKRERKRERK
KRANG!!
!?

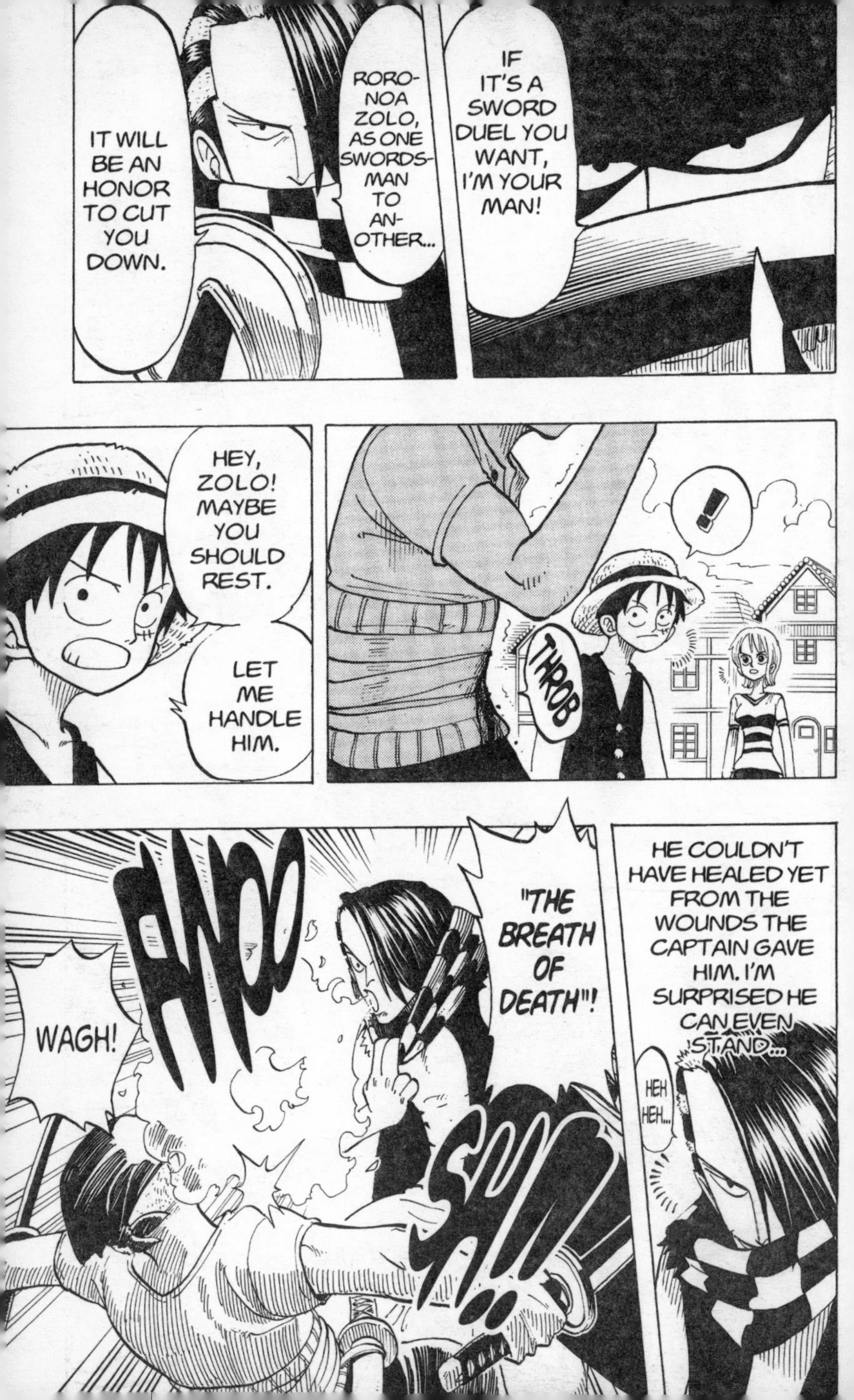

RORONOA ZOLO, AS ONE SWORDSMAN TO ANOTHER...
IT WILL BE AN HONOR TO CUT YOU DOWN.
IF IT'S A SWORD DUEL YOU WANT, I'M YOUR MAN!
HEY, ZOLO! MAYBE YOU SHOULD REST.
LET ME HANDLE HIM.
THROB
!
WAGH!
"THE BREATH OF DEATH"!
HE COULDN'T HAVE HEALED YET FROM THE WOUNDS THE CAPTAIN GAVE HIM. I'M SURPRISED HE CAN EVEN STAND...
HEH HEH...

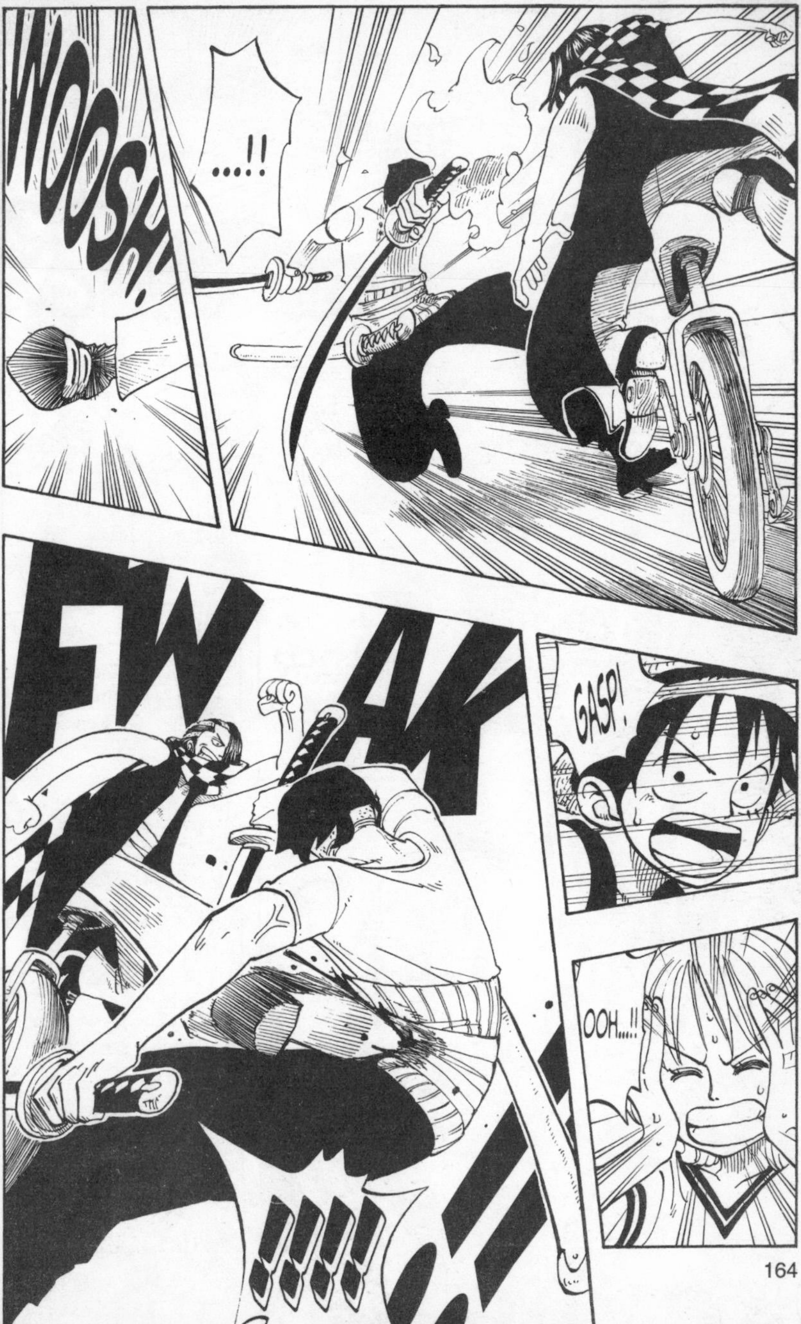
...!!
WOOSH!!
GASP!
OOH...!!
FWAK!!!!

READ THIS WAY

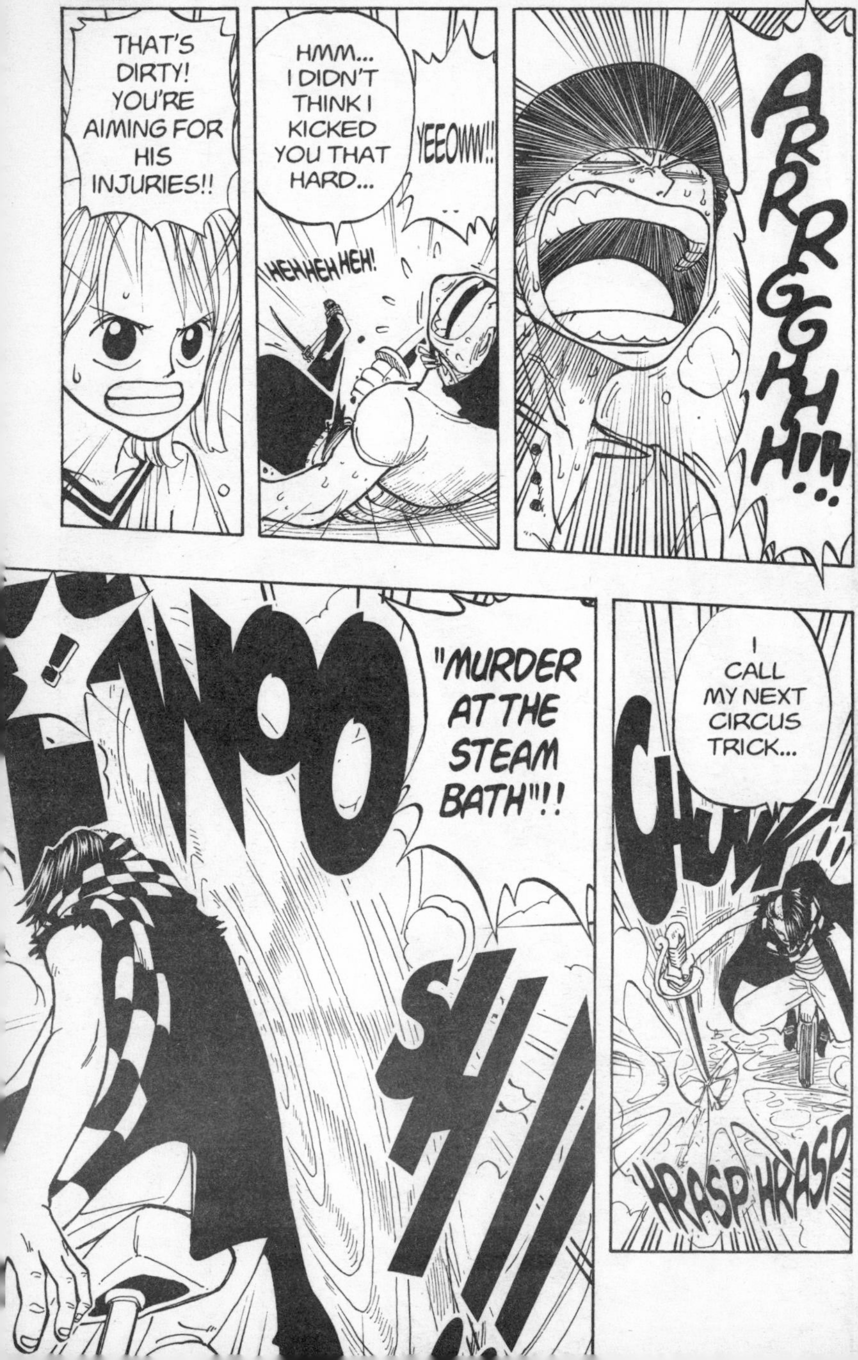
ARRRGGHHH!!
HMM... I DIDN'T THINK I KICKED YOU THAT HARD...
YEEOWW!!
HEHHEHHEH!
THAT'S DIRTY! YOU'RE AIMING FOR HIS INJURIES!!
I CALL MY NEXT CIRCUS TRICK...
CHUNK!!
HRASP HRASP
"MURDER AT THE STEAM BATH"!!
WOOSH

READ THIS WAY

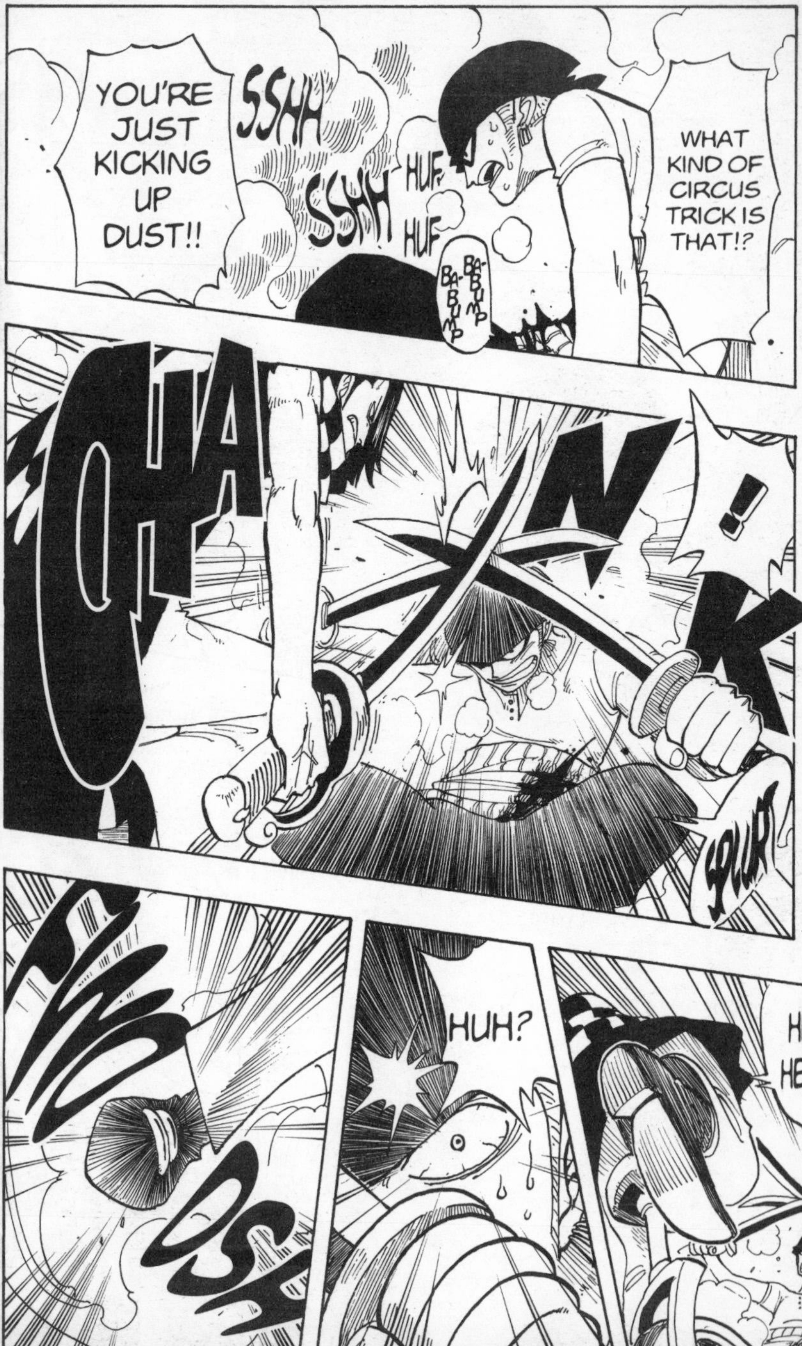

WHAT KIND OF CIRCUS TRICK IS THAT!?
HUF HUF
SSHH SSHH
BA-BUMP BA-BUMP
YOU'RE JUST KICKING UP DUST!!
CHANK!
SPLURT
HEH HEH...
HUH?

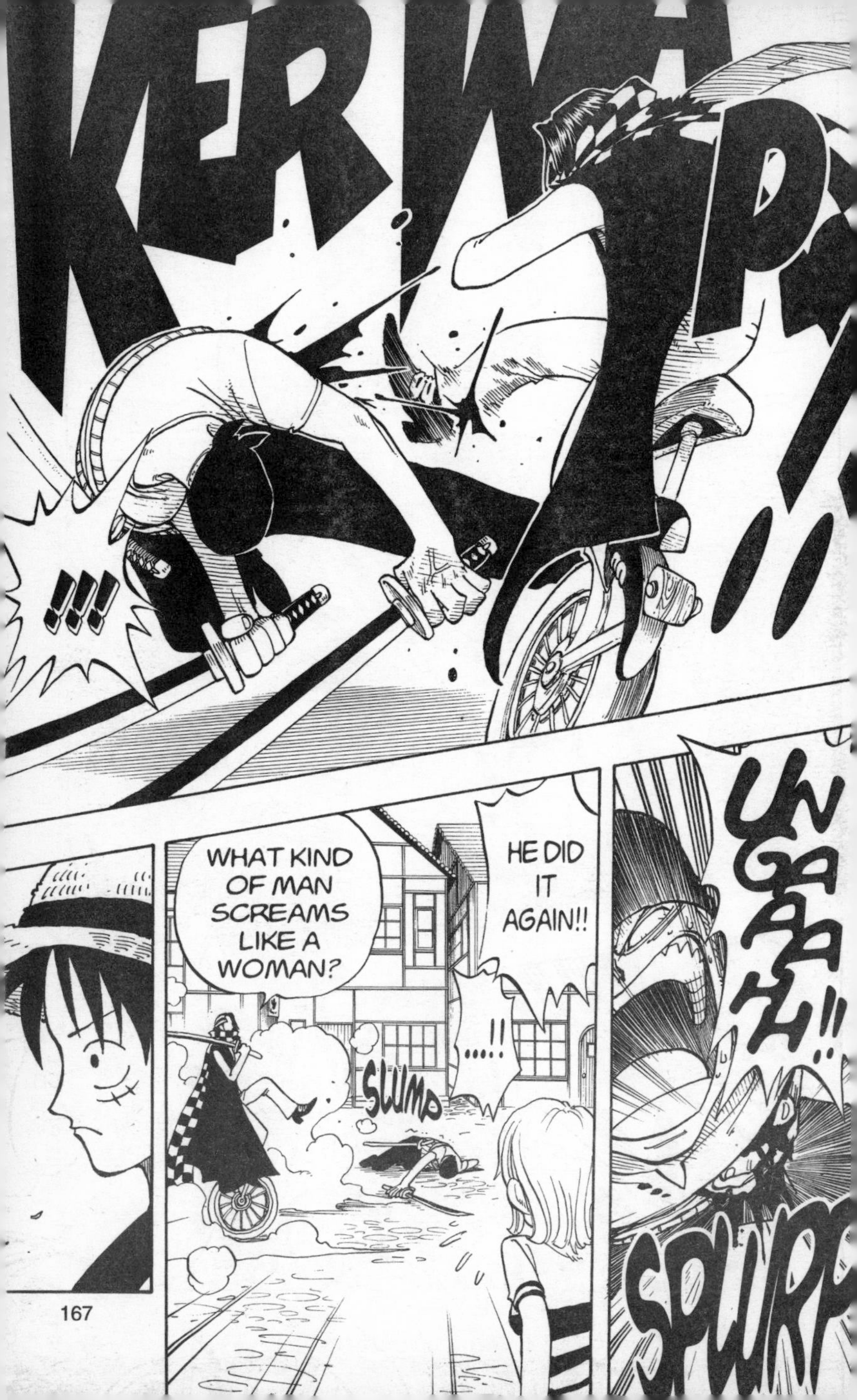
KERWAP!!
!!!
UNGAAAHH!!
SPUR
HE DID IT AGAIN!!
WHAT KIND OF MAN SCREAMS LIKE A WOMAN?
....!!
SLUMP

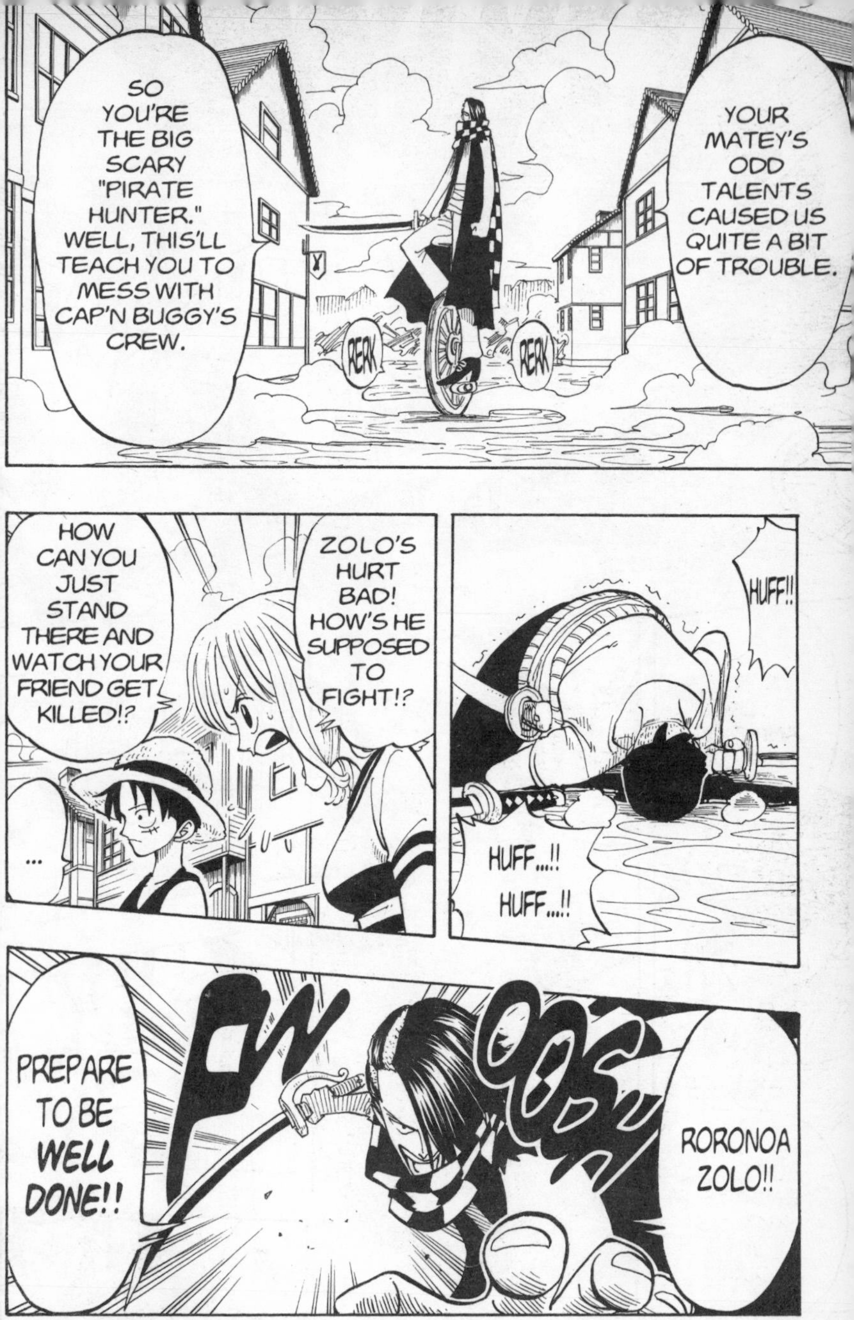
SO YOU'RE THE BIG SCARY "PIRATE HUNTER." WELL, THIS'LL TEACH YOU TO MESS WITH CAP'N BUGGY'S CREW.
RERK
RERK
YOUR MATEY'S ODD TALENTS CAUSED US QUITE A BIT OF TROUBLE.
HOW CAN YOU JUST STAND THERE AND WATCH YOUR FRIEND GET KILLED!?
ZOLO'S HURT BAD! HOW'S HE SUPPOSED TO FIGHT!?
...
HUFF!!
HUFF...!!
HUFF...!!
PREPARE TO BE WELL DONE!!
FWOOSH
RORONOA ZOLO!!

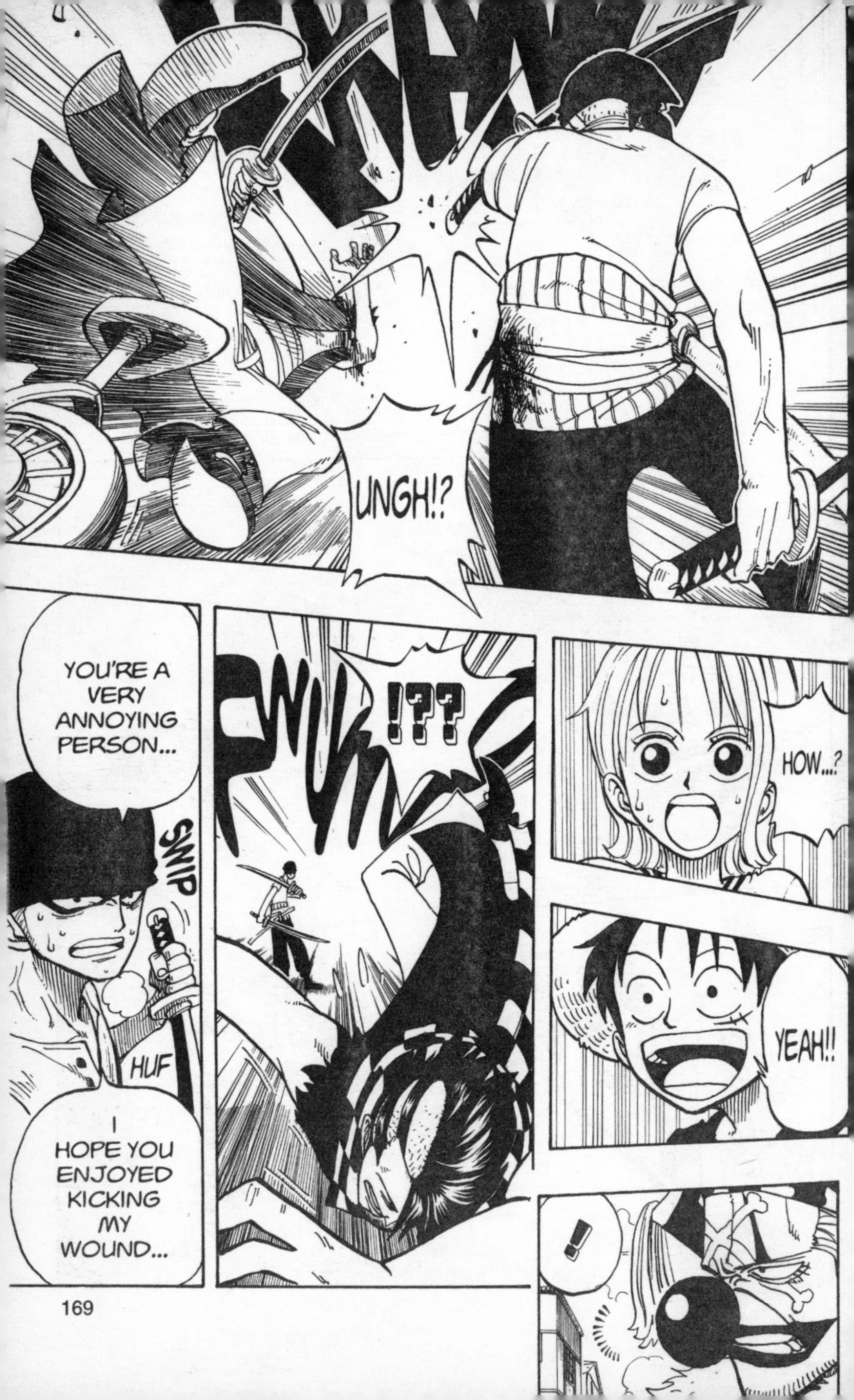
UNGH!?
YOU'RE A VERY ANNOYING PERSON...
SWIP
HUF
I HOPE YOU ENJOYED KICKING MY WOUND...
!??
HOW...?
YEAH!!
!

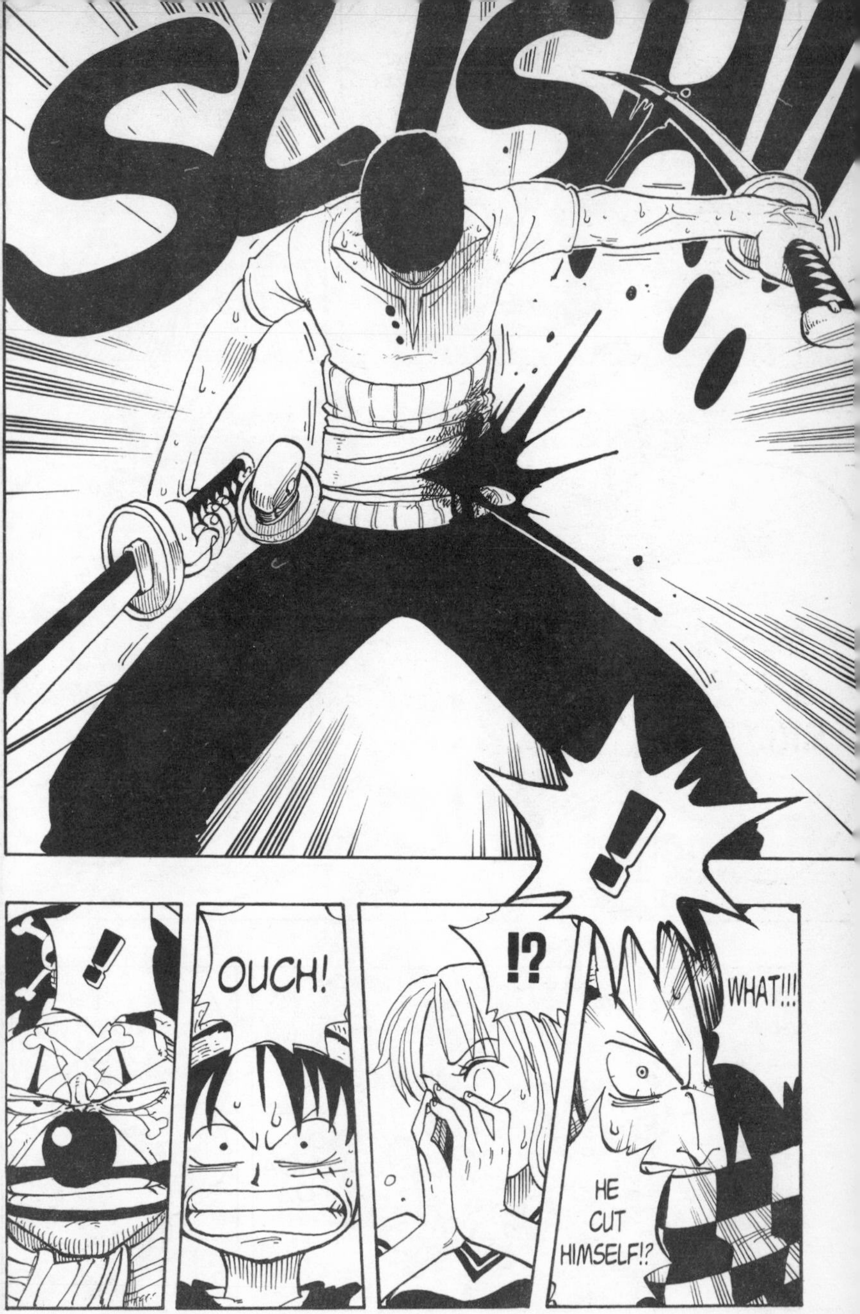
SLISH
!
!
OUCH!
!?
WHAT!!!
HE CUT HIMSELF!?

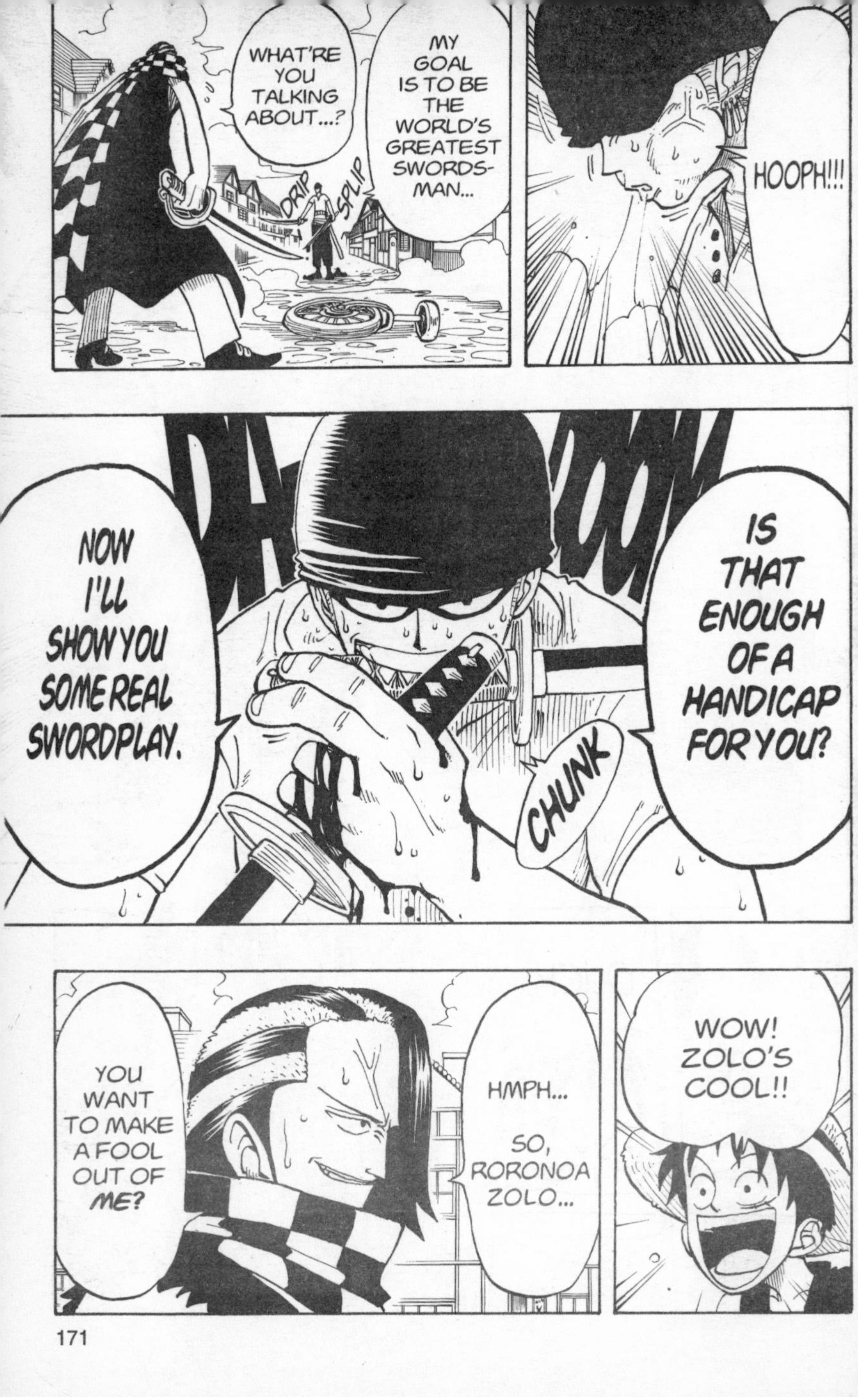
WHAT'RE YOU TALKING ABOUT...?
MY GOAL IS TO BE THE WORLD'S GREATEST SWORDS-MAN...
DRIP
SPLIP
HOOPH!!!
NOW I'LL SHOW YOU SOME REAL SWORDPLAY.
IS THAT ENOUGH OF A HANDICAP FOR YOU?
CHUNK
YOU WANT TO MAKE A FOOL OUT OF *ME*?
HMPH...
SO, RORONOA ZOLO...
WOW! ZOLO'S COOL!!

One Piece Rough Sketch!

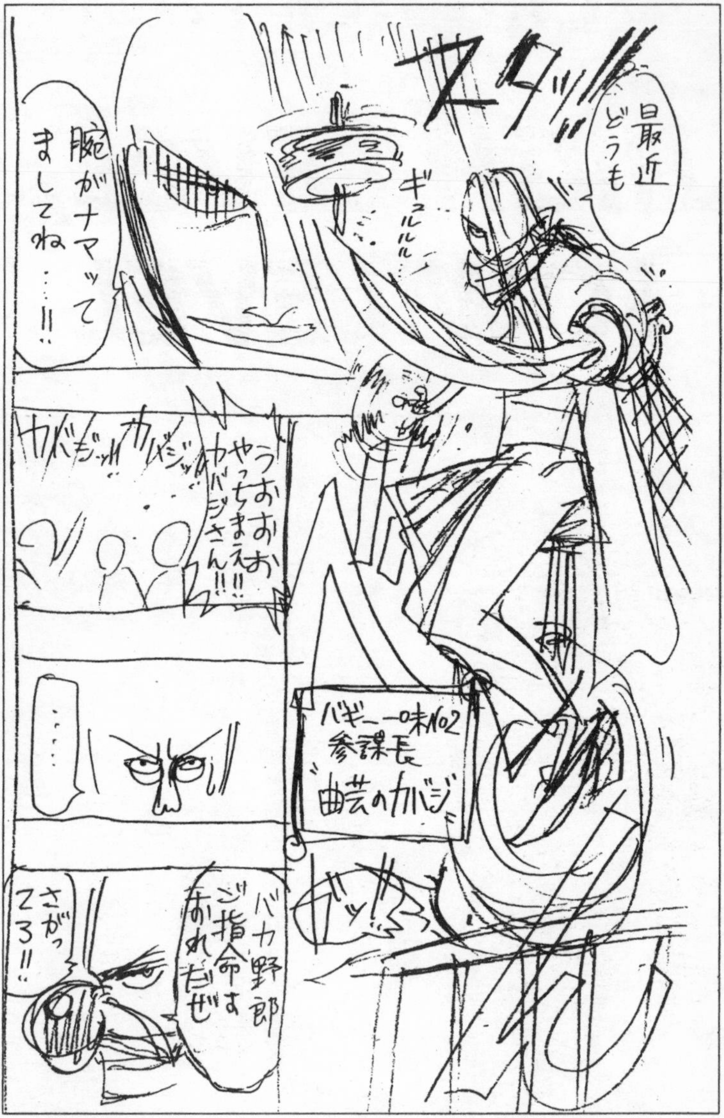
スタッ
最近どうも
ギュルルル…
腕がナマッてましてね……!!
うおおお やっちまえ!! カバジさん!!
カバジッ!! カバジッ!!
バギー一味No2
参謀長
"曲芸のカバジ"
……
バカ野郎 ご指命は おれだぜ
さがってろ!!
ガッ!

Chapter 17:

HIGH LEVEL, LOW LEVEL

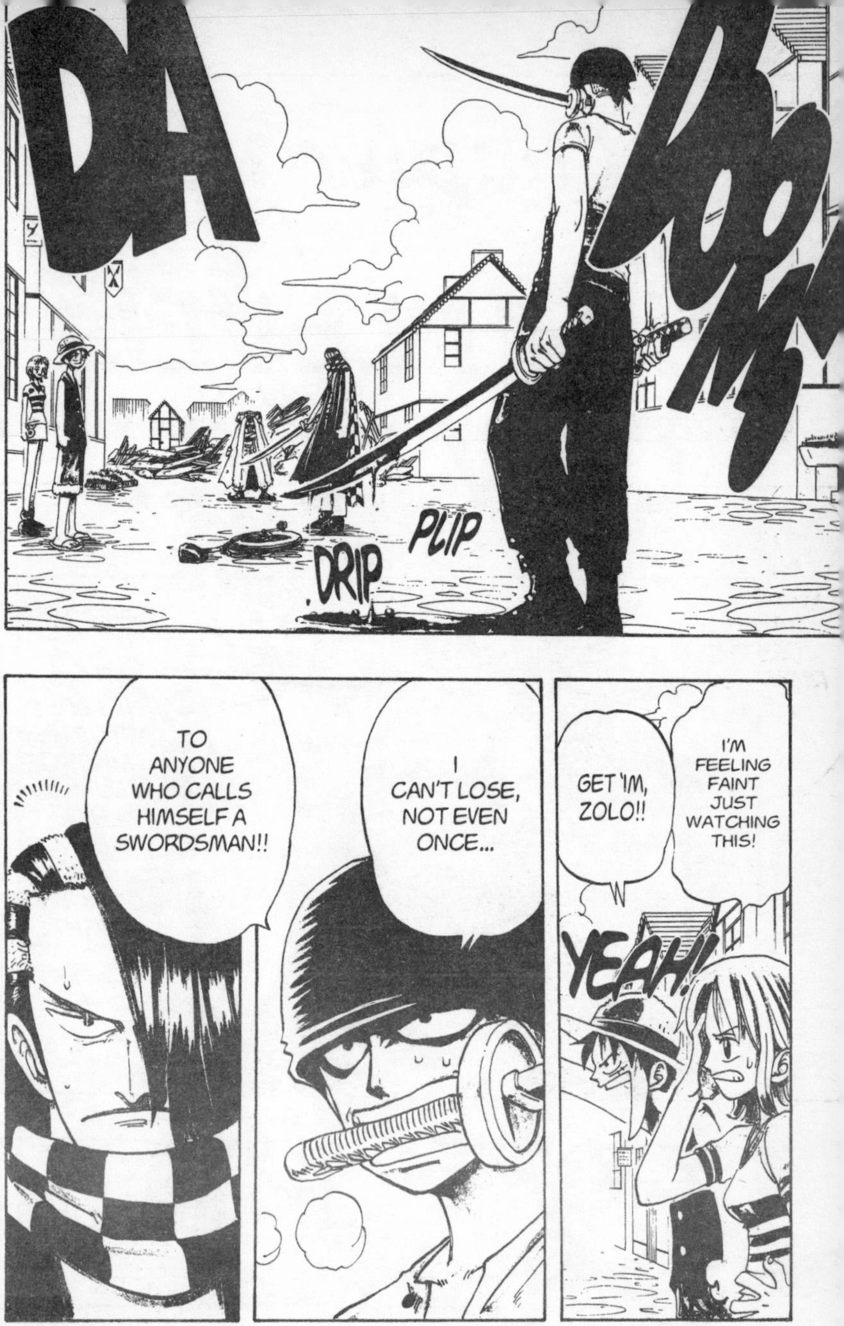
DA
DOOM
PLIP
DRIP
TO ANYONE WHO CALLS HIMSELF A SWORDSMAN!!
I CAN'T LOSE, NOT EVEN ONCE...
I'M FEELING FAINT JUST WATCHING THIS!
GET 'IM, ZOLO!!
YEAH!

READ THIS WAY

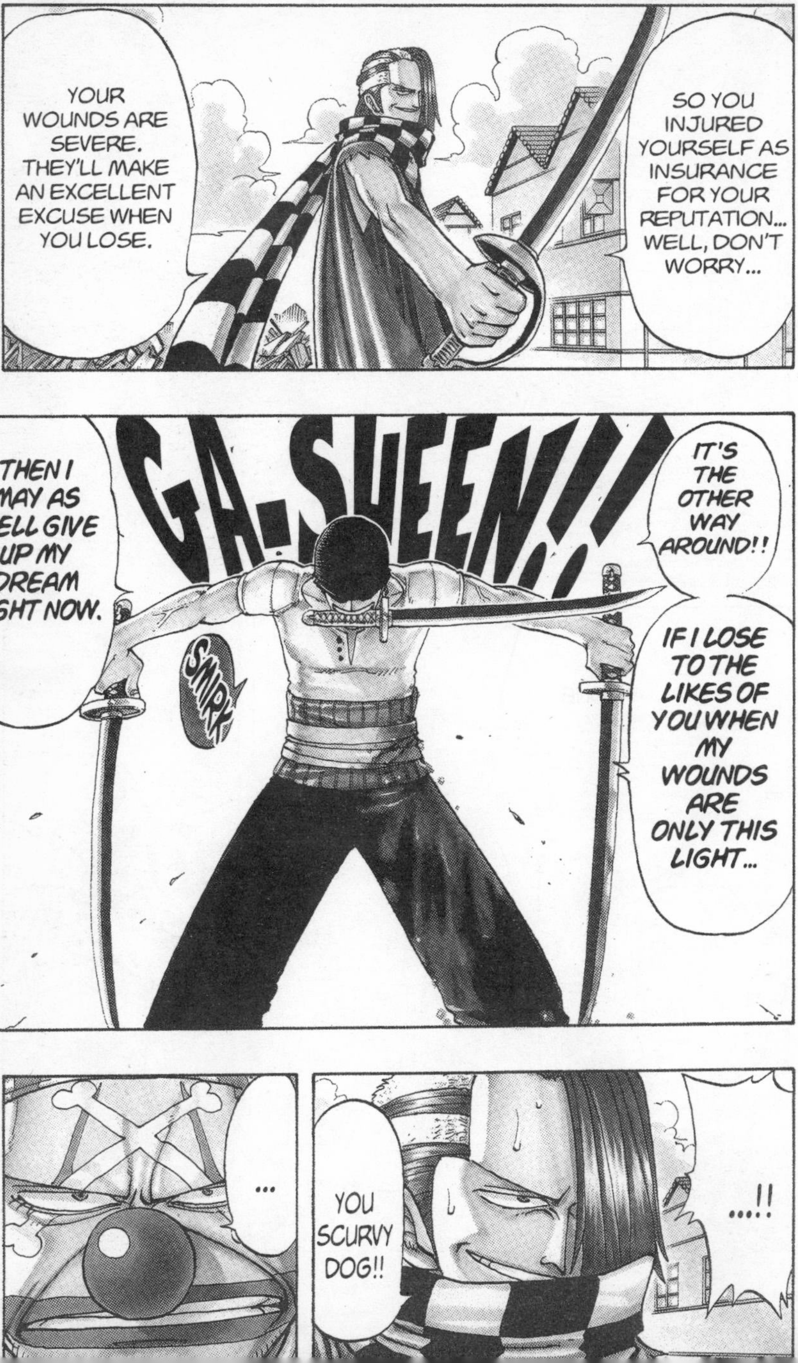
SO YOU INJURED YOURSELF AS INSURANCE FOR YOUR REPUTATION... WELL, DON'T WORRY...
YOUR WOUNDS ARE SEVERE. THEY'LL MAKE AN EXCELLENT EXCUSE WHEN YOU LOSE.
IT'S THE OTHER WAY AROUND!!
IF I LOSE TO THE LIKES OF YOU WHEN MY WOUNDS ARE ONLY THIS LIGHT...
GA-SHEEN!!
SMIRK
THEN I MAY AS WELL GIVE UP MY DREAM RIGHT NOW.
...!!
YOU SCURVY DOG!!
...

READ THIS WAY

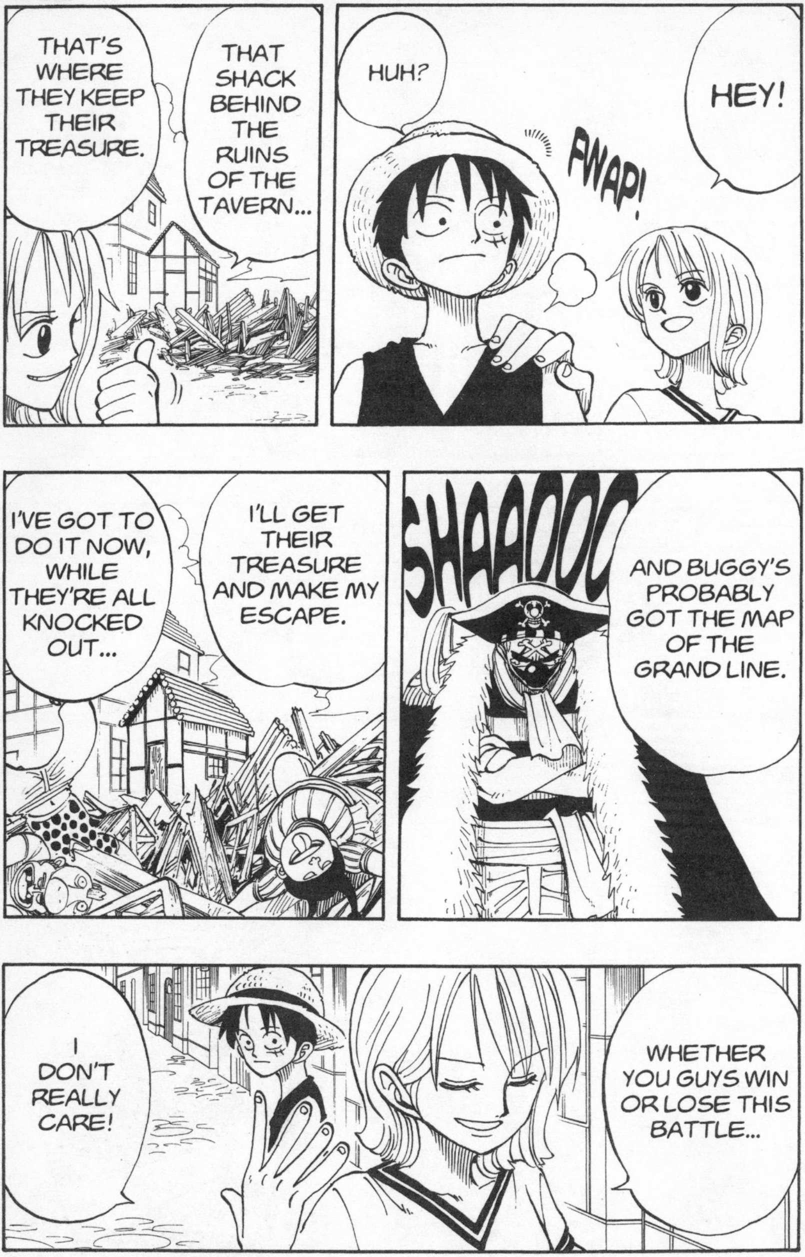
HEY!
HUH?
FWAP!
THAT SHACK BEHIND THE RUINS OF THE TAVERN...
THAT'S WHERE THEY KEEP THEIR TREASURE.
SHAAOOO
AND BUGGY'S PROBABLY GOT THE MAP OF THE GRAND LINE.
I'LL GET THEIR TREASURE AND MAKE MY ESCAPE.
I'VE GOT TO DO IT NOW, WHILE THEY'RE ALL KNOCKED OUT...
WHETHER YOU GUYS WIN OR LOSE THIS BATTLE...
I DON'T REALLY CARE!

READ THIS WAY

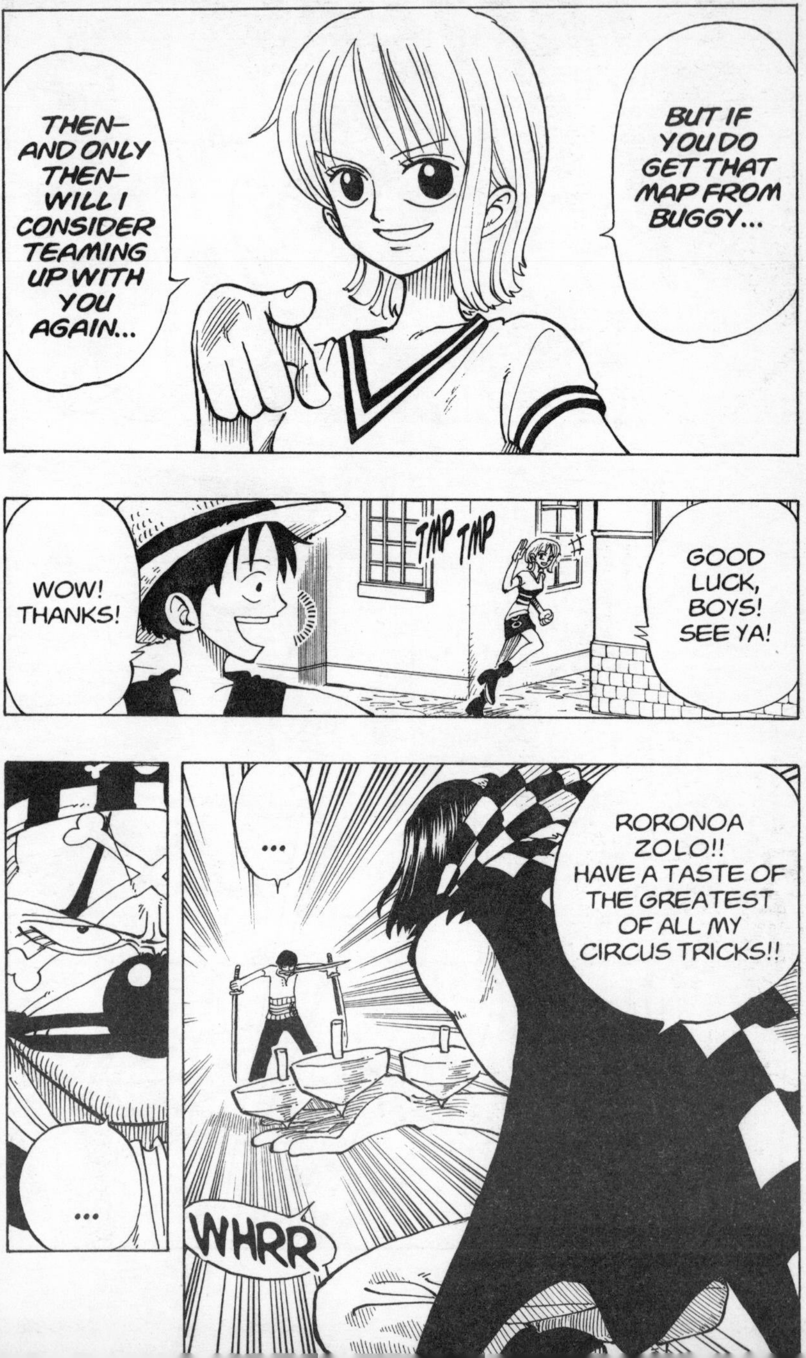
BUT IF YOU DO GET THAT MAP FROM BUGGY...
THEN— AND ONLY THEN— WILL I CONSIDER TEAMING UP WITH YOU AGAIN...
GOOD LUCK, BOYS! SEE YA!
TMP TMP
WOW! THANKS!
RORONOA ZOLO!! HAVE A TASTE OF THE GREATEST OF ALL MY CIRCUS TRICKS!!
...
WHRR
...

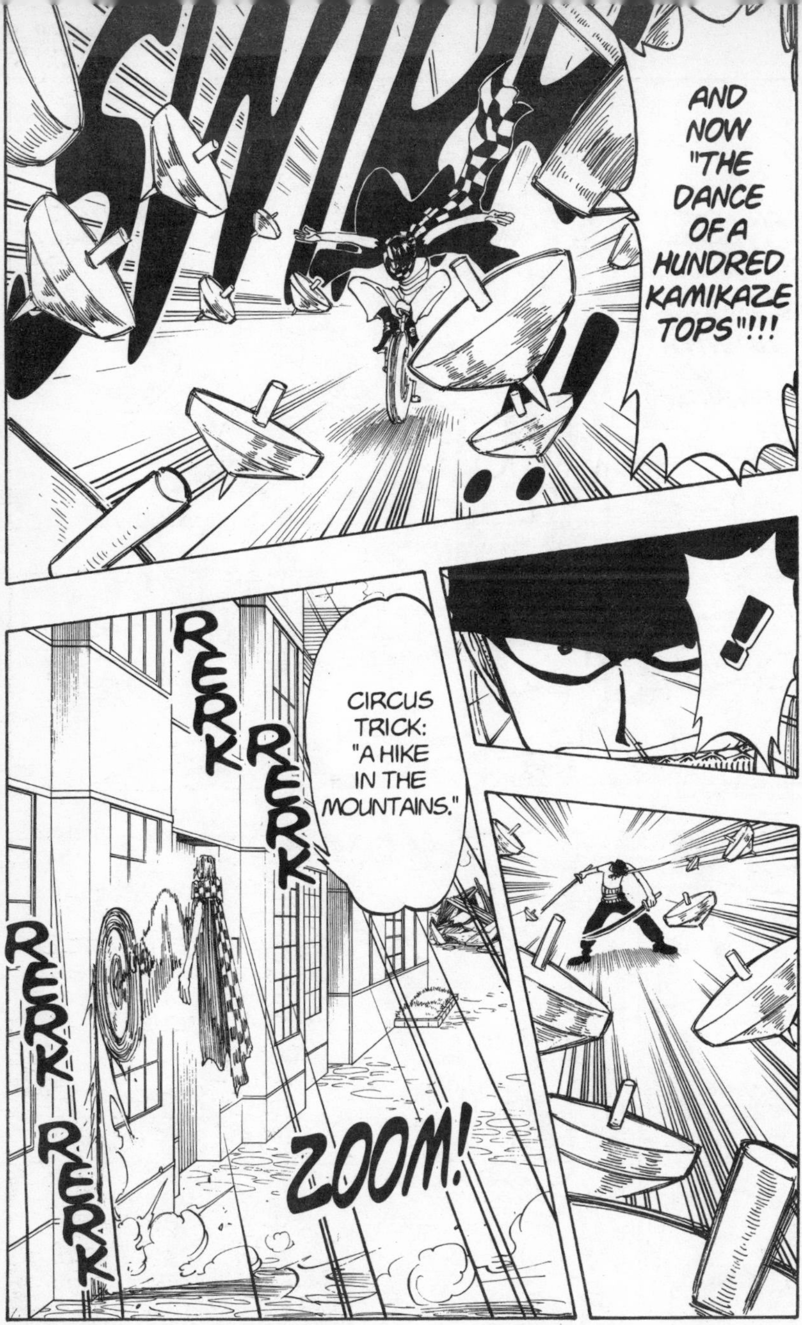
AND NOW "THE DANCE OF A HUNDRED KAMIKAZE TOPS"!!!
!
CIRCUS TRICK: "A HIKE IN THE MOUNTAINS."
RERK RERK
RERK RERK
ZOOM!

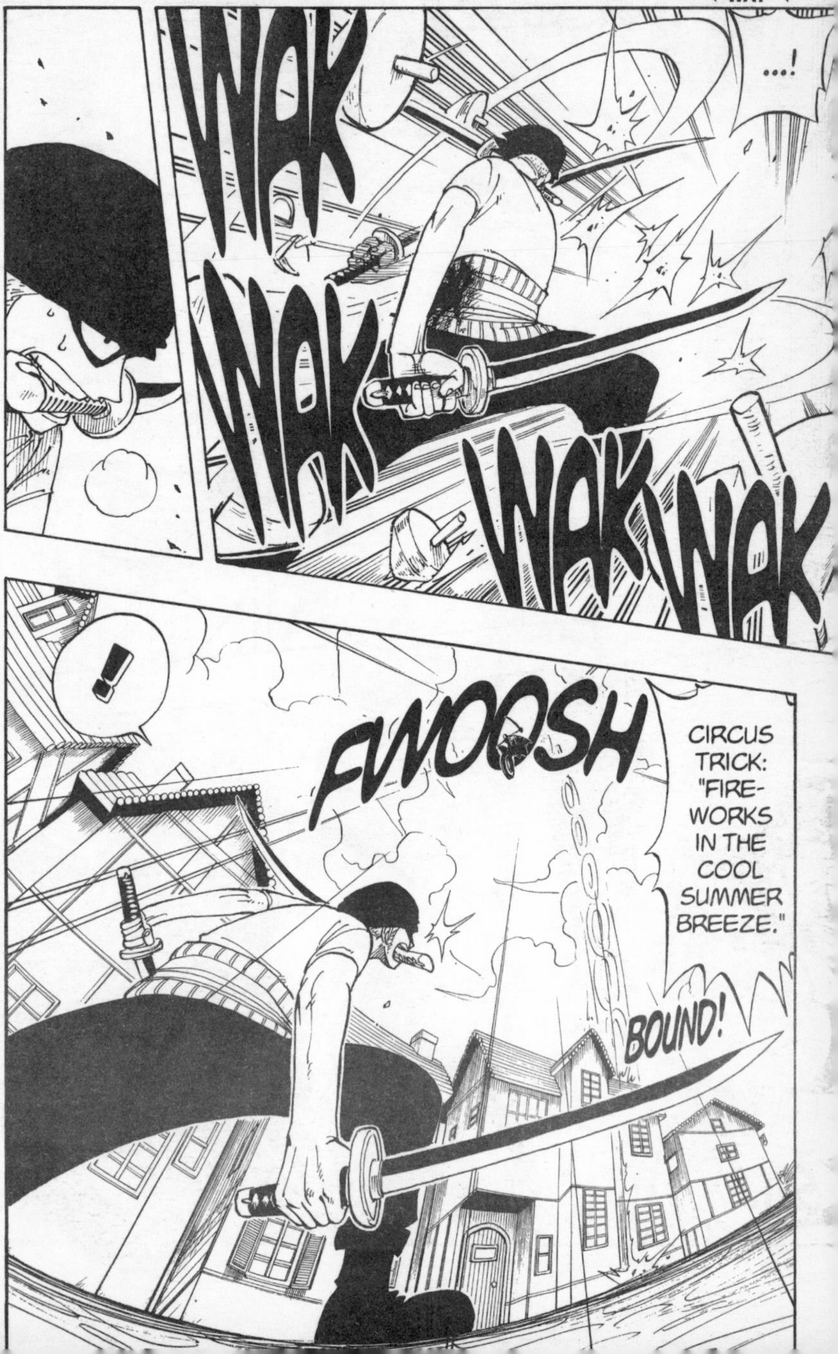
READ THIS WAY
...!
WAK
WAK
WAK
WAK
!
FWOOSH
CIRCUS TRICK: "FIRE-WORKS IN THE COOL SUMMER BREEZE."
BOUND!

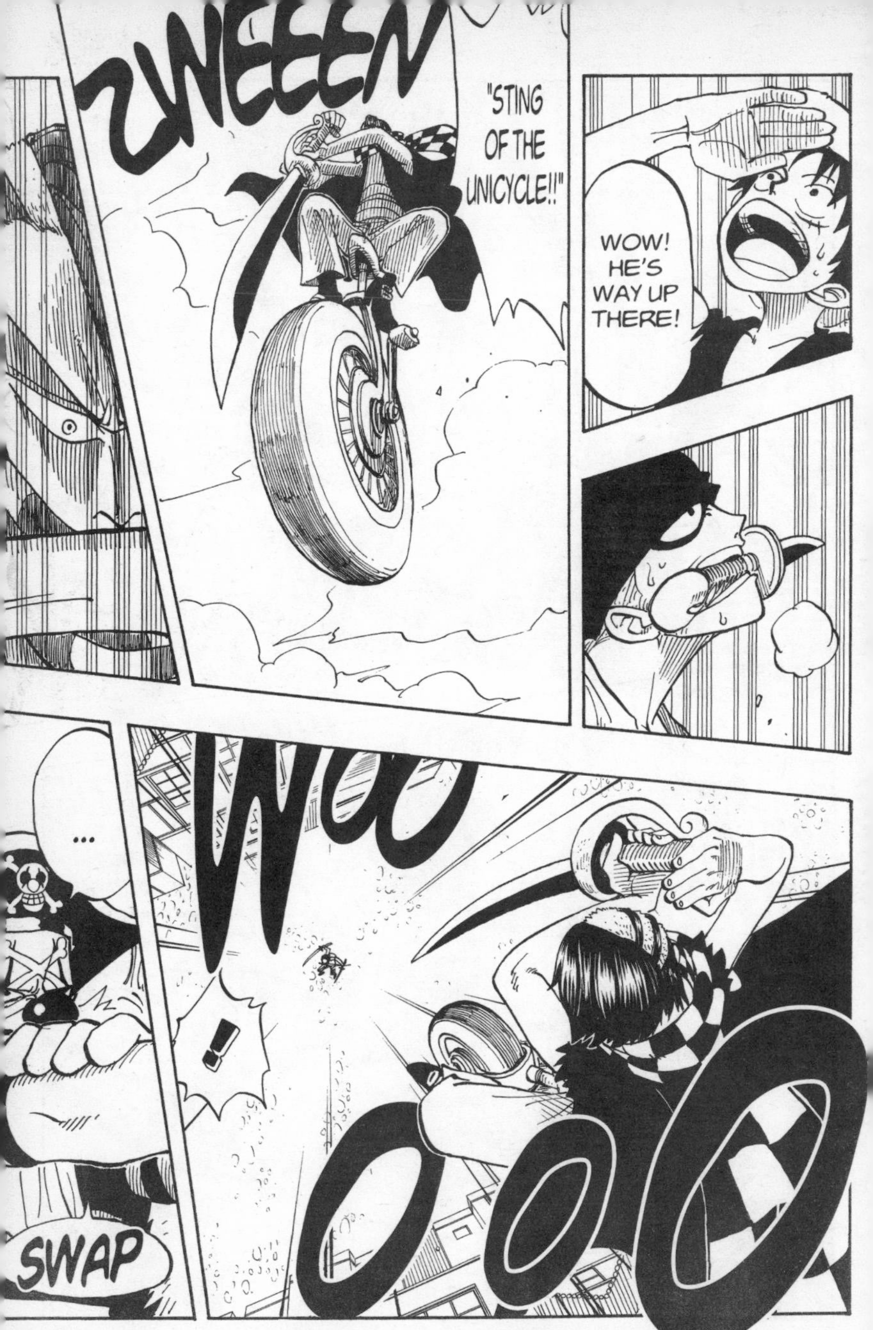
WOW! HE'S WAY UP THERE!
ZWEEEN
"STING OF THE UNICYCLE!!"
WOO
OOO
!
...
SWAP

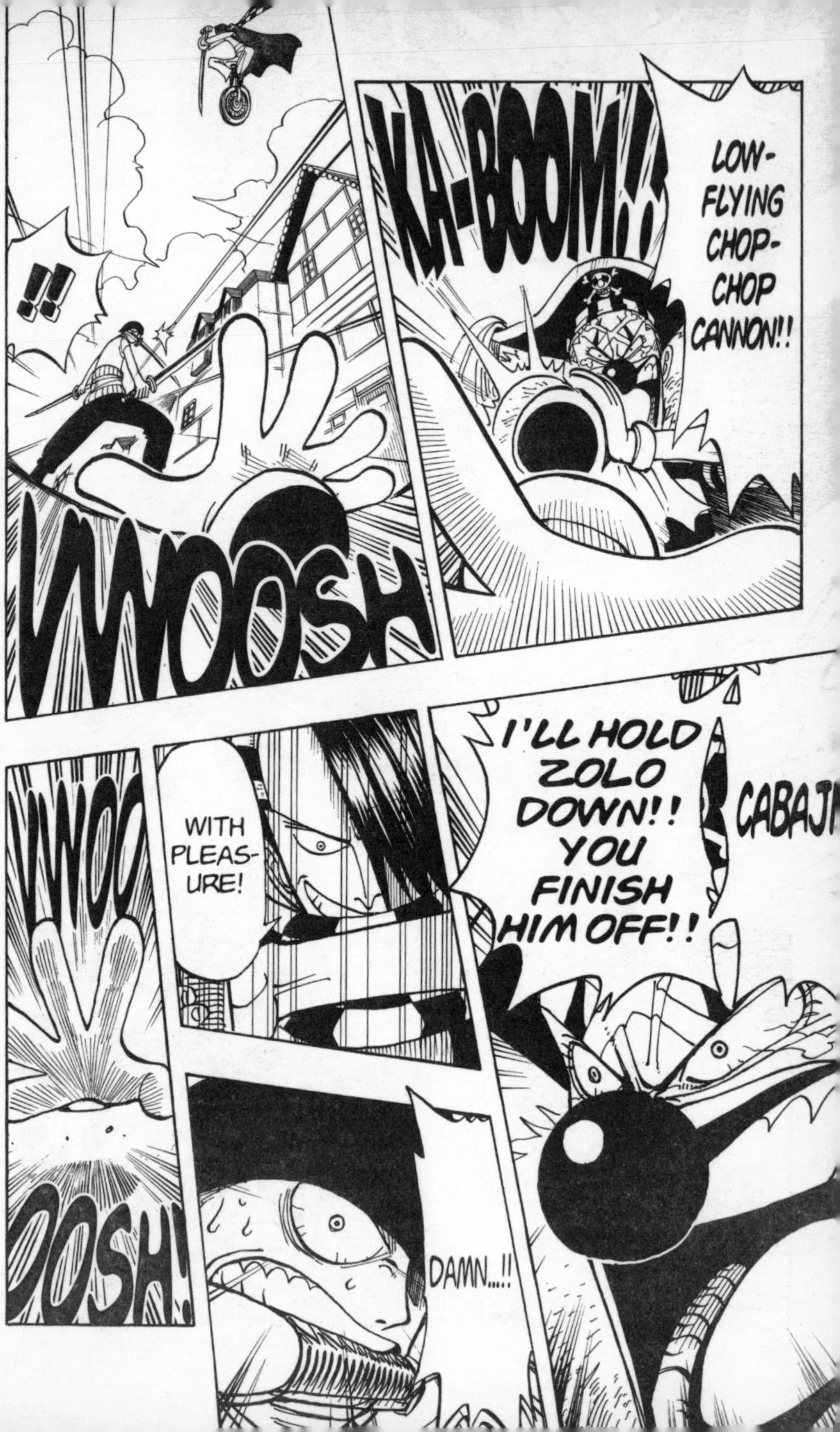

KA-BOOM!!
LOW-FLYING CHOP-CHOP CANNON!!
!!
WHOOSH
CABAJI
I'LL HOLD ZOLO DOWN!! YOU FINISH HIM OFF!!
WITH PLEAS-URE!
DAMN...!!
WHOO
OOSH!

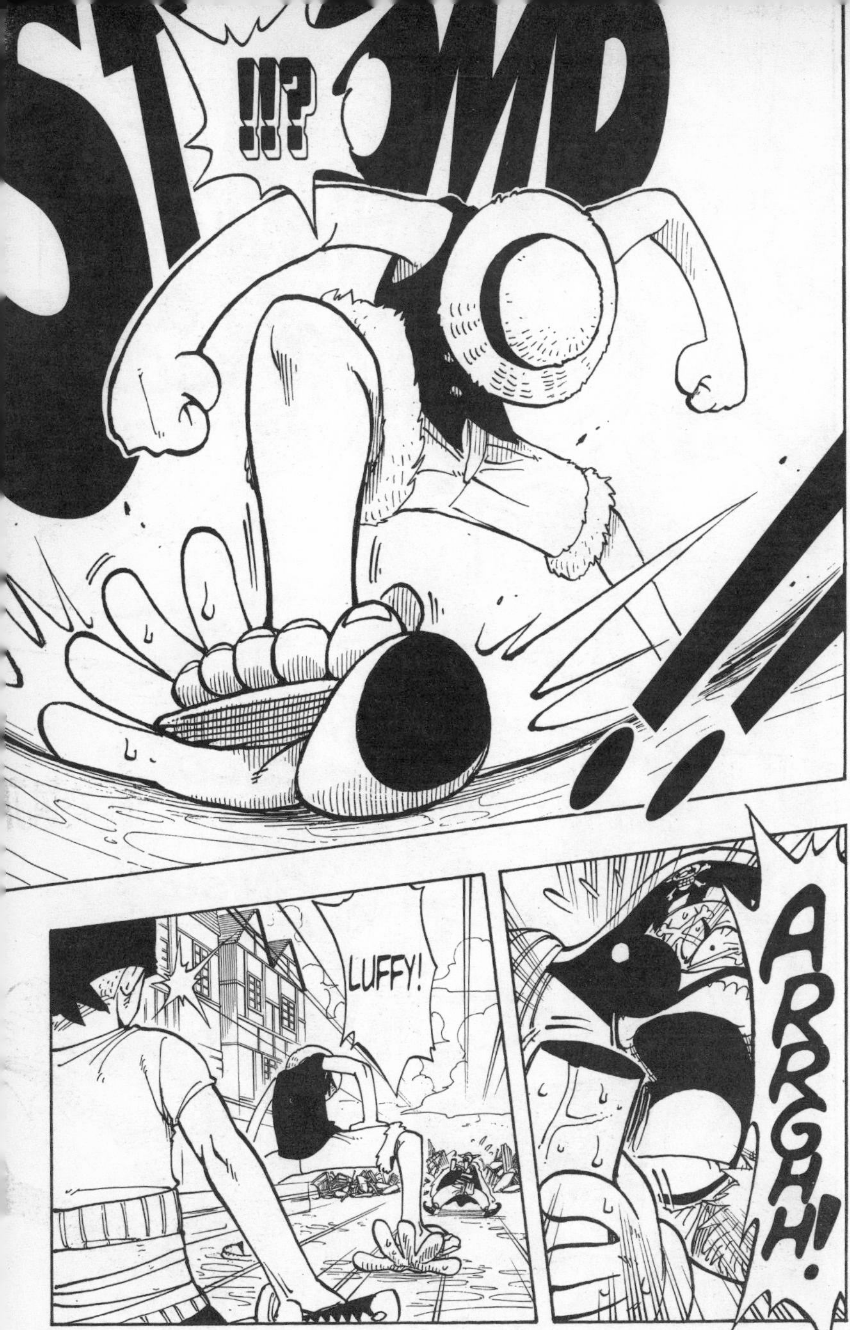
STOMP
!!?
LUFFY!
ARRGH!

KEEP YOUR MITTS OUT OF ZOLO'S DUEL!

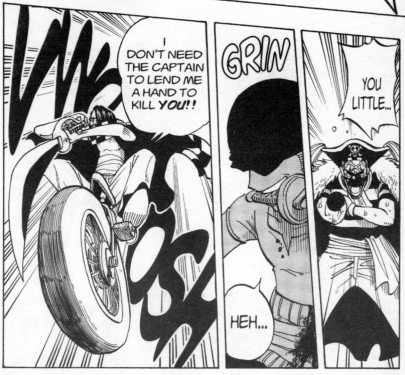

I DON'T NEED THE CAPTAIN TO LEND ME A HAND TO KILL *YOU*!!

GRIN

HEH...

YOU LITTLE...

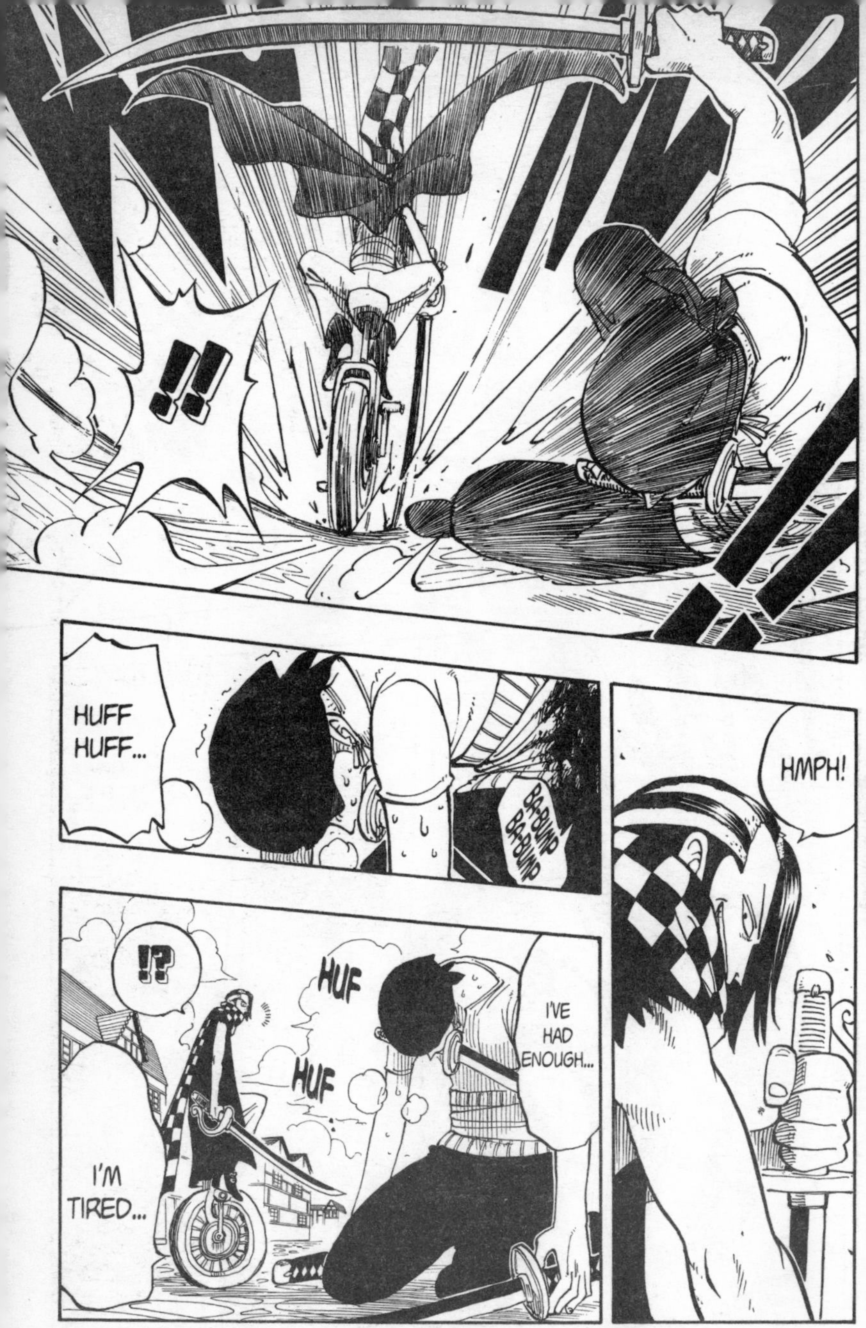

!!
HMPH!
HUFF HUFF...
BA-BUMP BA-BUMP
I'VE HAD ENOUGH...
HUF
HUF
!?
I'M TIRED...

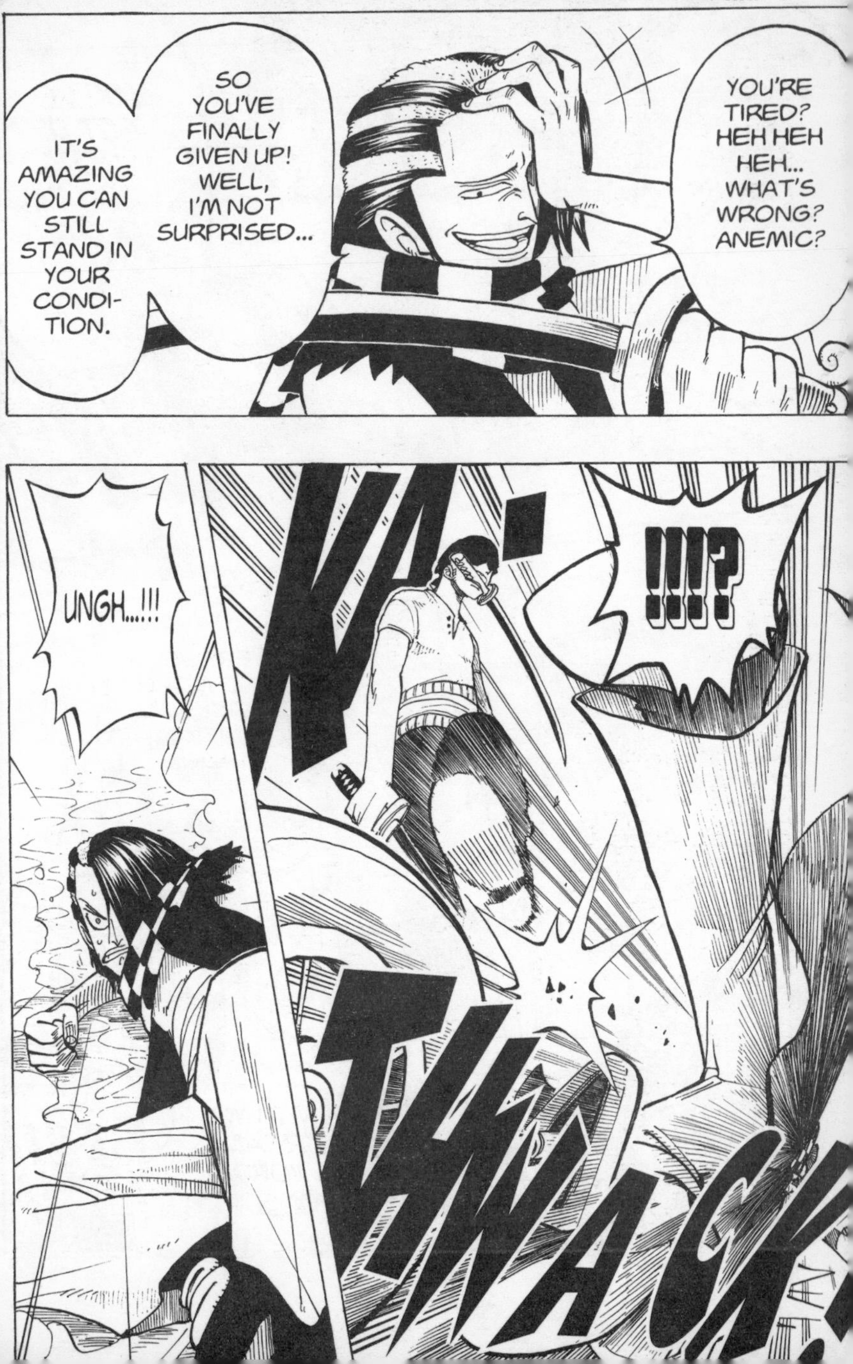
YOU'RE TIRED? HEH HEH HEH... WHAT'S WRONG? ANEMIC?
SO YOU'VE FINALLY GIVEN UP! WELL, I'M NOT SURPRISED...
IT'S AMAZING YOU CAN STILL STAND IN YOUR CONDITION.
KA'
!!!?
WHACK
UNGH...!!!

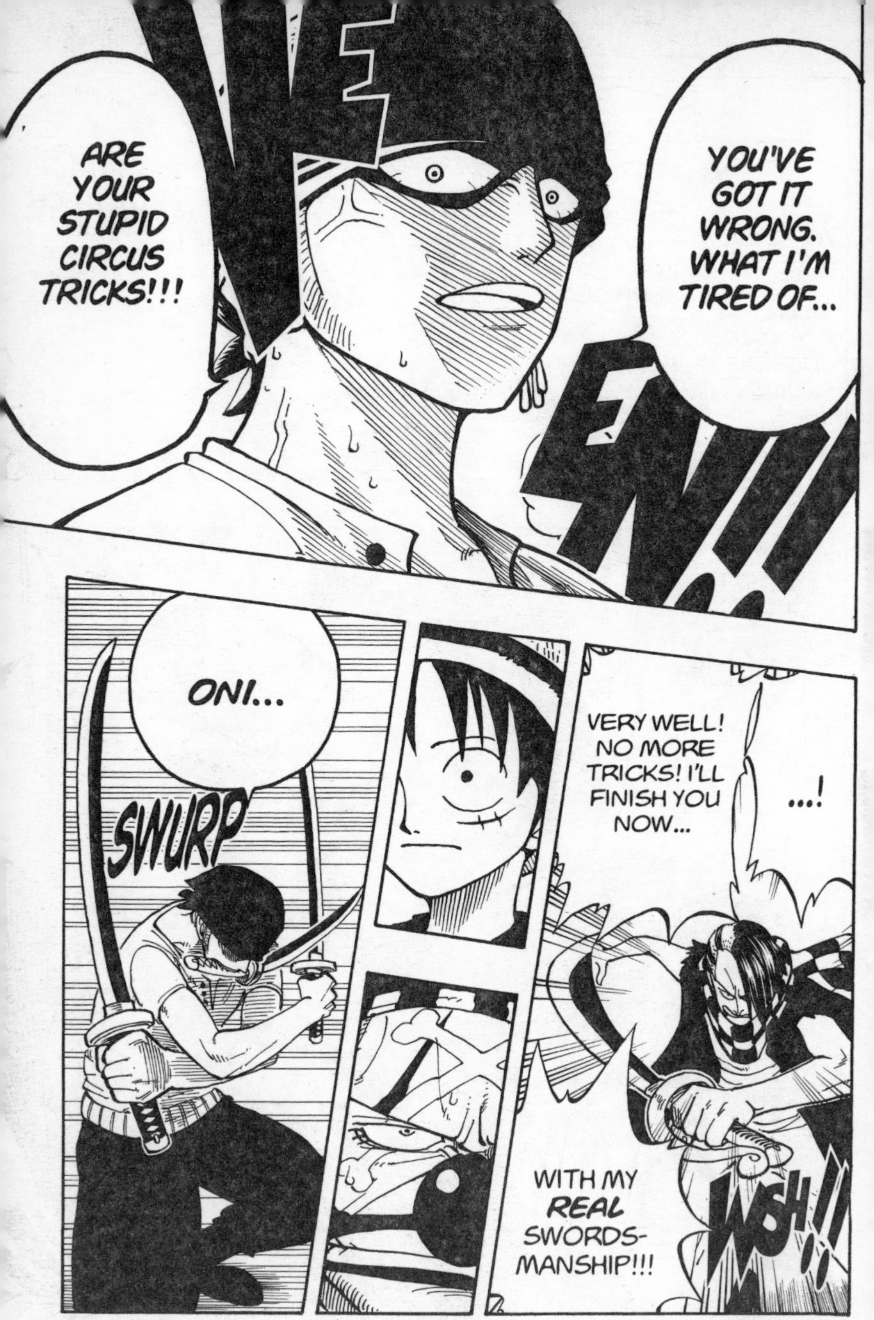
YOU'VE GOT IT WRONG. WHAT I'M TIRED OF...
ARE YOUR STUPID CIRCUS TRICKS!!!
ONI...
SWURP
...!
VERY WELL! NO MORE TRICKS! I'LL FINISH YOU NOW...
WITH MY REAL SWORDS-MANSHIP!!!
WSH!!

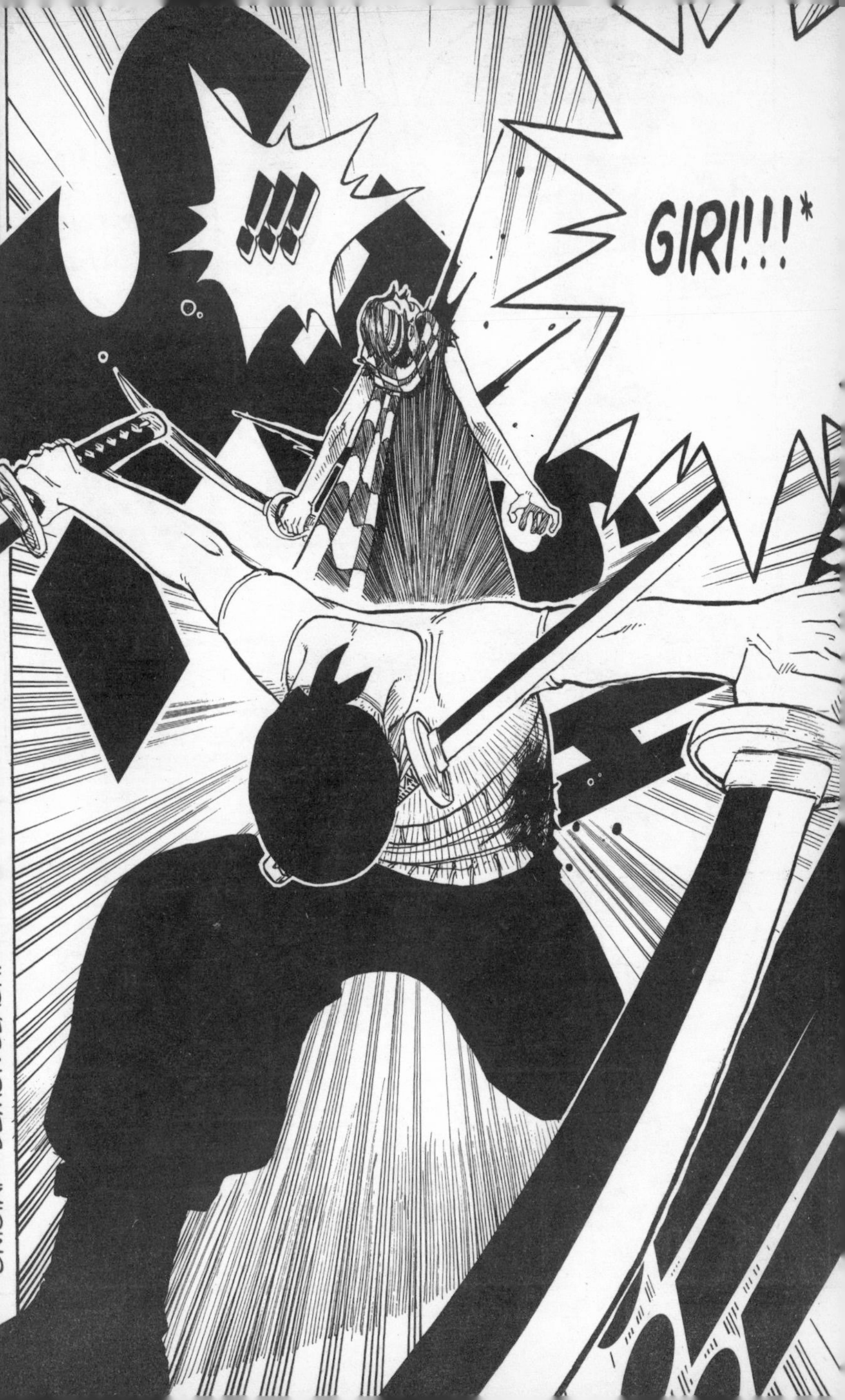
!!!!
GIRI!!!*

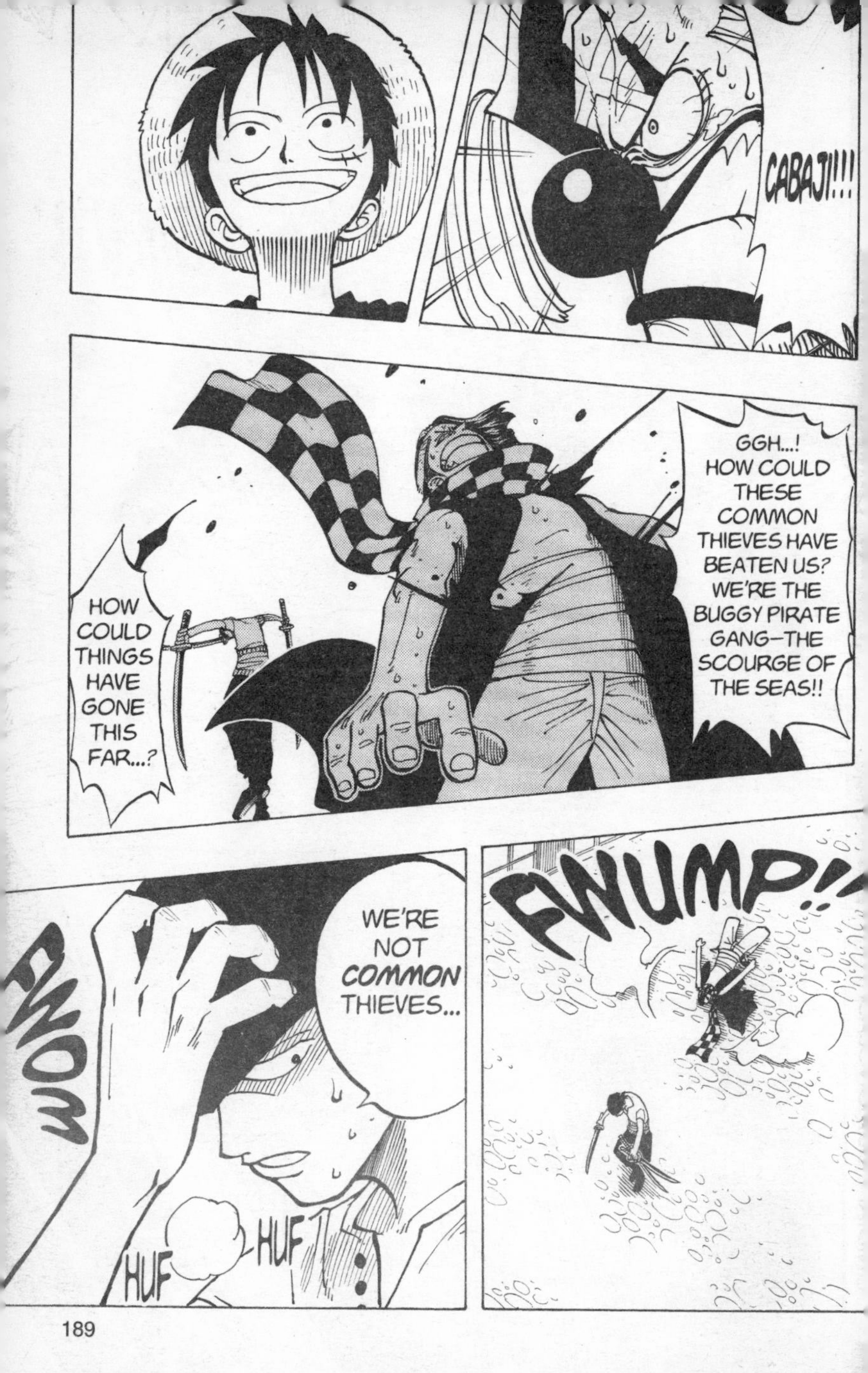
CABAJI!!!
GGH...! HOW COULD THESE COMMON THIEVES HAVE BEATEN US? WE'RE THE BUGGY PIRATE GANG—THE SCOURGE OF THE SEAS!!
HOW COULD THINGS HAVE GONE THIS FAR...?
FWUMP!!
WE'RE NOT COMMON THIEVES...
FWOM
HUF
HUF

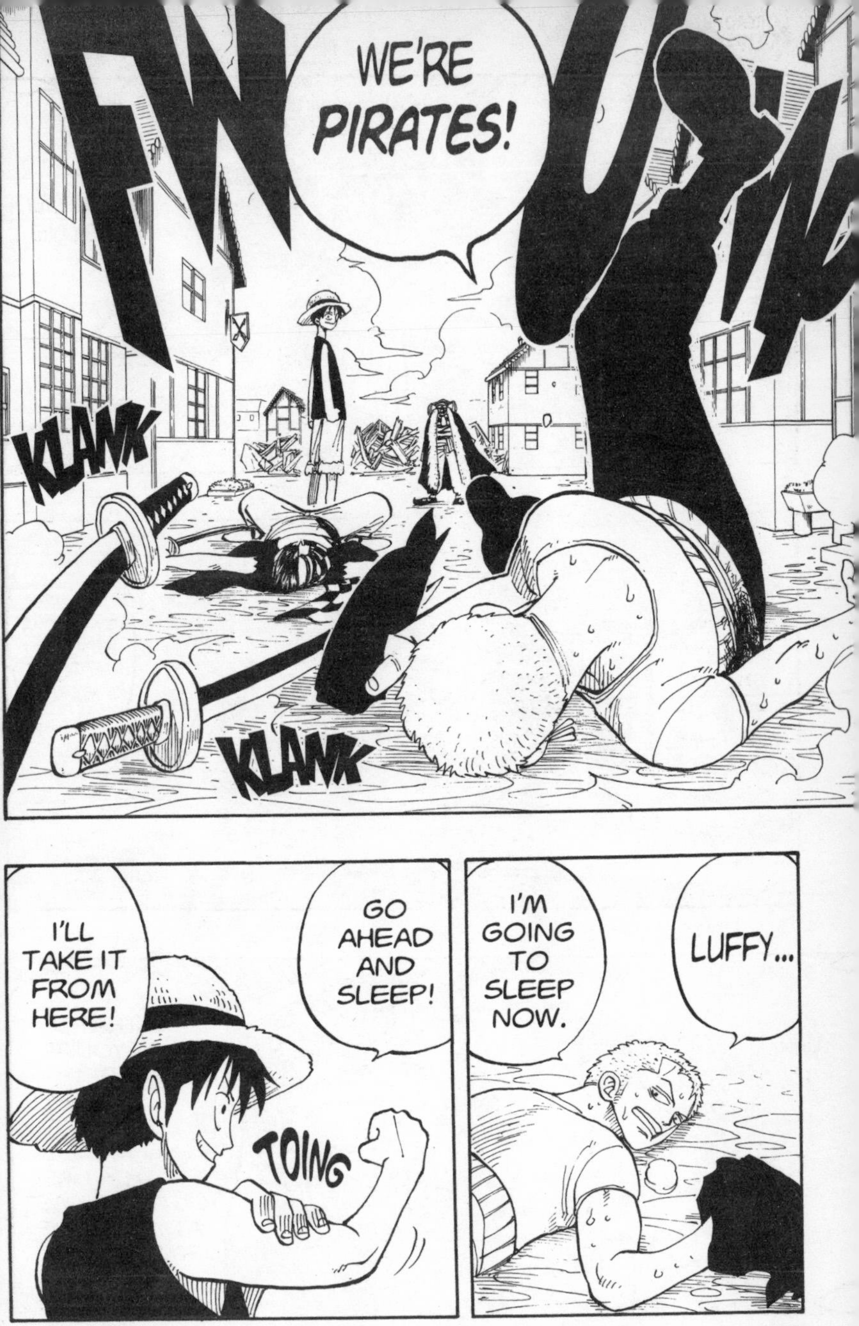
WE'RE PIRATES!
KLANK
KLANK
LUFFY...
I'M GOING TO SLEEP NOW.
GO AHEAD AND SLEEP!
I'LL TAKE IT FROM HERE!
TOING

READ THIS WAY

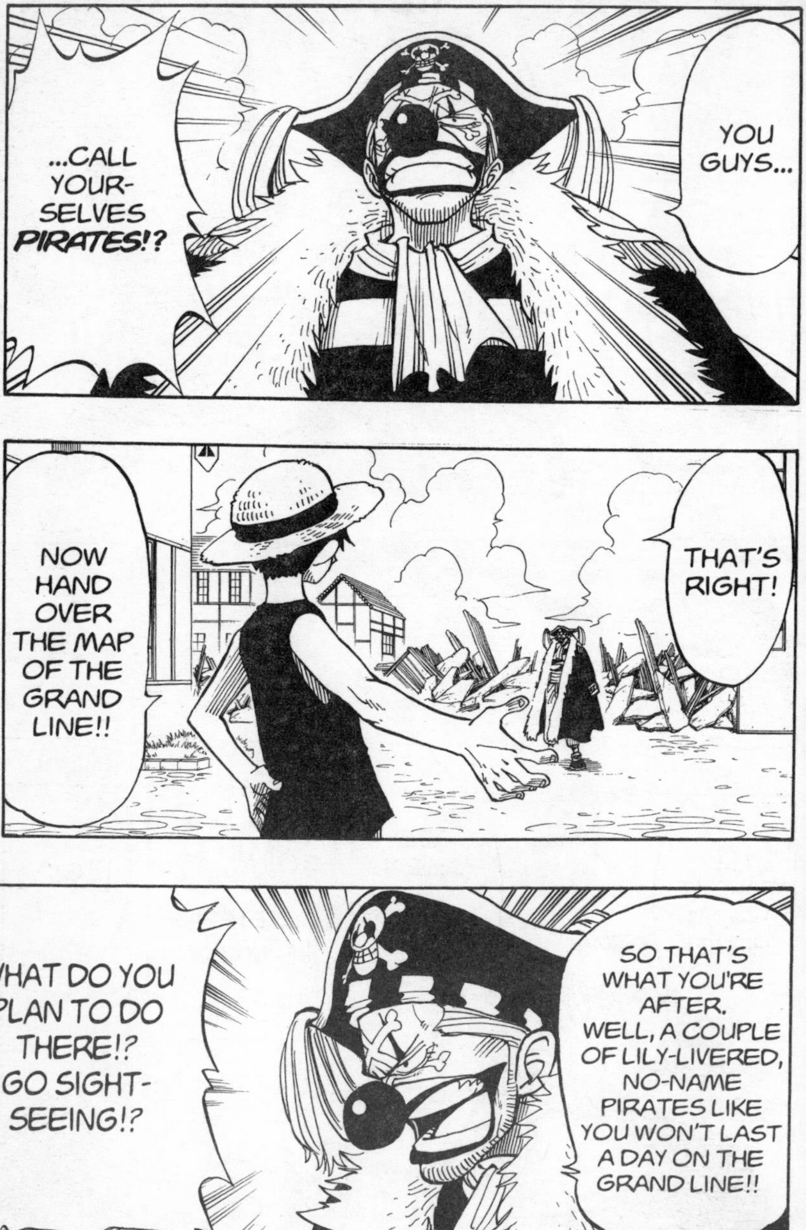
YOU GUYS...
...CALL YOUR-SELVES *PIRATES!?*
THAT'S RIGHT!
NOW HAND OVER THE MAP OF THE GRAND LINE!!
SO THAT'S WHAT YOU'RE AFTER. WELL, A COUPLE OF LILY-LIVERED, NO-NAME PIRATES LIKE YOU WON'T LAST A DAY ON THE GRAND LINE!!
WHAT DO YOU PLAN TO DO THERE!? GO SIGHT-SEEING!?

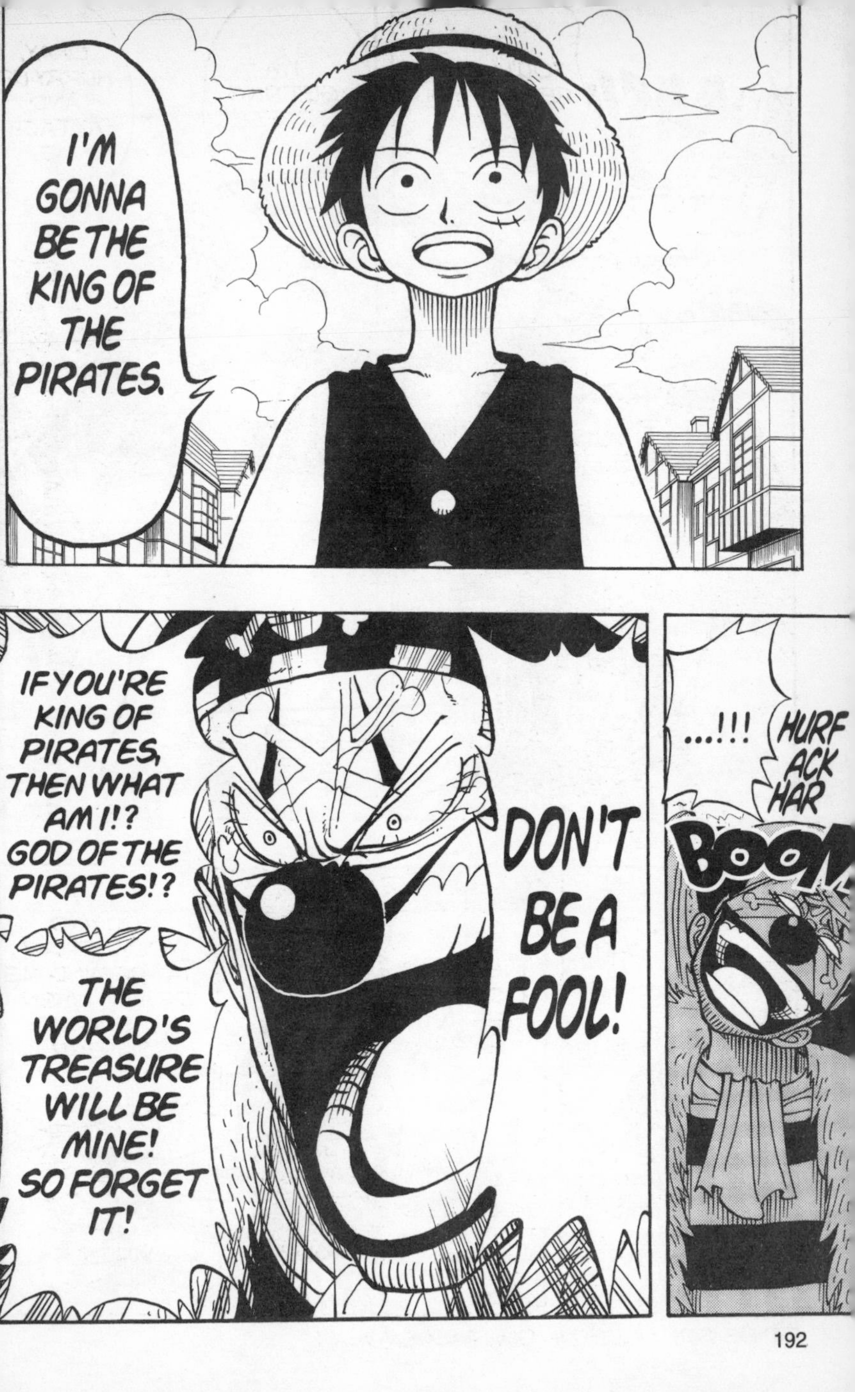
I'M GONNA BE THE KING OF THE PIRATES.
IF YOU'RE KING OF PIRATES, THEN WHAT AM I!? GOD OF THE PIRATES!?
THE WORLD'S TREASURE WILL BE MINE! SO FORGET IT!
DON'T BE A FOOL!
...!!!
HURF ACK HAR
BOOM

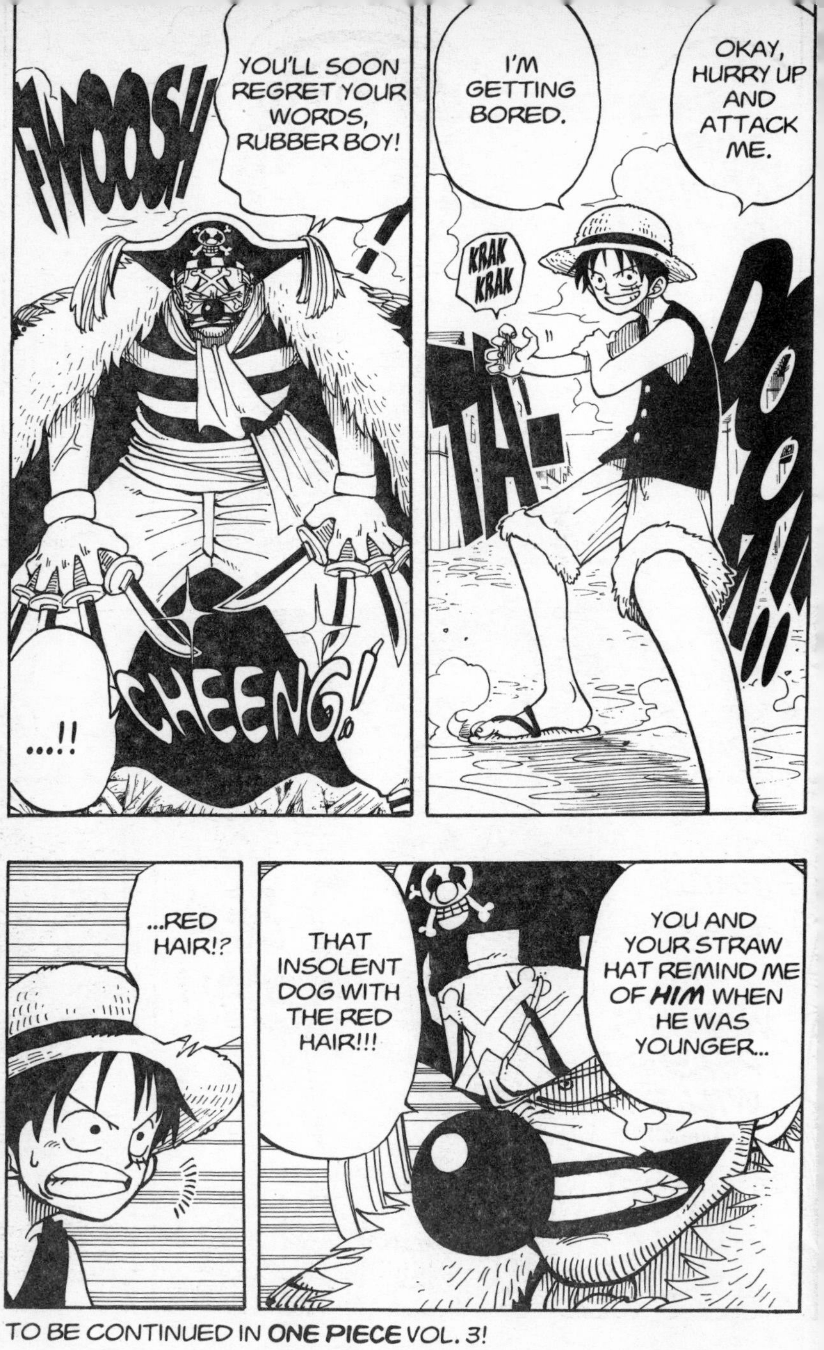
OKAY, HURRY UP AND ATTACK ME.
I'M GETTING BORED.
KRAK KRAK
YOU'LL SOON REGRET YOUR WORDS, RUBBER BOY!
FWOOSH
CHEENG!
...!!
YOU AND YOUR STRAW HAT REMIND ME OF HIM WHEN HE WAS YOUNGER...
THAT INSOLENT DOG WITH THE RED HAIR!!!
...RED HAIR!?

TO BE CONTINUED IN **ONE PIECE** VOL. 3!

Let's make a Sproingy Luffy!

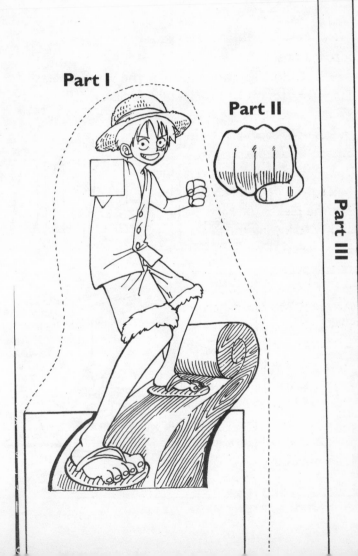

Part I

Part II

Part III

Part IV

How to make a Sproingy Luffy:

You need:
Scissors - Glue or paste - Crayons, markers, or colored pencils - Stiff paper - The strong will to make Sproingy Luffy

Instructions:

1. Color! To start out, color the various parts of Luffy. (Have fun!) Use flesh color for Parts II, III and IV. People who don't like messing up their books can make a photocopy to color and cut out instead.

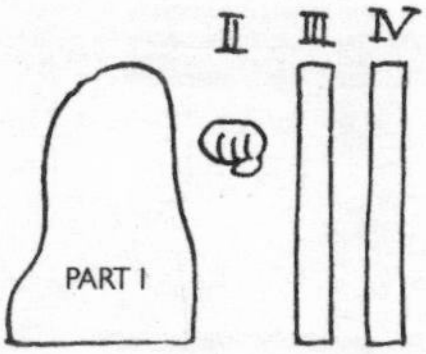
II III IV
PART I

2. Cut it out! Cut out Part I along the dotted line, and cut out the pieces for Parts II, III and IV, following the lines.
3. Paste Part I onto a piece of stiff paper.

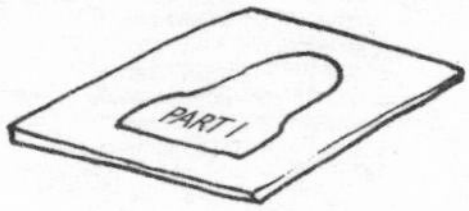
PART I

Let it Dry!

4. Wait for the glue to dry. Act cool. You can dance while you wait, too.
5. Cut out Part I (you'll be cutting the stiff paper, too), following Luffy's outline this time. Do it all powerful-like! Carefully cut the slots, following the thick lines around his legs, and make Luffy stand up.

Ta-Da!

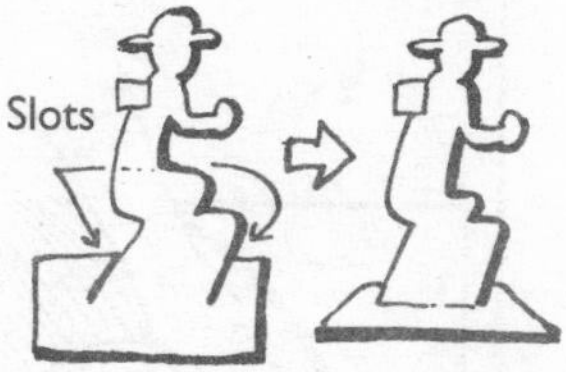
Slots

6. Glue Part III and Part IV at right angles to each other, just at the tips!

Glue tips together.
IV
III
and then
IV
Fold.
IV
III
Fold.
III
IV
IV
Fold.
IV

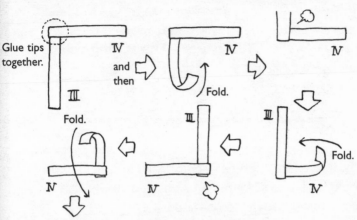

And so on and so forth, folding them over and over each other like you're weaving.

← You should get something sproingy like this thing.

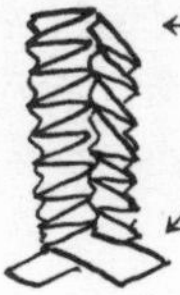

↙ Glue the other ends together, and then you're done with this part!

7. Assemble (Rise, Luffy, Rise!)

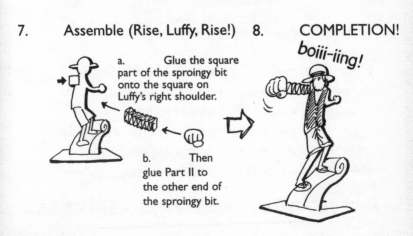

a. Glue the square part of the sproingy bit onto the square on Luffy's right shoulder.

b. Then glue Part II to the other end of the sproingy bit.

8. COMPLETION!

boiii-iing!

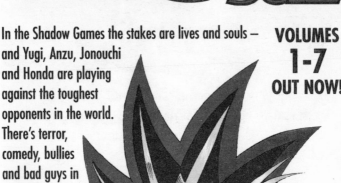

Yugi was just a normal boy — until he solved
an ancient Egyptian Puzzle and now, every game
is a life-or-death adventure!

DRAGON BALL™

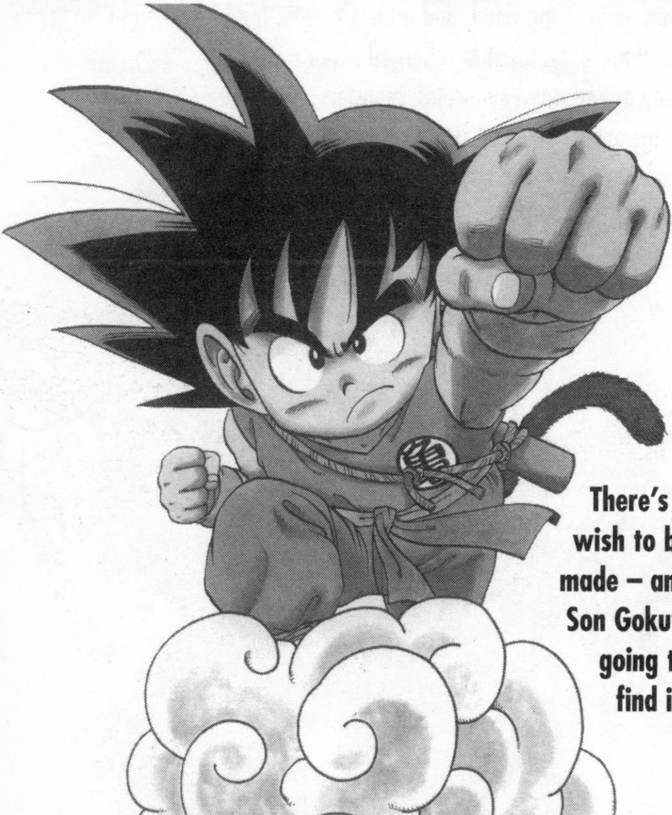

There's a wish to be made – and Son Goku's going to find it!

LET THE TOURNAMENT BEGIN!

The ultimate tournament is beginning, with games of wit, strategy and danger like no other . . .

COMPLETE OUR SURVEY AND
LET US KNOW WHAT YOU THINK!

❏ Please do NOT send me information about Gollancz Manga, or other Orion titles, products, news and events, special offers or other information.

Name: _____

Address: _____

Town: _____ County: _____ Postcode: _____

❏ Male ❏ Female   Date of Birth (dd/mm/yyyy): ___ / ___ / _____
                    (under 13? Parental consent required)

What race/ethnicity do you consider yourself? (please check one)

❏ Asian   ❏ Black   ❏ Hispanic

❏ White/Caucasian   ❏ Other: _____

Which Gollancz Manga series did you purchase?
❏ Case Closed   ❏ Dragon Ball   ❏ Flame of Recca   ❏ Fushigi Yûgi
❏ Maison Ikkoku   ❏ One Piece   ❏ Rurouni Kenshin   ❏ Yu-Gi-Oh!
❏ Yu-Gi-Oh! Duelist

What other Gollancz Manga series have you tried?
❏ Case Closed   ❏ Dragon Ball   ❏ Flame of Recca   ❏ Fushigi Yûgi
❏ Maison Ikkoku   ❏ One Piece   ❏ Rurouni Kenshin   ❏ Yu-Gi-Oh!
❏ Yu-Gi-Oh! Duelist

How many anime and/or manga titles have you purchased in the last year?
How many were Gollancz Manga titles?

Anime	Manga	GM
❏ None	❏ None	❏ None
❏ 1-4	❏ 1-4	❏ 1-4
❏ 5-10	❏ 5-10	❏ 5-10
❏ 11+	❏ 11+	❏ 11+

Reason for purchase: (check all that apply)

❏ Special Offer ❏ Favourite title ❏ Gift

❏ In store promotion If so please indicate which store: _____

❏ Recommendation ❏ Other _____

Where did you make your purchase?

❏ Bookshop ❏ Comic Shop ❏ Music Store

❏ Newsagent ❏ Video Game Store ❏ Supermarket

❏ Other: _____ ❏ Online: _____

What kind of manga would you like to read?

❏ Adventure ❏ Comic Strip ❏ Fantasy

❏ Fighting ❏ Horror ❏ Mystery

❏ Romance ❏ Science Fiction ❏ Sports

❏ Other: _____

Which do you prefer?

❏ Sound effects in English

❏ Sound effects in Japanese with English captions

❏ Sound effects in Japanese only with a glossary at the back

Want to find out more about Manga?

Look it up at www.orionbooks.co.uk, or www.viz.com

THANK YOU!

Please send the completed form to:

Manga Survey
Orion Books
Orion House
5 Upper St Martin's Lane
London, WC2H 9EA